COMPUTER
USER'S GUIDE TO
ELECTRONICS

No. 1899
$24.95

COMPUTER USER'S GUIDE TO ELECTRONICS

ART MARGOLIS

TAB BOOKS Inc.

Blue Ridge Summit, PA 17214

FIRST EDITION

FIRST PRINTING

Copyright © 1985 by TAB BOOKS Inc.

Printed in the United States of America

Reproduction or publication of the content in any manner, without express
permission of the publisher, is prohibited. No liability is assumed with respect to
the use of the information herein.

Library of Congress Cataloging in Publication Data

Margolis, Art.
Computer user's guide to electronics.

Includes index.
1. Microcomputers—Popular works.   I. Title.
TK7885.4.M37 1985   621.391′6   85-16402
ISBN 0-8306-0899-0
ISBN 0-8306-1899-6 (pbk.)

Contents

COMPUTER USER'S GUIDE TO ELECTRONICS

Introduction

Deep down, every computer user hopes that his machine will make him smarter. It will. It is a legitimate extension of your brain. It will think for you, in certain ways, thousands of times faster than would otherwise be possible. First, however, you must master your machine. There are a number of dimensions that must be built in your mental habit patterns before you are in complete control of the relationship between you and it.

Most of the areas of expertise you have probably been exposed to, and many of them you have mastered. Programming, word processing, speadsheet analysis, data filing, graphics, and so on are your daily fare and have become quite familiar. There is one facet, though, that is sadly neglected, and without it the machine still remains boss if you are not knowledgeable in it. That facet is electronics.

You cannot gain complete mastery over your computer until you have an understanding of the electronics of the thing. In truth, the computer is a digital electronic entity. It is not manual or analog.

It is an electronic purveyor of high and low voltages. If you can gain the understanding of how it works, you then will own the key to the mastery of your machine.

That is what this book is all about. It covers the typical components and their participation in circuits in your computer. Once you get this information under your hat, you will fill gaps and answer questions that constantly surface as a source of puzzlement about how your computer works. It will make you truly knowledgeable on your subject.

The book starts off with high level languages from the electronic point of view. The first chapter takes you from these type program lines to what they really are in terms of electricity in the machine. The next four chapters then go into actual electronic components that are in the machine. This includes resistors, capacitors, and transistors from their molecular composition to their fabrication as both discrete and microscopic parts. The chapters continue with the individual components being connected into the digital and analog circuits that you will find processing data.

Starting with Chapter 7, typical computer circuits are put together one by one to form a total computer. There are chapters on the clock, the microprocessor, ROMs, static and dynamic RAM chips, common I/O chips, and the inbetween chips that help the digital signals travel around the print board.

Chapter 14 covers in detail the way the computer puts together a composite TV signal that you can view on the TV display. Following that, Chapter 15 gives you the ability to actually figure out the way a memory map can be compiled.

Chapter 16 is a step-by-step description of a TV monitor. The way that color can be displayed is also discussed. Chapter 17 explains a typical power supply for a single-board computer.

The book winds up with one chapter on diagnosing computer troubles and easy repairs. The last chapter covers the safety measures you should take if you ever decide to take your machine apart.

With electronics as one of your computer dimensions, you will be a leg up on any computer user who does not have the knowledge. Besides being able to write high-level language programs, assembly and even machine-language programs become much easier to knock out. I hope the information to follow proves as useful to you as it has been for me.

Chapter 1

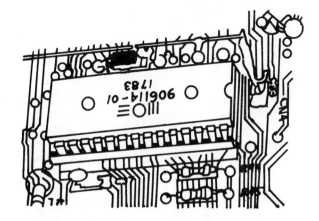

From Program
Lines to Digital Signals

THE AUTOMOBILE IS A MACHINE THAT IS AN extension of the human body. With the aid of a key, steering wheel, foot pedals and dashboard controls, you can travel at high speeds from one place to another. You do not have to know a blessed thing about how the machine operates internally to get it to perform its vital function. However, the more you do know about those mechanical things the more control you have over the car. In order to be a top notch professional driver, like a race car champion, you better understand the auto from one end to the other.

The computer is an extension of the human mind. With the aid of a keyboard, cassette tape, disk drive, and TV display you can input coded requests for it to perform tasks and obtain an output of completed jobs. In lots of cases, you do not have to know hardly a thing about how the electronics is taking the keyboard strikes, tape, disk and other inputs and producing finished jobs. However, the more you know about those electronic processes the more control you will have over your machine. If you have the desire to gain complete mastery over

your computer, you must know all about what happens internally when you program and execute a job in your pride and joy.

HIGH-LEVEL LANGUAGES

When you sit down at your computer, chances are that you start programming the machine in a high-level language. The language used the most is BASIC. All the high-level languages were created to make life easier for the programmers. There are many complicated electronic machinations that the computer goes through as it operates. When you program in low-level languages, you must take into consideration all the many details that the computer experiences as it works. Otherwise, the low-level language program won't work.

The high-level language is constructed as a cushion to automatically take care of the changing registers and confusing data paths and leave the programmer free to concentrate on the program lines. These levels of cushions are graphically illustrated in Fig. 1-1.

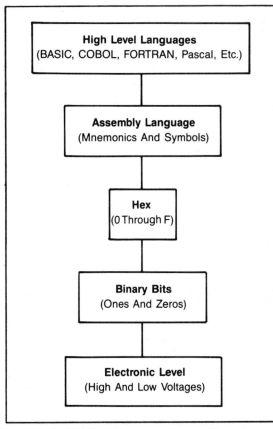

Fig. 1-1. The high level languages sit on cushions of codes that frees the programmer from having to understand the electronics in the computer in order to use it. However, mastery of your computer can only happen when you are able to also work at the electronic level.

In a BASIC computer, a ROM chip is installed on the print board that is able to translate the BASIC statements you type in to a machine-language routine that the computer insides can use. The only problem, though, is a waste of efficiency in the machine. All the little details you were able to avoid by using BASIC instead of machine language still have to be handled in order for the program to be successfully run. Instead of you doing the details, the computer is given the job. There are such details connected with the execution of each and every BASIC statement. This makes the execution of a BASIC program run many times slower than the same program written in the computer's native instruction set.

Suppose you are writing a program and at a certain time you want to clear the screen of light. On my TRS-80 Color Computer, I could write the following line in BASIC; as,

110 CLS(0)

As I entered the program, the CLS(0) was changed into voltage highs and lows. The voltages were routed to the microprocessor. The microprocessor in turn sent voltages to a place on the ROM chip that contains the translations from BASIC to machine language. The place on the ROM chip that the MPU contacts is a small program routine that is able to clear the TV display of light. The CLS(0) statement is a collection of four characters and two symbols. The screen clearing ROM routine has 13 individual byte locations. The CLS(0) statement triggers off the 13 byte routine, as shown in Fig. 1-2.

The beautiful part of the BASIC statement is that you can remember CLS(0) as a way to command the computer to turn the screen black. Never mind that the command in turn makes the computer execute a 13-byte program. It is easy for you.

The poor part of using the BASIC language is that the jobs you can do with BASIC are limited and, from a professional point of view, slow and unwieldy. BASIC is a casual language that was designed for beginners. It is a good place to start your computing career.

The connection between BASIC and the electronics of the machine is separated by a cushion of program layers. To form a connection of understanding between BASIC and the computer's electronics, you have to work down through the layers shown in Fig. 1-1. The layer below BASIC is the lower-level language called Assembly Language.

ASSEMBLY LANGUAGE

When you talk about assembly language, you must reference it with the computer's Instruction Set. As far as BASIC is concerned the Instruction Set is meaningless. BASIC is above all that. The Instruction Set is brought into play automatically when a BASIC program is executed.

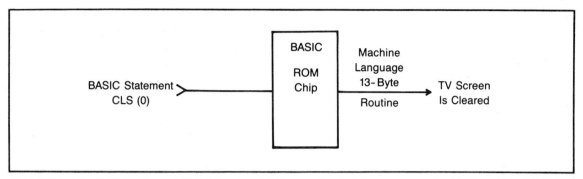

Fig. 1-2. When the BASIC statement CLS(0) is entered, it triggers off a 13-byte routine contained in the BASIC ROM interpreter.

If you write a program in assembly, though the Instruction Set is thought of at every step. What is the Instruction Set? I'll go into it in more detail as the book progresses, but at this point the following will suffice.

The MPU is able to do a number of jobs. Some of these jobs are easy to understand like add and subtract. There are a group of voltage highs and lows that, when they are applied to the MPU, force the MPU to add some of the numbers that are in the MPU at that time. The group of voltages that cause the addition in Fig. 1-3 is an instruction called ADD. In an Instruction Set there are many instructions. A typical small computer could have 72 instructions in its set.

Naturally, it would be a prodigious chore to try to keep track of 72 individual groups of voltage highs and lows. As a result, a language of mnemonics is assigned to the voltage instructions.

The mnemonic ADD is used to describe the addition group of voltages. Other mnemonics are used to clue you in to the other instructions. There is a mnemonic for every instruction. Table 1-1 shows the mnemonics for the 6800 MPU.

In BASIC, a statement word is designed to trigger off a routine stored in the ROM chip. One word can get many instructions of highs and lows to execute. With assembly language, a mnemonic doesn't usually set off a long routine. The mnemonics are just about one for one with an instruction. In fact, you could say that the mnemonic is an instruction, and be quite close to an exact definition.

The assembly language is applied to its own ROM chip for translation to machine language. When an assembly-language program is passed through its ROM chip, called an assembler, it is said that the program has been assembled. All that

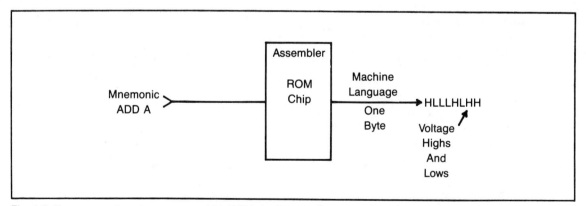

Fig. 1-3. If a mnemonic enters an assembler ROM, it triggers off a byte collection of Hs and Ls.

Table 1-1. Assembly Language Mnemonics.

Mnemonic	Meaning	Mnemonic	Meaning
ABA	Add accumulators, A to B	DES	Decrement stack pointer
ADCA/ADCB	Add with carry	EOR	Exclusive OR
ADDA/ADDB	Add without carry	INC	Increment
ANDA/ANDB	Logical and	INS	Increment stack pointer
ASL	Arithmetic shift left	INX	Increment index register
ASR	Arithmetic shift right	JMP	Jump
		JSR	Jump to subroutine
	BRANCH IF	LDAA/LDAB	Load accumulator
BCC	Carry Clear	LDS	Load stack pointer
BCS	Carry Set	LDX	Load index register
BEQ	= to 0	LSR	Logical shift right
BGE	> or = to 0	NEG	Negate
BGT	> than 0	NOP	No operation
BHI	Higher	ORAA/ORAB	Inclusive OR
BLE	< or = to 0	PSHA/PSHB	Push data onto stack
BLS	Lower or same	PULA/PULB	Pull data from stack
BLT	Less than 0	ROL	Rotate left
BMI	Minus	ROR	Rotate right
BNE	Not = 0	RTI	Return from interrupt
BPL	Plus	RTS	Return from subroutine
BRA	Always	SBC	Substract with carry
BSR	To subroutine	SBA	Subtract accumulators
BVC	Overflow clear	SEC	Set carry
BVS	Overflow set	SEI	Set interrupt
		SEV	Set 2's comp. overflow bit
		STAA/STAB	Store accumulator
BIT	Bit test	STS	Store stack pointer
CLR	Clear	STX	Store index register
CMPA/CMPB	Compare	SUBA/SUBB	Subtract
CBA	Compare accumulators	SWI	Softwear interrupt
CLC	Clear carry	TST	Test (Z or N)
CLI	Clear interrupt	TAB	Transfer accumulator A to B
CLV	Clear 2's comp, overflow bit	TAP	Transfer accumulator A to CCR
COM	Complement	TBA	Transfer accumulator B to A
CPX	Compare index register	TPA	Transfer CCR to A accumulator
DAA	Decimal adjust a accumulator	TSX	Transfer stack pointer to index register
DEC	Decrement	TXS	Transfer index register to stack pointer
DEX	Decrement index register	WAI	Wait for interrupt

#, means "immediate" addressing mode. $, means "HEX"

means is the assembly language has been transformed from mnemonics to voltage highs and lows.

If you write a routine in assembly language that will do the same job on my Color Computer that BASIC's CLS(0) will do, the mnemonics read in the following way:

```
SCNCLR    LDA     #$20
          LDX     #$400
```

```
SCN001    STA     ,X+
          CMPX    #$600
          BNE     SCN001
          RTS
          END
```

The center row of abbreviations are the mnemonics. The LDs are shorthand for load. The ST is a contraction of store. The CMP stands for compare. The RT for return and the END for end.

These names are just as easy to remember as the BASIC statement abbreviations. However as the example shows, it took seven assembly mnemonics plus the other characters and symbols to replace the one BASIC statement.

The assembly language is one code layer closer than BASIC to the physical voltages that are actually doing the computing. When a mnemonic is input to this assembler ROM chip for the most part, one byte of highs and lows is output. This one to one relationship is quite unlike the BASIC single statement input and 13-byte routine output.

In order to be facile with BASIC, there is little or no need to be concerned with the electronics of the computer. When you start using the assembly languages though, you are closely connected to the voltages and begin working with bits, bytes, and words. You must observe their travels through the computer circuits. The assembly language is simply a convenient code you use to handle the electronics of the computer.

HEX MACHINE LANGUAGE

Between the assembly code and the voltage signals that the computer actually processes is another layer of code. It is written in hexadecimal numbers normally referred to as hex. All hexadecimal means is decimal plus six. The hexadecimal numbering

system has 16 numbers instead of 10 as our ordinary decimal system does. The hex numbers are the same as decimal from 0 to 9. From there, 10 through 15 become A, B, C, D, E, and F. The hex number after F is 10. (Hex 10 = decimal 16).

Hex numbering has become very popular because it is much more convenient to use with the computer than any other numbering system. There will be more about hex throughout the book.

The Instruction Set of the MPU, which is in reality digital voltage collections, can be coded conveniently into hex. Typically two hex numbers can represent an instruction. A mnemonic is only a part of a total instruction. You need some additional symbols in the rest of the program line to form the entire instruction with mnemonics, as shown in Fig. 1-4. Two hex numbers, though, represent an entire instruction. Two hex numbers code all the information in the group of voltage signals that comprise an instruction. Refer to Fig. 1-5.

When you assemble a program the assembler chip outputs voltages, but if you read the assembly on the TV screen you will see the hex code. For example, our screen clearing program, when assembled will read the following hex on the screen.

3F00	86	20	3F07	8C	0600
3F02	8E	0400	3F0A	26	F9
3F05	A7	80	3F0C	39	

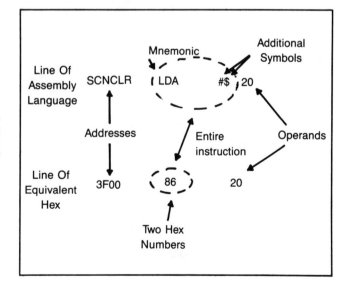

Fig. 1-4. The line of assembly language and the line of hex contain identical information. Two hex numbers are a complete instruction. They contain the information denoted by the mnemonic and the two symbols.

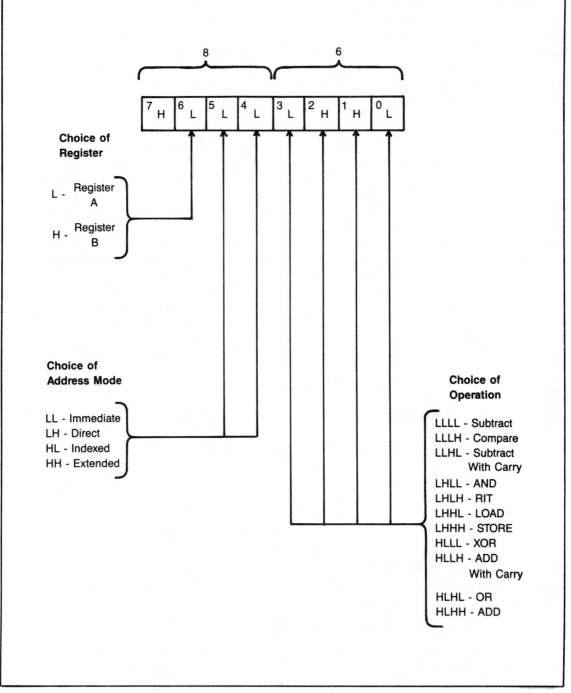

Fig. 1-5. A byte instruction of two hex numbers contains eight bits. Bit 6 provides a choice of two accumulator registers. Bits 5 and 4 gives a choice of four addressing modes. Bits 3, 2, 1, and 0 allows a choice of 16 operations.

The center column is composed of hex numbers from the Instruction Set. 86 and 8E are the two load instructions. A7 is the store. 8C is the compare and 39 the return. The first and last columns are not from the Instruction Set. The first column contains addresses and the last column has operands.

All of the columns are in hex and all are codes for voltages. In recent years, programmers often wrote their programs in hex. There are certain areas of computing where it is very convenient to write programs in hex. One such endeavor is performed by test technicians. In order to exercise circuits, technicians often must write small hex programs that test the performance of the various sections of the computer.

These programs in hex are said to be written in machine language. There are ROM chips like the ones that translate BASIC and assembly for the machine programs. They translate the hex numbers into voltage signals. The programs on the ROM in Fig. 1-6 change hex to voltage and are called *hex loaders*.

The Instruction Set that has the individual instructions coded in two hex numbers has a limit to the number of instructions. Just as two decimal numbers can count from 00 to 99, two hex numbers

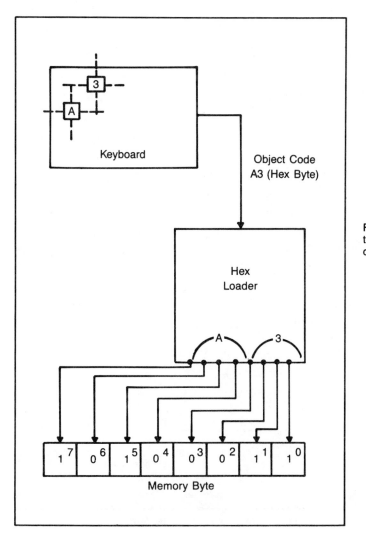

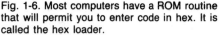

Fig. 1-6. Most computers have a ROM routine that will permit you to enter code in hex. It is called the hex loader.

can count from 00 to FF. The equivalent decimal of FF is 255. This gives the hex pairs 256 possible combinations as long as you count 00 as one of the possible pairs. This means that an Instruction Set that used all the possible pairs of hex digits cannot have more than 256 instructions.

The hex code is one layer closer to the voltages than the assembly language. However, you can take paper and pencil and translate a program from hex into the voltage that the hex code represents. You cannot do that with assembly language or any higher-level language. The ROM translator chips can, but you can't. This makes hex programs and the electronics of the computer closely connected. The next layer of code completes the connection.

BINARY MACHINE LANGUAGE

Everyone using a computer should have heard about bytes and bits. A bit is the basic (not BASIC) element in a computer. A bit is a single binary number. Just as there are 16 hexadecimal numbers 0 through F, there are two binary numbers. They are 0 and 1. A bit is either a 0 or a 1, nothing else.

A byte is a collection of eight bits. Many computers in use today are based on the byte. If you take half a byte, you have bitten off a nybble. Naturally, if a byte is eight bits, then a nybble is four bits. Figure 1-7 illustrates these ideas. The nybble is the most used piece of data in the computer. However, the nybble is rarely used alone. The nyb-

ble is used in pairs. Let me explain why.

The nybble is composed of four bits. Each bit can be in a state of 0 or 1. If we think about it, the four bits, each capable of two states, are able to form 16 different combinations. One set of hex numbers is made of 16 different numbers and letters. A code is easily formed between the hex integers and a nybble of binary digits. The coding goes like the following:

Hexadecimal	Binary
0	0000
1	0001
2	0010
3	0011
4	0100
5	0101
6	0110
7	0111
8	1000
9	1001
A	1010
B	1011
C	1100
D	1101
E	1110
F	1111

It is a good idea for anyone working with computers to memorize the hex-binary relationship.

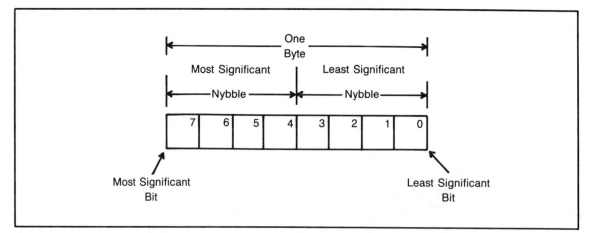

Fig. 1-7. Most computers contain registers that are based on the byte or multiples of the byte.

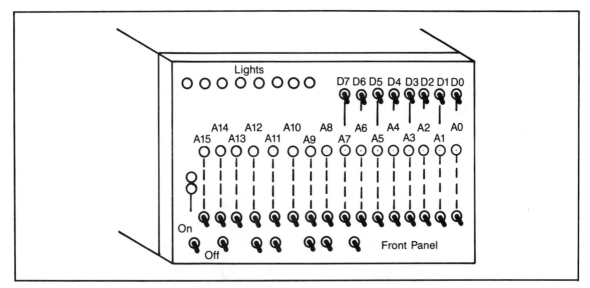

Fig. 1-8. The oldtime front panel permitted programmers to enter routines in the form of binary bits.

The single hex numbers and the nybble of four bits should be second nature. When you look at a hex number you should know that it is also a nybble. The memorizing will let you convert any size binary numbers to hex and vice versa. This is a very valuable technique when you are concerned with the electronics of the computer.

The bit is the natural indicator of the state of a digital circuit. The 0 and 1 can represent off and on, true and false, clear and set, zero volts and +5 volts, black and white, and so on.

There are 16 possible combinations of bits in a nybble. There are two nybbles in the commonly used byte. If you combine two nybbles into a byte, then the eight bits of the byte can form 256 (16 × 16) possible bit combinations. The two nybbles can be coded into two hex numbers. The two hex numbers also can form 256 combinations. For all practical purposes, the two-nybble byte and two-digit hex number are just two different descriptions of the same high and low voltages that travel through the computer.

In years past, computers could be programmed by installing the binary code bit by bit into the computer through a device called a *front panel*. The panel, shown in Fig. 1-8, was nothing more than a collection of switches and lights. There were 16

address switches numbered 0-15. There were eight data switches numbered 0-7. Each byte of program was installed bit by bit. The front panel was too slow to enter long programs, but it was useful to code small programs.

If we wanted to code our hex screen clearing program into binary in order to enter it into a front panel, the coding would look like this.

ADDRESSES		INSTRUCTIONS AND DATA	
Hex →	binary	Hex →	binary
3F00	0011 1111 0000 0000	86	1000 0110
3F01	0011 1111 0000 0001	20	0010 0000
3F02	0011 1111 0000 0010	8E	1000 1110
3F03	0011 1111 0000 0011	04	0000 0100
3F04	0011 1111 0000 0100	00	0000 0000
3F05	0011 1111 0000 0101	A7	1010 0111
3F06	0011 1111 0000 0110	80	1000 0000
3F07	0011 1111 0000 0111	8C	1000 1100
3F08	0011 1111 0000 1000	06	0000 0110
3F09	0011 1111 0000 1001	00	0000 0000
3F0A	0011 1111 0000 1010	26	0010 0110
3F0B	0011 1111 0000 1011	F9	1111 1001
3F0C	0011 1111 0000 1100	39	0011 1001

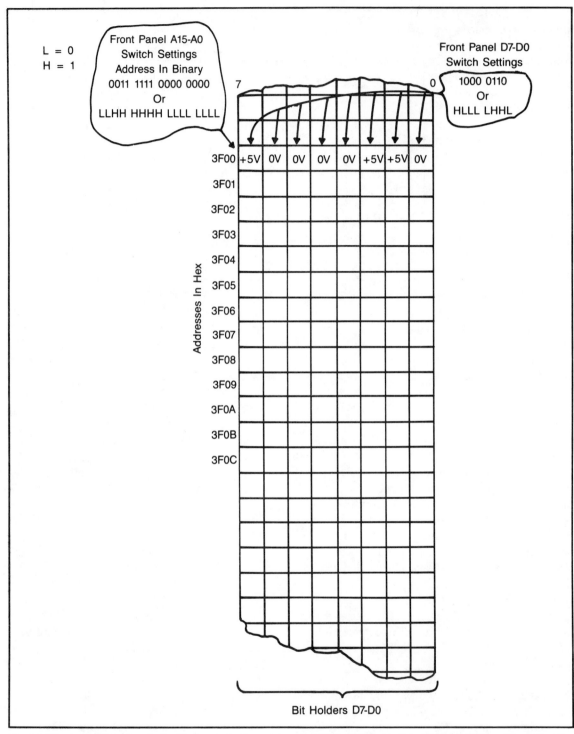

Fig. 1-9. Whatever the coding, in the final analysis, the program bytes are installed in the circuits as high and low voltages.

BINARY TO VOLTAGE

In today's computers, front panels are rarely if ever used. The typewriter style keyboard has become the important input device. As a result, computer people do not as a rule enter binary bits directly. If a program is written in bit form, it is usually coded into hex and entered through the keyboard and the hex loader.

As an example though, to see how the binary bits become voltages stored in a computer memory, let's enter a line of the screen clearing program we've been examining into a front panel.

The first line of the program shows an address in binary, 0011 1111 0000 0000. There are 16 bits, a collection of 0s and 1s. I put a space between each four bits to show that each four bits code one hex character. These 16 bits code 3 F 0 0 in hex.

In the computer, there is a memory. The memory shown in Fig. 1-9 is composed of rows and rows of RAM and ROM locations. Each memory location contains eight bit-holders. Each memory location has an address. The addresses can be described in decimal, hex, or binary. Whatever the description mode, the addresses, of course, are the same. In this computer, there are 65,536 individual eight bit locations. The addresses in decimal are numbered 0-65,535. In hex, the addresses are 0000 to FFFF. In binary, the addresses are 0000 0000 0000 0000 to 1111 1111 1111 1111.

The 16 binary bits can be arranged in 65,536 individual combinations. Each combination can dial up one location in memory. The electronics proceed in this fashion.

Notice the front panel has 16 address switches, labeled A15 to A0. When a switch is pushed up, a 1 is installed at that switch. If a switch is pressed down, a 0 is installed. The installation of a 1 closes a circuit and the switch outputs a voltage of +5 volts. When a 0 is installed, the switch outputs 0 volts. The +5 volts is called a high (H) and the 0 volts is called a low (L). The address 0011 1111 0000 0000 is described by technicians as LLHH HHHH LLLL LLLL.

When the address is finally switched into place, the voltages energize that location. All the other locations remain on hold. Contact is made so that eight bit-holders of the location can do some work. There will be a lot more about this procedure throughout the book.

Once the location has been energized, it is time to do something with the bit holders. They are called *bit holders* because they are capable of storing bits. The eight holders are numbered. On the front panel, the eight are contacted through switches D7 to D0. Each of these data switches are connected to its respective bit. All of the respective bits in the memory are connected together although only one memory location is energized at a time. The switches only can work with an energized location.

The data switches are like the address switches in that up is a 1 and down is a 0. To install the instruction or data byte into an activated address, the switches are pushed up or down. The first line of the program has the binary 1000 to 0110 instruction. The switches are pressed and the +5 and 0 voltages enter their respective bit holders.

In RAM, there are two common ways that the voltages can be stored after they arrive at their bit. In *static RAM*, the voltage arrives at a flip-flop circuit. The circuit receives the high or low and assumes that voltage state. There are detailed descriptions of the flip-flop in the next two chapters.

The other way to store voltage is used in *dynamic RAM*. Dynamic RAM is basically a grid of many tiny capacitances. Each bit has one of these capacitances. If the incoming voltage charges up the capacitor, the bit has a high. When the incoming voltage is 0 and does not charge the capacitor, the bit contains a low.

As the data switches are set, the instruction is installed into memory. The machine-language programmer calls the binary in the memory 1s and 0s. The technician calls the binary highs and lows. As we proceed through the book, I will use both descriptions interchangeably. They both mean the same thing, although the highs and lows are perhaps a better description as we discuss electronics rather than programming.

Chapter 2

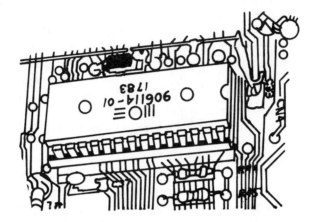

Inside the Digital World

T HE *DIGITAL WORLD* IS COMPLETELY EN-closed by an impenetrable wall. The only way anything can get in or out is through carefully guarded ports of entry and exit. Inside the digital world are a number of meticulously architecturally fashioned circuit structures. This world is microscopic and only a germ would be able to physically travel from one silicon building to another. The activity in the digital world consists of electrical impulses traveling from one building to another with timing that is precisely measured in billionths of a second. A typical small microcomputer has 100,000 or more individual circuits in the digital world. Figure 2-1 shows a simple map of the digital world.

In the digital world there are four types of structures. If you look down at the digital circuits on the computer printboard in Fig. 2-2, you'll see the structures as different size silicon chips. There are large chips with 40, 48, or even 64 little legs sticking out. There are smaller chips with 28, 20, 16, or 14 pins connected to the print board. There could be other chips with in between numbers of solderable legs.

The main building is the microprocessor itself. Without it, the system is not a computer. The MPU is the heart of the system. It performs practically all the computations. A typical 8-bit computer has 40 pins sticking out. The pins are numbered from 1 to 40, counterclockwise, starting from the end with the notch or paint dot. The pins are extended by copper traces on the print board and attach to all the other structures in the digital world.

The rest of the chips are all occupants of the digital world. As proof of occupancy, they are all given addresses. The addresses are listed on a document called the *memory map*. Refer to Fig. 2-3. The memory map is duly noted by the MPU. The MPU is the addressor of the map. The rest of the chips are the addressees. The 8-bit computer is able to have its MPU address 65,536 individual locations. That number is roughly called 64K.

If the MPU is the heart of the digital world, then the ROM is the source of intelligence. Typical ROMs contain 8K or 16K of the total 64K addresses. The ROMs contain programs that operate the computer. They contain all the programs that

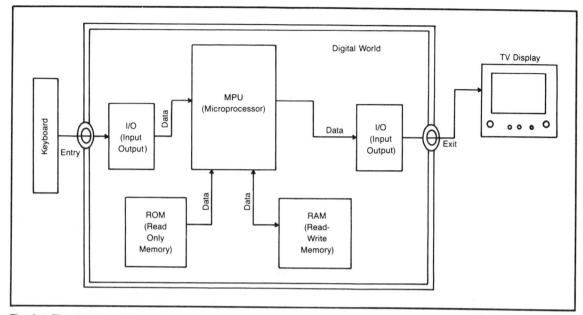

Fig. 2-1. The digital world consists of microscopic circuits built into silicon and involved in moving and processing electrical impulses from ports of entry to exits.

Fig. 2-2. The real structures in the digital world are different size silicon chips with dual in-line rows of solderable legs.

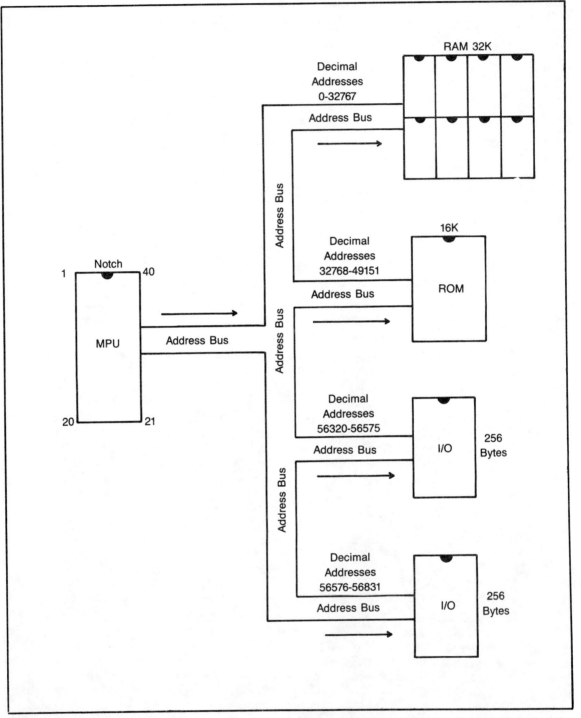

Fig. 2-3. The structures in the digital world consist of the addressor (the MPU) and the addressees (the residents of the memory map).

control the traffic of information that travels between the MPU and the memory map and the programs that transform the inputs from keyboard strikes into digital signals and other operating functions.

The next type of addressable chip are the RAMs. The RAM chips contain rows and rows of empty byte storage areas. Typically an 8-bit microcomputer contains anywhere from 4K to 32K of usable RAM locations. ROM chips can only be read by the MPU, but the RAM chips can be read and also written to. The ROM (read only memory) has its byte size rows of bit holders filled with permanent programs at the factory. That's why you can't write to it. It's bit holders are already occupied. The RAM (read/write memory) holders, on the other hand, are empty. You can write bits into the RAM bytes and then read them when it is necessary. There will be a lot of electronic detail about the two types of memory in Chapters 10 and 11. Incidentally, if you are wondering why I didn't call RAM, random access memory, even though that is what the letters R-A-M stand for, it's because read/write memory is a better definition.

The fourth party in the typical digital world is the input/output chips. These chips can be large 24-40 pin packages, but they require only a few addresses. They contain the ports to the outside world whereby the electrical signals can get entry and after processing obtain exit to do work for us.

BUS LINES

Between the MPU and the residents of the memory map are three groups of bus lines. They are the data bus, address bus, and so called control bus. In the 8-bit computer, illustrated in Fig. 2-4 the *data bus* has eight lines names D7-DO. In a 16-bit computer, the data bus has 16 lines called D15-DO. The data bus is connected simultaneously to every byte in the memory map. There is no conflict, however, since computers are designed so that only one byte can be energized at a time. That way, as long as the computer is operating normally, only the single byte being addressed can be read or written to by the MPU.

The data bus has two way lines. The bits of

communication can travel on the same lines from a memory location to the MPU during a read operation or from the MPU to the memory byte during a write.

The *address bus* in the 8-bit computer typically has 16 lines. The address bus in a 16-bit computer has more. In the 68000 for example, there are 24 lines active and another eight lines built into the chip for a future possibility of 32 lines. The 16 lines can address the 64K memory perfectly. When there are 24 address lines, the additional lines let the MPU address a possible 16M (16,777,216) memory locations directly. If there are 32 lines, the bus can address an astounding 4 trillion bytes of memory.

The set of *control lines* are all individual, unlike the data and address lines which are all identical. All of the lines are examined in detail later in Chapter 5.

PROGRAMS

The buildings in the digital world, except for the few input/output ports and the power supply have nothing to do with the rest of the computer or the periperals. All the work takes place as the MPU reads from and writes to the locations on the memory map. The computer really doesn't do anything much but run programs. A program that is to be run is installed somewhere in the memory map. Figure 2-5 shows a 10-byte program in RAM.

There are a number of ways that the program can be installed. The most common way is to have a program, which consists of byte after byte of instructions and data, typed on the keyboard into empty RAM byte holders. A second method is to plug a ROM into a cartridge holder in the side or back of the computer. This cartridge holder has addresses on the map just like the permanent ROMs on the print board. A third method of installing a program is to enter it by means of tape or disk. The tape or disk input is interpreted by circuits and is installed into RAM.

Once the program is installed in memory, it is run. The MPU runs the program by reading byte after byte of memory, in sequence, analyzing each instruction as it receives it, processing the data as

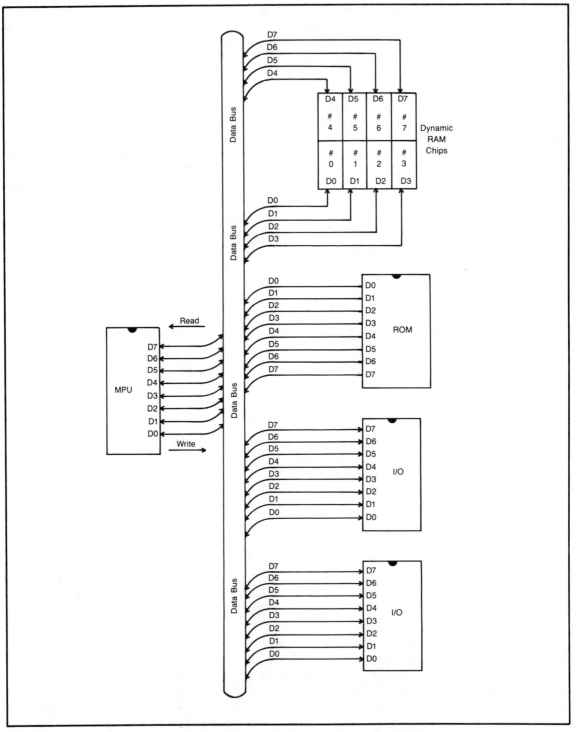

Fig. 2-4. In the so-called 8-bit computer, the data bus has 8 two-way lines named D7-D0.

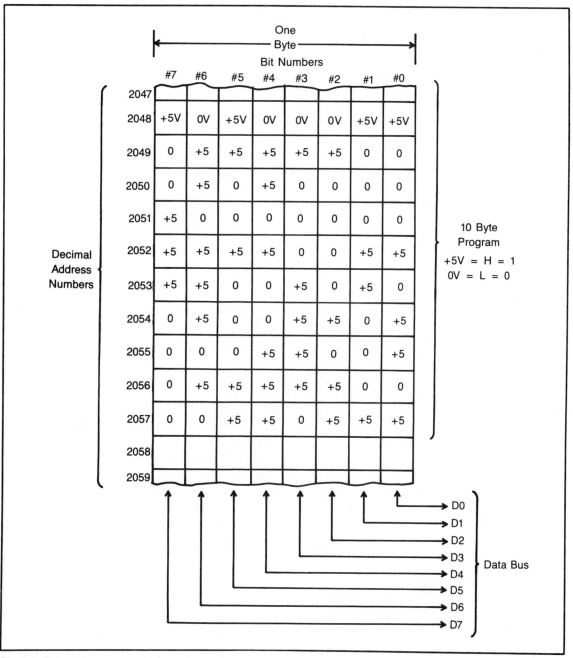

Fig. 2-5. This 10-byte program is installed in decimal map locations 2047-2059.

the instruction directs, and then outputting the results to the outside world. All of the program running takes place between the MPU and the memory map locations inside the digital world.

SQUARE WAVES

The digital world deals in square waves. It does not do anything else. All the digital activity is concerned with is moving and processing streams of

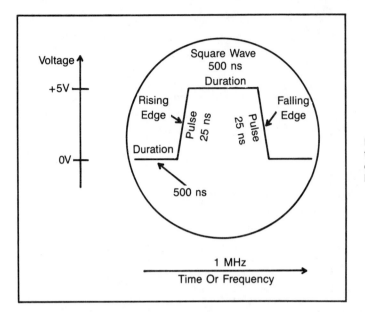

Fig. 2-6. This square wave is a voltage level that passes through time and periodically changes levels from 0 volts to +5 volts and back.

square waves. What exactly is a square wave?

From an electronic point of view, a square wave is plotted on paper or seen on the face of an oscilloscope as the image formed by the two parameters: voltage and time. Voltage is vertical, and time is horizontal. The typical digital square wave is depicted as a voltage level passing through time and changing levels periodically from 0 volts to +5 volts and back. A square wave is depicted in Fig. 2-6.

This action, if viewed on a scope will trace a line from left to right on the scope. The horizontal trace part is called the *duration* of the wave. The vertical tracing is usually called the *pulse*. The dura-

tion of the wave, as it travels, takes up time. It is measured as time. The pulse of the wave, for instance as it changes from 0 to +5 volts, doesn't seem to take up any time. It looks like it is instantaneous.

Clearly the pulse must take up some time, it can't be instantaneous. However for all practical purposes, you can consider it instantaneous most of the time. In a typical square wave, the duration could be 500 nanoseconds while the rising edge of the pulse takes 25 ns from 0 to +5 volts. The 25 ns timing is usually inconsequential. It is only 5% of the duration of the wave.

One full wave can be considered to have one

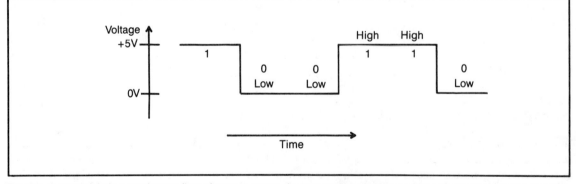

Fig. 2-7. A wave train is a continuous flow of square waves. An assortment of highs and lows in any pattern can appear.

18

rising edge, one duration at a +5 volt level, one falling edge, and one duration at a 0 volt level. A wave train is a continuous stream of square waves. The levels do not necessarily have to be in order; that is, the same waveshape one after another. The train can and does have the subsequent individual levels in any order according to the intent of the signal. Figure 2-7 is an example.

The +5 volt level is considered the high voltages (H) and the 0 volt level the (L). This means, of course, that the +5 volt level is electrical code for a binary 1 and the 0 volt represents the binary 0. Examination of the square wave in Fig. 2-6 shows that it can store two binary digits during the time of one full square wave. A 1 is created when the rising edge of the wave occurs. The 1 remains as long as the wave shape is held high. A 0 is produced as a falling edge happens. The 0 stays as long as the wave shape is held low.

The digital world only processes these square waves. It deals in highs and lows. There are only two states to work with during programming. The digital signal is finite and not like the familiar analog electronics that you are used to. A typical analog signal is the sine wave. It is viewed on a scope with time as the horizontal sweep and voltage as the vertical. In comparison to the two voltage levels in a digital signal, the sine wave in Fig. 2-8 has an infinite number of voltage levels. Every point on the sine wave is at a different voltage level. There will be a lot more detail about the sine wave and other analog signals in Chapter 6.

You can easily test the circuits in the digital world with a specially designed device called the *logic probe*. The test probe in Fig. 2-9 shows the logic state at a test point by means of tiny LED lights. Typically a probe has one light for a *high*, one for a *low*, and a third called *pulse*.

If you attach the probe into the circuit by connecting one clip lead to +5 volts and the second clip lead to 0 volts, you can touch down on an energized chip pin and receive an indication. If the

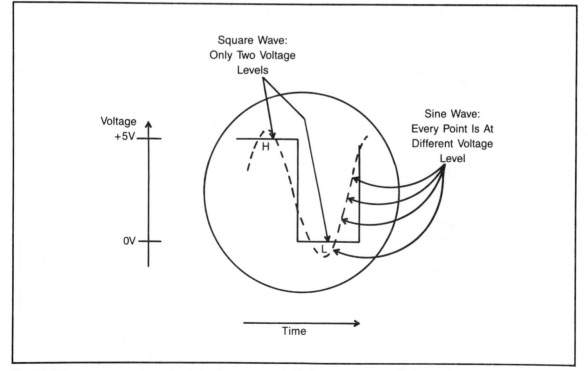

Fig. 2-8. When a square wave and a sine wave are compared, the square wave only has two levels. The sine wave has a different level at every point on the wave for an infinite number of levels.

19

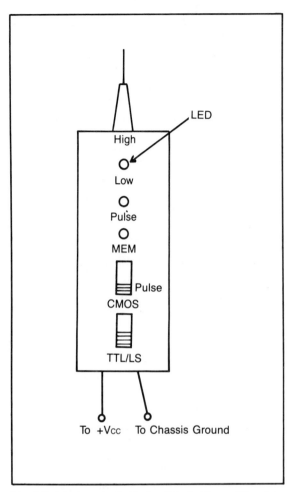

Fig. 2-9. A logic probe is a test unit that will reveal the state of a test point; high, low, or pulse.

pin is being held high, the high LED will light. When the pin is held low, the low LED will light. If a wave train is pulsing at the test point, the pulse LED will blink or just simply light up. A high-frequency pulse makes it blink and a low-pulse frequency will just light it up. My probe blinks at frequencies above 100 kHz.

The probe is useful to pick out the two logic states and the wave train indication. It does not reveal the third logic state. Did I say the third state? Yes, there is one more.

THIRD LOGIC STATE

The third logic state is called Tristate or three-state by technicians and engineers. It is the state of nonstate. It is the state that a test point assumes when it is turned off but the computer is otherwise energized. If you touch the logic probe to a chip pin that is three-stating, none of the LEDs will light. The pin will appear dead to the logic probe.

That is why the old faithful vom is so useful to a digital technician. If you touchdown onto a three-stating TTL chip pin with a vom you'll get a voltage reading somewhere between 0.8 volts and 2.4 volts as in Fig. 2-10. What is this third voltage that can be in the digital world? Examine the simple circuit in Fig. 2-11 that is designed around the phenomena of three-stating.

There are a lot of bus lines in the computer. Suppose you have a bus line with three chips attached to it. Also the three chips are designed so

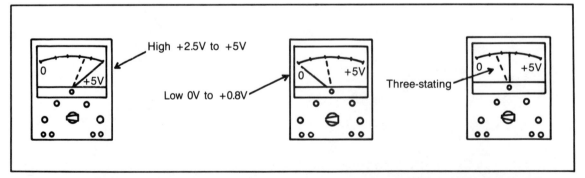

Fig. 2-10. The vom will reveal one of three possible logic states at a test point in the digital circuits. A voltage between +2.5 volts and +5 volts is the high state. Voltage between 0 and 0.8 volts is the low state. When the reading is above 0.8 and below 2.5 volts, the test point has no digital state, is developing a static noise voltage, and is said to be three-stating.

that only one chip at a time is permitted to input to the bus. The other two chips must be turned off while the remaining chip is inputting.

All three chips in Fig. 2-11 are made with a three-state control pin. That way only one chip can input to the bus without interference from the other two. Three-stating is common in computers.

Another way that a test point can be found to be three-stating is when as open circuit has developed in a chip. The indication is there and is quickly located with the vom. Unfortunately, most logic probes are lacking in the ability to read a three-state condition.

The reason the three-state condition produces a voltage is as follows. If the computer is not energized, there is no voltage developed. However, if the computer is energized and a chip is three-stating, the pin is in a high impedance condition. The voltage in the computer surround the three-stating pin. Static electricity builds up due to the electrical noise bristling around the pin and forms a static charge that reads on the vom between the

high and low. The three-state indication is an important test and design piece of information.

SQUARE-WAVE BYTES

In the digital world most of the activity takes place in the form of bytes. If the movement of a byte is parallel, such as occurs when the MPU reads a memory location, then the eight bits of square wave voltages all move at the same time over the data bus from the memory to MPU. Parallel movement of a byte of data is shown in Fig. 2-12A. When the movement is serial, as when the byte travels from the computer to the serial input of a printer, then the eight bits travel one at a time, in proper sequence, one byte after another. Figure 2-12B shows a serially moving byte.

In the digital world, most of the work is based around the byte-sized register. The registers can be single bytes, double bytes or more, but they are all forms of bytes. The register is the instrument that runs the computing. When you think about computing, you are mostly concerned with

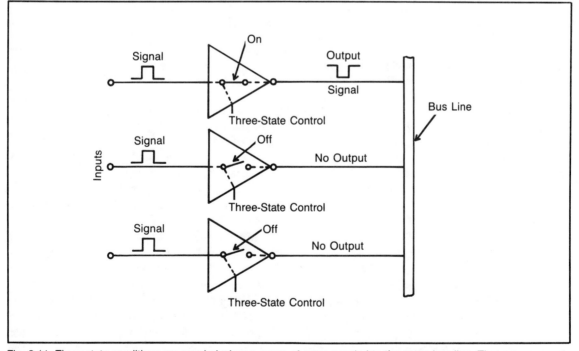

Fig. 2-11. Three-state conditions are needed when a group of gates are tied to the same bus line. That way, one gate at a time can output while the rest of them stay off.

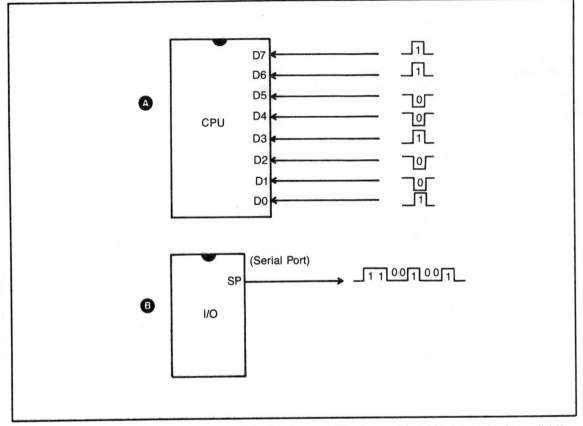

Fig. 2-12. When a byte travels on all eight lines of the data bus as 8 bits abreast, it is said to be moving in parallel (A). If a byte travels over only one line in single file, it is serial movement (B).

registers. Registers are capable of doing a number of operations. The MPU, ROM, RAM, and I/O chips are all loaded with registers that have byte related numbers of bit holders. What are the few jobs these registers do? The jobs break down into two categories: movements and manipulations.

Byte Movements

First of all, a register can move its bit contents to another register. If the bits in a byte are numbered from 7 to 0, one register can transfer bits 7-0 to the same bit positions in a second register. The bits are transferred in parallel fashion from register to register over a data bus that is also numbered 7 to 0 to match up with the register bit positions. Registers normally transfer bits in a byte

batch, as in Fig. 2-13, not one at a time.

Another movement that job registers can perform is an exchange of contents. For instance, Fig. 2-14 shows two accumulator registers, A and B. During the running of a program it might be necessary to put the bits of A into B, while at the same time take the contents of B and shuttle them over to A.

Moving the bytes from register to register is the most popular activity the computer performs. Better than 70% of the computing is moving the bytes from MPU to memory and back. The bytes are also moved from MPU to the I/O ports and back. They can also be moved from memory location to memory location. Register content movement requires exact electronic timing. The circuit details are covered in the next chapter.

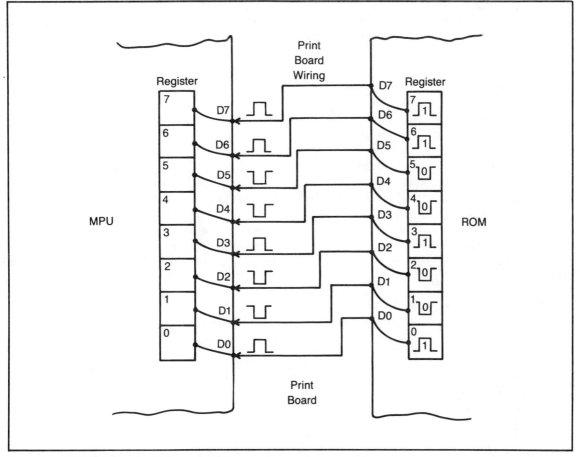

Fig. 2-13. A ROM register is sending the MPU register a parallel byte of data.

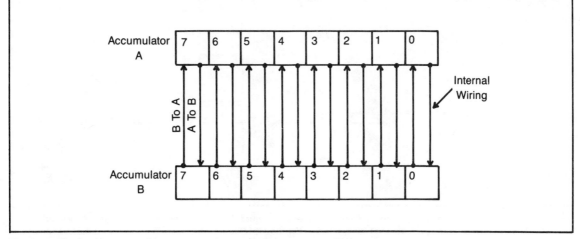

Fig. 2-14. These two accumulators can exchange their contents easily.

Byte Manipulations

Once a byte arrives in a register in the MPU it can be manipulated. The first type of work that can be done to it is simple mathematics. The byte can be added to, subtracted from, multiplied by, divided by, or whatever else you'd desire in the realm of elementary math. Most small computers can really only perform addition. The subtraction is, with a bit of trickery, called two's complement, accomplished with addition procedures. Multiplication and division capabilities are produced by using a software routine contained in ROM.

The register electronics enables the computer to perform math because a register can count as shown in Fig. 2-15. The counter circuits are discussed in later chapters.

The next group of register manipulations are logic abilities: NOT, AND, OR, and exclusive-OR. In order to do the logic jobs, the register circuits must use NOT gates, AND gates, OR gates, and XOR gates in addition to the flip-flop bit holders. Figure 2-16 shows the symbols of all the logic functions.

There are some other logic functions that computers perform, such as YES, AND, NOR, and XNOR. However, by combining the NOT, AND OR and XOR gates in specific wirings, all the logic functions can be accomplished. The gates are covered in detail in the next chapter.

The next way a register is manipulated is called complementing. Figure 2-17 has all the 1s changed to 0s and the 0s changed to 1s. Once the complement instruction is executed, the bits in a complemented register are reversed.

Another simple register manipulation called clear is shown in Fig. 2-18. Clear is another word for the logic state of L or 0. When a bit is clear, it has a low stored in its flip-flop circuit. When a reg-

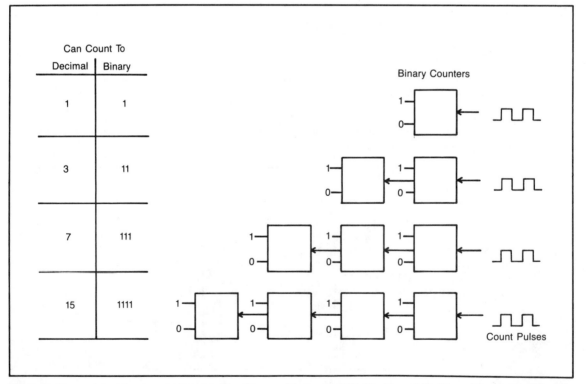

Fig. 2-15. One register bit can count 0 and 1. Two bits are able to count 00, 01, 10, and 11. Three bits counts 000, 001, 010, 011, 100, 101, 110, and 111. Four bits, or a nybble, can count 0000, 0001, 0010, 0011, 0100, 0101, 0110, 0111, 1000, 1001, 1010, 1011, 1100, 1101, 1110, and 1111.

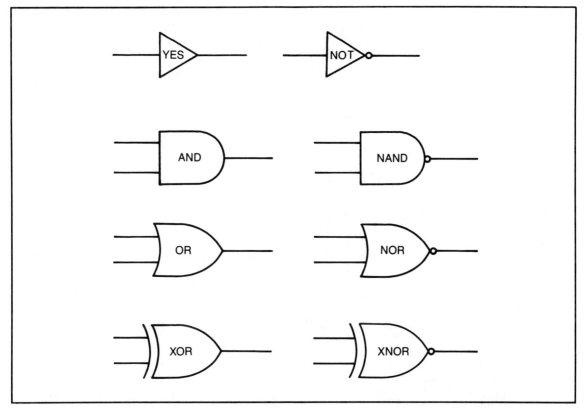

Fig. 2-16. The schematic symbols for the logic components are triangles, bullet shaped objects, and circles.

ister is cleared all the bits, no matter their value, end up at the end of the instruction in a low-voltage state of 0.

Two more register bit manipulations are called incrementing and decrementing. As Fig. 2-19 shows, *incrementing* means increasing the value of the register. *Decrementing* decreases the value of the register. Incrementing and decrementing can be done by one step, two steps, or more. If you want to increment a register by one, you add a high to bit 0 of the register. This adds one to the total value of the register. This adds one to the total value of the register. To decrement, you remove one from bit 0 of the register. This deducts one from the total

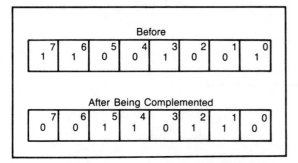

Fig. 2-17. When all the 1s in a register are changed to 0s and the 0s to 1s, the register has been complemented.

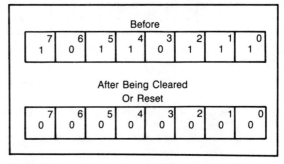

Fig. 2-18. If a register is cleared, all bits, no matter their state, are made into 0s.

25

	MSB 15	14	13	12	11	10	9	8	7	6	5	4	3	2	1	0 LSB
1st	0	0	0	0	0	0	0	0	0	0	0	0	0	0	0	0
2nd	0	0	0	0	0	0	0	0	0	0	0	0	0	0	0	1
3rd	0	0	0	0	0	0	0	0	0	0	0	0	0	0	1	0
4th	0	0	0	0	0	0	0	0	0	0	0	0	0	0	1	1
5th	0	0	0	0	0	0	0	0	0	0	0	0	0	1	0	0
6th	0	0	0	0	0	0	0	0	0	0	0	0	0	1	0	1
7th	0	0	0	0	0	0	0	0	0	0	0	0	0	1	1	0
8th	0	0	0	0	0	0	0	0	0	0	0	0	0	1	1	1

Fig. 2-19. Incrementing a register means raising its value. Decrementing lowers the value. Although the operation is usually performed one step at a time, multiple steps can also be done.

value of the eight bits in the register.

The final job that a register can do is *shift*. Pure shifting, as in Fig. 2-20, occurs when the Hs or Ls in the eight bits are all moved at the same time one place. If you shift them left, all the bits move one place left, bit 7 falls out of the register, and bit 0 is given a low. Should you shift the register right, all the bits move one place, bit 0 falls out of the register, and bit 7 has a low installed.

Actually, during computing, shifting a register can be combined with the operation of another register and the end bits are manipulated and not lost. However, you get the idea of shifting with this definition.

That is about all the registers do during computing. They move and manipulate their contents. The registers in the MPU are a lot more versatile than the memory location bit holders. The registers

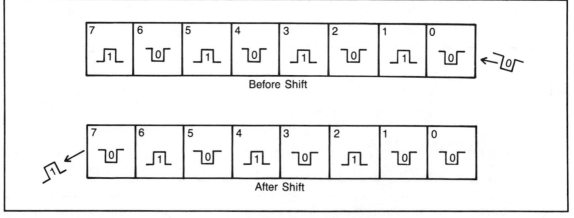

Fig. 2-20. A register is able to shift bits to the left or to the right upon command. Bits can be pushed in and can fall out.

in the MPU are all assigned various jobs. The MPU accumulator registers are the most agile of all. They can perform every job I mentioned. The rest of the MPU registers can do some of the jobs but not usually all of them. The MPU registers are discussed in detail in Chapter 8.

The RAM and ROM registers cannot usually do much more than store and move the binary bits to the MPU. The RAM can also receive bytes from the MPU. The ROM, of course, can't receive from the MPU since its locations have bits burnt permanently into the holders. The ROM is a read only location.

Some computers have MPUs that follow instructions to transfer bytes directly from memory location to memory location. However, a lot of computers cannot do that directly. In order to transfer a byte from one RAM location to another RAM location, the byte must be routed though the MPU.

ADDRESSING

All of the byte movement and manipulation concerned itself with data. The data is the bits that are contained in the registers. As you know, registers have addresses. On the memory map, addresses are numbered in decimal starting at 0 on up. An 8-bit computer is able to address a total of 64K addresses. 64K means 0 through 65,535 individual addresses on the memory map.

Figure 2-21 shows the registers in the MPU. In a small MPU you could have addresses like accumulators A and B, index registers X and Y, stack pointers U and S, condition code register CCR and program counter PC. These addresses are just as important as the memory map and must be thought

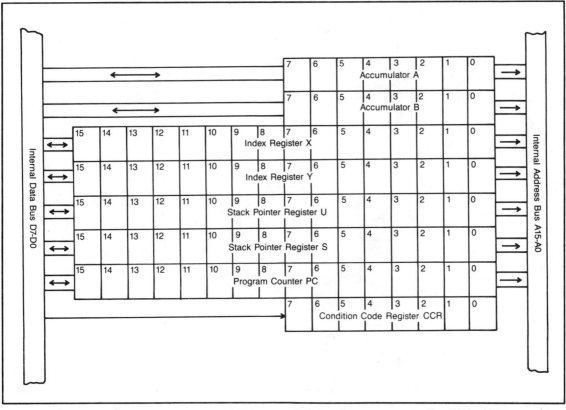

Fig. 2-21. The addresses of the registers in the MPU are not listed on the memory map. The MPU addresses and accesses them internally.

of under the category of addressing even though they are not listed on the memory map.

When writing a program the memory map locations are defined by their number in decimal or hex. The MPU register addresses are defined by bits in an instruction (Fig. 1-5). Either way both types of addresses are located by means of a set of bits.

The addressing of a register in the MPU is performed internally in the MPU. When an instruction arrives at the Instruction Decoder circuit in the MPU, the decoder can quickly address the correct internal register by one, two, or three highs and lows of the address imbedded in the byte or bytes of instruction, as seen in Fig. 2-22. If only one bit

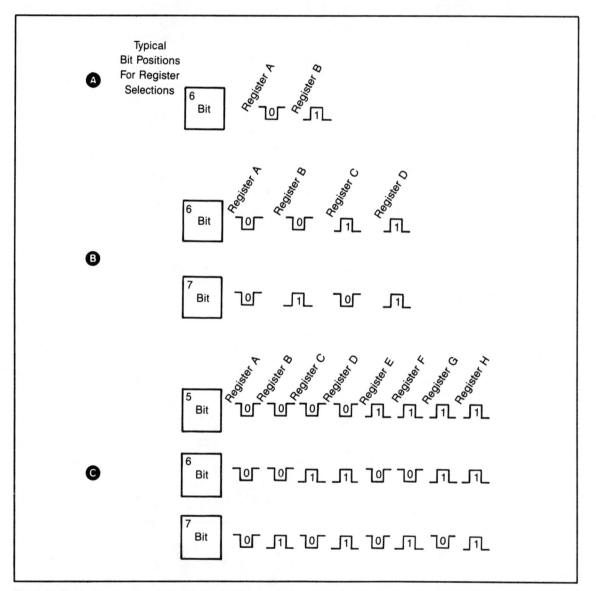

Fig. 2-22. The instruction decoder inside the MPU uses bits from incoming instructions to address MPU registers. A) One bit can choose from two registers. B) Two bits have a choice from four registers. C) Three bits can choose among eight registers.

is used for the register address, then one of two registers can be chosen. When two bits are used for the register address, then one of four registers can be picked out. Should the instruction use three to choose a register then one of eight registers can be addressed.

The addressing of a memory map location is different than addressing a register inside the MPU. The MPU and the instructions figure is on the map addressing, but they have to address external chips. The MPU extends 16 address lines in a bus to the memory map residents.

The main addressing mechanism in the MPU is the 16 bit (two byte) register called the program counter, or PC. The PC is connected bit by bit to the 16 address lines. The lines are named A15-A0. The PC is built to be able to be incremented, added to, and subtracted from. These are the three abilities the PC needs to conduct its addressing chores.

Since all the PC does is address the locations of the memory map, it is a one way bus. As Fig. 2-23 shows, the addresses are able to travel from the MPU to the memory locations but not back. There is no need for the addresses to return. This contrasts with the data bus since data must be able to travel from the MPU to the bit holders for a write operation and then the other way (from the memory bytes back to the MPU) during a read. The address bus only conducts a form of a writing operation, MPU to memory.

Address Sequencing

The PC is built to constantly sequence as a program is run. The PC starts addressing at its current state and continues to address each sequential program location, in turn, as the program progresses. For example, suppose the PC is started at, or as it is called initialized at, 0000 0000 0000 0000. As the program begins running, the PC puts out the 16 zeros onto the address bus. The electronics decodes the starting address as decimal 0 and activates the first location in memory. All of the other locations remain in a three-state condition. Only the one location is turned on.

If the program instruction is a read, whatever highs or lows are in the location's bit holders are flashed into the data bus and head for the MPU. Should the instruction be a write, whatever highs or lows are in the accumulator of the MPU are placed on the data bus and go to the activated location's bit holders.

As the data speeds one way or the other, the PC is incremented to 0000 0000 0000 0001. After the data is transferred and is settled comfortably into its destination, then the PC is permitted to place the next address onto the address bus. The cycle repeats itself. It keeps repeating itself over and over again until the program has all its instruction executed. The address sequencing is automatic and is one of the staples of the computer operation.

Even though I used 0s and 1s to describe the contents of the PC as it addresses, the 16 bit holders of the PC are in reality working with voltage highs and lows. It is these voltages that are actually placed on the address bus and open up the coding circuits of the memory chips. Each address line carries a voltage of +5 or 0 to designate the address. The addresses are highs and lows just as the data is composed of highs and lows.

As the PC increments, it starts at decimal 0. Each increment adds a binary 1 to the contents of the PC. You can add a binary 1 65,535 times to a 16-bit register before the register cannot go any higher and returns to 0000 0000 0000 0000 the second time. That is why the 16-bit register is capable of addressing a 64K memory bank in the digital world.

Address Changing

Besides having the automatic power to sequence addresses, the MPU is able to, under instruction, give the PC a change of address. There are many instances in most programs where sequencing the addresses by itself, won't permit a program to successfully do a job. There are many times in a program where the addressing must stop sequencing and jump or branch to another part of memory. These changes of address are installed in the program by the programmer. When these changes of address program lines arrive at the MPU, complex manipulations take place in the

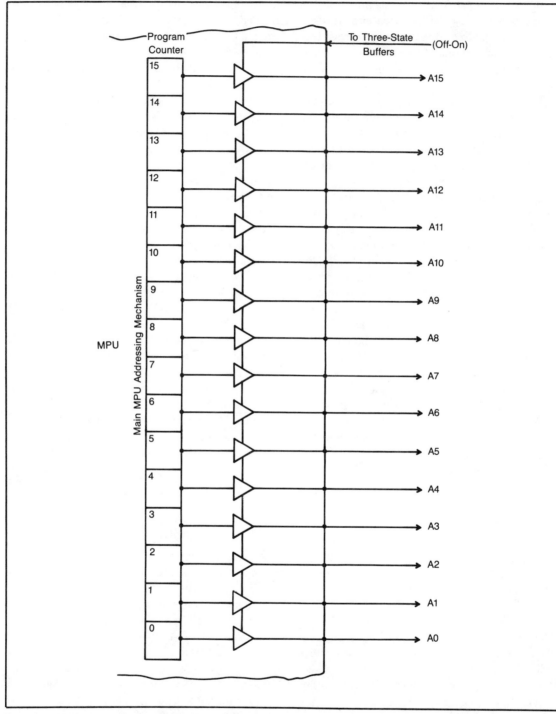

Fig. 2-23. The program counter register in the MPU conducts a form of write operation from the MPU to the memory map addresses.

registers. One way the PC address changes is with a branch instruction. The PC gets a binary number added to or subtracted from a current address. The new binary total is then placed on the address bus and another address, not in sequence, produced by combining the current address in the PC + or − an offset number (+2). The PC outputs this change of address to the address bus and the out of sequence memory location is opened as shown in Fig. 2-24.

Another change of address procedure is less complex. A jump instruction orders this second type. The instruction commands the MPU to place this new address into the PC bits in its entirety as in Fig. 2-25. There is to be no adding or subtracting of offsets. The next address follows the jump instruction. The 16-bit address is in the next two locations.

When the PC changes the address in these ways, then the new address formed becomes the program location. That change of address becomes the new start address. The PC does not switch back to the old addresses it had been sequencing. It continues sequencing at this new area in the memory that it has been switched to.

If you are a programmer, you will recognize these manipulations. In BASIC, the statements GOTO, IF-THEN and so on are change of address

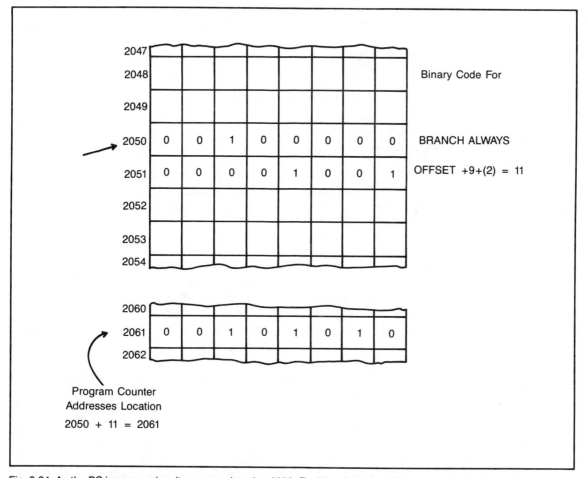

Fig. 2-24. As the PC is sequencing, it accesses location 2050. Residing there is a binary code for the instruction "Branch Always". The PC then accesses the next location for the offset, which is binary 9. The PC then adds +2 to the 9 and branches 11 locations ahead for the next program byte.

31

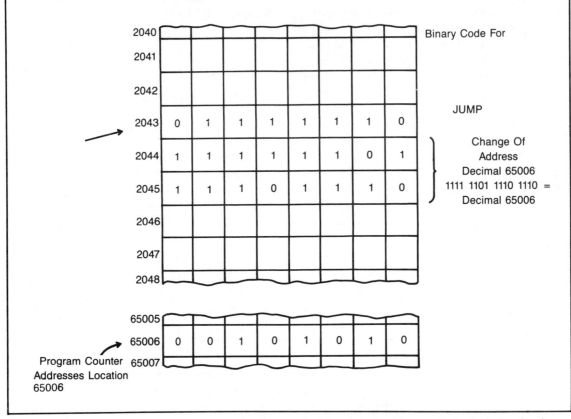

Fig. 2-25. As the PC is sequencing, it accesses location 2043. Residing there is a binary code for the instruction Jump. The PC then accesses the next two byte-sized locations for the new 16-bit address.

instructions. With assembly language, the change of address mnemonics are grouped in the jump and branch instructions. The electronics though are affected as the highs and lows are grouped as bytes and cause the circuit to respond in the way they were designed to operate. Actual circuit details of the digital world will be covered in the next chapter.

Addressing Modes

Computing is seen as cycles of MPU and memory action, whereby the PC addresses a location, data is read from the location, processed in the MPU and then written back into locations. Data is stashed in many areas of the memory map at many locations. The MPU must be able to address all locations for the data, even the most out of the way places on the map.

The computing will proceed in the most advantageous way if the data can be located with the least number of steps. Some data stashes are different than others and require different modes of addressing to locate them. For example, data can be installed in the program itself right after the instruction.

If you have an instruction byte that says "load accumulator A", the question is, with what? There are addressing modes that answer that question. In the 6800 MPU, there are four addressing modes whereby you can load accumulator A. The programmer knows them as Immediate, Direct, Indexed, and Extended. The four LDA modes are found in the hex machine instruction bytes, 86, 96, A6, and B6. The bytes look like this in binary:

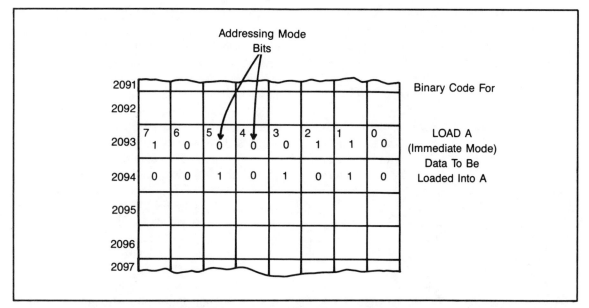

Fig. 2-26. The Immediate mode of addressing is ordered when instruction bits 5 and 4 are 00. This tells the Instruction Register that the needed data itself will be located in the next program byte.

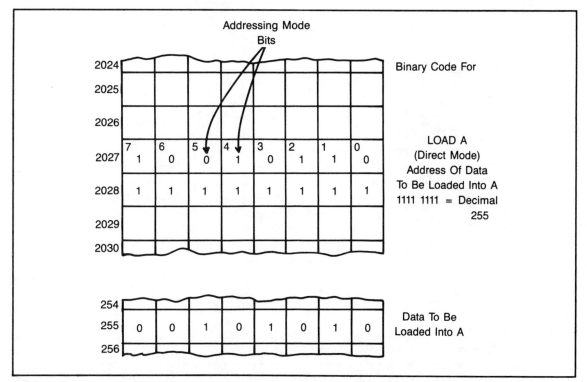

Fig. 2-27. The Direct mode of addressing is ordered when bits 5 and 4 are 01. This tells the IR that the address of the needed data can be found in the next program byte. The single-byte address limits the location to decimal addresses 0-255.

LDA	Bits	Hex
Immediate	10000101	86
Direct	10010101	96
Indexed	10100101	A6
Extended	10110101	B6

Notice the bits are identical in all four LDA instruction except for bit positions 5 and 4. These are the address mode bits. As the program is being run, these highs and lows appear at the instruction register of the MPU. When LL appears the IR decodes it as LDA in the Immediate mode. This alerts the MPU that the byte of data it is to load into the accumulator A is the next byte in the next address in the program. The LL, or 00 as in Fig. 2-26, tells the MPU where the data stash is.

If bits 5 and 4 are LH, it tells the MPU the addressing mode is Direct. This is shown in Fig. 2-27. This means that the next byte of the program is not data. The next byte of the program is the address where the data will be found. The MPU then places the address into the PC and the data is fetched with the Direct addressing mode.

Notice that in this mode the address is only the single next byte of data. One byte can only count from 0 to 255. This means the location is in the lower address numbers from 0 to 255 only.

If the Extended mode is used, the address mode bits will be HH. This tells the MPU that the address of the data will be found in the next two bytes of the program. This is exactly the way the Direct mode is designed except Extended points to the next two bytes instead of only the next one byte. By containing the address in two bytes, 16 bits, the address containing the desired data can be placed anywhere in the 64K map. To obtain the data, the MPU places the two byte address in the PC, the location is opened up, and the data is read out of the bit holders. Figure 2-28 gives an example.

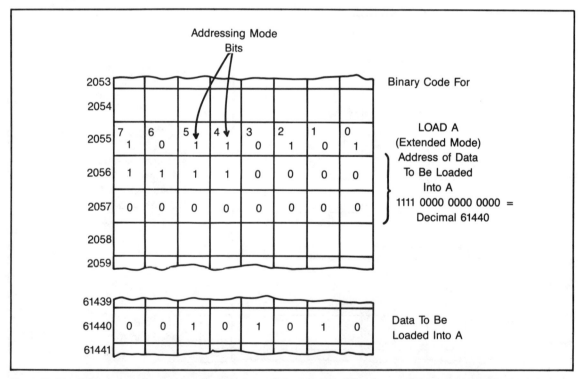

Fig. 2-28. The Extended mode of addressing is commanded when bits 5 and 4 are 11. This tells the IR to place the contents of the next two bytes of the program into the program counter. The two bytes are the address of the next location to be accessed. The two-byte address gives the PC the ability to address any location on the 64K map.

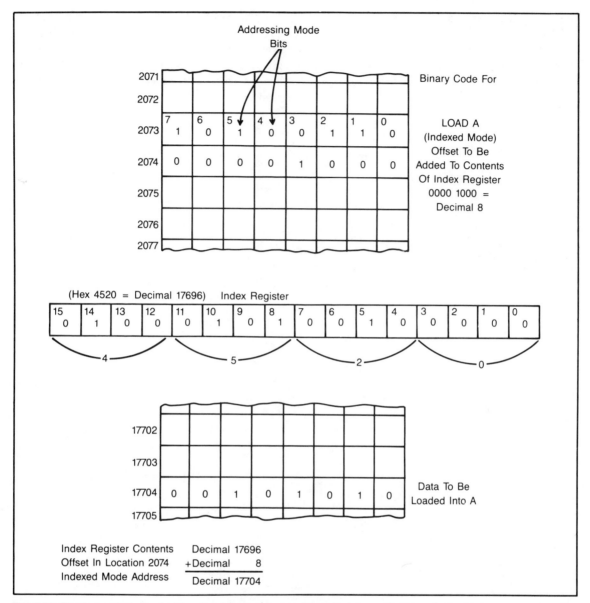

Fig. 2-29. The Indexed mode of addressing is ordered when bits 5 and 4 are 10. This tells the IR that the next program byte is an offset to be added to the contents of the index register. With the addition of the offset, the index register forms an address in its 16 bits. This address that is placed on the address bus.

The fourth addressing mode is executed by the MPU when the 5th and 4th bits of the instruction contains bits HL. This mode is called indexed and is a very handy way of addressing the memory map to locate a byte of data. The study of indexing and the development of indexing techniques by the pro-grammer is a study all by itself. We are, at this time, only interested in examining the mode to understand the electronics involved.

Specifically, when the MPU receives the index-mode bit-code HL, it knows that the byte after the instruction byte containing the HL is an indexed offset. The indexed offset is a byte that is added to the contents of another MPU register, the Index register. (The Index register, covered in Chapter 9, is a 16-bit register like the PC. The Index register also concerns itself with addressing. Figure 2-29.)

The result of the addition forms an address. That address is placed on the address bus. That address is then activated and the bit holders either give up their highs or lows or receive highs and lows, according to whether the instruction was a read or write.

Chapter 3

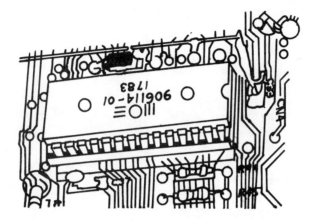

What Makes It Tick

I N THE DIGITAL WORLD, ABOUT ALL THAT HAP-
pens is voltage states (in the form of highs, lows,
and pulses) moving from place to place. The states
are changed from high to low or kept the same.
They chug through relatively long distances and
follow intricate pathways. Sometimes they travel
one route and other times they take a different
route. As they journey, they can be buffered,
latched, stored, counted, NOTed, ANDed, ORed,
and exclusive-ORed. They are powered by electricity and timed by a clock that runs courtesy of
a crystal oscillator.

As you write programs, the overall program job
you want to accomplish is lost to the circuits running the machine. The hardware has no versatility.
It runs every program in the same way following
the same rules. One program is the same as another
to the circuits. All the circuits know is to process
the voltage states in the way they are designed. As
far as the circuits in the digital world are concerned,
your word processor software gets the same treatment that Space Invaders gets.

This makes understanding the hardware easy
in comparison to the software. Once you master the
circuits in your computer, you got it. No further effort is needed. This is unlike programming the machine, which requires a new effort for every fresh
project that you want it to perform.

The vital basic circuits that you must com-
prehend are astoundingly small in number. The
digital world operates almost exclusively with only
gates and registers. You'll run into only about eight
variations of gates although they are really only the
combinations of three gates, NOT, AND, and OR.
Gates are circuits that route the traveling voltage
states from place to place. According to what states
enter a gate determines what states leave a gate
or is stopped at that point.

Registers are circuits that are able to store a
state. The states are stored in circuits called flip-
flops. This type of storage is called static. Other
circuits that are also able to store states are the
dynamic type. The states in these storage areas are
kept as capacitor charges.

The gates and the registers are intermingled to perform most of the digital world jobs. They are aided in their efforts by some additional electronic switching circuits. Let's explore these digital world circuits.

THE LOGICAL COMPUTER

The circuits in the digital world are designed to do a simple job. They turn off and turn on. They don't do anything else. They could be replaced with a set of on-off switches or relays. In fact, computers right after WWII did use relays and vacuum tubes to do the job. The same jobs are being done today except for the fact that those thousands of circuits have been shrunk down into chips.

Computers are logic machines. Logic is a science and not particularly new since most of the beginning work was perfected by Aristotle. Logical work can be performed by many other means besides electronics. For example the older model automatic washing machine is an example of logical work being done mechanically. The cycles the machine goes through are the result of a wheel with notches being slowly turned. As particular notches arrive at the control point, switches are caused to be opened or closed, producing the various cycles.

New washing machines have eliminated the old notched wheel control. The new machines control the timing with a small electronic real-time circuit. As the cycles proceed from start to finish, the internal cycle switches are opened or closed electronically.

Either way, the same logical controlling is being used; the old one was mechanical, and the new one is electronic. The designer can describe them both with the same logic.

The entire washing machine operation is an exercise in the correct turning off and turning on of the wash cycles. That is what all logic systems do; turn off and turn on. Of course there are literally millions of the offs and ons during a computer program run but that is all that is happening.

Logic Operations

There are really only three logical operations.

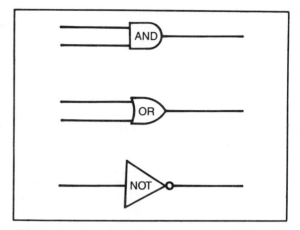

Fig. 3-1. The three basic logic operations are NOT, AND, and OR. By combining them, all the other operations can be created.

They are illustrated in Fig. 3-1. All the other logic types can be produced by combining these basic three. If you study the science of logic, one of the first things you'll learn is DeMorgan's Theorem. It states that any logic gate can be built with two combinations of the three basic gates: AND plus NOT or OR plus NOT.

In your computer, all of the gates are found. The gates jobs are to receive highs and lows at their inputs and logically, as a result of the inputs, produce a predictable output. Besides the three basic types, you'll find gates called exclusive-OR, NAND, NOR, and exclusive-NOR. (See Fig. 3-2.) The various gates could be hidden in many circuit variations. Often, the only way that you will know that a circuit is configured as a particular type gate is by its inputs and output. If the inputs and outputs results in the predictable action of a NAND gate, then the circuit is a NAND gate no matter what it looks like or is called.

Digital Circuit Materials

The digital circuits in your computer are built in and around chips. Outside the chips, next to numbers printed on the computer board shown in Fig. 3-3 are discrete color coded resistors. They are designed as R23, R14, etc. Numbers such as C14, C31, etc. are discrete color coded capacitors. Alongside numbers like PN2222, 2N4401, etc. are

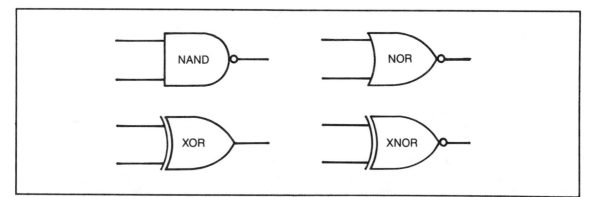

Fig. 3-2. The remaining basic gates are exclusive-OR (EOR), NAND, NOR, and exclusive-NOR (ENOR).

Fig. 3-3. Printed next to the component on most modern computer boards is the same part number as is found on the schematic and parts list.

discrete transistors. You are able to see the small bodies of the components, snip them out of the circuits and solder new ones into their place. It takes a bit of care to do it right, but it is not overly difficult.

These discrete components are wired to nearby microscopic integrated circuits installed by photographic chemical means onto silicon chips. They are contained in what is known as a Dual Inline Package, abbreviated as DIP. The DIP is a tiny rectangular component with little sturdy legs sticking out. The legs are arranged in dual, inline rows on either side of the rectangle.

Inside the chip are complete circuits with more resistors, capacitors, and transistors. However, you can't physically contact these components. They are not discrete. You can run tests on them and sometimes even pinpoint which of these germ size parts are defective. That might be interesting, but you can't replace it. The entire chip must be changed when one component in one circuit in the DIP is upsetting your computing.

The only difference between the discrete components and the internal chip components in the circuit is their size. Resistors are resistors whether mammoth or as big as a virus. There are some limitations as far as the amounts of resistance possible in the tiny chip, but both types are resistors.

The same goes for capacitors. They both do the job a capacitor is supposed to do. Transistors also

act out transistor type duty whether they are hidden in the DIP or sit boldly in view on the print board.

RESISTORS

The discrete resistors in your computer are mostly needed for pull up jobs. They are usually carbon resistors. That is, the body of the resistor is made of carbon. To the carbon is added an insulator like a resin. The amount of resin determines how much resistance the resistor will afford. Figure 3-4 and Table 3-1 explain the resistance color code. But resistance to what?

The resistor impedes the flow of electrons in a circuit. The greater the resistance the fewer electrons that can pass through the carbon-resin body. A typical pull up resistor in the computer has a resistance of 1500 ohms, 3300 ohms, etc. It is installed between a voltage source of +5 volts and a pin of a chip. The +5 volts is supposed to hold the pin high at +5 volts. This arrangement is shown in Fig. 3-5A. While the pin is high, both sides of the resistor are held at +5 volts. There are, in effect, no electrons passing through the resistor.

When no electrons flow through a resistor and a voltage like +5 volts is applied to one end of the resistance, the voltage at both ends of the resistance are the same. The voltage potential exudes through the resistance without any dropoff. The voltage potential acts just like water pressure. When the

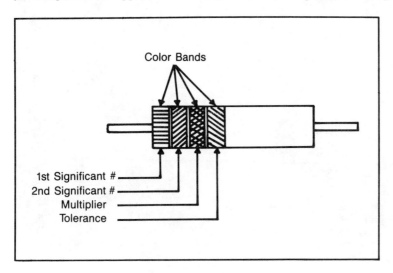

Fig. 3-4. The resistance in ohms of a discrete resistor is painted in bands on the body.

Table 3-1. Color Code Chart for Resistors

| Color Code | OHMS | | | 4th Band |
| | 1st Band | 2nd Band | 3rd Band | |
	1st Significant Number	2nd Significant Number	Decimal Multiplier	Percent Tolerance
Black	0	0	1	
Brown	1	1	10	
Red	2	2	100	
Orange	3	3	1,000	
Yellow	4	4	10,000	
Green	5	5	100,000	
Blue	6	6	1,000,000	
Violet	7	7	10^7	
Gray	8	8	10^8	
White	9	9	10^9	
Gold			0.1	± 5%
Silver			0.01	± 10%
No Band				± 20%

faucet is turned off, the water pressure is there even though no water is flowing. Voltage is nothing more than electromotive pressure.

When electrons start flowing through the resistance, as in Fig. 3-5B, the voltage situation at the two resistor ends changes. The voltage at the end connected to the +5 volt source remains at +5 volts. The voltage at the other end falls. The more electrons that flow the further the voltage falls. If only a few electrons flow the voltage could fall slightly, perhaps to +3 volts. This would be determined by the amount of current flow and the

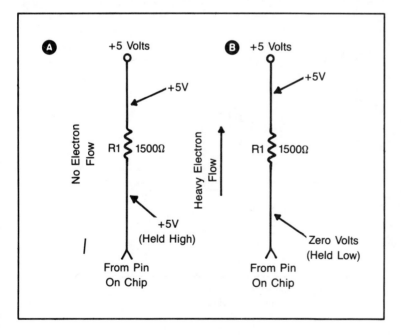

Fig. 3-5. A) When there are no electrons flowing, the voltage at both ends of a resistor is the same. There is no voltage drop across the resistor. B) When electrons flow, the voltage drops at the end of the resistor where the electrons enter.

amount of resistance in the carbon-resin body. The more current and resistance there is, the more the voltage drop will be. If the current is really heavy, the voltage could easily drop down near 0 volts.

These resistance facts of life are used in digital circuits. Let's examine the circuit in Fig. 3-6 that uses a pull up resistor. The sample circuit consists of two resistors and an off-on switch. The two resistors are connected in series. The resistor, named R1, has 220 ohms. The other is R2, a 330 ohm resistor. R1 connects to +5 volts and R2 to the chassis ground which is at a potential of zero volts. Connected from the junction of R1-R2 to ground is the off-on switch. When the switch is open, as in Fig. 3-6A, the following happens.

A circuit is formed between +5 volts and ground zero. Electrons are attracted by the +5 volt potential and leave ground, travel in a direct current, first through R2 and then through R1 to the +5 volt source connection. The two resistors in se-ries form a Voltage Divider circuit. The +5 volt potential is divided as the electrons flow through the carbon bodies. If you test the voltages, the source is of course, +5 volts. At the junction be-tween R1 and R2, you'll find +3 volts. At the ground connection, there is zero volts. The switch plays no part since it is open.

As long as the circuit is energized and the switch is open the electrons will flow through the resistors and the switch connection between R1 and R2 will remain "pulled up" to +3 volts. +3 volts is considered a high just as +5 volts is. Computer techs would say that the junction between R1 and R2 is being "held high."

When the switch is closed, as in Fig. 3-6B, the situation drastically changes. Since the resistance of a closed switch is near zero ohms and the switch is between the R1-R2 junction and ground, all of the electrons will flow through the switch and R1, which takes R2 completely out of the circuit.

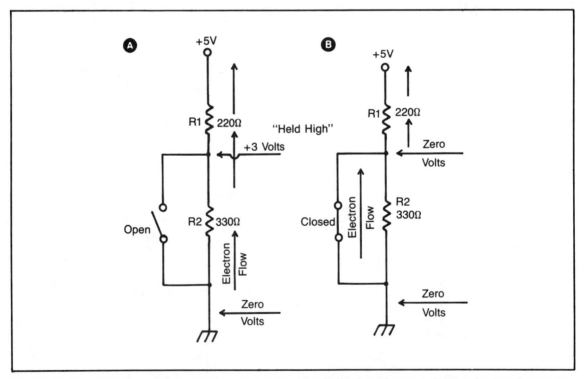

Fig. 3-6. A) R1 and R2 form a Voltage Divider between the +5 volt source and ground. About +3 volts will be at the midpoint between the resistors. B) When the switch is closed, R2 is taken out of the circuit since the switch has a resistance of zero ohms. It shorts out R2.

With R1 being the only resistance in the circuit, all of the +5 volts will be dropped across R1 as a heavy electron flow goes through the R1 body. The electrons will come up out of ground, pass through the switch, and then through R1 and on into the source attraction.

When this happens, the R1-R2 junction is pulled down to near 0 volts. This is a low. Closing the switch changes the condition where the junction was held high to a state where the junction is forced to go low.

These pull up and pull down jobs will be found going on in many places in the computer. The pull up circuits can use discrete components or microcomponents found in the internal wiring of some chips.

CAPACITORS

Capacitors are the second important component found in the digital world. A capacitor, whether discrete or fabricated on a chip, contains the same

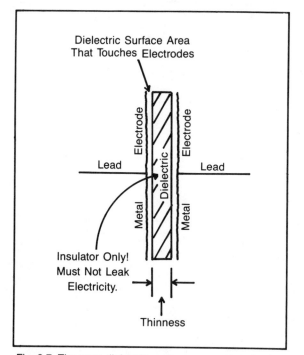

Fig. 3-7. The more dielectric surface area a capacitor has the larger the capacitance will be. Also, the thinner the dielectric the larger the capacitance.

parts, as shown in Fig. 3-7. There is first of all a dielectric. This is an insulator. The size and thinness of the dielectric determines the amount of capacitance in the unit. The more surface area there is to the dielectric the more capacitance the piece will exhibit. The thinner the dielectric the more capacitance the unit will have. Capacitance is typically measured in picofarads (pF), and microfarads μF. Figure 3-8 explains the color code markings for capacitors.

The dielectric is usually contained as the center of a sandwich. The outside sections of the sandwich are two conductors such as silver foil. The dielectric must absolutely keep the two conductors from touching each other. If they should make contact, even the skinniest sliver touching, the capacitor becomes shorted and useless.

Capacitors are able to store an electric charge because of the dielectric. If a dc voltage is impressed on one of the conductors, an electron attractive force will be on that conductor. Dielectrics are very thin. They must be to produce measurable capacitance in the unit. The effect of +5 volts is felt strongly on the other conductor in the sandwich.

Often when +5 is impressed on one conductor in a capacitor, the other conductor is connected to ground, as in Fig. 3-9. The +5 volts will attract electrons right up out of the zero volt potential at ground. The electrons will run up the connection till it reaches the dielectric. If the dielectric insulation does not spring a leak, the dc flow of electrons must halt at the dielectric. However, a lot of electrons will collect on the conductor. The larger the surface area of the conductor the more electrons can assemble. Electrons are little negative charges. The more that collects the larger the charge will be.

With +5 volts of attraction on one conductor and an assembly of electrons on the other conductor, the capacitor is charged up. It is storing a measurable amount of electricity.

In the digital world there are a few discrete capacitors. Capacitors with values such as 0.1 μF or 360 pF usually have dielectrics made of insulators such as mica, paper, and some ceramics. Capacitors that have values like 10 μF at 25 working volts (WV) are electrolytics. They are usually

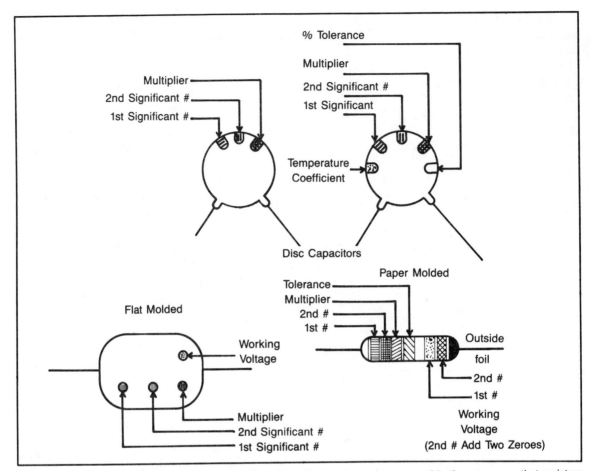

Fig. 3-8. There are a number of discrete types of capacitors. Their color codes are read in the same way that resistors are read, except that the values are in picofarads.

polarized, which means they can only be installed one way. Should you install an electrolytic backwards it could explode on you or cause other troubles.

The electrolytics are able to contain those enormous amounts of microfarads because their dielectric is only a few molecules thick, not measurable under normal circumstances. Remember the thinner the dielectric the higher the capacitance. You can't get much thinner than a few molecules.

The electrolytics are named from the electrolyte conductive paste that is filled in between the aluminum foil plates. The dielectric is formed on one of the plates by a reaction between the electrolyte and the aluminum as a dc voltage is applied.

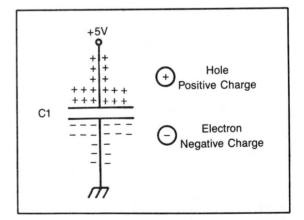

Fig. 3-9. If +5 volts is connected to one end of a capacitor and the other lead is grounded, a charge will be stored.

44

Refer to Fig. 3-10. That is why it is polarized. If you install it into a circuit with the dc voltage going the same way as when the dielectric was formed, all will be well. Should a reverse voltage be impressed, the electrolyte will heat up as it reacts with aluminum in the other direction.

Most of the jobs that the capacitors are called upon to do is bypass or filter out any electrical interference that could develop during computing. Figure 3-11 shows how high-frequency ac voltages that develop in the +5 volt line are eliminated. Capacitor C1 bypasses the unwanted ac to the chassis ground. When low frequency hum enters, electrolyte C2 filters out the interference.

The circuit is the same little pull up one discussed in the Resistor section. If we install a 0.1 μF capacitor from the +5 volt source to ground, any high frequency ac noise will be bypassed to ground. It will never arrive at the junction of R1-R2. If the bypass capacitor wasn't there, ac noise could possibly cross over R1 and interfere with the open switch condition that is holding the junction high. If the switch was closed, the noise would interfere

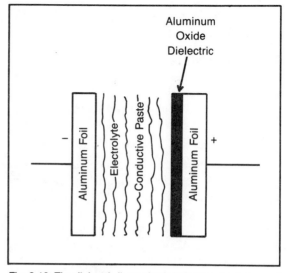

Fig. 3-10. The dielectric in an electrolytic capacitor is formed as an aluminum oxide coating on one of the aluminum foil electrodes. The dielectric is only a few molecules thick.

with the low. The ac noise could drive the high low for a time or the low into a high state.

If a 10 μF at 25 WV is also installed, it would

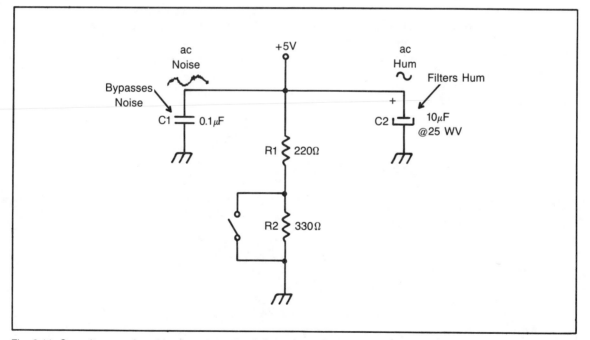

Fig. 3-11. Capacitors are found in computer +5 volt lines. A small capacitor like C1 will bypass ac noise before it can interfere with the logic states. A large capacitor such as C2 will filter out power supply hum.

connect with its + side attached to +5 volts and its common side to ground. Should some low-frequency interference like 60 cycle hum make it into the +5 volt line, it would act to filter the hum before it could interfere with the +5 volt source input. In order for the computer to operate properly, that +5 volts must be very well regulated.

SEMICONDUCTORS

Everyone knows something about insulators and conductors. A good insulator will not allow electricity, in the form of electrons, to pass through it. The insulator possesses a very high resistance that measures way up in the millions of ohms. A good conductor will allow electrons to easily pass through. A conductor has practically no resistance. A small length of copper wire could measure a fraction of an ohm.

The semiconductor is an element that is neither an insulator nor a conductor but something in between. One of the most familiar is made from silicon. Silicon by itself is an insulator. It has to be doped with other elements before it becomes a semiconductor.

Silicon can be made into one of two types of semiconductors. If it is doped with a material such as arsenic, it becomes a piece of n semiconductor material. If it is doped with aluminum, it becomes a piece of p material. It doesn't require much doping. One atom of doping substance to millions of atoms of silicon will do the trick nicely.

N Material

To understand what is happening in the arsenic-doped silicon, a silicon atom that has combined with an arsenic atom must be looked at. The silicon molecule shown in Fig. 3-12 is a tiny universe of two atoms each with four electrons in the outer orbit around two nuclei. When an arsenic atom combines with the silicon, it replaces one of the four electron silicon atoms. The new semiconductor molecule consists of one silicon atom combined with one arsenic atom. Refer to Fig. 3-13.

The arsenic atom is not the same as the silicon. It has five electrons in outer orbit. Four of the arsenic atoms electrons fit into the silicon type orbit exactly. The fifth electron though, is extra baggage. It has no set orbit. It is loose from the nucleus. It roams free around the molecule. With very little energy, it can even leave the molecule and take a tour around the nearby molecules.

In a piece of n material there are millions upon millions of these footloose electrons. Each one is a small negative charge. A small amount of light,

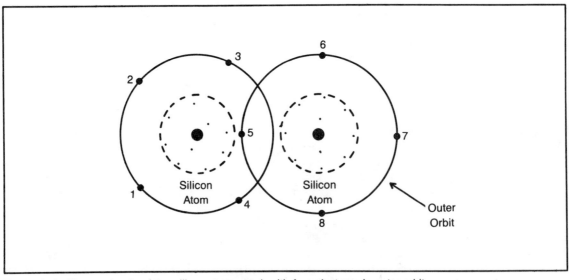

Fig. 3-12. A silicon molecule of two silicon atoms, each with four electrons in outer orbit.

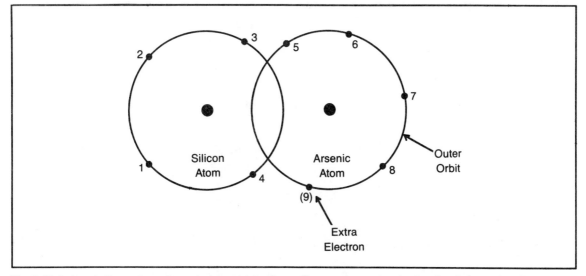

Fig. 3-13. A doped silicon piece of n-material consists of one silicon and one arsenic atom bonded together. The arsenic atom has five electrons in outer orbit. This fifth electron is in an unstable orbit.

heat, or electric current causes considerable random movement of these electrons about a piece of n material at all times. The only way to stop the electron roaming is to place the piece of n material in a deep freeze.

These fancy free electrons are current carriers. If you take a battery and attach the terminals to two ends of a piece of n material, these electrons will line up and get on the move as in Fig. 3-14. Battery electrons will leave the negative end of the battery and enter the semiconductor. These electrons will repel the free electrons and herd them toward the positive end of the battery. The electrons then will enter the + side of the battery and

new electrons will enter the n material. A current will flow from one end of the n material to the other as long as the battery is connected.

P Material

When p material is made, the same kind of silicon is doped but the doping substance is different. Aluminum is often used. The reason why the silicon develops p characteristics is because the aluminum only has three electrons in comparison to the arsenic's five. Figure 13-15 shows an aluminum atom combined with one of the silicon atoms.

Fig. 3-14. If a battery is attached to a piece of n-material, electrons will flow from the − end of the battery, through the n-material to the + end of the battery.

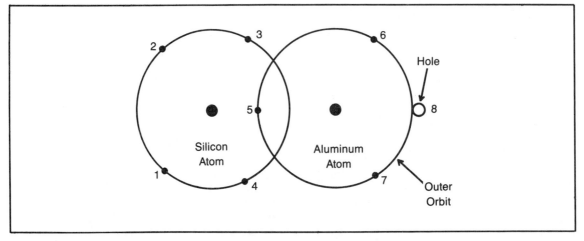

Fig. 3-15. A piece of p-material is formed by doping silicon with aluminum. Aluminum only has three electrons in outer orbit. This leaves a hole in the orbit space.

The combination puts seven electrons in outer orbit. There is room in orbit for eight electrons. This leaves an electronic *hole*. Since an electron is a charge, the hole is the lack of that negative electron charge. That makes the hole that is in orbit the opposite charge of the electron. If the electron is considered a negative charge the hole becomes a real positive charge.

In a piece of n material, the doping causes a lot of extra electrons to abound. These extra electrons moved easily around the material and their movement constituted an electric current. In a piece of p material the doping caused a deficiency of electrons or a lot of holes in orbit.

A hole is a specific positive charge, just as an electron is a specific negative charge. Both the hole and the electron are affected by voltage potential. A hole is attracted by a negative charge and repelled by a positive charge. Holes seem to move around the p material just as electrons usually move around the n material.

The movement of holes is not really happening. Electron movement is causing the effect. Holes remain in their respective orbits. Each hole represents a positive charge. If a battery is attached to a piece of p material, Fig. 3-16, in the same way that it was connected to the n material, electrons in orbit are attracted to the + terminal. However, since they are not floating free, the only paths they can take to the + voltage are the holes. The electrons, are made to jump from one hole to the next in the direction of the + terminal of the battery. This type of current flow is illustrated in Fig. 3-16.

When an electron jumps out of a hole, the hole becomes a + charge. The next hole it jumps into, which had been a + charge then loses its charge. The effect is exactly as if the hole had moved in the opposite direction to the movement of the electron. That is why I said "holes seem to move." They aren't moving, but their + charge is moving. The + charge in a piece of p material, for all intents and purposes acts like the electron-charges in a piece of n material. It is said that holes move one way in p material and electrons move the other way in n material. This is the fact that all chip activity and thus your microcomputer is based on.

PN Junction

The two types of semiconductor material are not very useful as separate pieces. They only become something special when they are joined together. If a piece of n and a piece of p are melted together they form a pn junction at the point where they are joined. The pn junction forms a solid-state diode. A diode, one of the staples of electronics, is a device that rectifies alternating electric current.

When the electric company sends you 110 volts, it is ac at a rate of 60 cycles per second in the U.S. In other countries it is 50 cycles. These cycles are sine waves and the voltage changes from a positive value to a negative and then back. A heavy duty diode is able to rectify the sine wave, which means chopping off one of the deviations and retaining the other. The rectifier in Fig. 3-17 eliminates the negative part of the cycle and retains the positive. To put it another way, a rectifier changes ac to a pulsating dc. The little pn junctions on a chip can't handle power applications, but they can and do rectify the tiny little chip currents.

A pn junction forms a diode complete with cathode and anode due to a phenomena that takes place. At the junction, the free moving electrons are confronted with holes. Since the electrons are – charges and the holes are + charges, the two different static charges are attracted to each other.

As a result some of the free electrons in the n piece jump into holes in the p. Every loose electron that jumps causes the orbit it came from to lose its negative charge and become more stable. Every hole the electron jumps into causes that orbit to lose its positive charge and become more stable. This jumping of electrons from n to p (shown in Fig.

3-18) produces a very stable junction that is no longer semiconductor material but once again silicon, which is an insulator. This produces a barrier to àny other heavy electron movement.

The electrons have plenty of energy though and a few of them are able to burst through the barrier. Also as these few electrons do get through some of them leave holes. As a result on the p side a slight negative charge builds up. On the n side a tiny positive charge is formed. A tiny potential of about 0.1 volts stays at the junction. It's like a tiny battery voltage from the negative to the positive. Perhaps you've heard of the names *barrier region, space charge region,* or *depletion region.* They all are talking about the pn junction.

The pn junction is the basis for all diode, transistor, and integrated circuit action in the computer. Without it, the vacuum tube would still be ruling the scene and microcomputers would not be in existence.

DIODES

If you attach a battery across a pn junction the barrier region is affected. According to the connections

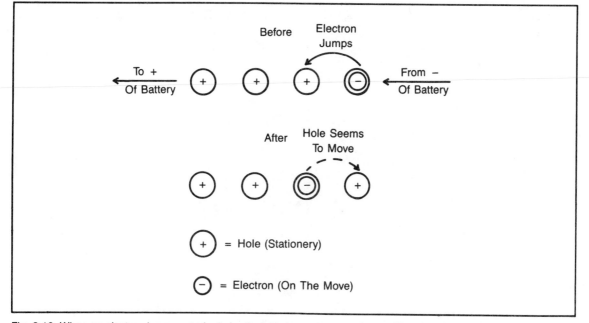

Fig. 3-16. When an electron jumps out of a hole, the hole becomes a + charge. The effect is as if the hole has moved in the opposite direction of the electron movement.

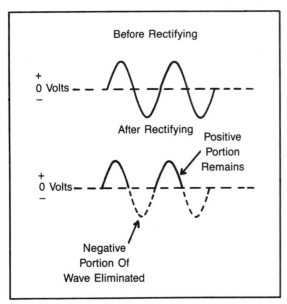

Fig. 3-17. A rectifier is able to let the + voltages of the sine wave pass while it eliminates the − voltage portions.

the junction will receive a reverse or forward bias. When the + end of the battery is connected to the n material and the − end to the p material the junction is reverse biased. If the + battery goes to the

p material and the − to the n, the junction is forward biased.

During reverse biased condition shown in Fig. 3-19, the electrons in the n material are attracted to + and the holes in the p piece move toward the −. This movement of the electrons and holes is away from the junction and lessens their numbers. The barrier widens as more of the junction turns into more of an insulator and increases in resistance. The voltage charge across the junction gets larger and larger and approaches the battery voltage. When the voltage equals the battery, all current flow ceases. This is the reverse bias condition with no current flow.

There is a limit to how much reverse bias a junction can stand. If the reverse voltage gets too high, the crystalline structure of the silicon can fall apart and be destroyed. When that happens, the junction is said to be shorted and a heavy current can then flow.

The opposite of reverse bias is forward biasing. This condition is shown in Fig. 3-20. The battery connections are switched. The + end goes to the p material and the − to the n. The electrons at the junction are attracted to the + and repelled

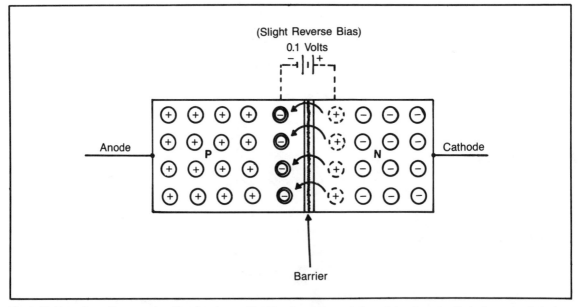

Fig. 3-18. Upon formation, a pn-junction develops a slight barrier charge of about 0.1 volts opposite to the normal electron flow. This tends to retard the cathode to anode electrons. This charge can be varied.

50

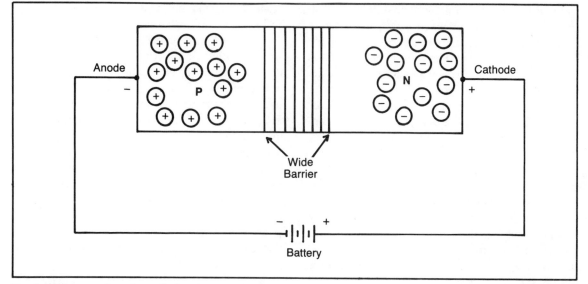

Fig. 3-19. If a + voltage is applied to the pn cathode, the barrier widens and the junction is reverse biased. Electron flow is retarded.

from the – end of the battery. Electrons leave the – end of the battery and skip across the n material, repelling the loose electrons in front of them towards the junction. The electrons then pour over the junction into the p material. Then they pick their way through the p piece from hole to hole and exit the semiconductor into the battery.

As long as the battery is attached in the

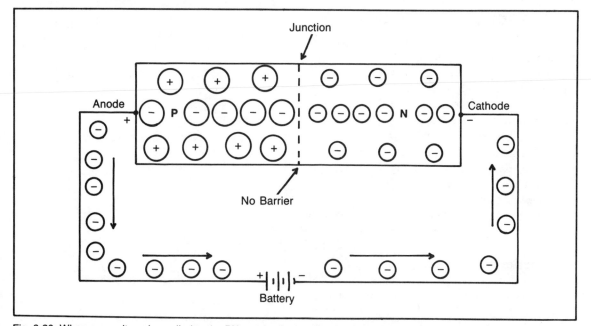

Fig. 3-20. When a + voltage is applied to the PN anode, the barrier shrinks and the junction is forward biased. Electrons flow freely in the n-material and from hole to hole in the p-material.

forward bias condition a continuous flow of electrons continues. The pn junction narrows down to practically nothing. The junction in this state becomes a conductor. The only danger is if too much voltage is applied and too much current flows. The junction will overheat and be destroyed.

The pn junction in forward bias is a conductor but not as good as a piece of copper wire. The copper has a resistance of a tiny fraction of an ohm. A junction has a forward resistance of a few ohms. This is a few hundred thousand times more resistance than copper. That is why the current flow must be watched and restricted so a lot of heat isn't created to destroy the junction.

The junction is a conductor when forward biased and becomes an insulator when reverse biased. One pn junction is a diode. The n side is always the cathode of the diode. The p side is always the anode. Under ordinary circumstances electron conduction should take place from cathode to anode and not from anode to cathode. The biasing is able to turn on or turn off the cathode-to-anode conduction. Forward biasing lets the diode conduct while reverse bias shuts the diode off.

BIPOLAR TRANSISTORS

One pn junction is a diode. Two pn junctions become a bipolar transistor. There are two types of bipolar transistors: the npn and the pnp. They are both shown in Fig. 3-21. If you take a piece of n material and a piece p material that has been melted together and melt on another piece of n so that the p is sandwiched between, you have created an npn transistor. In the same way, if you take the pn and melt on a piece of p making the n the meat in the sandwich, you have built a pnp transistor.

A bipolar transistor is basically two pn junctions back to back. The npn has two junctions with the p material joined up at either end with n. The pnp is the opposite. It is still two junctions but the n is melted to the two p pieces.

One reason that the transistors are called bipolar is because the two end pieces are made of the same material. Another reason is because, there are both electrons and holes on the move in opposite directions. In any case, bipolar transistors are the

npn and the pnp types which are different than the FETs, which are discussed later in this chapter.

Transistors have many versatile uses. However, in digital circuits they are used as switches. They are fast acting electronic switches. They turn on and off, which, by this time, you know is the main work of the circuits in the computer. I'll dwell on that aspect in these discussions. Other transistor applications are covered in Chapter 6 and later chapters.

In both npn and pnp types, the names of the inputs and outputs are the same. There are two inputs and one output. The inputs are the emitter (E) and the base (B). The output is the collector (C). In an npn, the materials are connected as three blocks one on top of another. The p is in the middle. The bottom n piece has the emitter connected

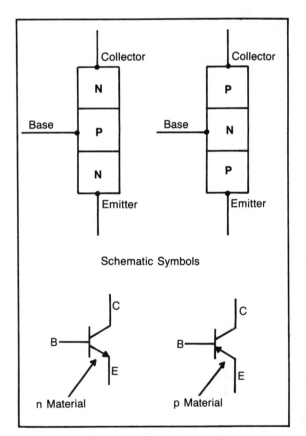

Fig. 3-21. A bipolar transistor is two pn junctions connected back to back. The schematic symbol shows the diode symbol in the EB section.

to it. The center p block has the base attached. The top n material has the collector connected. Figure 3-21 also shows the schematic symbols.

Note that the emitter in the npn has what looks like an arrowhead pointing downward. Forget that it looks like an arrowhead. It indicates a piece of n material. That is where the ground return connection is usually made to the npn. Any electron conduction in the npn is always opposite to the way the arrow is pointing. The symbol for the pnp transistor also shows a triangle. However the symbol points the other way and is drawn with the point at the other end of the line. That indicates a piece of p material.

Electron conduction in the pnp is opposite to the npn as the point on the triangle shows. The emitter, base, and collector, however, are connected to the same position blocks even though the blocks are also the opposite. In the pnp, the emitter is connected to the bottom block, which is p material. The base is connected to the center block and the collector to the top block.

NPN SWITCH

A typical npn switch circuit is shown in Fig. 3-22. E is connected to the chassis ground. C is the output line and is also attached through a pullup resistor to +5 volts. B is the input from a signal source. B delivers the control signal to the switch. The control signal is a high or a low.

With power applied, the npn goes to work. Electrons leave ground and attempt to seek out the +5 volt attraction. The electrons enter E which is a piece of n. They skip across the orbits with the excess electrons. The first obstacle they arrive at is the junction between E and B. In a switch, the pn junction will be either in an insulator or conductor stage, not in-between.

When a low is applied to the base in Fig. 3-23, which is a piece of p, the diode junction between E and B will go into a reverse bias and become an insulator. The barrier in the EB junction widens out. What about the other junction between C and B? It is the mirror image of the EB junction. The two junctions share the same piece of p material attached to B. The low on the base also reverse biases the BC junction. It's barrier also widens.

With the two junctions reverse biased, the electron conduction in the npn cuts off. If there is no conduction, the pullup resistor has no voltage drop from +5 volts to the collector connection. That makes the npn output a +5 volts which is a high. The result of a low being input to the base of the switch is the inversion of the low to an output high.

When a high is applied to B, as in Fig. 3-24, the EB junction becomes forward biased. There is zero volts at E which is grounded and a positive

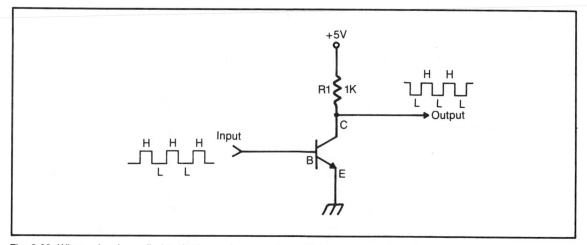

Fig. 3-22. When a low is applied to the base of a transistor, a high appears at the collector. A wave train of highs and lows will produce and output a wave train of inverted highs and lows.

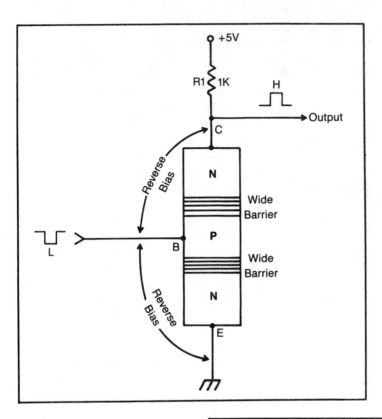

Fig. 3-23. When a low is applied to B, both pn junctions are reversed biased and the collector goes high to the +5 volt source level. The switch is effectively cutoff.

Fig. 3-24. When a high is applied to B, both pn junctions are forward biased and the collector falls to a low due to the voltage drop across R1. The switch is in saturation or on.

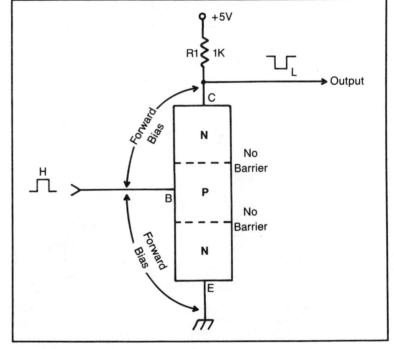

voltage at B, which is receiving the high. The forward biasing narrows the barrier down to practically no barrier. Electrons rise up out of ground and travel the n piece easily. With no barrier in the junction, the electrons flood over into the p material. They pick their way from hole to hole and arrive at the BC junction.

There is a barrier there. However with +5 volts on C, some electrons are pulled through and the conduction through the pullup resistor causes a voltage drop so that the collector drops from +5 volts toward zero. This forward biases the BC junction. The junction becomes a conductor without any barrier. The electrons then continue their movement towards the resistor to the +5 volt source. This keeps the collector saturated with the flood of electrons as long as the high remains on the base input.

With the collector at saturation, the collector drops to about zero volts, which is a signal low. The base-input high results in a collector-output low.

An npn transistor switch goes off and on, putting out either a low or high according to its base input. A low cuts off the npn producing a high, and a high causes the npn to saturate causing a low.

The pnp switch works in exactly the same way except that everything is reversed. The +5 volt source is at the emitter and the ground return at the collector. However, the only difference is that the electrons are going the other way. The npn conduction is from emitter to collector. The pnp conduction goes from collector to emitter. The inputs are still usually at the base and the output at the collector. Figure 3-25 shows several typical circuits.

Cutoff still happens when the barrier widens out and stops the electron flow. Saturation still is produced when the barrier narrows down to near nothing. All that is needed is to put the correct voltages on the pieces of material to control the EB and BC junctions.

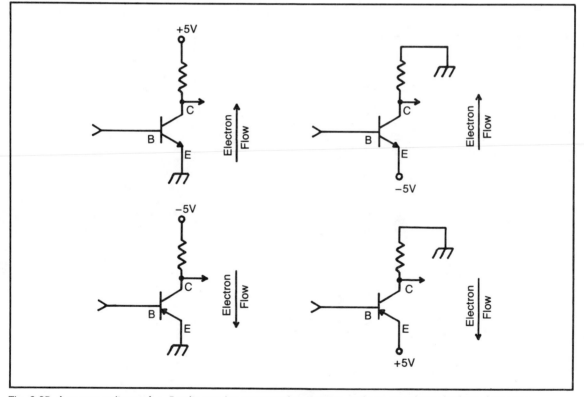

Fig. 3-25. A source voltage of ± 5 volts can be connected to the npn and pnp transistors in these four ways.

In Fig. 3-26, the emitter has +5 volts. A low at the base will cause the junctions to be forward biased and the pnp will saturate. When a high arrives at B, as in Fig. 3-27, the junctions will reverse bias and cut off. The transistor switches can be forced to turn on or turn off by either pulse waveforms or a steady dc high or low.

FIELD EFFECT TRANSISTORS

The Field Effect Transistor, or FET, is a unipolar transistor. This contrasts with the bipolar types just discussed. The bipolar transistor has n and p materials joined together in a sandwich. Electrons move in the n material and holes appear to move in the p material. In the unipolar transistor, only one type of semiconductor acts to conduct current. There is the n channel FET that conducts electrons and the p channel FET that has the effect of moving holes. In various FETs, either electrons or holes move, not both. Thus the unipolar description in the name.

On computer chips, IGFETs are the type of transistors that are used. The IG stands for Insulated Gate. This is not the gate that is used in logic applications. It is simply an unfortunate use of the same word to describe two different objects. Figure 3-28 shows the construction of an IGFET.

The IGFET is a device built around a bar of semiconductor material. For instance, a bar of n material can be an n channel. The bar on n material is then joined to a substrate of p material. If you connect a 5 volt battery to the ends of the n bar, electrons will start flowing from the negative end to the +5 volt end. The negative end is then assigned the name source (S), and the +5 volt end the name drain (D).

The electrons will flow nicely with this arrangement but without any special control. To take control of the current flow, a gate (G) is installed. A thin insulator, such as a piece of glassy silicon dioxide is laid on the bar. Then a metal lead is connected to the insulator but not through it. A voltage applied to the gate will induce an equal but opposite

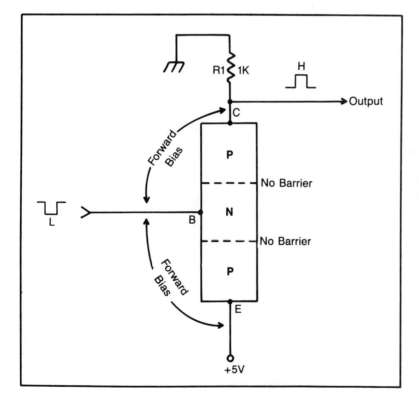

Fig. 3-26. A low at the base of a pnp forward biases the junctions and the transistor saturates placing a high at C.

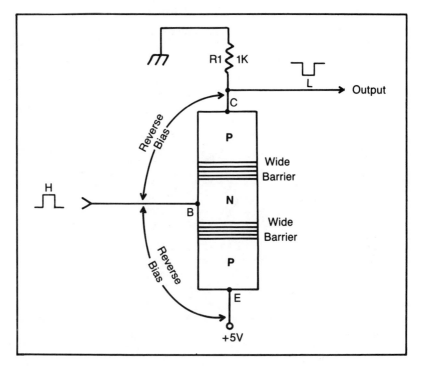

Fig. 3-27. A high at the base of a pnp reverse biases the junctions and the transistor cuts off.

R1 1K

L

Output

Reverse Bias

P

Wide Barrier

N

B

Wide Barrier

P

C

E

H

Reverse Bias

+5V

effect on the electron flow. If a high is applied, the + charge attracts electrons from the source and makes the channel saturate with an enhanced current flow. when a low is applied, the − charge repels the electrons back to the source and attracts hole + charges from the p substrate. This closes the channel which cuts off or depletes the current.

This effect is also called pinch off.

In a p channel IGFET with a +5 volt battery connected to the channel, the electrons still move. However, their movement from hole to hole gives the electrical effect of holes moving from the +5 volt connection to the − end of the p material bar. The same type of insulated gate is connected and

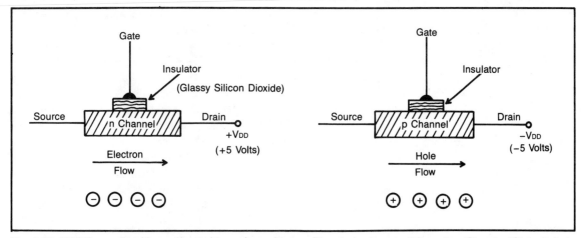

Fig. 3-28. IGFETs can be either n-channel or p-channel types. The electrodes are the source (S), gate (G), and drain (D). N-channel conduction is by means of electrons. P-channel conduction is with the use of holes.

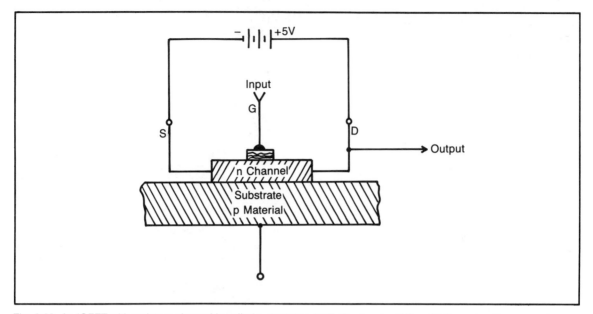

Fig. 3-29. An IGFET with an intact channel is called a depletion FET. Electrons will flow till the gate attracts + charges from the substrate and pinches off the channel.

the high or low input will switch the current off and on.

These IGFETs with an intact channel, as in Fig. 3-29, are called *Depletion FETs.* That is because they are able to conduct even if there is no charge applied to the gate. All the gate can really do is deplete or pinch off the channel flow. There is another type of IGFET used more often than the depletion mode kinds. They are called Enhancement FETs.

Enhancement IGFETs do not have a channel. They are configured something like the bipolar transistors and contain both n and p materials where the current must flow. For instance, in the n channel enhancement FET, the S and D connections are made to pieces of n material but the insulated gate is not. It is connected above a piece of p material sandwiched between the two Ns. Refer to Fig. 3-30.

The p material there blocks off any current flow that would normally go even if there is no charge on the gate. In the depletion mode, FET current flows as long as the channel is connected to the battery. This can't happen in the enhancement mode FET because the piece of p forms two pn junctions

and blocks it off. This incidentally is the important difference between the two modes.

Normally then, if there is no charge on the gate or if a low is applied, this FET is switched off. To turn the FET on, a high can be placed on the gate electrode. The + charge on the gate attracts electrons to fill the holes and form an excess of electrons in the p material beneath the insulation of the gate. This makes the p material beneath the gate then act as n material. That connects up the source and the drain. Electrons start flowing from source to drain. The FET is switched on. A high on the gate turns on the FET. A low shuts it off.

These IGFETs are more commonly known as MOSFETs. The MOS stands for Metal-Oxide Semiconductor. The metal refers to the gate lead, the oxide to the gate insulator and the channel is a piece of semiconductor.

The glassy insulator is a very important item in computers. First of all it is sensitive and needs special attention. If some static electricity should come along, the voltage can easily pierce the oxide and kill the FET. When technicians work with MOSFETs, either in discrete form or as chips, they take extra special care to avoid static charges. The way to avoid static charge troubles is shown in Chapters 18 and 19.

The insulator, between the gate lead and the semiconductor, forms a capacitance. It becomes the dielectric. The gate and the semiconductor constitute the two ends of the capacitor. Sometimes this capacitance is unwanted and can cause design problems. Other times, design people are able to use the capacitance. In dynamic RAM chips this capacitance becomes the storage area for the highs and lows. This is discussed in detail in Chapter 11.

INTEGRATED CIRCUITS

The circuits on a chip can be made from microscopic resistors, capacitors, diode pn junctions, bipolar transistors, and FETs. The chips in your computer are termed monolithic. A monolithic integrated circuit is one that uses the substrate or base of the chip as one of the active elements. In Fig. 3-29, an n depletion FET uses p material as the substrate. It draws + charges from the substrate to pinchoff the current flow in the n channel. The schematic symbols for FETs are shown in Fig. 3-31.

The monolithic chip begins life in a slice of silicon about 0.005 inches thin and about an inch in diameter. One slice could produce a few or hundreds of individual identical chips, according to the complexity of the design. The circuits are produced through high tech applications of high-temperature gas diffusion, photoresist masking, chemical etching, glassy silicon dioxide installation, and vacuum evaporation for the lead pads.

The individual chips are then scribed apart and wired into a package. It is tested, and if it works, it is sealed. When the chip only has a few components on it, it is known as SSI, for small scale integration. If it has 10 to 100 circuits on it, then it is MSI, or medium scale integration. Over a hundred circuits makes it an LSI, or large scale integration. Over 1000 is VSLI, for very large scale integration. As the density of circuits continues to increase, designers will come up with more names to define the chips.

On your print board, there are dozens of chips. They are each one of two types. There are either TTL or MOS chips. The TTLs use bipolar transistors, and the MOS use IGFETs.

Transistor-Transistor-Logic

The TTL chips as mentioned are designed around bipolar transistors. Besides the conventional npn and pnp transistors, there is a third type of

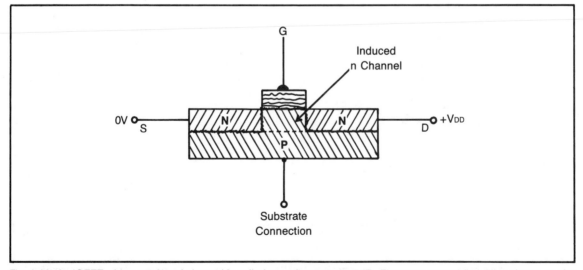

Fig. 3-30. An IGFET with a sectioned channel is called an enhancement FET. Electrons cannot flow till a charge on the gate induces an n-channel between the other two pieces of n-material.

bipolar. It is recognized by its emitter section. Instead of a single emitter it can have two, three, or more emitter inputs. This multi-emitter transistor was invented in 1961 by a scientist named Thompson. It is shown with two emitters in Fig. 3-32. It was devised in an effort to replace extra input components like resistors and diodes.

In early chips, the inputs to the bipolar transistors were typically made through series resistors or pn diode junctions. The resistor-input chips were termed RTL, for Resistor-Transistor-Logic. The diode input chips were called DTL, for Diode-Transistor-Logic.

Transistor-Transistor-Logic chips are so named because of the multiple emitters in the input transistor. The TTL chips are the ones you'll find in your computer. RTLs and DTLs are outdated. They can still be obtained but they are not used in computers anymore.

There is an entire family of TTLs. They are the generic 7400 family. They come first of all with numbers that go from the 7400 to 74490 and up. This is the oldest TTL product category. Technically it is referred to as the gold-doped double-diffused type of chip. It is in general use.

Another TTL category is the 74LS00 family. This is the most popular group of TTL chips. They are like the 7400 except for the L and S features. The L stands for low power. This means the chip is able to operate with 80 percent less power than its 7400 counterpart. However, the power dissipation is at the expense of a slower chip switching speed.

That is where the S enters the scene. The S stands for Schottky-diode clamped. There is a Schottky barrier-diode clamp in the base circuits that speeds the switching action back up. Actual TTL chips are discussed throughout the book.

Metal Oxide Semiconductor

In the 1960s when chips were first introduced into digital circuits, the TTL types were the ones

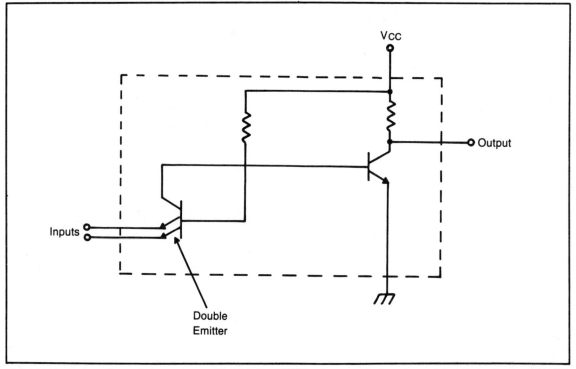

Fig. 3-31. The schematic symbols are drawn with depletion FETS having an unbroken channel, but the enhancement FETs have their channels in three parts.

60

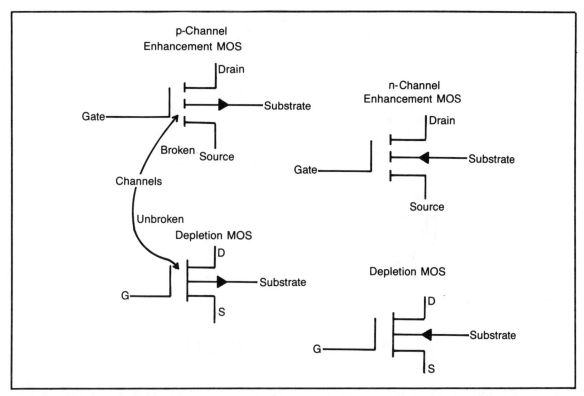

Fig. 3-32. A TTL is so named because there is a multiemitter on the input transistor. The TTL stands for Transistor-Transistor-Logic.

used. The bipolar circuits were the ones that concerned designers and technicians the most.

As the 1970s arrived, the MOS chips began to appear. The FETs became popular to design circuits around. The first group of them copied the generic 7400 number. The chips were labeled in the 74C00 family. For the most part, the 74C chips are MOS versions of the 7400 family.

In addition to the 74C generic naming, another family of MOS chips was introduced in the 4000 family. These generic numbers indicate at glance whether the chip is TTL or MOS.

Chapter 4

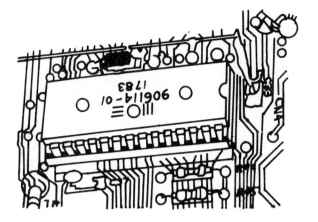

Digital Circuits

R ESISTORS, CAPACITORS, DIODES, BIPOLAR transistors, and FETs are what makes your computer tick. A few of them are discrete parts that you can see soldered on the print board. They are easily identified and it is not too difficult a task to test them or replace them. The great majority of the components in the computer though are microscopic. They have been shrunken down into a different dimension. They are completely inaccessible.

No matter how tiny they might be they still require attention when you consider the electronics of your computer. The individual components do make up the content of the circuits you use to run programs. However, the components are at the bottom of a circuit type hierarchy. The components are able to do certain electronic feats. Resistors can impede the flow of electrons. Capacitors can store a group of electrons. Diodes will let electrons travel in one direction but not in the other. Bipolar transistors can switch from passing a heavy flow of electrons or cut off the flow, obeying a signal input. FETs can do the same thing as the bipolar but with

varying characteristics. These jobs are the abilities of the basic digital components, the bottom of the hierarchy.

The next step up is the wiring together of the components, discrete or microscopic, to create a circuit that will perform digitally. When you wire up the components, you then have the gates and the registers that are needed. That is what this chapter is all about.

The basic electronic components that were covered in the last chapter are the lowest level of the chip hierarchy. These components are connected up to form circuits. The circuits are nothing but gates, registers, and electronic switches to enable and disable more gates and registers. Switches are in the next level of the hierarchy.

Up one more level brings you to the logic. At this level, the digital states travel through gates. The states are latched into registers and move over bus lines. This is the level that receives most of the attention when considering the electronics in the computer. At this level, the vom can take voltage readings, the logic probe can test inputs and

Table 4-1. Digital Hardware Hierarchy

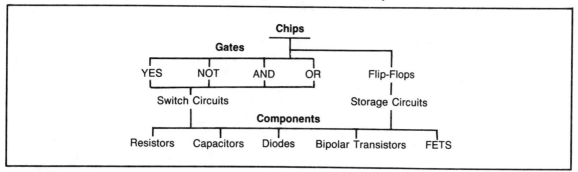

outputs, and logical signal tracing can take place. Below this level, the electronics is so miniscule in size that discussions must be, for the most part, academic. This logic level is where most of the rest of the book will dwell.

The top rank of the digital hierarchy is the large chips. The large chips contain all the gates and registers in great numbers. On some chips, a complete computer could reside. A large special MPU could have a clock, memory, and I/O ports. About all you do with a chip of this nature is examine its many inputs and outputs. What goes on inside the chip is beyond human physical access. Refer to Table 4-1.

The word digit in digital means integer. The binary number system uses two integers. The circuits represent the digits by switching off the flow of electrons or turning them on. The off mode is known as cutoff, and the on mode as saturation. There is no in-between flow. The electron movement is either completely cutoff or fully saturated. In fact, that is the difference between digital and analog. Digital works with circuits that are either cutoff or saturating. Analog uses circuits that can have an infinite variation of current flow amounts from cutoff to saturation. Analog computer circuits are covered in the next two chapters.

Digital circuits operate on pure logic. This means that every operation that goes on is absolutely predictable as long as the computer is working ok. Whenever you enter a program, the computer will predictably run it. The computer does not make a mistake. Let's go into the logic circuits.

YES

The buffer circuit, the amplifier mentioned earlier is also a logical YES gate. The amplification it performs has no logic to it. Amplification is an analog function. The logic is derived from the voltage state that enters the input of the buffer and the predictable voltage state output. The states represent digits. The digits are passed through the buffer. They must exit the buffer in a predictable state or the buffer is not being logical.

The YES gate in Fig. 4-1, logically works this

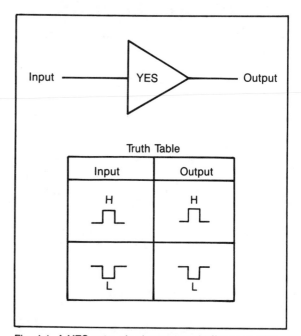

Fig. 4-1. A YES gate, also known as a buffer or amplifier, outputs the same logic state that it receives at its single input.

Table 4-2. Various Binary Descriptions.

1	0
True	False
High	Low
+5 V	0 V
⎍	⎍
Yes	No
Set	Reset
Set	Clear

way. Whatever state enters the gate leaves the gate. Therefore, if a high enters the gate, a high must leave the gate. Should a low enter the gate, then a low must exit. The YES gate must perform those ins and outs every time it is used.

Every gate has what is known as a *truth table*. It is called a truth table because the highs and lows are sometimes referred to as trues and falses as Table 4-2 shows. All the truth table shows is the input and output of a gate. The illustration, Fig. 9-1, shows the table for the YES gate.

Schematically the Yes gate is drawn as a triangle. It has one input at the flat side and one output at the pointy end. The gate symbol is the next step up on the circuit hierarchy. It designates a lot of internal wiring. Inside the triangle could be many transistor circuits. However they will have one input to all the components and one output from the YES configuration.

A YES circuit could be built around an npn transistor as shown in Fig. 4-2. The input would then be made at the emitter. The collector is connected through a pullup resistor to +5 volts. The output is also from the collector. If a high is input to the emitter, the EB junction would be reverse biased. That would cutoff the npn. The collector voltage would then rise to +5 volts since no electrons would traverse the pullup resistor to +5 volts. The output from the collector at that time would be +5 volts which is a high. When a high enters the input, therefore, a high leaves the output. This meets the requirements of the YES gate.

If a low is input to the emitter, the EB junction would be forward biased. This makes the npn go into saturation. A lot of electrons flow through the npn through the pullup resistor and on into the +5 volt source connection.

All those electrons across the pullup makes the voltage across the resistor drop drastically. The

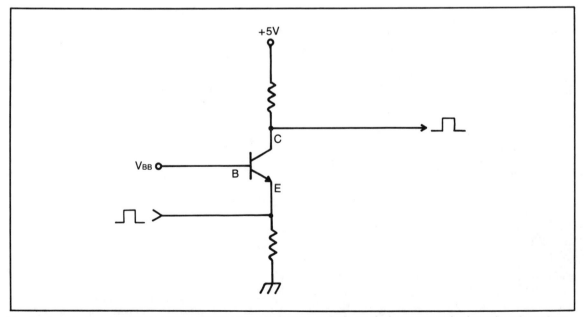

Fig. 4-2. In order for an amplifier output to have the same logic state as the input, the input connection is made at the emitter.

voltage at the collector will drop down near 0 volts. This constitutes a low. The low is then passed on to the next stage. Therefore, as a low enters the emitter, a low will leave the collector. This is the way the YES gate is predicted to pass logic, and it does.

When you look at a computer schematic, you'll never see the internal wiring of the gates. The wiring has been cast in silicon and is committed to the microscopic world. The schematic will show the triangle with the one input and the one output.

If you wanted to replace a YES gate, you would then encounter the next level in the hierarchy. For instance, the YES could be installed on a 7417 TTL chip like the one shown in Fig. 4-3. There are six buffers on the chip. You can't just replace one buffer. All six must be changed since they are all an integral part of the chip. The 7417 is called a Hex Buffer since there are six Yes gates mounted upon it.

To sum up, the YES gate is an amplifier stage that also exhibits logic characteristic. Besides amplifying the current level of the signal, it also passes the logic state that is input without change from the output.

NOT

If you look at the schematic symbol of the NOT gate in Fig. 4-4, you might mistake it for the YES gate. The symbol is the same triangle with the same single input and single output. The only difference is the small circle on the pointy output end between the output lead and the point. This is a NOT circle. It makes the YES symbol into a NOT gate, or as it is called, an Inverter.

As the name implies, the logic state is inverted from input to output. A high at the input predictably produces a low at the output. A low at the input always produces a high at the output. The internal circuits can be thought of as very similar to the YES gate. The only difference in Fig. 4-5 is the location of the input. It is connected to the base instead of the emitter.

The emitter is tied directly to ground, which

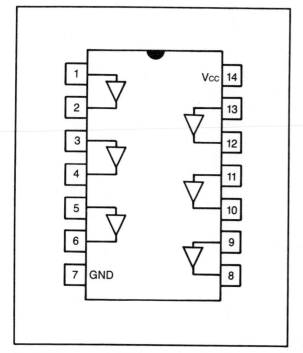

Fig. 4-3. There are six YES gates on a 7417 Hex Buffer chip.

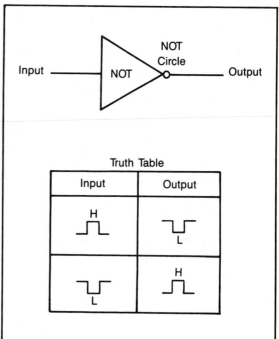

Fig. 4-4. The only schematic difference between a YES gate and a NOT gate is the NOT circle at the output.

65

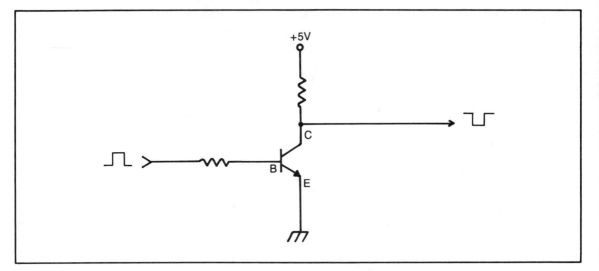

Fig. 4-5. The only circuit difference between the YES gate and the NOT gate is the input occurs on the base.

is at 0 volts. If a high is input to the base, the EB junction will be forward biased, and the transistor goes into saturation. This sends a lot of electrons through the pullup resistor to +5 volts. The voltage at the collector drops to near 0 volts, or a low. The high input causes a low output. The input high has been inverted to a low.

When a low is input to the base, the EB junction becomes reverse biased and conduction in the npn cuts off. The stoppage of electron flow through the pullup causes the collector side of the resistor to rise to the +5 volt level, which is a high. Again the gate has performed logically. A low input becomes a high output. The inversion is complete.

A commonly used TTL chip that houses inverters is the 7406. It is shown in Fig. 4-6. It is a 14-pin DIP called a Hex Inverter Buffer/Driver with open-collector outputs. Let's take its description one part at a time.

The 14 pins are arranged on the rectangular package, seven on a side, in line. Hex means the chip contains six inverter gates. Each gate has an input and an output. That uses up 12 of the 14 pins. Pin 7 is needed to connect the chip to chassis ground. Pin 14 is the attachment to Vcc, the voltage for the internal wiring of the circuits contained in each of the six gates.

The word buffer and the word driver both re-

fer to the fact that these circuits in the 7406 are all able to perform amplification along with the inverting of the logic state. The six inputs all receive a voltage high or low. If a gate is input a high, it amplifies the current, not the voltage state, and outputs a low.

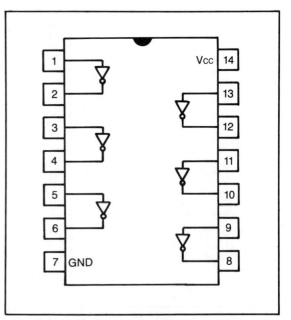

Fig. 4-6. A commonly used set of six NOT gates is the 7406. It features an open collector output.

The last part of the 7406 description mentions open collector. This is a common circuit in gates. Each of the 7406 gates has its own internal circuitry based around bipolar transistors. The six inputs are pins 1, 3, 5, 9, 11, and 13. Following the inputs are six identical circuits that buffer the logic state and then invert it. The Vcc +5 volt input at pin 14 and the ground connection at pin 7 power the circuits. After the inversion, the circuits are ready to output the finished logic.

The six output transistors have their collectors attached to pins 2, 4, 6, 8, 10, and 12 as Fig. 4-7 shows, the collectors are left open at the pins. The output transistors in the gates are purposely made heftier than the rest of the gate transistors. The 7406 output transistors are each able to pass a relatively large 30 milliamperes of current.

These open-collector output transistors are usually connected to external discrete pullup resistors on the print board. That way they have the electrical strength to be able to drive LEDs and relays. The pullup or load resistance used with a 7406 is 1000 ohms.

If you are testing a chip like the 7406, you test each gate as an individual. The only circuit the six gates have in common is the +5 volts they share from pin 14 and the common ground at pin 7.

AND

The first thing you'll notice about AND gates is that they have two or more inputs in comparison to the YES and NOT gates which only have a single input. The AND output though remains single no matter how many inputs are installed. The inputs are processed by the internal wiring of the AND gate into one output.

Logical AND is implemented electronically by combining voltage states in a circuit. The AND gate will output a high only when all inputs are high. If any or all of the inputs are low, the AND gate will

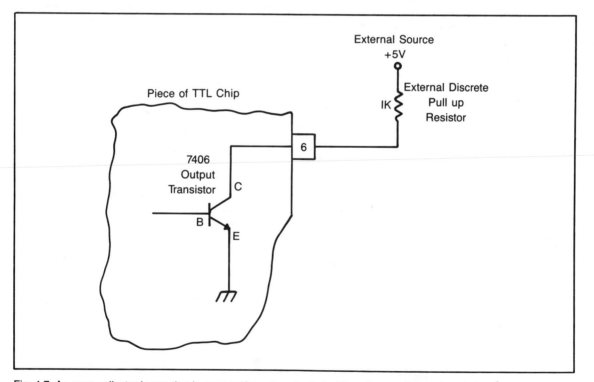

Fig. 4-7. An open collector is one that is open at the gate output pin. There is no pullup resistor inside the chip. In order to operate the gate, an external discrete pullup resistor and +5 volt supply is needed. This permits the gate to process large amounts of current.

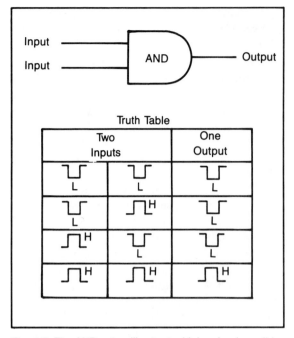

Truth Table

Two Inputs		One Output
L	L	L
L	H	L
H	L	L
H	H	H

Fig. 4-8. The AND gate will output a high only when all inputs are high. If any or all inputs are low, the output will be a low.

output a low. Figure 4-8 provides the truth table.

On a schematic, the AND gate is drawn as a bell. It is usually lying on its side, but it can be found pointing in any direction. The bell has a flat side and a rounded end. The inputs attach to the flat side and the single output to the round end.

In operation, the AND gate acts as a switch to turn on some circuit in its output. Typically, the inputs to the AND gate contain one low which keeps the output held low or off. Then when it is necessary to enable (which means turn on) the circuit, a high is sent to the low AND input. As the high enters the input, the gate switches states. The change of gate output from low to high in turn switches on the external circuit.

The truth table of the AND gate is also a little service checkout chart. The table shows the way a two input AND gate should output results. When the inputs contain a low, the output is always a low. When both inputs are high, the output must be a high. If you test the two inputs, you can predict the output. Should the output be incorrect that indicates trouble in the chip.

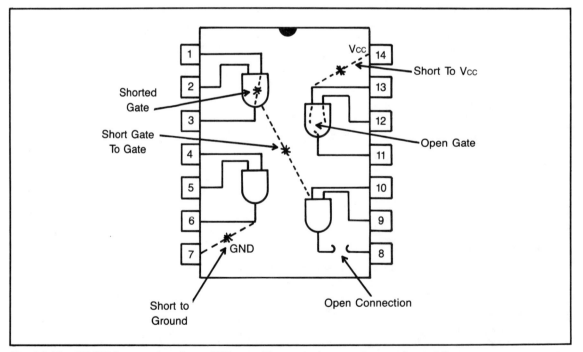

Fig. 4-9. The 74LS08 is a quad two-input AND gate. There are six common ways it can fail.

68

Figure 4-9 shows a common chip that houses AND gates. The 74LS08 is a Quad Two-Input AND gate. It contains four LS AND gates each with two inputs. It is a 14-pin DIP. The four sets of inputs are 1-2, 4-5, 9-10, and 12-13. The respective outputs are 3,6, 8, and 11. Pin 14 is the +5 volt source and pin 7 is ground.

If the gate connected to input pins 1 and 2 and output pin 3 and 3 reads a high even though one of the inputs is low, the gate could be shorted. If you tested the gate at pins 4, 5, and 6 and it is outputting a low even though both inputs are high, it could be shorted to ground. If you are reading voltages at pins 8, 9, and 10 and it reads low with both inputs high, the output pin could have disconnected internally. Or if you are reading pins 11, 12, and 13 and it is reading an output high with both inputs low, the gate could have shorted to the source of +5 volts.

Figure 4-9 illustrates these failures. The truth table on a three input AND gate works in the same way, except for the three inputs. Figure 4-10 shows a typical three input chip. The 74LS15 is a Triple Three Input. The Triple means there are three

gates on the chip. All gates have three inputs. It is still a 14-pin DIP, but each gate needs one more pin.

The truth table for the two input chip only had four rows of data. That is because there were only four possible combinations of inputs. When there are three inputs available, there are eight possible combinations of inputs you can inject.

Inputs
L-L-L
L-L-H
L-H-L
L-H-H
H-L-L
H-L-H
H-H-L
H-H-H

When the AND gate has four inputs, there are 16 possible combinations. Five inputs makes 32 possible logic states and so on.

An AND gate though, no matter how many inputs there are, will always be held at a low output unless all the inputs are high. This can be accomplished electronically by wiring pnp transistors in parallel, as in Fig. 4-11. Their collectors are connected to ground. The emitters are tied together and are powered with +5 volts. The emitter is the output. The bases are the inputs. You can connect as many input transistors together as needed. If three inputs are required three pnp transistors can be installed.

As long as any or all of the base inputs are low, an EB junction of a pnp will be forward biased. That transistor will saturate and a lot of electrons will flow through the pullup resistor and drop the emitter side of the resistor to a low voltage. The gate output will result in a low. Only when all of the bases are receiving highs will all of the EB junctions be reverse biased. At that time, all of the pnp transistors will cutoff, and no electron flow will take place in the pullup resistor. This results in the +5 volts appearing on the emitter side. The +5 volts, or high, will be output.

There are many different circuit arrangements

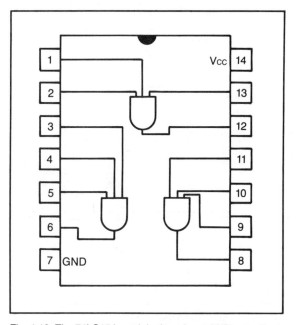

Fig. 4-10. The 74LS15 is a triple three-input AND gate. Each gate has three inputs but still only one output.

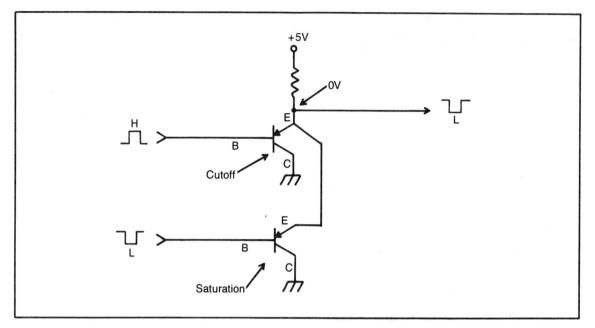

Fig. 4-11. Two pnp transistors can be wired as an AND gate. A high will cause cutoff, and a low will cause saturation. When both pnp transistors are cutoff, the circuit will output a high. If either one or both is in saturation, the output will be a low.

that will perform the AND gate function. The important requirement is to have a circuit that will output a high only when the multiple inputs are all highs.

OR

Logical OR is somewhat the counterpart of logical AND. The AND gate will only output a high when all inputs are high. The OR gate, which has multiple inputs and one output like AND, will only output a low when all inputs are low, Fig. 4-12. If any or all of the OR inputs are high, the OR gate will only output a high. In the circuits, OR gates are often held high. This is the off position. When it is desired to enable the gate, lows are sent to any of the inputs that are high. The gate will respond by going low. The truth table and schematic symbol are shown in Fig. 4-12.

The OR gate schematic symbol resembles the AND gate except it has a pointy end where the AND was rounded. Also it does not have a flat bottom but one that is gently rounded and comes to a point at either side. The rounded bottom is the

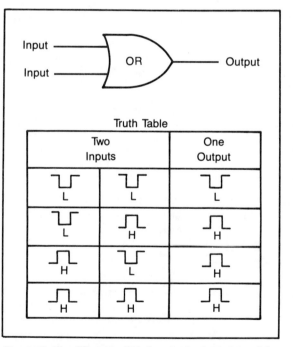

Fig. 4-12. The OR gate will only output a low when all inputs are low. If one or more inputs are high, the gate will output a high.

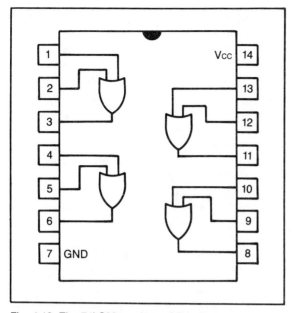

Fig. 4-13. The 74LS32 two-input OR gate is wired pin for pin with its AND counterpart the 74LS08.

a Quad Two-Input OR Gate grouping. The pins are arranged exactly like the 74LS08 AND gate. If you find it necessary to test the four sets of inputs and outputs, the truth table will predict what should be present on a good energized chip.

The OR gate is wired up easily. It does not even require any transistors. Diodes alone with a load resistor will do the job, as Fig. 4-14 shows. The diodes have all their cathodes wired together and are attached to ground. The output is also at the cathode common connection.

With ground connected to the cathodes, any highs at the anode inputs will cause conduction. Refer to Fig. 4-15. Electrons will leave ground and go through the forward biased pn junction. This will cause a high to develop at the junction of the cathodes atop the load resistor. This high will be output as long as one of the diodes is conducting because of a high.

When all the inputs are low, then all the pn junctions have a reverse bias. Therefore only when all of the inputs are low will the gate output be low. The truth table dictates the activity.

NAND

Quite simply, if you take an AND gate and

input lead area and the pointy end is where the output connection is made.

A commonly used OR gate is shown in Fig. 4-13. The 74LS32 chips are 14-pin DIPs and house

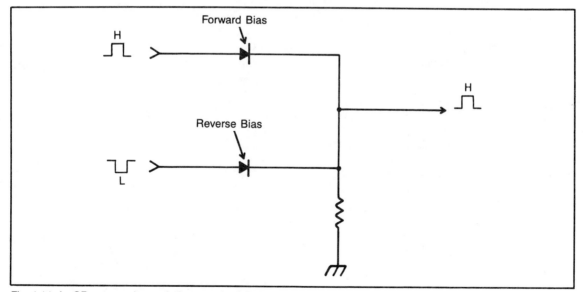

Fig. 4-14. An OR gate can be made from a pair of diodes and a resistor. A high input at either or both anodes will produce a high output. Only two lows will output a low.

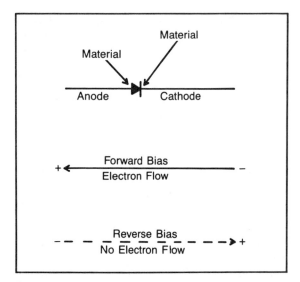

Fig. 4-15. A diode will conduct when it is forward biased. It will cut off when reverse biased. In Fig. 4-14, a high forward biases an input diode. A low reverse biases an input diode.

connect a NOT gate in series with it's output, you have created a NAND gate. Refer to Fig. 4-16. The NAND gate is nothing more than a NOT AND gate, which is where the name came from. If you examine the truth table of the NAND gate in Fig. 4-17, you'll find it permits the output of a low only when all inputs are high. This further demonstrates that the NAND gate has the same outputs as the AND gate but inverted.

The NAND gate is much more than simply an AND gate plus an inverter. The NAND gate circuits are used to form all of the TTL chips. All the TTLs start out from the universally accepted NAND configuration shown in Fig. 4-18. It is composed of five subcircuits. All gates, flip-flops, and the rest of the TTL groups are constructed with this universal building block.

The first subcircuit is an npn type of AND gate, Fig. 4-19. I say "type of npn" because the transistor has at least two emitters and possibly three or more. All of the emitters are made of n material and are n parallel. Each emitter forms an individual EB junction with the same base. The base is made of p material. The multiemitter-base junctions are all diodes with their anodes connected to the rest of the transistor. Refer to Fig. 4-19.

This ties all the anodes together. In Fig. 4-14 an OR gate was shown with the key to the OR function; diodes with their cathodes tied together. To change the OR gate to an AND gate all that is needed is to reverse the diodes. This multiemitter circuit reverses the diodes forming the AND gate.

Each emitter is one input. If there are only two emitters, then there are only two inputs. When the need arises for more inputs, additional emitters are built into the input transistor. The name TTL is derived from the multiemitter arrangement: Transistor-Transistor-Logic. In years past when the inputs were through resistors, the chips were called RTLs. If the inputs were through diodes the chips were called DTLs. The TTLs are a takeoff on the DTLs.

The multiemitter npn outputs to the second subcircuit in Fig. 4-19 is a NOT gate. The collector of the input npn connects directly to the base of the inverter, which is also an npn. With the first stage an AND gate and the second stage a NOT gate, the two stages form a NAND gate. While it is NOTing the AND input,the inverter goes ahead and provides some amplification so the voltage state is beefed up to a higher current rating.

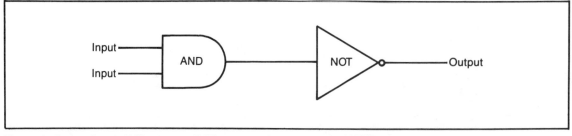

Fig. 4-16. If you wire an AND gate to a NOT gate, you have created a NAND gate.

The remaining three stages do not operate on the state of the voltage. They are the TTL output stages and consist of three more npn transistors that condition the voltage state so it may be applied to subsequent stages or computer bus lines. These circuits will be covered later in the book.

NOR

It can be seen that a NAND gate is easily fabricated out of an AND gate and a NOT gate. The NOR gate is formed in a similar manner but using an OR and a NOT. Refer to Fig. 4-20. The NOR can be built with two diodes a couple of resistors and an npn transistor. Figure 4-21 shows that the two diodes are wired in parallel with their cathodes connected. This is the configuration of an OR gate. The cathodes are then connected to the base of the npn. That is the way a NOT receives input. A pullup resistor is then attached from the collector to Vcc, the emitter is grounded and the base is returned to ground through a base bias resistor. The output is from the collector

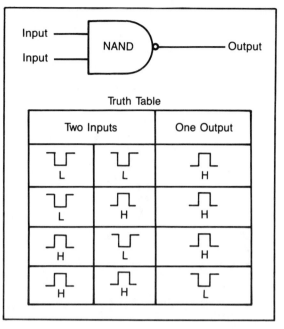

Fig. 4-17. The NAND gate will only output a low when all inputs are high. This is the inverted output state of the AND gate.

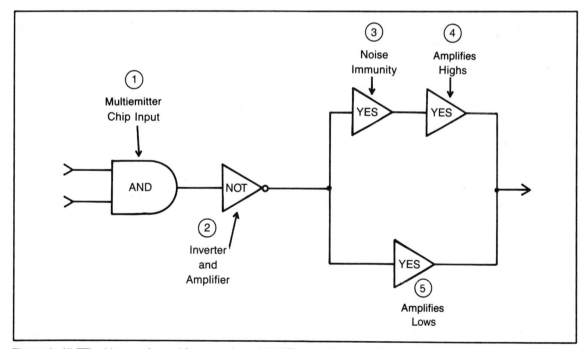
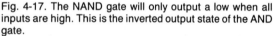

Fig. 4-18. All TTL chips are formed from a universal NAND gate. There are five subcircuits that comprise the NAND. There is one AND, one NOT and three buffer YES gates.

73

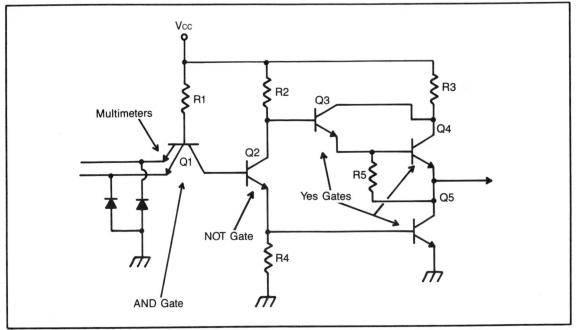

Fig. 4-19. The NAND gate subcircuit has multiemitters. Each emitter acts the role of a diode input. With the cathodes of the diodes receiving the inputs, the configuration is AND. Following the AND is the NOT circuit. After the NOT are the three buffers.

This NOR gate is held high if in the off position. If two lows are at the diode anodes, the pn junctions will be reverse biased and lows will be at the cathodes. With a low at the cathode, the base of the npn is low, and the npn is cutoff. The lack of electron flow pulls the collector voltage up to +5 volts, an output high.

Should a high appear on one or both of the diode inputs, one or both of the diodes will start to conduct. Electrons are drawn up out of ground through the base bias register. This puts a + voltage on the base, which makes the npn conduct and saturate. All the electron flow through the collec-

tor resistor causes a voltage drop across the resistor. The +5 volts that was on the collector drops down near zero volts. The NOR gate thus outputs a low.

The truth table in Fig. 4-22 shows that this is the way a NOR gate should act. The gate outputs a high as long as both inputs are low. If one or both of the inputs goes high, then the collector output goes low. This output activity is then the exact opposite of the OR gate.

The NAND gate appears on schematics as an AND gate with a little NOT circle on its rounded output. The NOR gate appears on schematics as

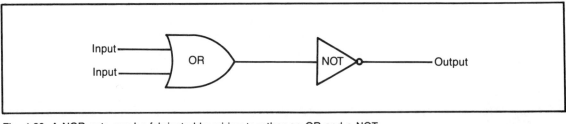

Fig. 4-20. A NOR gate can be fabricated by wiring together an OR and a NOT.

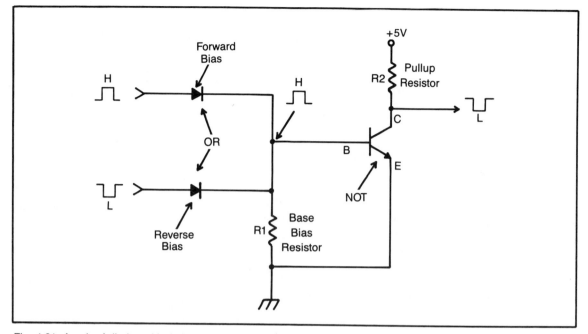

Fig. 4-21. A pair of diodes with their cathodes connected and an npn produces a NOR gate.

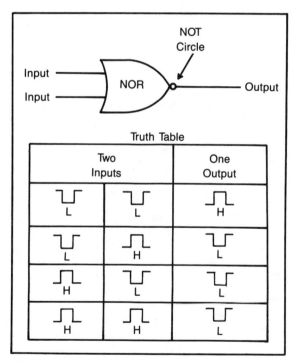

Truth Table

Two Inputs		One Output
⊔ L	⊔ L	⊓ H
⊔ L	⊓ H	⊔ L
⊓ H	⊔ L	⊔ L
⊓ H	⊓ H	⊔ L

Fig. 4-22. The NOR gate will output a high only if all inputs are low. Otherwise, the gate will output a low.

an OR gate with a NOT circle on its pointy output. The NOR symbol is also shown in Fig. 4-22.

The NOR gates, like all the other common gate types are found as sections of chip packages. The 74LS02 in Fig. 4-23 is a Quad Two-Input NOR gate. It is also a 14-pin DIP with the pins assigned in the same way as the other quad type chips. There are three pins to each NOR gate. Pin 14 is Vcc and pin 7 is ground.

EXCLUSIVE-OR

At first glance the exclusive-OR schematic symbol in Fig. 4-24 looks like the ordinary OR symbol. A second glance reveals the difference. The input curved base line proves to be twin parallel lines with a space between the lines. The input leads attach to the outermost line. The output lead though is the same as the OR gate.

The truth table at first glance also looks like the OR gate but again a closer look finds a difference. The OR gate dictates that if two highs are input a high must output. With exclusive-OR, that order is remanded. When two highs are input, a low

75

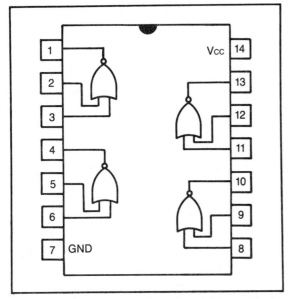

Fig. 4-23. A commonly used set of four NOR gates is the 74LS02, a quad two-input NOR gate.

exits the gate. All the rest of the inputs and outputs are identical to OR.

If you think about it, the outputs of the OR gate are not logically OR. The OR definition is, if one OR the other of the inputs are high, then the output is high. This proves true when the OR inputs are L-L, L-H, and H-L. For L-L neither input is high so the output, following the definition, is L. For L-H and H-L one of the inputs is high so the output must be H. This is true.

However, in the last possible case H-H, both of the inputs are high, not one OR the other, yet the output is still high which does not follow logically. That is the nature of the OR gate, logical or not.

The exclusive-OR is the variation of the OR gate that is made to follow the logic. When the four possibilities of a two input gate is considered, they are logically like the OR gate except for the last possibility H-H. When two Hs are input to the EOR

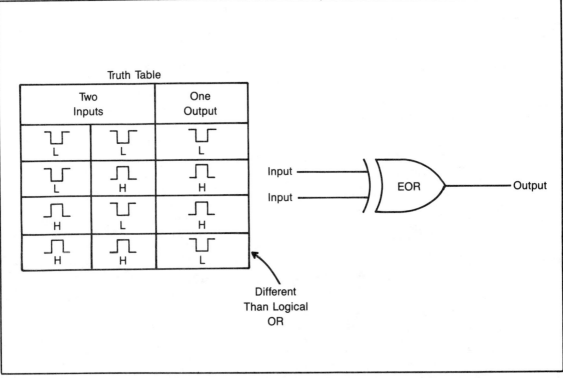

Fig. 4-24. The exclusive-OR gate symbol differs from the OR due to a separated base. The EOR truth table differs from the OR truth table. When two highs are input, a low is output.

76

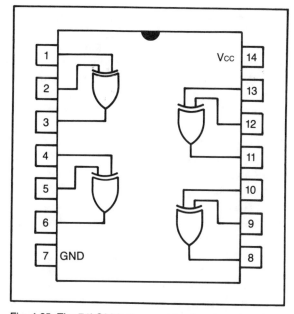

Fig. 4-25. The 74LS86 is the quad two-input version of the EOR gate.

gate will output the inverted result of the EOR gate.

Note that the ENOR gate in Fig. 4-26 was put together tinkertoy style with a gate from the EOR 74LS86 and a gate from the 7404 Inverter chip. This is common practice. A gate can be fabricated by logically putting together gates from one, two, or more chips. Another way an ENOR gate could be put together is with five NAND gates. Take two 7400 chips, both quad NAND gates, and connect-ING up four gates on one chip and one of the gates on the other as shown in Fig. 4-28. The result is an ENOR gate.

UNIVERSAL NAND GATES

The 7400 type chip is very handy. Figure 4-29 shows how a single 7400 can be wired to form an AND, OR, NOT, EOR, and NOR. It covers the NAND also since it contains four NAND gates. This wiring feat illustrates the DeMorgan theorum that states that any logic function can be produced with only NOTs, ANDs and ORs. Since NANDs are nothing but ANDs and NOTs, the 7400 type chip can do it all.

For instance, two of the NANDs can be wired to form an AND. First the inputs are installed at pins 1 and 2. The output 3 is wired to 4 and 5 of the inputs of the next NAND. The output is taken from pin 6. Any input at 1 and 2 ends up ANDed at pin 6.

This happens because when you short the in-puts of a NAND gate together, it becomes a NOT gate. You are changing the two inputs to a single input. After the inputs at 1 and 2 are NANDed, they enter the shorted pins 4 and 5 and become NOTed. The total result is ANDing.

The ORing is also easily accomplished with the same chip using three NAND gates. The pins 1 and

gate, the output is logically L. The EOR gate only outputs a high when one OR the other of the inputs are H, not both. That one input possibility, H-H, with its low output is the difference between OR and EOR. You will also find exclusive-OR ab-breviated XOR.

The Quad Two-Input exclusive-OR gate in Fig. 4-25 is the 74LS86. It is a 14-pin DIP resembling the other quad chips discussed.

EXCLUSIVE NOR

If you take an EOR gate and add a NOT gate to its output as in Fig. 4-26, the result is an ENOR gate. The truth table in Fig. 4-27 shows the final

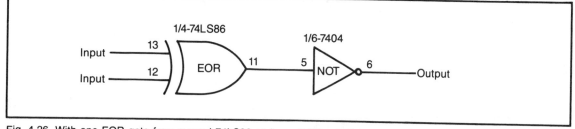

Fig. 4-26. With one EOR gate from a quad 74LS86 and one NOT gate from a hex 7404, an ENOR gate is formed.

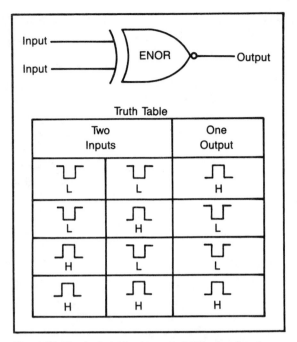

Truth Table

Two Inputs		One Output
L	L	H
L	H	L
H	L	L
H	H	H

Fig. 4-27. The truth table shows that if the two inputs are identical a high will result. Only when the inputs are mixed will a low output result in an ENOR gate.

2 are shorted together making the gate a NOT. Then Pins 4 and 5 are shorted producing a second NOT. The outputs of the NOT, pins 3 and 6, are connected to pins 9 and 10, the inputs of another NAND. If inputs are injected at pins 1-2 and 4-5 they will exit pin 8 in an ORed condition. The results of first being NOTed and then NANDed is OR.

On a schematic, you will encounter all sorts of gate symbols. The NOT, AND, OR, NAND, and NOR are straightforward and require no further interpretation. It should be realized though, that the little NOT circle and the complete triangle and circle of the NOT gate mean the same things and could even be representing the same sort of internal wiring.

Besides these straightforward symbols, schematics also are found with alternative symbols that represent gates. Refer to Fig. 4-30. An AND gate might be drawn as an OR gate with NOT circles at both inputs and at the output. This indicates that even though the total result of the gate is AND, the circuitry accomplishes the logic by first

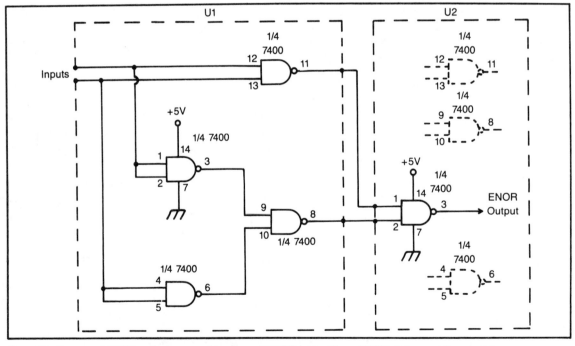

Fig. 4-28. Two quad NAND gates are used to wire an ENOR gate. Three NAND gates remain unused.

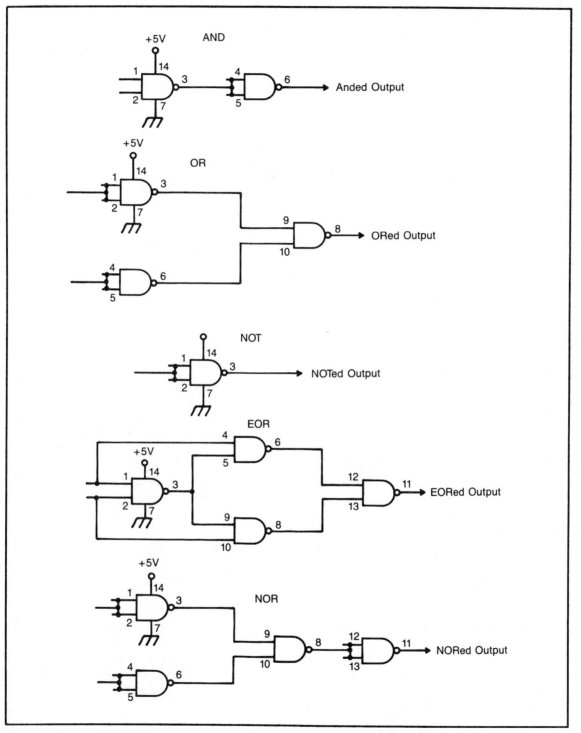

Fig. 4-29. The quad 7400 NAND gate is very useful. Any types of gate can be wired from it.

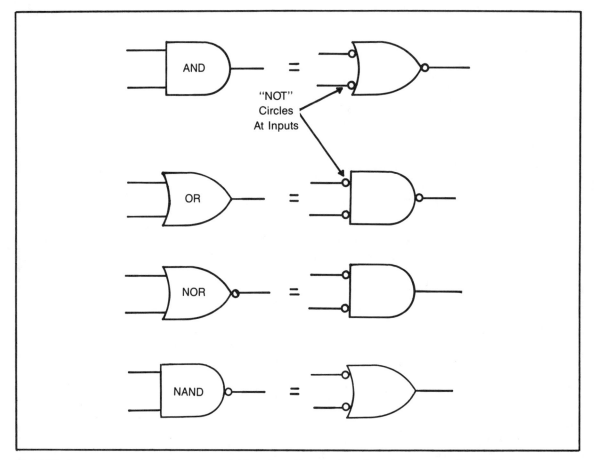

Fig. 4-30. On computer schematics, you are liable to find all sorts of symbol arrangements. The NOT circles could be at the inputs as well as the outputs. An AND could look like an OR with NOT circles at all connections. An OR could be drawn as an AND with NOT circles at the inputs and outputs. A NOR could look like an AND with NOT circles at the inputs. A NAND could appear as an OR with NOT circles at the inputs. Take care reading schematics.

inverting the inputs and then inverting the outputs.

An alternative OR gate is drawn as an AND gate with NOT circles at the inputs and at the output. The NOT gate could have the NOT circle at the input instead of at the output. A NOR gate could be found as an AND with NOTed inputs. A NAND gate might be drawn as an OR with NOTed inputs.

This demonstrates the close relationship that all the gates have with each other. All the gates are nothing but voltage/logic state changers. They change the states by switching the electron flow and/or holes off and on by means of diodes, bipolar transistors, and FETs. The gate circuits are massive mazes of these electronic switches.

REGISTERS

Besides the logic gates, there is the other category of TTL and MOS circuits called Registers. They are used in jobs such as RAM, ROM, latches, shift registers, and flip-flops. The main difference between a gate and a register is that a register is able to store the logic state and a gate cannot. This difference is illustrated in Fig. 4-31. As soon as a high or low arrives at a gate, it receives immediate processing and quick passage to the output. It can't stop and wait in the gate, it is forced in and out. A register on the other hand, is a place of storage. When the high or low arrives, it can stay as long as it wants, just so long as the electricity stays on.

The logic state is called a bit. Eight bits is, of course, a byte. Registers can be single-bit types, nybble size, byte size, or whatever is needed. Each bit holder is a complete circuit of its own. A multiple-bit register contains a number of bit holders all wired together. As mentioned earlier, the bit holders come in static and dynamic form. The static bit holders are based around flip-flop circuits. The dynamic types use capacitors to hold the logic states. Static storage areas are built in both TTL and MOS chips. Dynamic storage is found only in MOS technology.

FLIP-FLOPS

A flip-flop circuit needs two active devices. It can be formed from two bipolar transistors, two FETs, or even two NAND gates as in Fig. 4-31. The idea is to cross couple the two devices. With the cross coupling, one of the two is cutoff and the other is saturated. This state can be designated as a high. Then if the devices receive an input pulse, they can be made to switch their cutoff and saturation conditions. The new state can then be the low.

Figure 4-32 shows an actual circuit with two identical pnp transistors called Q1 and Q2. The emitters of the two are grounded. The base of Q1 is wired to the collector of Q2 through a resistor. The base of Q2 is wired the same way to the collector of Q1 with the same value resistance. The base to opposite collector wiring is the cross

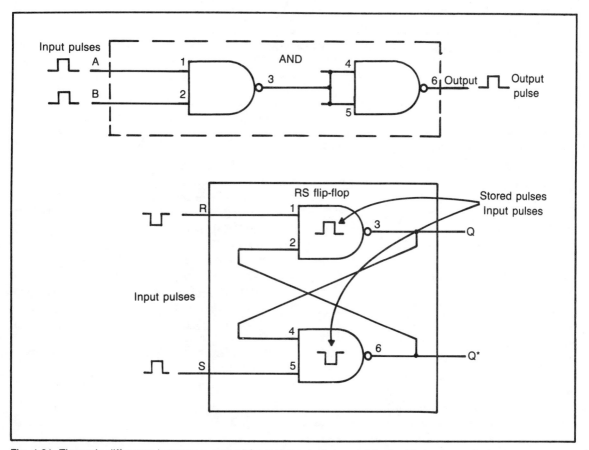

Fig. 4-31. The main difference between a gate and a register is that a register is able to store a logic state and a gate cannot. These NAND gates are wired as examples. The top shows two NAND gates wired as an AND gate. The bottom circuit is the same two NAND gates wired as a register bit. The AND gate passes an input pulse immediately to the output. The register bit receives the pulse and holds it in storage till it is time to output it.

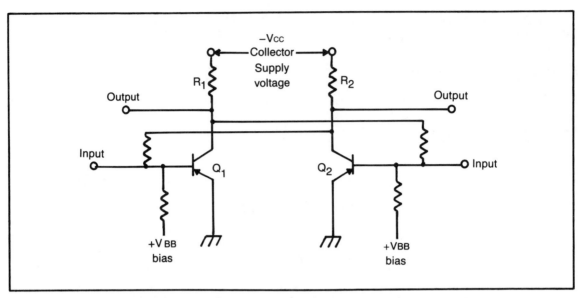

Fig. 4-32. The basic flip-flop circuit consists of two pnp transistors. They are wired so when one is saturating the other is cutoff. This is one state. If they are pulsed, they will flip-flop and switch states. The one saturating will cutoff and the one cutoff will saturate. This inverts the stored state.

coupling that is going to make the circuit do the flip-flopping.

The collectors are then connected to − Vcc through two load resistors. A base bias voltage + VBB is attached to the two bases through two more load resistors. That is a basic flip-flop circuit. It is known as a bistable flip-flop.

The bistable means that one stage will go to cutoff as the other stage saturates and vice versa. The bistable also indicates that the circuit will hold that stable condition unless it is upset by a pulse. If the proper pulse does come along, the stages will swap their voltage states and again hold stable.

If the circuit is energized, both transistors try to turn on. With the − Vcc on the collectors and the emitter grounded, electrons try to flow from collector to emitter in both circuits. However, no two transistors are perfectly matched and one transistor draws slightly more current than the other. This makes the collector voltage slightly more positive than the other. If Q1 draws a bit more collector current than Q2, then the Q1 collector voltage becomes more positive.

This positive voltage is coupled to the base of Q2. This reverse biases the Q2 EB junction. Q2 is

forced to cutoff. The collector voltage on Q2, as it cuts off, goes more negative approaching − Vcc. This negative voltage is coupled to the base of Q1.

As a result of the negative bias on the base of Q1, the EB junction goes into a forward bias. This causes the electrons to saturate Q1. The action comes to a stable end as Q1 becomes saturated and Q2 is cutoff. This activity takes place at blinding speeds that is measured in billionths of a second, called nanoseconds.

This stable state is one of two possible. The other state possible is attained by flip-flopping the circuit. The circuit can be flip-flopped in one of two ways. The first method is to apply a high to the base of the saturating stage, Q1. If a high is applied to Q1 the equilibrium is upset. The base of Q1 is low as it saturates. If the high is applied, Q1 will instantly cutoff. As it cuts off, its collector current stops and its collector voltage falls toward − Vcc. This low voltage is then coupled to the base of Q2. The − Vcc derived voltage forward biases the EB junction and Q2 goes into saturation.

In the same way, you can start the flip-flop by applying a low to the base of Q2. The low to Q2 will turn on Q2 as it forward biases the Q2 EB junction. As Q2 turns on, it saturates. All the electrons flowing in from − Vcc source causes the collector of Q2 to develop a positive voltage.

This + voltage is coupled to the base of Q1. The high on the Q1 base reverse biases the EB junction and Q1 cuts off. The flip-flop is complete. The circuit is now containing the second possible stable state. Either condition will hold the state steady till forced to change to the other state.

If you apply a low to the saturating state, nothing will happen. The stages will continue their condition. Should you apply a high to the cutoff pnp again nothing will occur. Only a low to the cutoff stage will turn it on or a high to the saturating pnp will cut it off.

You will never come in contact with these basic circuits in computers. They have been reduced to microscopic entities. The flip-flop is found on schematics as little squares with the letters FF in the symbol. The FF comes with it's own truth table. The simplest form of FF is the RS flip-flop. Another common type is the D flip-flop. The important thing to note is they are single bit registers that are able to store logic states and operate with the gates to do digital computer work.

D Flip-Flop

The D is for Data. It is a simple latch for data. It can hold one bit, a high or low. In a group of eight, it can store a byte of data. Four bit-holders

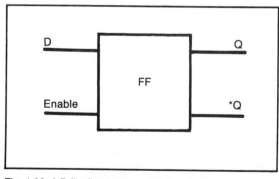

Fig. 4-33. A D flip-flop has one data input (D) and an enable input. These can be thought of as base inputs. There are two outputs Q and *Q, analogous to the collector outputs. The logic state the FF is holding will be on Q. The inverted result of the logic state is on *Q.

form a nybble holder.

Figure 4-33 shows the schematic symbol of the FF. It is a square with four connections. There is one input for the data, D. A second input is called Enable. The word enable in computerese means *turn on*. This is the opposite of disable which means *turn off*.

The FF has two outputs that are complementary. One is Q and the other is *Q. Whatever is on Q, its complement, or its opposite, is on *Q. If the stages in the FF were single bipolar transistors, Q would be the output of the second stage and *Q the output of the first stage.

The 74LS75 in Fig. 4-34 is an example of a TTL chip that contains four bit-holders. It is a 16-pin DIP and is described as a Four-Bit Bistable Latch. It is able to receive a nybble of data and either pass it on or store it till needed. It has a truth table for each flip-flop just like the gates do. There are two inputs just like the gates, but the FF has two outputs. Gates only possess one output.

Each latch is independent of the others except for the enable connections. There is one enable for a pair of latches. The D input and the outputs though have their own pins.

One latch contains two AND gates, one NOR, and two NOTs. The logic diagram in Fig. 4-35 shows only gates. There are no resistors, capacitors, or transistors in sight. This is the way the schematic drawings of the chips are made. The internal wiring has been committed to the world of the microscope and is only needed in some special cases. For the most part, the electronics of the computer is thought of in terms of the gates being the basic component rather than the actual npn or FET transistors that are buried in the silicon.

A 74LS75 works like the following in gate terms. When a bit of data enters the D pin it arrives at one of the inputs of an AND gate. The second input is the enable bit. When the D input is a low and the enable is a high, the AND gate outputs a low. This low is output to one of the inputs of the NOR gate.

The other NOR input is coming from the other AND gate. The second AND gate has two inputs. One is coming from a NOT gate in series with the

83

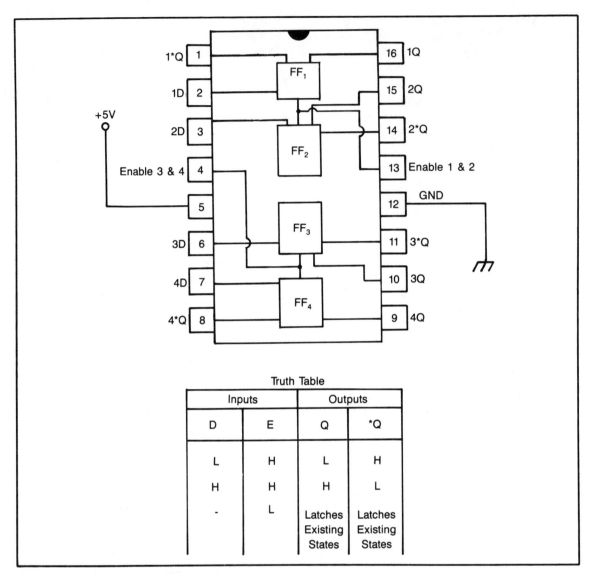

Fig. 4-34. The 74LS75 quad FF chip has two inputs and two outputs for every FF. A nybble can be stored in the quad.

enable. In the case where the enable is a high, the NOT gate inverts it to a low. Since the low is input to the AND gate, a low must be output. The AND gate can only output a high when both inputs are high.

The low leaves the AND gate and enters the second input of the NOR gate. This puts two lows into the NOR. Two lows into the NOR produces a high. The high encounters a crossroad. Straight

ahead through the NOT gate is the output. The high goes through the inverter and ends up on Q as a low. The other part of the intersection is a piece of wire connected directly to *Q. The high ends up on *Q. It can be seen that when a low enters D and is enabled, a low appears on the important output Q. At the same time, a high appears on the complementary output *Q. This is exactly what the truth table in Fig. 4-34 predicted would happen.

Both Q and *Q are available at pins. If all you wanted to do was pass the state through the latch, it is accomplished in this way. At the outputs, there is the choice of either the input state or its complement. If the D input is a high the same modus operandi takes place, except the Q ends up with a high and *Q ends up with a low.

When the enable goes low, the latching ability takes over. Whatever data is present at the input is held in limbo. The low on the enable pin stops the latch from flip-flopping. The enable low is applied to the top AND gate which forces it to output a low no matter what the D input is. The NOT gate input to the second AND gate inverts the enable bit to high. The feedback bit, if it is a high, makes the AND gate output a high. The high causes the NOR gate to output a low. This keeps Q a high and *Q a low. If the feedback bit is low, the AND will send a low to the NOR. Two lows into the NOR outputs a high. This keeps Q as a low and *Q a high. The states will hold that way till the enable finally goes high again.

The 74LS75 is a latch. It is not in the strict definition of the term, a D flip-flop. The latch has an enable pin. The enable is typically held low. A bit of data, when enable is low is stored as it arrives. When it is time to release the data, then a high is applied to the enable.

The D flip-flop is practically the same configuration except the enable pin is a clock input. The clock enters a square wave that goes from high to low and back in time with the frequency of the clock. This enables and disables the latch in time with the clock. The D flip-flop is thus triggered by the rising or falling edge of the square wave or the high or low level of the wave. As a result, the D is called a pulse edge-triggered device and the other is a voltage-level sensitive FF.

RS Flip-Flop

The RS flip-flop is a direct takeoff from the pnp flip-flop circuit discussed earlier. There is no enable input. The inputs are called R and S. The outputs are still Q and *Q. Refer to Fig. 4-36. They are still complements of each other. The RS can be fabricated from two NAND gates. Although the gates themselves cannot store a state, a pair of cross-coupled gates can, as Fig. 4-31 showed.

If the two NAND gates are powered up they could come on storing a low. By convention, this means there is a low on Q and a high on *Q. The states will stay there as long as they are not disturbed and are powered. In Fig. 4-37, a low is applied to R and a high is applied to S, and the circuit flip-flops. The low on Q will go high, and the high on *Q will go low. Should a high then be

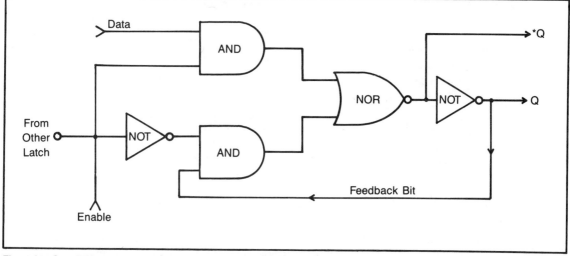

Fig. 4-35. One FF latch in the 74LS75 has five internal gates.

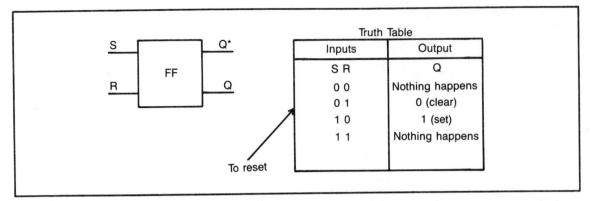

Fig. 4-36. The RS flip-flop has four possible sets of inputs. Two of them are useful and the other two are meaningless.

applied to R and a low to S, then the circuit will switch states again and the original states return. The truth table predicts what will occur.

This RS flip-flop can also be made with a clock input. It is called the T type. The T stands for toggle which is just another name for setting, clearing, and setting once again. The circuit is sensitive to an edge on the incoming square-wave clock signal. The clock signal is used when it is necessary to sync the FF in time with other clock driven circuits. Usually though, the clock driven circuits use another form of FF, the JK flip-flop.

JK Flip-Flop

The JK looks like the RS clock driven T type. In fact, it is sometimes said that the T-type RS

shown in Fig. 4-38, is a form of the JK-type flip-flop. The J input is likened to the S. (S means set and R is reset). The truth tables of the JK are about the same as the RS table. Probably the main difference is that additional gates are connected in the internal input circuits to provide more isolation between the inputs and outputs.

A typical JK flip-flop is the 7470 chip in Fig. 4-39. It is a 14-pin Dip and contains one JK flip-flop circuit. However the JK only takes up five pins. Also on the chip are two three input AND gates and two YES gates with NOT circles at their inputs. The chip is named a JK Positive Edge-Triggered with Preset and Clear.

At pins 8 and 6 are the outputs Q and *Q. Pin 12 has a clock enabling input. Pin 13 is an input called preset and pin 2 is the input clear.

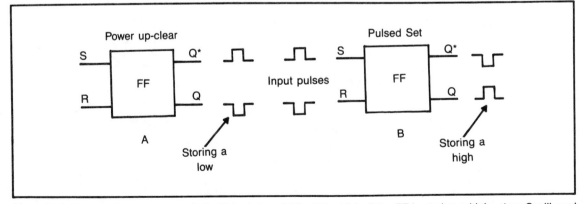

Fig. 4-37. When an FF is storing a low, Q will be low and *Q will be high. If the FF is storing a high, then Q will read high and *Q low.

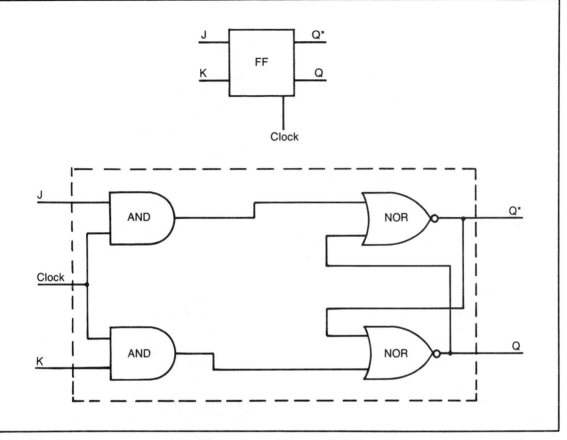

Fig. 4-38. The JK FF is quite like the RS. Here is a JK that uses two AND and two NOR gates crosscoupled to produce the storage ability.

The preset input is a control line. It is an S line. It works the same as the S line in an RS flip-flop. In this chip, if you inject a low into preset, the FF will flip into a cutoff-saturated condition that leaves Q set with a high. When that happens, *Q must assume a low.

The Clear input is also a control line. It is an R-type line. It too operates in the same manner as the R in an RS flip-flop FF. If you insert a low into Clear, the FF will switch itself into a condition that leaves Q reset or cleared to a low. *Q again will assume the complementary position which is a high.

The value of these two control inputs is to get the chip ready for action. With Preset and Clear you can switch the FF into having whatever state output is needed for a particular application. You can

also lock up the chip by holding the pins high or low.

This is a positive logic chip. That means the control into the FF itself must be positive or a high. Yet the inputs to affect the control are lows. A low into preset or a low into Clear. Look closely at the chip drawing. There are NOT circles at the preset and Clear inputs on the internal FF. The NOT circles invert the low inputs to highs before application to the FF.

The inputs to the J and K connections on the FF have AND gates wired internally. The AND gates each have three inputs. Two of the three inputs are wired directly to chip pins. The J AND gate is connected directly to pins 3 and 4. The K AND gate has two inputs to pins 10 and 11. That leaves one more input to each AND gate.

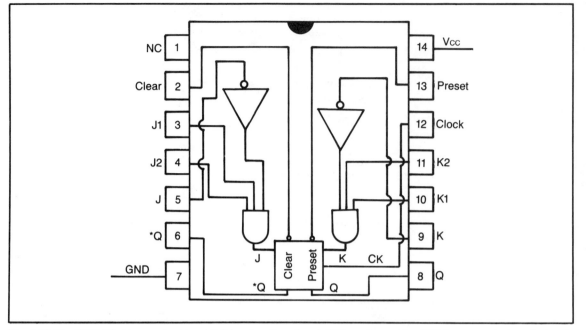

Fig. 4-39. The 7470 FF chip can store one bit. It has two three input AND and a couple of NOT gates to isolate the inputs from the outputs.

Both of these inputs are coming from NOT gates. The J input is at pin 5 and the K input is at pin 9. The AND gates will not output a high unless all three inputs are high. This means the two direct inputs have to be actually high, but the third input through the inverter must enter the pine as a low. The inverter will then change the low to a high.

The truth table for the JK flip-flop FF is essentially like the RS flip-flop except for the fact that the circuit inputs data by means of the JK connections rather than RS connections. The RS connections (Preset and Clear) in this chip are used for control, not data transfer.

When the AND gates input two lows into J and K, nothing happens. The states that were on Q and *Q remain. If the J input is a low and the K input a high, then Q goes low and *Q becomes high. Should J receive a high and K a low, then Q goes high and *Q low. Lastly if both J and K receive highs, the FF switches and the states that were on Q2 and *Q change. This is an important quality.

Besides being able to store states, the JK can

be used as a counter because of this ability. With highs on both the J and K, the clock input can switch the FF. Every clock pulse is able to toggle the circuit. If you count the toggles, you are counting the clock input pulses. This counting ability is the basis for a lot of the calculating that the computer is able to perform. There will be more about this ability in Chapter 8.

THREE-STATE LOGIC

As highs and lows are processed through the digital maze, it is often necessary to turn off some pathways and turn on other pathways. For example, the data bus is a two way single-lane street. While data is being written to memory, the data travels from the processor to memory. Data that is being stored in memory is not permitted to go from memory to the MPU while the traffic is moving the other way.

In the eight-lane data bus in Fig. 4-40, there are 16 buffers installed. Eight of them amplify the data that goes one way, and the other eight amplify the data going the other way. These buffers are of the three-state or three-state variety. They can be turned off and on at command. There is an extra little transistor circuit in them that does the enabling or disabling. Refer to Fig. 4-41.

When data travels from MPU to memory, the eight buffers aimed at memory are enabled, and the buffers pointed from memory to MPU are disabled. When the MPU is reading from memory, the eight buffers that had been disabled are turned on and the remaining eight are turned off.

This enabling and disabling ability is the three-stating. The highs and lows a chip processes are states number one and number two. The disabling is the third state. The third state is a measurable voltage. If you check an output with your vom and the test point is three-stating, the voltage will read somewhere in between a high and a low. If the high is near +5 volts and the low is just above zero, the three-state voltage will be above 0.8 volts and just below 2.4 volts.

This voltage is the result of a buildup of static noise voltages in the circuit. It has no logic. It is meaningless. The vom is able to display the three-state voltage as its sensitive meter responds to the dc buildup.

Should you use a logic probe to test the same three-state output, there will be no indication. The logic probe only reads high, low, and pulse. The static dc three-state buildup fails to excite the probe.

In a TTL a typical three-state circuit is built like the illustration in Fig. 4-42. The three-state transistors are able to enable and disable a common NAND circuit. The NAND is the top circuit and is based around Q1, Q4, Q6, Q7, and Q8. The Disable stage uses Q2, Q3, Q5, and D1.

Without the disable stage, the NAND gate will process any logic inputs that enter its twin-input emitters. The NAND output will follow the dictates of the NAND truth table. With the disable stage, though, the NAND can be forced to quit logic processing, and its output will go into a high impedance nonlogical state, as described.

The disable stage has a single input into the emitter of the npn Q2. When the emitter input of Q2 is held low, and the base has a + voltage on it, the npn will saturate. With Q2 saturating, Q3 and Q5 will be cutoff. This keeps a high on the cathode of D1 and on the third emitter of Q1.

As long as D1 is not conducting, Q4 is unaffected by the disable stage. Also, as long as there is a high on the third emitter of Q1, the NANDing of logic states being input will be allowed to continue without interruption. The NAND gate can process logic correctly.

However, if a high is input to the disable stage, Q2 will cutoff. Q3 and Q5 in turn will saturate. The collector of Q5 will go low. This puts a low on the cathode of D1 and on the third emitter of Q1. D1 conducts so that the output current of Q4 falls

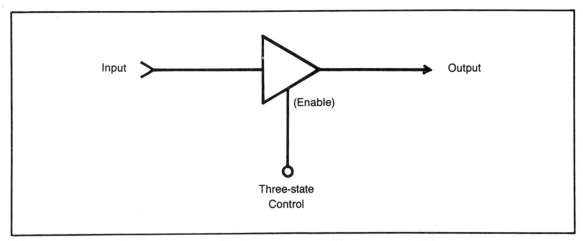

Fig. 4-40. In a three-state buffer, a three-state input connection is able to enable or disable the gate.

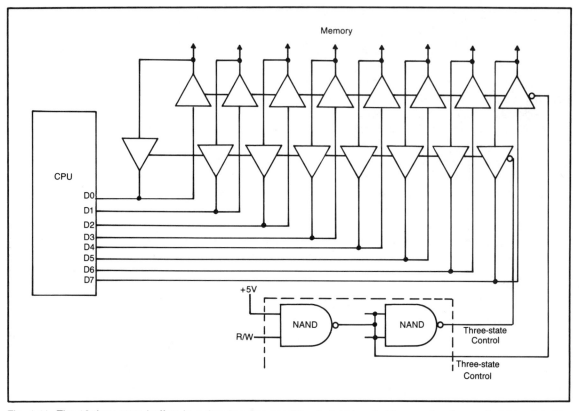

Fig. 4-41. The 16 three-state buffers in a data bus line consists of eight headed in one direction and eight pointed in the other direction. Only one set is on at a time permitting data travel only in one direction.

sharply. At the same time, the low on the third emitter of Q1 causes the NAND activity to cease. The NAND gate is disabled. The output at the junction between Q7 and Q8 becomes the undefined static. This cannot be passed on in the logical digital circuits. The output of the disable stage is a switch on the data stage.

GERMS EYE VIEW

Figure 4-43 shows a closeup of a microscopic resistor and capacitor. The resistor is constructed by placing a resistive element on top of the subtrate and connecting metal electrodes at either end. As electrons passed from one electrode to the other they have to traverse the resistor.

The capacitor is constructed in somewhat the same way. The dielectric was placed between two electrodes but with as much surface area touching the electrodes as possible. The thinner the dielectric and the more surface area, the more capacitance the miniscule capacitor has.

These two basic components are among the group shown at the bottom of the Digital Hierarchy in Table 4-1. The other basic devices are the ones that need a pn junction to operate. They are the silicon diodes, the bipolar transistors and the insulated gate FETs. All of the components are fabricated on substrates made out of pieces of p or n material and wired together to form the gates and registers shown in the higher rankings of the hierarchy.

The pn-junction devices are fabricated somewhat differently than the resistors and capacitors. If the substrate is a piece of P material, tubs of n material are installed in the p substrate as in Fig. 4-44.

90

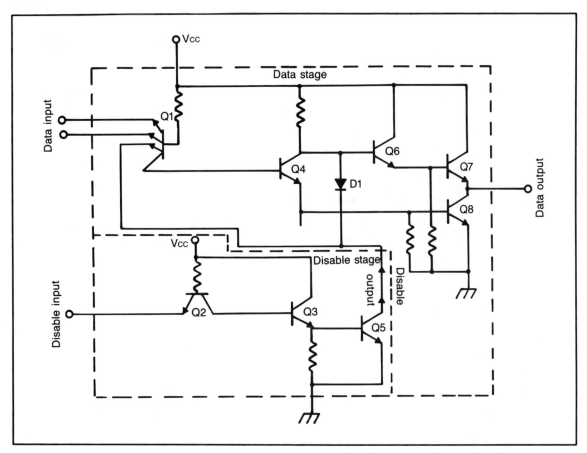

Fig. 4-42. A typical three-state circuit can be designed around a few npn transistors. This TTL NAND gate uses D1, Q2, Q3, and Q5 to do the job.

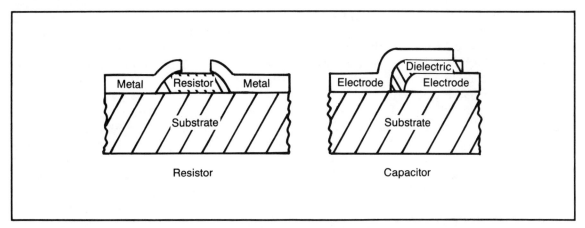

Fig. 4-43. In a chip, microscopic resistors and capacitors can be found. The resistor is a resistive element on top of the substrate with metal connectors on the end. The capacitor is a dielectric sandwiched between two metal electrodes on top of the same substrate.

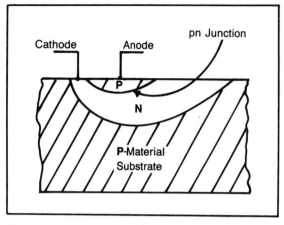

Fig. 4-44. A diode on a chip is fabricated by installing a tub of n-material on a p-material substrate and then diffusing another little p region in the n. The pn junction formed is the diode.

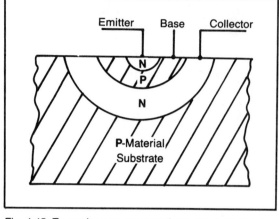

Fig. 4-45. To produce an npn transistor, the diode is taken one step further. Another little n region is installed in the p.

The size of the n material and its depth is determined by the amount of material used and the heat applied to diffuse the n into the p. The n tubs are the beginning of the components. The p substrate is only the casing of the chip. There is a pn junction formed between the tub and the substrate but it must not be used. Designers take great care not to allow this junction to turn on. If it does the chip won't process logic.

To produce a diode, another little p region is diffused into the n tub. If a lead is attached to the lower layer of n and another lead is connected to the higher layer of p, a diode is created. This diode can be used in the chip circuit.

To produce an npn transistor, the same procedure is used with one more step. The lower layer of n is called the collector and receives a lead. The next higher layer of p becomes the base. A third layer of n is then diffused into the base. It receives a lead too and is called the emitter. A tiny npn transistor is formed. Refer to Fig. 4-45.

The resistors shown in Fig. 4-43 can be installed in the tubs somewhat like a diode is made. In the n material, a p area is diffused. Then leads are attached to either end of the p section. Whatever the resistance value of the p section, it becomes the resistance. The resistors cannot attain high resistances. Only small values are possible.

To protect the tiny sensitive circuits a coating of silicon dioxide is placed on top of all the diffusions. The capacitors are made by using the oxide as the dielectric. Two leads are installed with the dielectric awkwardly sandwiched inbetween. That arrangement possesses capacitance.

Of course the chip making and arrangement of components has a lot more engineering details than I've covered, but essentially that is the way the electronics is built onto a chip using bipolar transistors. FETs are build in the same way.

The most complicated MOS chip is the CMOS. It stands for Complementary MOS in comparison to the NMOS and the PMOS. The CMOS contains both NMOS and PMOS components. It starts out in production as an n substrate. The n substrates usually are used to form PMOS circuits (shown in Fig. 4-46) and p substrates are used to produce NMOS chips. The CMOS starts out as n so the first step is to build the p-channel FETs. This is easy, two little sections of p material is diffused into the N substrate. Refer to Fig. 4-47. Leads are attached to each to become the source and drain. In-between the S and D connections the insulated gate is attached. A p-channel FET is made. What about the n-channel FETs?

They are started by diffusing a relatively large pocket of p material onto the n substrate. Then two

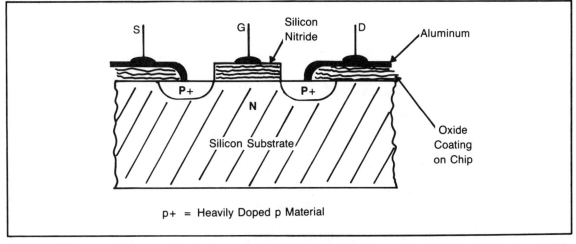

Fig. 4-46. All the components on a chip are microscopic. This PMOS FET has p + material which is heavily doped p material.

smallish pockets of n material is diffused into the p material. The S and D leads are attached to the small n pockets and an insulated gate over the channel. The n-channel FET is installed onto the CMOS chip.

These basic structures are the lowest level of the chip hierarchy. These components are connected up to form the gates, registers, and electronic switches that this chapter has discussed.

A digital world exists in every one of our computers. All it does is process the highs and lows that are entered. These logic states are codes for the analog entities that humans want to manipulate. The next two chapters discuss how electronics is able to change our analog world entities into digital codes for entry into the digital world and then how electronics changes the digital codes back to analog once they have been processed.

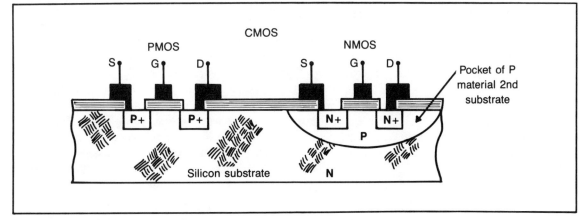

Fig. 4-47. This CMOS chip is able to have both NMOS and PMOS FETs on the same substrate.

Chapter 5

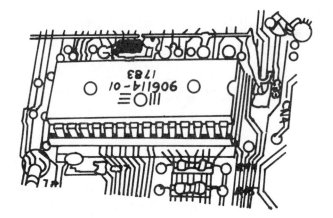

Digital-to-Analog Connection

T HE WORD ANALOG, WITH RESPECT TO COMputers, refers to the analog computer that is very different from a digital computer. An analog computer is a device that sets up a mathematical analogy of a problem. It then solves the analogy and has the answer to the problem. A digital computer, on the other hand, has the problem broken down into arithmetic. The arithmetic, which consists of counting digits, is run off. The answer to the problem is in the resultant digits.

If that explanation is confusing let's explore it further by examining two mechanical, nonelectronic computers. The instrument panel of your car contains a digital computer and an analog one, both mechanical. Refer to Fig. 5-1. They are dedicated to two different jobs. The digital computer is the mileage indicator, dedicated to counting miles. It is driven by a cable connected to the drive shaft. As the drive turns the indicator moves. After every mile the indicator increments by one. This is a digital measurement.

The speedometer, on the other hand, is an analog computer dedicated to indicating speed, not distance. It is attached to the same cable and as the drive shaft rotates the speedometer needle indicates the rate of rotation. Theoretically there are an infinite number of possible speeds the needle can point to. When the car stops, the needle falls to zero. The needle is the analogous measurement of the physical speed of the car over the road.

The mileage indicator is the handiest way to count the miles as they whiz by. The fact that a running count is needed lends itself to digital means. The speedometer needle is an excellent mechanical measuring way to keep you aware of the speed you are traveling at in real time. If you wanted to replace the analog needle with a mechanical digital device, while it could be done, it would be hard to come up with the digital display that could show the rate of rotation of the cable.

However, with digital electronics the replacement of the needle by a digital display is easy and even superior to the analog needle against a scale of mph. That is because the electronics has been made microscopic and acts, as far as we are concerned, instantly. The digital display speedometer,

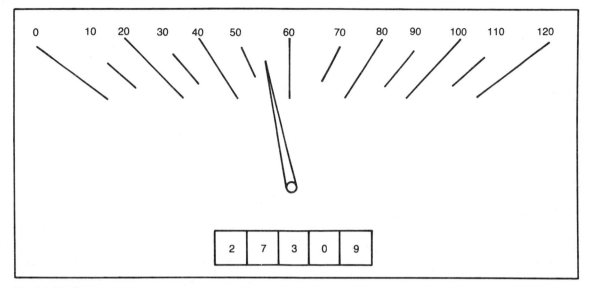

Fig. 5-1. The dashboard of your car contains an analog computer and a digital one. The analog computer is the speedometer, and the digital computer is the mileage indicator.

although a thousand times more complex than the needle display, is gradually replacing the analog needle as the speed indicator.

We humans live in a world that runs in real time and most of the things we do on a job have been measured, until recently, by analog means. The slide rule, needles on meters, volume controls, scales, radio and TV signals, calculations involving physical volume, length, width, and height, etc. Were all made using an analogy of the problem and coming to a conclusion by means of the analogy. Trying to perform any lengthy calculation by mechanical counting has been the hard way to go.

Digital electronics has changed all that. It is so fast that the seemingly cumbersome counting procedure is now the best approach. It is now easier in lots of cases to take a problem and forget about setting up an analogy to solve it. The digital approach converts the problem into arithmetic. Next the arithmetic is coded to binary. Then the binary 1s are made into highs and the 0s into lows. The highs and lows enter the digital world and get quickly processed. After processing, the answers are displayed on a TV screen. Hard printed copy is made, or the answers are stored on cassette tape or disk.

ANALOG-TO-DIGITAL

In the analog world, there are all sorts of problems the digital computer is called upon to solve. In order for the computer to do its job, the first thing that must be done is to transform the given information regarding the problem into highs and lows. The information can be in many forms. It could be the speed, temperature, and navigational position of a missile in the sky. It might possibly be the specific gravity of a chemical being produced. Maybe it is an electronic waveshape that contains video or audio. It might be the position of a shaft connected to a potentiometer. The possibilities are unlimited. Most of the information comes from analog sources that vary from a top to a bottom with many positions in between. The information must be changed to a digital voltage that has a top level, a bottom level and no in between. This is what changing an analog situation to a digital one is all about.

Since the computer is electronic, the first step to converting analog to digital is preparing all the physical information into terms of analog voltages and current. For example a sound can be input to a microphone and move a coil in a circuit or a shaft can be attached to a potentiometer and the movement of the shaft can change the voltage output of the variable resistor in the pot. All of the potential inputs for the computer can be made into electrical forms in similar ways.

Once the information has been prepared into voltage, it can be entered into an analog-to-digital converter circuit. Refer to Fig. 5-2.

DIGITAL-TO-ANALOG

After the A/D converter circuit converts the analog to digital states, it injects the highs and lows into the digital world. The inputs are then processed, the problem is solved; and the computer wants to get rid of all the answers and get on to the next task. In some cases, outputs are to emerge from the computer in digital form. Other outputs need to be converted back into analog voltages for use in the analog world. These voltages are passed through digital-to-analog circuits. The output of these circuits are the solutions to analog problems.

At first glance, this procedure of first changing analog to digital, computing the digital, and then changing the digital back to the original analog might seem like a lot of unnecessary trouble. It is considerable trouble to set the system up, but digital computing operates at such blazing speeds

and can process utterly amazing amounts of data, that at the present time and for the foreseeable future, there is no other practical way to go.

DIGITAL-TO-DIGITAL

Not all of the inputs to the computer are analog in nature even though they originate in the analog world. In addition, not all of the outputs of the computer have to be analog. Some of the outputs of the computer have to be analog. Some of the other outputs feed digital equipment outside the computer.

Your computer uses typical inputs such as joysticks and a cassette tape player. These are analog devices. When the computer receives a joystick input it is essentially reading the position of the stick in relation to the stick container box. This is an analog value since the stick can be pushed into an infinite number of positions around the box. The cassette player is also an analog device because the tape contains audio frequencies. The frequencies are code for digital signals but they are audio nevertheless. Place a computer cassette tape into a player and listen to it. The noises are unintelligible audio. I'll discuss these circuits later in this chapter.

On the other hand, the keyboard is a digital

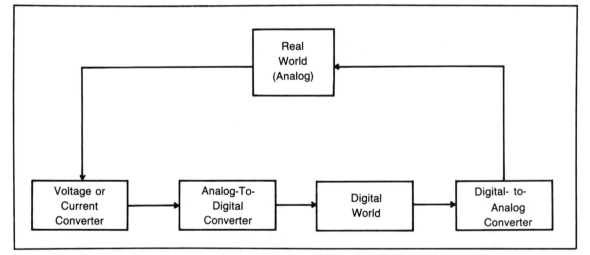

Fig. 5-2. To solve one of our real world problems with an electronic digital computer, the steps are the following. First, code the analog given information into voltage or current. Second, convert the analog electricity into highs and lows. Third, process the logic states. Fourth, convert the processed bits into analog electricity. Lastly, send the analog back to the real world.

INPUT device. When you strike a key, you are shorting together two wires. The keys have two states. When they are not touched, they are open. If one is stuck, it is closed. It is a switch. When it is open, it is dormant. As it is struck it conducts voltage. This is a digital situation. The keyboard is able to input information into the computer without need for an analog-to-digital conversion since it is already digital in nature.

The same type of mixup is present in the outputs too. Of the various outputs possible, some are analog and others are digital. For instance, the video you display is an analog signal. The video input to the TV display is a composite TV signal just like the signals that come over the air or through the cable company. The same goes for the audio your computer might create. The programs you save to tape are also analog. The program lines might be digital information but there are circuits in your computer that converts them to an analog form.

The output to the printer though is digital. The printer receives it's input directly from the digital circuits without needing the conversion to analog. Inside the printer the circuits do some analog work, but your computer outputs digital. Your computer is able to display your digital keyboard strikes by TV analog means and print the characters on paper through digital outputs.

DIGITAL-TO-ANALOG CONVERTERS

I'll begin the circuit explanations with a D/A converter because the A/D converter is more complex and is based around a D/A converter. Most digital-to-analog circuits consist of a collection of electronic switches and resistors. There is a switch for every bit that is used in the digital processing. If the computer is processing four bits, then the D/A circuits have four switches. As an example, Fig. 5-3 shows a scheme for converting a 4-bit digital signal to an analog output.

In a nybble signal, there is a steady stream of four parallel data bits. The four bits travel abreast over four lanes in a data bus. The four bits are output into a 4-bit D/A converter circuit. The four bits could be an audio signal like a siren the computer creates as sound effects. The D/A converter has four separate inputs, one for each of the bits.

In order to produce a siren type sound, the steady stream of nybbles must vary smoothly from a low to a high pitch and back. As the pitch goes from a low to a high, the sound can be produced digitally by using the following stream of nybbles:

LLLL
LLLH
LLHL
LLHH
LHLL
LHLH
LHHL
LHHH
HLLL
HLLH
HLHL
HLHH
HHLL
HHLH
HHHL
HHHH

Four bits at a time are input at the four switches of the D/A converter. The switches are connected to the resistors. The resistors are wired as a voltage divider. The resistors have a source voltage of +5 volts, and at the bottom end, returns to ground.

Each nybble, as it enters the D/A circuit, produces a slightly different voltage output. The effect of the resistors is to permit the input nybble states to be converted into an analog voltage between 0 and +5 volts.

The LLLL nybble does not open up any of the electronic switches. All four of the switch connections to the voltage divider are at 0 volts, a low. They do not have any effect. According to the wiring of the divider, the four Ls could place the total divider output voltage down near 0 volts.

As each subsequent nybble enters the switch circuit, the H's start turning on the switches. According to which switches are turned on and the number of +5 volts, through series resistors, that

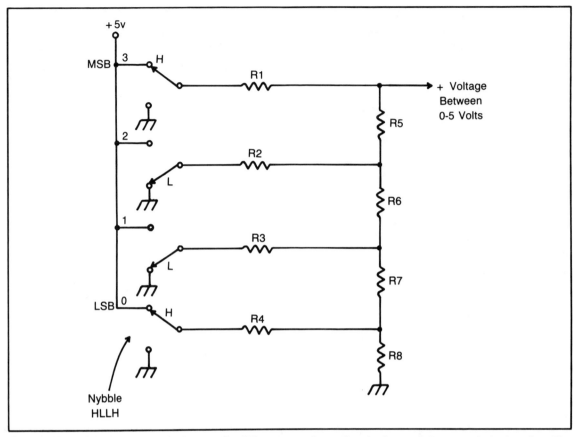

Fig. 5-3. Four bits at a time can be input to the D/A converter by setting the four switches to a desired setting. The switches connect to a resistive voltage divider. Each different setting of the switches produces a different output voltage between 0 and +5 volts.

are introduced to the divider, the output voltage varies. When the nybbles vary from LLLL to HHHH the output voltage can be made to vary in steps from near 0 to near +5 volts. As the nybbles then decrease in binary value, from HHHH to LLLL the output voltage in turn will decrease back down to near 0 volts.

If the varying voltage is then input to an analog oscillator circuit, the siren type sound will emanate. All sorts of audio sounds can be produced with this type of D/A converter.

Take note of the fact that the 4-bit input produced 16 different voltage levels of output. If there had been five inputs, there could have been 32 different voltage levels available at the output. A 6-bit input could produce 64 output levels, and seven in-

puts, 128 levels. This is the very core of D/A techniques. It is the attempt to convert a seeming few digital inputs to a great multitude of voltage output levels.

ANALOG-TO-DIGITAL CONVERTERS

Converting digital to analog is helpful to the computer to get its digital results out to the analog world. Getting the analog world information into the digital computer is a mite harder. The D/A converter circuit, in addition to converting digital to analog is also the centerpiece in the analog to digital effort. It plays a major part in the total A/D circuit. It is located in the middle of the A/D circuit network shown in Fig. 5-4.

98

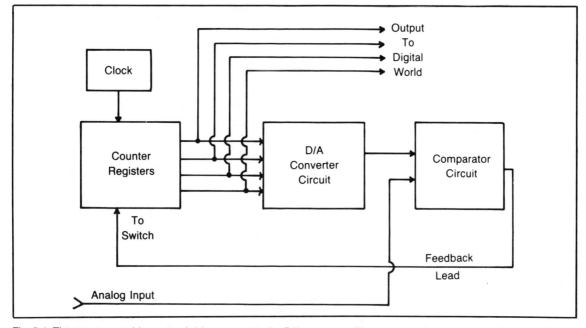

Fig. 5-4. The counter provides a steady binary count to the D/A converter. The converter in turn sends a constantly changing voltage to the comparator. Also input to the comparator stage is the analog signal. It is compared to the count signal and logic states are output as the count compares with the analog. The comparator signal is then fed back to the counter.

Besides the D/A circuit, the A/D needs a counter input circuit and an output into a comparator. The counter is a register arrangement that begins with 0 and counts up to its potential. For instance, a nybble counter can count the four bits from decimal 0 to 15. A byte-sized counter can count from 0 to 255. A two-byte counter can go from 0 to 65,535, and so on. The counter inputs its bit sets into the D/A inputs. The switches in the D/A respond accordingly and the voltage output of the D/A changes gradually as the count goes on.

Comparator

The voltage produced is output to a comparator. A comparator is a voltage controlled device. It has two inputs and one output. Refer to Fig. 5-5. Inside the LM339 chip in Fig. 5-6 are four comparators. They all have a + and − sign by their inputs. The + and − signs have a confusing meaning. They do not indicate positive or negative voltages. The − sign shows where the reference voltage is input. The + sign designates the place

to input a signal voltage. In the A/D converter, the reference voltage comes from the D/A converter stage. The input signal arrives from the analog circuit. It is the signal that wants conversion from analog to digital.

A simplified version of a comparator stage, is built around a pair of pnp transistors in Fig. 5-7. The circuit almost looks like a flip-flop but there are important differences. The inputs though are not really legitimate states. They are two voltages

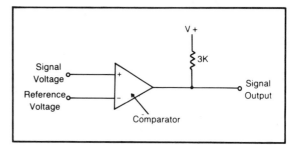

Fig. 5-5. The comparator is a voltage controlled device. A signal voltage is compared to a reference voltage to produce one of two output voltage states.

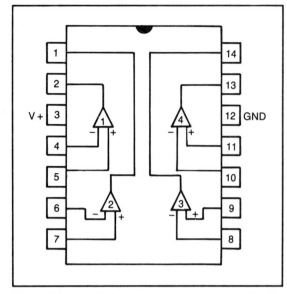

Fig. 5-6. The 339 chip has four comparators on a 14-pin DIP.

input. As a result of the inputs, the comparator will either saturate or cutoff. If it saturates, the output becomes a low. Should it cutoff, the output is a high. Note that there is only one possible output. Recall that a flip-flop has two complementary outputs.

The emitters are tied together and returned to ground through a common resistor. This makes the two base input signals control the outputs of both transistors. Both transistors will respond to the more negative of the two inputs. If the reference voltage is more negative than the analog input voltage, Q2 will saturate and Q1 will cutoff. The output voltage, as Q2 saturates will become about the same voltage as the negative base input.

If the analog input is more negative into Q1, then Q1 will saturate and Q2 will cutoff. With Q1 saturating, the voltage output will switch and become about the same as the $-V$ source.

The actual comparator circuit in Fig. 5-8, although essentially the same and based around a pair of transistors, has added diodes and transistors to give it stability. Comparators are sensitive to temperature variations. The illustration shows an internal circuit found in one of the comparators on an LM339.

that are anxious to become one logic state. They are the reference and analog signals.

The two transistors can be called Q1 and Q2. A reference signal is applied to the base of Q2, the $-$ input. The analog input is connected to the $+$

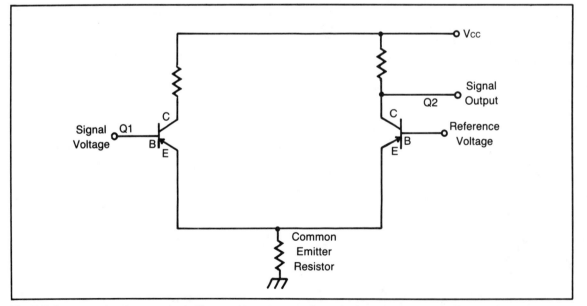

Fig. 5-7. A comparator stage can be built around two pnp transistors and a pair of resistors. The one output state is a result of the two inputs.

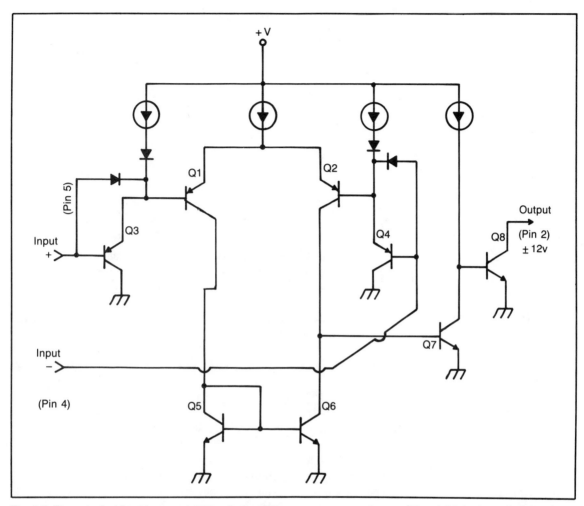

Fig. 5-8. The actual wiring of one comparator in the 339 uses two npn transistors, Q5 and Q6, in the emitter circuits of the pnp comparator, Q1 and Q2. This provides better temperature control to the stage.

The LM339 has the ability to switch from +12 volts to −12 volts as the input analog signal changes the base voltage of Q1 from a condition of being more negative than the reference voltage to being more positive than the reference voltage. This swing from +12 volts to −12 volts can then be used for all sorts of purposes. In the A/D converter, the comparator output is coupled back to the counter stage.

Counter

In the A/D circuit, the counter is counting away at a steady pace. If the counter is a nybble register, it outputs four bits to the four input switches of the D/A converter. It keeps counting from LLLL to HHHH and the D/A converter receives the steady stream of nybbles. The D/A converter changes the nybbles to varying voltage levels. The analog output from the converter is thus continually applied to the comparator's reference input.

The counter is driven by a clock. The clock is an oscillator circuit. It runs at a prescribed frequency and its final output is a square wave. The complete clock circuit is discussed in detail in Chapter 8.

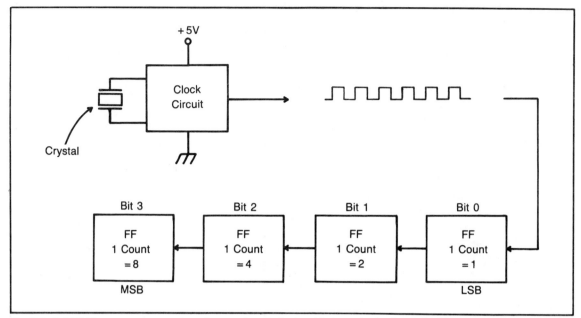

Fig. 5-9. A 4-bit binary counter counts pulses as the clock signal is input to the least significant bit.

The square wave input drives the counter. The continual wave train of highs and lows in Fig. 5-9 keeps pushing into the counter. Every pulse of the wave train forces the counter to count once. There is no let up in the counter as long as the wave train keeps being injected.

This nybble counter is a circuit containing four flip-flops wired together, side by side. The flip-flops start off by being *initialized.* All that computer term means is that the four flip-flops have their states arranged so that they begin at LLLL. This is the same thing that you do when you initialize your trip mileage indicator at 000 0 before starting on an auto trip.

One FF, in order to count from 0 to 1, often needs the help of two AND gates. The gates are needed when the FF wants to be able to output an arithmetical carry in addition to counting. Refer to Fig. 5-10 for the following explanation.

One FF, as it is powered up, develops an initial total state of 0. The 0 state comes about as the two cross-coupled circuits adopt the following states: the set-*Q side becomes a high, and the Reset-Q goes to a low. That is the convention. When Q is held low, the entire FF is considered to

be containing a binary 0. *Q is always the complement of Q, and when the FF is storing a 0, *Q is high.

The two AND gates have their outputs connected to Set and Reset. One input from the top gate is connected to an input on the bottom gate. The input for the entire stage is attached to this mutual input. The other AND inputs are wired to Q and *Q. They are cross coupled as shown in Fig. 5-10. The output of the stage is coming from the AND output attached to Reset. This output conveys the arithmetic carry.

With Q low and *Q high, the ANDs have the Set-*Q with one low input and the Reset-Q with one high input. If a high clock pulse is input at their common connection, a high will be input at Reset-Q. The pulse will cause the stage to flip-flop and a high will exit the stage. The high is an arithmetic carry of 1. The stage at this point in time now stores a 1 due to the flip-flop. Set-*Q is now held low and Reset-Q is in a high state. The counter has successfully counted from 0 to 1.

One FF can only count from 0 to 1. If you attach a second FF to the output of the first, the two FFs can count pulses, 00, 01, 10, 11, which is 0,

102

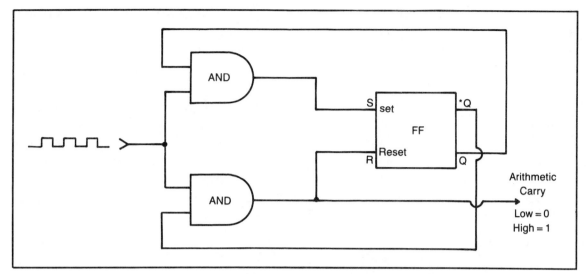

Fig. 5-10. Two AND gates will help out when a bit must be able to forward an arithmetical carry.

1, 2, and 3 in decimal. Then it starts over. With three FFs, the binary count goes from 000 to 111 which is 0 to 7 in decimal. Four FFs count 0000 to 1111 or 0 to 15 in decimal. This idea was introduced earlier in Fig. 2-15.

The arithmetic carry output line on each FF is connected to the next stage's common AND input. The clock drives the first FF. The rest of the FFs are flip-flopped by the output carry line of the previous stage.

Table 5-1. Nybble Counter Output.

	Count in Binary	Significant Values	Decimal Results	Hex Results
Nybble Counter 4 Bits	LLLL	0+0+0+0	0	0
	LLLH	0+0+0+1	1	1
	LLHL	0+0+2+0	2	2
	LLHH	0+0+2+1	3	3
	LHLL	0+4+0+0	4	4
	LHLH	0+4+0+1	5	5
	LHHL	0+4+2+0	6	6
	LHHH	0+4+2+1	7	7
	HLLL	8+0+0+0	8	8
	HLLH	8+0+0+1	9	9
	HLHL	8+0+2+0	10	A
	HLHH	8+0+2+1	11	B
	HHLL	8+4+0+0	12	C
	HHLH	8+4+0+1	13	D
	HHHL	8+4+2+0	14	E
	HHHH	8+4+2+1	15	F
5 Bits	(H)LLLL	(16)+0+0+0+0	16	10
	(H)LLLH	(16)+0+0+0+1	17	11
	(H)LLHL	(16)+0+0+2+0	18	12

The nybble counter output in Table 5-1 shows clearly how four binary numbers are coded into one decimal number. Four bits is the basic relationship that binary has to one decimal or hexadecimal number. The nybble counter is designed to count from 0 to 15. The rightmost FF in Fig. 5-9 contains the smallest value in binary. That is why it is called the least significant bit, or LSB. The leftmost FF contains the highest value of the binary count. That is why it is known as the most significant bit, or MSB.

In the A/D converter, the counter continually runs from 0 to 15 and then starts over again as the clock keeps pumping pulses into it. Each FF outputs its state to switches in the D/A part of the A/D converter. The resistive divider network converts the input states to an analog voltage.

The graph of the digital-state inputs to the resultant analog-voltage output in Fig. 5-11, draws what is known as a *stairstep* waveform. The 16 4-bit inputs each produce a different voltage level in the resistive output. The stairstep comes about because

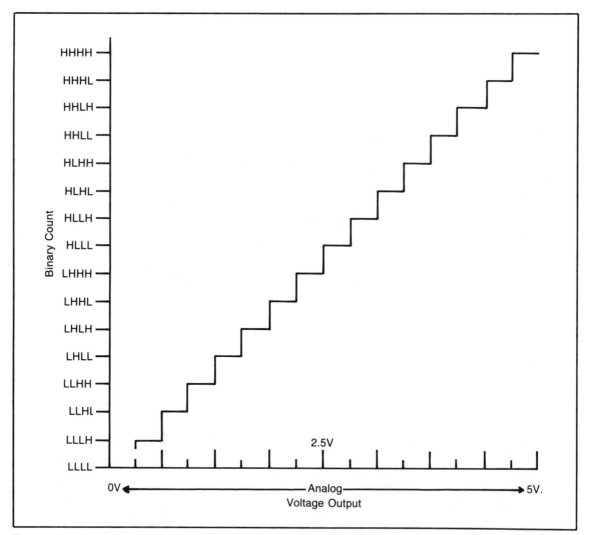

Fig. 5-11. The input to the reference voltage pin of the comparator is coming from the counter that is counting out the stairstep voltage.

the counter is continually counting from LLLL to HHHH. Each step is produced in turn on a regular basis.

The input to the Reference Voltage pin of the comparator is the stairstep analog voltage levels. As long as the counter keeps flip-flopping, the stairstep continues to enter the comparator. The output of the comparator remains at about the source voltage. The Reference Voltage is designed at that time to be more negative than the other signal input. Under those conditions nothing else is going on.

The counter FFs in Fig. 5-4 have another input and another output that hasn't been mentioned as yet. The input is a feedback lead from the output of the comparator to a switch in the counter chip. The switch can enable the other output. This second output connects to the same four bits that the original output is getting its count from. The second output though, goes to the digital world. It does not dead end at the comparator as the original output does. The second output is going to be the digital representation of the analog input from an analog device. For instance, it could be an analog input from a joystick.

JOYSTICK INTERFACE

The joystick is a device that is able to change the position of the shaft into an analog voltage. As you move the graphics across the screen, the joystick is varying a voltage.

The mechanism in some joystick assemblies is a stick connected to two potentiometers. Refer to Fig. 5-12. The potentiometers are nothing but two resistors with wiping arms. There is +5 volts attached to one end of a resistor and ground to the other end. A wiping arm slides over the resistor and varies the resistance to the arm. As a result the voltage out of the arm can vary from 0 to +5 volts, an analog voltage. It can be one of an infinite number of voltages.

This analog voltage is input to the signal input pin of the comparator. It will be any voltage between 0 and +5 volts. Meanwhile the Reference input is receiving the stairstep voltages. As long as the stairstep is more negative than the joystick out-

put, the comparator remains dormant and the feedback of its output to the counter is inactive.

As soon as the stairstep voltage inputs a value that is more positive than the joystick input, the comparator switches. The switch changes the comparator output to a different state. This new state is fed back to the counter. The counter switch is enabled and the count, at that instant, is output to the digital world. That is it! The analog voltage level from the joystick is input to the comparator and the digital count at that instant, which corresponds to the voltage, is output in digital form. The analog has been converted to digital.

CASSETTE INTERFACE

The cassette tape machine is an analog device. As you know, it is one of the important staples of a computer repertoire. The cassette requires three circuits in a computer in order to perform. First of all, it needs to be controlled. This is a digital function. The controlling only consists of turning it on and off.

Secondly, the cassette needs a D/A circuit. After computing, it is often necessary to save your work to tape. The D/A circuit will convert the digital computing data into an analog audio voltage that can be securely stored on tape.

The third interface that the cassette needs is an A/D circuit. When you want to run a program that you have stored on tape, the program must be placed into RAM so it can be run. An A/D circuit is able to take the computer coded audio containing the program and convert it to digital bits and bytes that can be stored in RAM.

Motor Control

The cassette can't do a thing till it is turned on. The motor control circuit in Fig. 5-13 is typical of most computers. It consists of an npn transistor that controls a relay. The transistor is able to saturate or cutoff. The collector of the transistor is connected to +5 volts through the windings of the relay.

The relay is the off-on switch for the cassette motor. When the relay is not activated, the motor

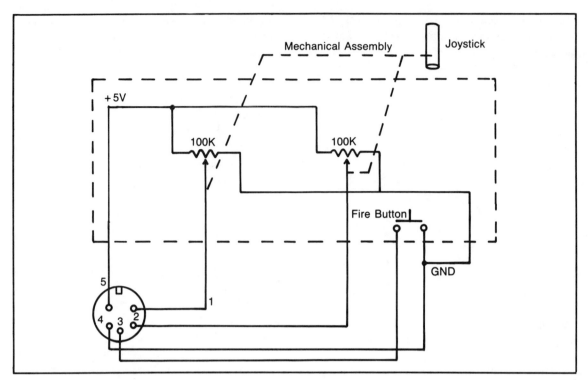

Fig. 5-12. The mechanism in the joystick assembly is a stick attached to two potentiometers. As the joystick is moved, the voltage across the two pots is varied.

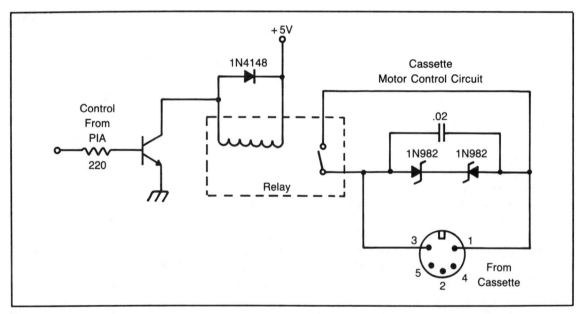

Fig. 5-13. The relay is the off-on switch for the cassette motor. The npn transistor controls the switch as it is made to saturate or cutoff.

is off. If the relay is energized, it forms a closed circuit and the motor goes on. A diode is placed across the relay to shunt off any surge currents that might occur as the relay opens and closes. There are two more diodes and a .02 μF capacitor in series with the relay to also dispel surges in voltage or current.

The motor control is a relatively straight forward circuit. The npn base input comes from the digital world. It is designed in software. When a high is input to the base, the npn saturates and the relay in the collector circuit is energized. The relay closes the motor circuit and the motor starts turning.

When the base receives a low, the npn cuts off. The relay opens up without the current flow and the motor turns off. The software in the program or in ROM provides the highs and lows at the appropriate times.

D/A Converter

After you have completed your day's programming you might want to save it to tape. In order to accomplish that end, you must convert the digital data to analog audio. Most computers accomplish this task in the following manner.

With the aid of software, every H bit you have produced is coded into HL. Every L bit is made into HHLL. These codings are then sent to the D/A converter. There are only two codes used, one is HL, which represents binary 1 and the second is HHLL, which represents binary 0. The bits are then fed serially to the D/A converter.

In the resistance network, the square waves are transformed into output sinewaves. At the rate of flow determined by the computer clock, the sinewaves emerge from the D/A in two frequencies. The 1s leave the D/A at a frequency of about 2400 hz. The 0s, which are twice as long as the 1s exit at the slower frequency of 1200 hz. The sinewave in Fig. 5-14 has a voltage top of about +2.5 volts and a bottom around −2.5 volts. An attenuator network consisting of a series resistor and a resistor and capacitor in parallel lowers the voltage to about 1 volt. These are audio frequencies and voltages. The tape has no problem in storing them.

A/D Converter

The cassette needs an A/D converter to put its contents into RAM. The cassette tape holds the magnetic representations of the 2400 and 1200 Hz sinewaves. The sinewaves are input directly to the typical comparator circuit in Fig. 5-15. The signals first encounter a connection between two resistors.

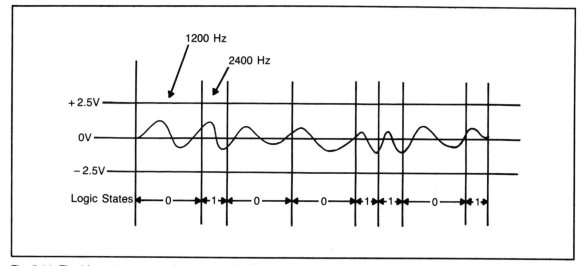

Fig. 5-14. The binary 1s are transformed to 2400 Hz pulses, and the 0s are made into 1200 Hz signals. The cassette tape can store these audio frequencies.

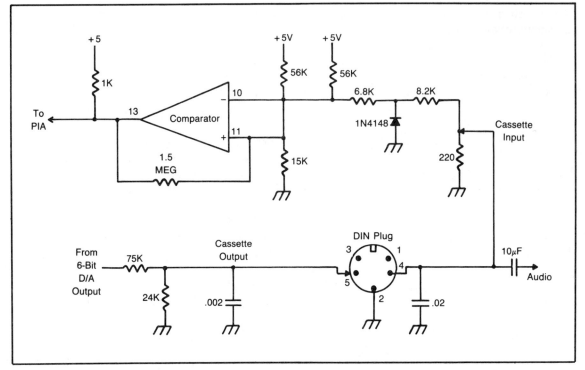

Fig. 5-15. The cassette tape contents are input to a comparator circuit. The comparator will change the audio pulses into digital highs and lows.

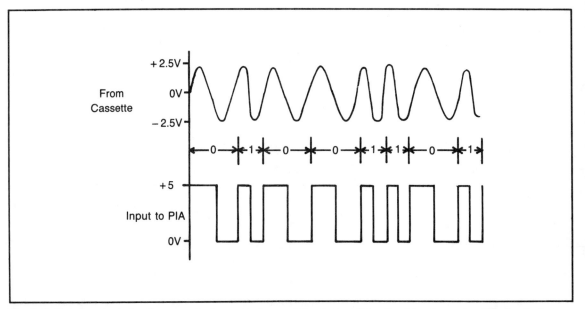

Fig. 5-16. The signal entering the computer is varying from + 2.5 volts to − 2.5 volts. A zero-crossing detector diode conditions the comparator input so the comparator will output a high from the + 2.5 volts and a low as the − 2.5 volts arrives.

A low resistance such as 220 ohms to ground terminate the cassette input line. Then the signal must pass through two series resistors and over a diode to the signal entry pin of the comparator. The pin is held at about 1 volt through a resistor to +5 volts.

Meanwhile the reference voltage pin is connected to the midpoint of a voltage divider of a 15K resistor to ground and a 56K to +5 volts. This holds the reference voltage also to 1 volt. With this configuration, the output of the comparator is held low. It stays low as long as there is no input from the cassette. When the cassette sends signal to the comparator, however, the following happens.

The signal is a series of analog sinewaves that go to a high of about +2.5 volts, crosses over zero and goes to a low of about −2.5 volts. A waveshape is shown in Fig. 5-16. The sinewaves occur in one of two frequencies: 2400 hz for a binary 1, and 1200 hz for binary 0. During the positive excursion of the signal, the diode, which has its cathode connected to the input line, is reverse biased. The voltage on the input pin at the comparator rises above the 1 volt it is held at. This makes the reference pin more negative. The comparator outputs a low.

As the sinewave goes negative, the diode becomes forward biased and the input-pin voltage drops down to about 0.5 volts. This makes the input pin of the comparator more negative than the reference pin. The comparator switches states and outputs a high. This circuit is called a *zero crossing detector*.

The comparator is thus changing sinewave inputs to logic state outputs. The 2400 Hz sinewave inputs are producing a steady stream of HL double bits. The HLs are cassette code for binary 1. The 1200 Hz inputs are producing HHLL outputs. HHLL is code for binary 0. These logic states are sent to the digital world where software decodes the cassette code into normal highs and lows for storage in RAM.

The output of the comparator is open collector. This allows you to install a pullup resistor. If a 1K resistor is installed between the comparator output and the +5 volt source, the logic states will have enough current to be put into a TTL chip easily.

Chapter 6

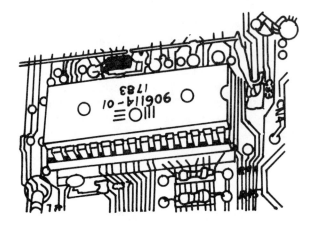

Analog Circuits

IF THERE IS ONE WORD TO DESCRIBE WHAT circuits in the digital world do, it is *switch*. All of the components, the capacitors, resistors, diodes, and transistors aid and actually perform all sorts of complex switching patterns. The switching from high to low voltage levels and back is what digital computing is all about.

Before you allow information into the digital circuits and after you receive the processed results, switching is the least job performed by the external analog circuits. In a flying missile the varying temperatures, pressures, fuel amounts, altitude, etc. all vary from one value to another, not switch from the maximum to the minimum and back. Chemical processes gradually dissolve materials into a finished batch. They do not take one instaneous jump from start to finish. Even your joystick pushes and pulls the potentiometer from 0 volts to +5 volts and through every in-between voltage. It doesn't switch from low to high. The analog voltages that these computer input processes develop must be handled in analog circuits before they can be converted into digital equivalent values.

In the analog output circuits, the same type of situation exists. After the digital circuits have processed the input data and the data has been converted back into analog voltages, analog circuits must be used to further the results on their way. The results usually must be displayed on a TV display. In order to make the information appear on the screen, the video information must be passed through video circuits. If there is computer audio to go with the video, the sound must be also amplified in order to be heard.

Should the computer be the type that uses an ordinary TV receiver as the display, the sound and picture has to be installed on a carrier wave, usually the commercial channel three or four. An rf modulator with an rf amplifier is used.

Besides the information handling analog circuits, some of the support circuitry in the computer is also analog in nature. For instance, the clock that drives and controls the speed of the computer is analog. It is an oscillator circuit. It produces an analog oscillator sinewave at its prescribed frequency. This in turn drives a square wave generator to produce the needed highs and lows. The clock circuits are discussed in detail in Chapter 8. The power supply is also an oldtime analog type circuit. It produces voltages like, + 5 volts dc, − 5 volts dc, + 12 volts dc, 9 volts ac, and so on. Typical microcomputer power supplies are covered in Chapter 17.

Therefore, it is necessary for the computer user to have some familiarity with these analog circuits as well as an in depth understanding of the digital electronics. Although the knowledge of the analog amplifiers, detectors, oscillators, and filtering methods won't be as valuable to your programming skills as the digital knowhow, it will aid in your quest to master your machine.

DIODES

There is absolutely no composition difference between the resistors, capacitors, and components with pn junctions used in analog circuits as in digital. The circuit wiring is the medium that makes them act differently. The wiring forces the com-

ponents to be switches in digital designed circuits and do analog jobs in analog circuits. The design brings out the different facets of their abilities.

The pn junction was discussed in detail in Chapters 3, 4, and 5. The junction in those digital circuits was one of the main actors in the switching operations. In analog circuits the diode is used for other duties. The diodes are needed in rectifier circuits, used as detectors, used as variable capacitors and act as zener diodes. All of these jobs can be found in computers. Some of these duties are built into chips and others are in discrete diodes.

The simple diode is symbolized by a line and a triangle. Refer to Fig. 6-1. The line is the n material and the triangle is the p. The cathode of the diode is the input to the line. The anode is the connection to the flat side of the triangle. The triangle symbol has no relationship to the logical YES or NOT symbols which are also triangles.

The silicon diode becomes forward biased when a voltage of about + 0.6 volts is applied to the anode and the cathode is at zero volts. Electrons are drawn from the cathode across the narrowed

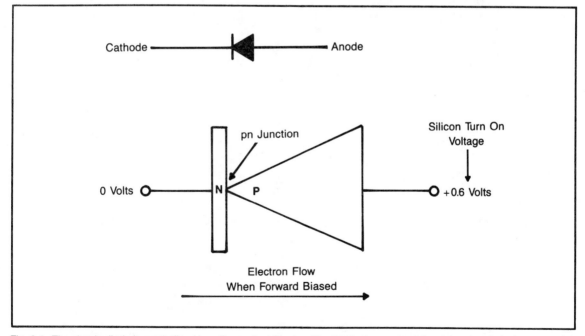

Fig. 6-1. The simple diode is symbolized by a line and a triangle. The line is the n-material and the triangle is the p-material. Electrons, except under special circumstances, travel from n to p as soon as a potential of 0.6 volts is on the anode.

pn junction to the anode. The +0.6 volts turn on is a fixed characteristic of silicon. If the diode is made of germanium, the turn on voltage is only +0.2 volts.

The electrons, attracted by the + voltage on the anode, move through the n material as excess negative charges and then pick their way through the p material, jumping from hole to hole. The effect of their movement through the p material is the same as if the positive charged holes were moving toward the cathode.

Silicon rectifiers are hardy, reliable components. They can pass large numbers of electrons easily. A power silicon rectifier can pass as much as 400 amperes with voltage pressures up to 130 volts in a temperature environment equal to the boiling point of water. They are small, lightweight, shockproof, and efficient.

When a silicon diode is reverse biased, there is a forward-to-reverse resistance ratio of 100 to 1. Any tiny amounts of current that do manage to flow is due to the presence of a few holes in the n material. They permit the electrons to pick their way through to the + voltage now on the cathode. With the reverse bias, the amount of current that does manage to make it from the zero volts on the anode to the cathode is measured as just a few microamps, or millionths of an amp. This is just a minute fraction of the full amperage that can pass during forward biasing.

Power diodes are usually referred to in terms of the amps that they can pass when forward biased. Typical values are 500 mA, 1 A, 25 A or 50 A.

An important rating of diodes is called its *peak inverse voltage*, or PIV. This is the safe amount of reverse-bias voltage that a diode can withstand. If the voltage is more than the PIV rating, the silicon crystal lattice structure will collapse from the strain. When that happens, the pn junction fails and the materials lose the qualities they received when doped. The diode just becomes a low resistance and acts like a piece of wire. The diode is ruined. (This is true except in the case of zener diodes which are designed around PIV. This is discussed later in this chapter.)

Diode Capacitance

The pn junction, when it is reverse biased becomes a capacitor. During reverse biasing the junction acts exactly the same way that a dielectric does. Refer to Fig. 6-2. If a + voltage is on the cathode and zero volts or a negative voltage is on the anode, the junction widens out and blocks the electrons from jumping the junction. The cathode will attract the electrons in the n material. Electrons will be attracted from the p material too. They will pile up on the p side of the wide junction and form a negative charge. Across the junction on the n side a dearth of electrons will take place forming a positive charge. This storing of charges is the work of a capacitance. It is aptly called *junction capacitance*.

The amount of capacitance a capacitor can store is a direct result of the thinness of the dielectric and the amount of dielectric surface area. In the pn junction, there isn't too much surface area, but the distance from one electrode to the other is only a few molecules thin. This produces useful amounts of capacitance.

The capacitance of a diode places a limit on the frequency at which it can work. In a discrete diode that has a relatively large surface area, the frequency range of the diode can be quite high. On a chip where the surface area is microscopic, even though the dielectric is so thin, the capacitance developed at the junction is tiny and the frequency range is limited. There will be more about these facts in the varicap discussion later in this section.

Zener Diodes

The zener, named after the scientist who invented it, is a special, very useful type of pn junction that works because of the peak inverse voltage breakdown characteristics. It has no other use. It does not rectify or do anything else tht other diodes do. Zeners are made of silicon and are made with various power ratings. However, when they are referred to, they are called 6-volt, 9-volt, 12 volt, 25 volt, etc.

This voltage identification designates the voltage level in the zener characteristic curve where

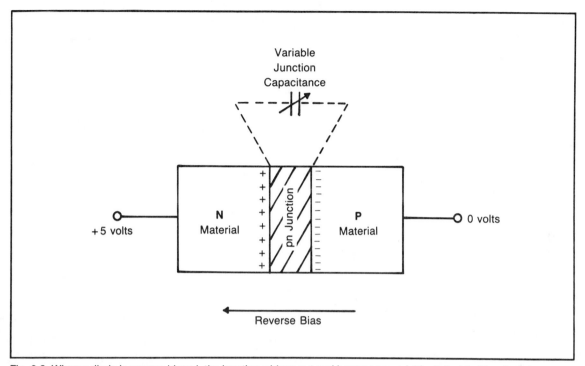

Fig. 6-2. When a diode is reverse biased, the junction widens out and becomes a variable dielectric. The diode becomes a capacitor.

the peak inverse voltage causes the sudden breakdown of the diode. It reverts to acting as a piece of wire. At that voltage breakdown point, the zener makes a sudden change from having no reverse electron flow to maximum electron flow.

The zener, though, does not break apart or short when this happens. It simply stops being a reverse-biased diode and becomes a dead short. When the peak inverse voltage is removed, the zener goes right back to being an ordinary diode and no harm is done.

A diode is made into a zener during manufacturing. It is doped in ways that produce the effect. The amount of doping decides the amount of voltage it will take to produce the zener effect. The heavier the doping, the lower the zener voltage point will be. Figure 6-3 illustrates the voltage points.

The zener characteristic curve starts at a zero point of current in the vertical axis and voltage or bias in the horizontal axis. The right side of the

curve in Fig. 6-4 is the normal diode reaction of current to forward bias. The left side of the curve shows what happens when reverse bias is applied. Figure 6-4 shows the sudden surge of current when 20 volts reverse bias is applied. The current surges and forms a place in the curve that looks like a knee. That is why that voltage point is called the zener-knee voltage.

Once a zener begins conducting in that way, the voltage level at that spot in the circuit becomes fixed at the knee point. No matter how much voltage you apply at the circuit spot, as long as it is more negative than the knee voltage, the knee voltage remains the same. If you do crank up the voltage, the only thing that happens is more current will flow through the zener. The voltage at the cathode will not waver.

The zener diode is always placed in the circuit with the n material or cathode attached to the voltage point that is to be controlled. Refer to Fig. 6-5. Typically the zener is installed in a power supply

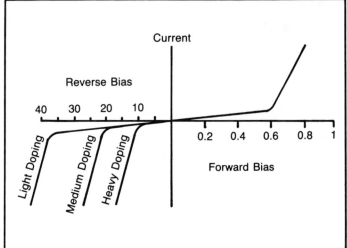

Fig. 6-3. The zener diode is doped to produce the zener effect. The heavier the doping the lower the zener voltage rating.

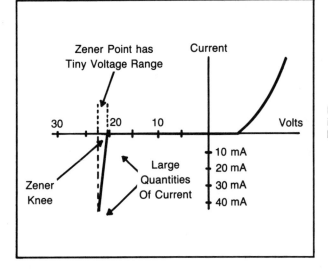

Fig. 6-4. At the zener knee, the diode starts drawing a lot of current, which stops the voltage from becoming any higher.

Fig. 6-5. The zener diode is typically wired into the circuit with the cathode at the + voltage and the anode at ground.

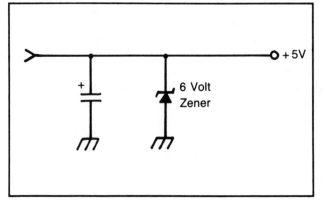

114

situation with the cathode connected to the + voltage and the anode to ground. If it is a 6-volt zener, it will keep that point at six volts no matter what the voltage will try to rise to. For instance, if there is a peak of nine volts that enters the + line, the zener will instantly conduct heavily at the knee level and hold the voltage at the prescribed six volts.

Varicap Diodes

As mentioned earlier in the chapter, the diode becomes a legitimate capacitor when reverse biased. The capacitance is formed by the junction acting as a variable dielectric. As the dc reverse bias is varied, the size of the barrier varies. As the reverse bias increases, the barrier enlarges. As the reverse bias lessens, the barrier shrinks. This changing of the junction is in effect changing the surface area of the capacitor's dielectric.

As the total junction becomes larger, it increases the amount of capacitance. The larger the capacitor plates become, the more capacitance is delevoped. As the junction shrinks and loses some of the reverse bias effect, the dielectric in turn loses surface area and lessens the amount of capacitance. The chart in Fig. 6-6, gives some idea of the actual

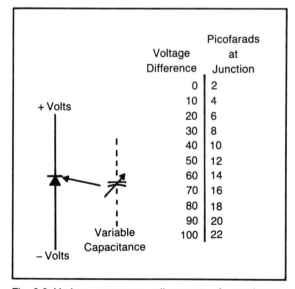

	Voltage Difference	Picofarads at Junction
	0	2
	10	4
	20	6
	30	8
	40	10
	50	12
	60	14
	70	16
	80	18
	90	20
	100	22

Fig. 6-6. Varicaps possess small amounts of capacitance. This is variable from 2 to 22 picofarads as the voltage is changed from 0 to 100 Vdc.

amount of capacitance that the varicap can produce.

A varicap is just an ordinary silicon diode. It does not need any doping or other measures to make it do its job as a variable capacitor. All it needs is the proper level of reverse biasing.

About the only characteristic the varicap needs is a high Q. The Q is determined by the amount of leakage current through the diode when it is reverse biased. If the leakage is excessive, (which is in effect a short) the Q will be low. A diode with a low Q is not good enough to act the part of a varicap. It could be ok for some other applications but not a varicap.

Detectors and Rectifiers

The diode applications, such as the zener and varicap diodes are able to do, are relatively speaking, new uses for the units. There are two other uses, though, that date back to the beginning of the century. One is the detecting of radio waves, and the other is rectifying of ac voltages. They both use the ability of the diode to pass one voltage state, for example + , while rejecting any − voltages. The diode determines which state to pass and which to reject by the way it is wired into the circuit.

Rectifying an ac voltage has been discussed and will be further covered in Chapter 17. The detection of radio waves hasn't been mentioned as yet. Radio waves or TV waves are very similar and are detected in exactly the same ways. It is not necessary to perform any radio or TV wave detection in many computers because there aren't any. When these computers process data, they turn the data into pure video or audio. A typical portion of pure video is shown in Fig. 6-7. This video and audio is then inserted directly into the display. The signals are not installed onto carrier waves and transferred to a TV receiver.

Other computers, though, use commercial TV sets as the display. They use an rf modulator to generate a carrier wave and install the video or audio that the computer produces onto a carrier wave of either TV channel three or four. Before the TV is able to display the data or emanate the computer sound, the signal must be detected and the carrier wave must be eliminated. All this is

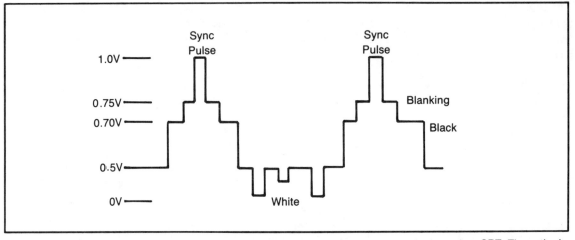

Fig. 6-7. Pure black and white video or as it is called, the Y signal, operates on the cathode ray in a CRT. The cathode ray runs full blast when the varying signal has a voltage near zero. This produces white on the screen. The cathode ray shuts off when the signal is +1 volt. This produces black on the screen.

accomplished in any commercial TV. The following is the part the detector diode plays in the TV.

If the rf modulator uses its channel three carrier wave, then the audio and video signals are installed in the station frequency range of between 66 and 72 megahertz, a six MHz TV band. Refer to Fig. 6-8. The video signal is placed around 67.25 MHz. The audio around 71.75 MHz. The carrier forms an envelope around the two signals. The video takes up near 4 MHz of the band and the audio a smallish 25 kHz.

In the TV, the carrier and its passengers are amplified in the TV tuner and i-f amplifiers. Then the carrier is injected into the detector stage. The stage is based around a detector diode, as shown in Fig. 6-9.

The video detector has the job of demodulating the composite TV signal that was modulated by the rf modulator circuit in the computer. The rf modulator has placed the video and audio generated by the computer into the carrier envelope. The detector must remove the envelope and restore the video and audio to it's former analog condition.

The detector accomplishes this mission in two steps. When the modulator placed the signal onto the carrier, the carrier has the form of a sine wave and continually moves from a midpoint to a high peak, back to a midpoint, to a low peak and back

to the midpoint again. As a result, the average change of the wave train is zero. This cannot be. If you try to use zero amounts of signal current, you will end up with nothing.

To rectify the situation, either the positive side is used or the negative. Some TVs rectify the signal leaving positive going signals and other TVs detect the negative going section of the wave train. This detecting is the first part of the demodulation process. It is also the more complicated, but it is not that complex.

A simple video detector circuit using a diode detector is shown in Fig. 6-9. If you want to end up with the signal positive going, then the diode has its anode connected to the input and the cathode to the output. To obtain a negative going signal, the diode is reversed.

As the incoming wave train enters the detector circuit, the diode will conduct during the positive part of the train if the anode is at the input. The diode will not conduct during the negative part of the train at that time. This cuts off the negative part of the train and the average change in current will be positive and not zero. To get a negative change, as mentioned before, simply reverse the diode.

Once the carrier wave has been rectified, the next step is to get rid of the carrier and leave the pure video and audio signals. This is easily accom-

116

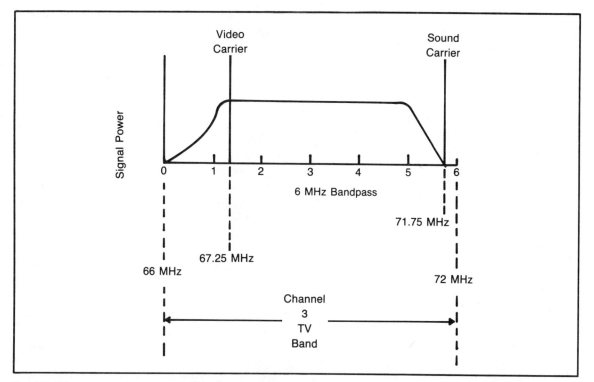

Fig. 6-8. When a computer uses a home TV as the monitor, it generates a 6 MHz carrier wave at the Channel 3 or 4 frequency. The video and audio signals are installed in the carrier.

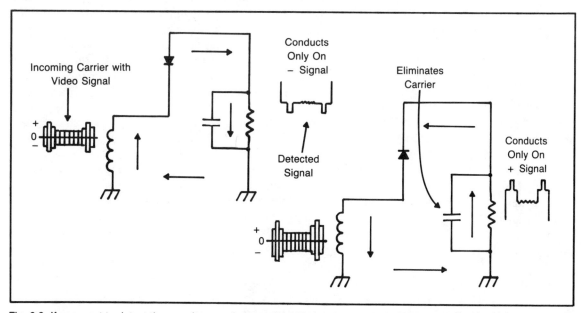

Fig. 6-9. If you want to detect the − voltage variations of the Y signal, the detector diode's cathode is connected to the input coil. To detect the + voltage variations, the diode's anode is connected to the input.

plished with a series filter capacitor that is accross the load resistor in the circuit. The signal that is rectified is developed across the resistor. As the signal changes in current through the diode, the voltage across the resistor changes in accordance to the signal change. The signal can be tapped off and sent on to video and audio amplifiers.

If a capacitor, large enough to be sensitive to the 64 MHz carrier frequency but not so large as to respond to the 3.5 MHz video frequency, is placed across the load resistor, the 64 MHz signal will be smoothed out and eliminated. The video and audio signals will pass on unscathed. The capacitor performs the second part of the detector action.

Diode Clamping

Clamp diodes are often used in computer circuits. They are needed in control circuits that use a transistor to turn an external device on and off. For example, a cassette motor circuit can have that arrangement. The clamp diode is an escape valve for surges of voltage that might develop and kill the control transistor.

In a motor control circuit, there can be a relay coil like in Fig. 5-13. The transistor turns off and on. The coil can be in series with and a part of the emitter circuit of an npn control transistor. The coil is connected to −5 volts. When the transistor turns on, the coil is energized because electrons leave the −5 volt point and are attracted to the grounded collector. Since the −5 volts source is more negative than ground, it has an excess of electrons and they are attracted to the more positive ground connection. The electrons move and the relay closes.

When the transistor turns off, the emitter blocks off any more current flow. However the coil has a lot of an electronic quality called *inductance*. The inductance is a quality that tries to keep electrons flowing even after the circuit is opened. The electrons surge a the npn cuts off. If left alone, they would impact the emitter and probably destroy the npn.

To save the day, a diode is installed across the relay coil. The cathode is connected to the npn side. When the surge of current occurs, the diode forms a cathode to anode escape path back from the diode to the −5 volt source. This is called clamping, and the agent is the clamp diode.

AMPLIFIERS

In the last few chapters, bipolar and field effect transistors have been discussed in some detail. However, all the discussions have been about how they are used as switches. Actually, aside from computer usage, the transistors are not primarily used as switches. The main job a transistor performs is amplification. In the analog applications such as radio, TV, etc., transistors are thought of as amplifiers and oscillators rather than switches. Switching, in analog uses, is the least thing transistors do.

If you examine the range of control a base exercises over the electron flow that takes place between an emitter and a collector, the switching goes on at the top of the square wave and at the bottom. In Fig. 6-10, the top could be the turn on part of the wave and the bottom the cut off. What about the in-between control area? It is used when the transistor is charged with the responsibility of performing amplification.

Between the digital switch voltages of off and on lies the analog infinite number of voltage points that can gradually change the electron flow from cutoff to saturation and back. Refer to Fig. 6-11. This is the basis by which amplification is able to take place. Let's examine the amplification electronic mechanism in more detail.

Common Emitter Amplifier

The common-emitter amplifier is so named because the emitter is returned to ground. The circuit in Fig. 6-12 shows the emitter is returned through an emitter resistor is bypassed with a small capacitor so no signal can develop across the resistor. The capacitor smooths out any signal variations that might occur.

The collector is attached to −5 volts also through a resistor. This resistor is not bypassed, as is the emitter resistor. That is because the signal that is developed across the resistor is desired. That signal, as will be shown shortly, is going to be the

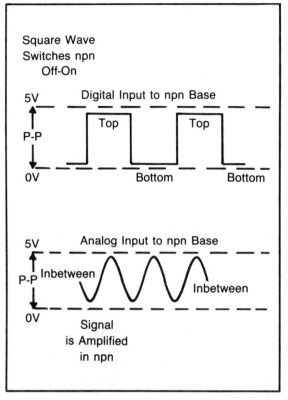

Fig. 6-10. The square wave is designed to operate at the top and bottom of its voltage changes. The sine wave operates in-between those voltages.

end result of this amplifier. The output of the stage emerges directly from the collector.

The base inputs the signals to be amplified directly to the n material sandwiched between the two pieces of p. The base is between two resistors, one going to − 5 volts and the other to ground. They form a voltage divider, and according to their values, B can be biased at any voltage between 0 and − 5 volts. The base is appropriately biased to handle the incoming signal.

If you wanted to switch this common-emitter circuit off, 0 volts or a + voltage will accomplish that end. A + voltage on the base will reverse bias the EB junction and stop electron flow. To switch the circuit on, − 5 volts on the base will forward bias the EB junction and get the flow moving again. All well and good. To take the exercise one step further, suppose you find it necessary to get the

flow running at some middle rate of electron flow.

If you can completely cut off the pnp with zero volts on the base and saturate it with − 5 volts, it follows that a voltage somewhere between the two will turn on about half the flow from the collector to the emitter. As you can see, the amount of electrons can be changed between cutoff and saturation in any amount. It is simply a matter of varying the base bias.

These bias changes are only dc variations, but ac fluctuations will vary the flow too. If you have an audio wave varying around a midpoint of − 2.5 volts with a peak-to-peak voltage of two volts, the audio signal will vary between one peak of − 1.5 volts and the other peak of − 3.5 volts. In accordance to the biased incoming audio signal, the electron flow will increase as the bias becomes more negative towards − 3.5 volts and decrease as the bias goes in a positive direction toward − 1.5 volts. The audio signal will, therefore, be found reproduced in the collector to emitter rate of electron flow. This is the first step in the amplification process.

Once the audio is reflected in the electron flow, it can be increased in voltage. This voltage amplification is not needed in switch circuits. All that was needed in switches was to transfer the digital voltage states from input to output correctly. It was not necessary to increase the highs or lows, in fact it would cause troubles if they accidently had their voltage state changed. Not so with amplification. If the audio voltage is not increased, it might never be able to drive the cone of speaker.

This brings us to the base-collector junction of the pnp. If you'll notice, the voltage that turns on the emitter-base junction forward biases the junction. The base is n material. The emitter is p. A negative voltage on B with E near ground (zero volts) is a forward bias. This same bias on B does not forward bias the BC junction. The collector has a voltage of − 5 volts, which is even more negative than the base audio signal. Since the collector is p material, the BC junction is reverse biased. This means that the BC junction has a large barrier region and a high resistance in ohms to the electrons. Figure 6-13 graphically shows this situation.

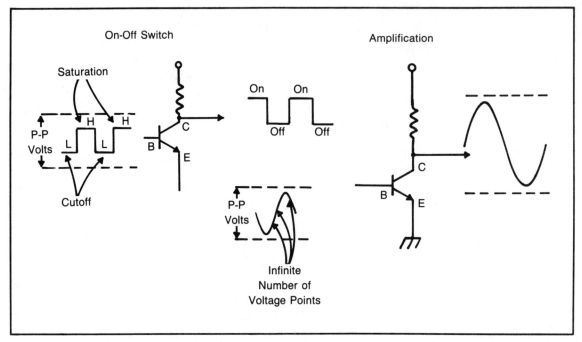

Fig. 6-11. When a square wave is input to an npn, the top of the pulse can turn on the switch and the bottom of the pulse can turn it off. When a sine wave is input, the npn stays on and amplifies the signal.

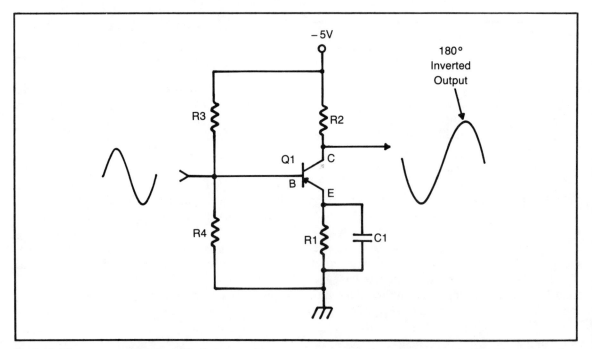

Fig. 6-12. The common-emitter amplifier has the emitter common to both the input and output circuits. The electron flow travels between the base and the emitter at the same time it travels between the collector and the emitter.

120

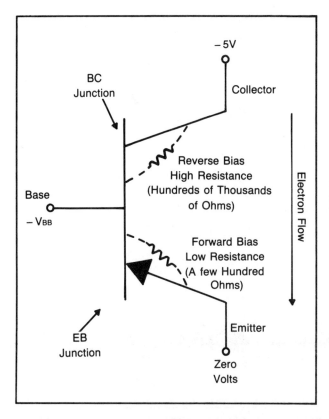

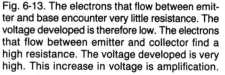

Fig. 6-13. The electrons that flow between emitter and base encounter very little resistance. The voltage developed is therefore low. The electrons that flow between emitter and collector find a high resistance. The voltage developed is very high. This increase in voltage is amplification.

The electron flow through the pnp is the same at both the EB and BC junctions. The resistance of the two junctions however are quite different. BC has a resistance of hundreds of thousands of ohms. EB has a resistance of a few hundred ohms. This makes the voltage drop (IR drop, electron flow × resistance in ohms) about two hundred times larger at BC than at EB. This is the voltage amplification. This large voltage gain allows the output voltage of the pnp to drive a speaker while the input voltage cannot.

This common-emitter circuit arrangement is the most used type of discrete transistor amplifier. It is called common emitter because the emitter is common to both the input and output circuits. The emitter in the pnp receives electron flow from both the base input and the collector output circuits.

Other Common Connected Amps

Figure 6-14 and Fig. 6-15 show the configura-

tions for the common base and the common collector circuits. Table 6-1 lists the important characteristics that these two amplifiers can provide.

Amplification refers not only to voltage but to current and power. Current is measured in amps, milliamps, and microamps. Power is nothing more than voltage × current and is the familiar watts, milliwatts, and microwatts. Table 6-1 shows the relative amounts.

The common-base amplifier in Fig. 6-14 has the input at the emitter rather than the base. It operates with somewhat the same amplification abilities at the common emitter. The voltage gain is about the same. One important difference, though, is the state of the output in comparison to the input. The output of the common emitter has a 180 degree phase reversal, but the common-base inputs and outputs retain the same phase.

The common-collector circuits are quite different than the common emitter and common base

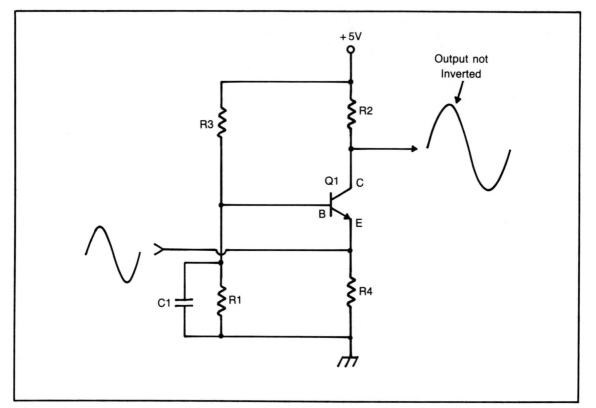

Fig. 6-14. The common base amplifier uses the emitter as the input and the collector as the output.

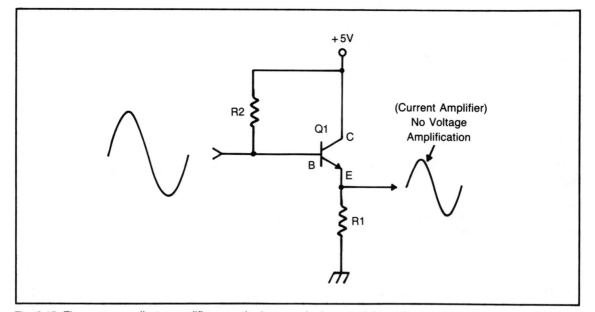

Fig. 6-15. The common collector amplifier uses the base as the input and the emitter as the output.

Table 6-1. Characteristics of the Common Transistor Configurations

Characteristic	Common Emitter	Common Base	Common Collector
Input Electrode	Base	Emitter	Base
Output Electrode	Collector	Collector	Emitter
Voltage Amplification	Large	Large	Less than 1
Current Amplification	Large	Less than 1	Large
Power Amplification	Large	Medium	Small
Voltage phase shift, input to output	180°	No phase shift	No phase shift

circuits. The common emitter and base circuits are used, for the most part to amplify voltage and power. The common collector circuit is usually employed to amplify current. The output of the common-collector circuit is like the common emitter and unlike the common base. The common-collector circuits typically have their inputs at the base and the output at the emitter.

When voltage is amplified in computers, it is the peak-to-peak voltage of a signal that receives the amplification. For instance, a high that has a voltage of +5 volts with a corresponding low of 0 volts might not be large enough to drive a device. The device might need +12 volts to indicate the high and −12 volts to show the low. A voltage amplifier could be used that receives a stream of +5 volt and 0 volt waveshapes. The amplifier could be a common base amp. With the proper voltages applied, it will amplify the range of the +5 to 0 V input to a +12 to −12 V output. The phase of the input will remain the same during the amplification and exit intact with only the size of the waveshape changed.

It is necessary to amplify the current of a signal when the amount of signal current that a device outputs is not enough to drive the subsequent chips. In those cases, the highs and lows are output with the same peak-to-peak voltage. The +5 to 0 V peaks are not changed. The waveshape is passed through a common collector amplifier. The output exits at the emitter. In the emitter leg, a load resistor is connected to ground. The signal enters at the base. The collector is connected to Vcc without benefit of a load resistor.

In an npn connected in this way a +5 volt high at the base input turns on the EB junction. A weak current flows from ground through the load resistor to the base. This turns on the emitter-to-collector current flow. The E-to-C flow also travels through the load resistor. However, the EC flow is many, many times heavier than the EB flow. This heavy flow is induced by the high at the base. Even though the current through the resistor has become high, the voltage peak on the resistor still remains about the same. In other words, the current through the resistor has been amplified and the voltage remains just about the same or a bit lower.

An output connection is made at the top of the resistor. The heavy current with the correct voltage state is tapped off and sent to the next stages that require the additional current.

OSCILLATORS

In computers, the most conspicuous oscillator is the clock circuit. Chapter 8 covers the clock circuits in detail. The clock is based around a crystal oscillator circuit and operates in ranges well into the millions of cycles per second, called megahertz (MHz). Another less obvious oscillator is found in the rf modulator circuit in computers that use an ordinary home TV as the display device. These oscillators also operate in the megahertz ranges. They have to produce the frequency for TV channels 3 and 4.

An oscillator is an electronic circuit that turns off and on at a nonstop, continuous rate. The number of times it turns off and on per second is called its frequency. Frequency used to be measured in cycles per second, but the word cycles has been modernized to hertz. One full cycle per second is called one Hz.

The frequency can be set by a designer. It comes about as a quartz crystal and a capacitance, and a transistor are wired together. The crystal will oscillate at a relatively fixed frequency if electricity is applied to its surface. The frequency is a direct result of how thick the crystal is cut. The thinner the cut, the higher it is able to oscillate.

A simple circuit can be made by installing a crystal cut to a computer frequency, for instance around 14 MHz, and connected collector-to-base, emitter-to-base or base-to-ground. The crystal is hooked into a feedback leg of the transistor.

In its natural state, a quartz crystal is shaped like a hexagonal prism with each end coming to a hexagon point. Refer to Fig. 6-17. This end to end *optical axis* is named the z-axis. From one flat side directly through the crystal to the center of the opposite flat side, is another axis called y. This flat-to-flat is the *mechanical axis*. From a point on the hexagon to the opposite point is the x-axis also known as the *electrical axis*.

If an ac voltage is connected across the x-axis, the crystal will start expanding and contracting. It starts vibrating mechanically at the frequency that corresponds with the voltage. Depending on the thickness of the crystal between the points, the vibration will assume a natural resonant frequency.

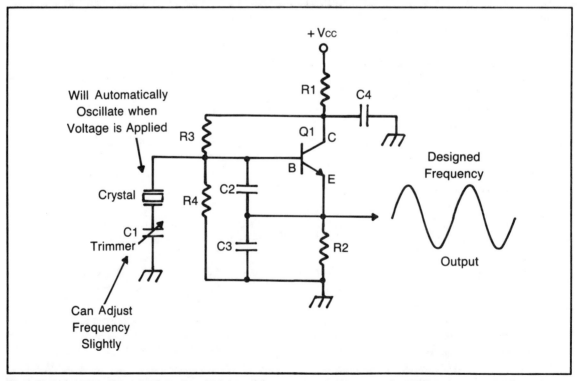

Fig. 6-16. A crystal oscillator circuit can be wired around an npn connected to a crystal and other components. The oscillator will run at the natural frequency of the crystal.

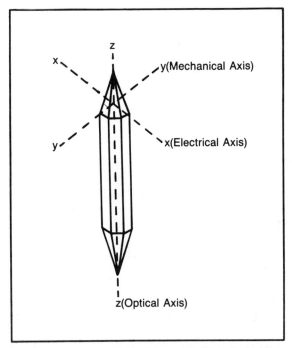

Fig. 6-17. A quartz crystal has three axis. There is the electrical axis, X, the mechanical axis, Y and the optical axis, Z.

A thin crystal will vibrate naturally at a high frequency and a thicker piece of crystal will vibrate at a lower frequency.

If the ac frequency matches the resonant frequency of the crystal, the crystal will maintain that frequency with practically no deviation. It will stay right on the tuned spot. A well-designed circuit can hold a frequency with less than 1 Hz drift. Oscillator crystals are cut like a piece of valuable jewelry along either the x- or y-axis. The z-axis is not voltage sensitive.

Crystals are very sensitive to heat. If the temperature of a crystal rises, it causes the resonant frequency to drift from its cut value. Of course, you try to keep the crystal oscillator in an environment near room temperature. However, the ambient temp is not the main consideration. The amount of voltage applied is. If too much voltage is applied, the crystal will heat up. Large amounts of voltage could even make the crystal burst.

Small amounts of excess voltage can cause the frequency to drift. Crystals are given a temperature

coefficient rating to allow you to intelligently use them. The rating is in MHz per degree centigrade changes. X-axis connected crystals have a negative-coefficient rating; as the voltage increases, the temperature rises and the frequency will go negative or decrease. Y-axis connected crystals have a positive-coefficient rating. As the voltage rises the frequency it will resonate at rises. If you cut a crystal at a midpoint between the x- and y-axis you can obtain the best of both worlds. That cut will tend to have no frequency change as the crystal heats. All three cuts are made for different applications.

The ability of an oscillator is measured in a value called Q. If an oscillator has a high Q, it oscillates very easily and will be very reliable. Should it have a low Q, it will be hard to get the oscillator rolling, and it will try to stop oscillating on the slightest provocation. Crystals have a very high Q.

The classic example of an oscillator is shown in Fig. 6-18. It is a series circuit consisting of a capacitor, a coil, and a resistor with a second capacitor across all three of them. The amount of resistance is the main factor in the Q of the configuration. A high resistance lowers the Q. The crystal acts as all three of the electronic components. It is mounted between two metal plates that hold it snug but makes allowances for the mechanical vibrating. The two plates act as the capacitor, using insulation qualities of the crystal itself as the dielectric. This is the parallel capacitor mentioned before.

The series string is the internals of the crystal. Inside the crystal there is a certain amount of capacitance, inductance (like a coil), and resistance. Together they form what is known as a tank circuit. The qualities of quartz cause the amounts of inductance to be high while the amounts of capacitance and resistance are tiny. This high ratio of inductance (L) to capacitance (C) and resistance (R), results in a very high Q.

If a crystal is placed into a collector-to-base feedback circuit arrangement, the voltage impressed on the crystal will start it vibrating. The oscillations are pushed into the base and the entire

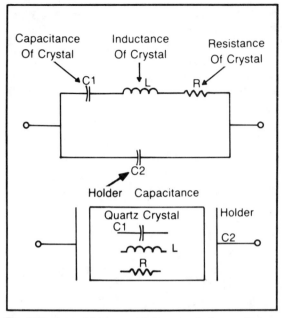

Fig. 6-18. A crystal has a certain amount of capacitance, inductance, and resistance. That is why it has a resonant frequency.

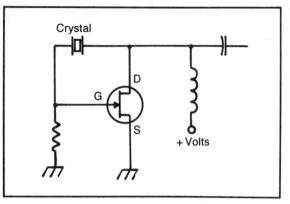

Fig. 6-19. A FET can work with a crystal just as easily as the bipolar transistors.

stage turns on. The circuit continues to oscillate at the stable resonant frequency of the crystal.

A crystal could also be placed into the feedback line between the drain and the gate of a FET. This approach is shown in Fig. 6-19. The same thing will happen. As the voltage is impressed into the LCR series circuit that is found naturally inside the crystal, the crystal starts oscillating. The frequency gets the FET turning on and off. The entire circuit continues to run at the resonant frequency of the crystal.

Crystal oscillators are not tunable. They operate best at a particular fixed frequency. For instance, a typical crystal is cut to run at 14.31818 MHz. It runs beautifully right at that five decimal place frequency. If you try to tune even two or three MHz away, the crystal will quickly lose its effeciency and could even shut down altogether.

In order to obtain the different frequencies needed in different sections of the computer, tuning is not used. The technique is to set up a master frequency and then divide it by two or four or eight or even 16 to get the other frequencies. These techniques are discussed in more detail in chapters concerning the clock and other frequency dependent circuits.

Chapter 7

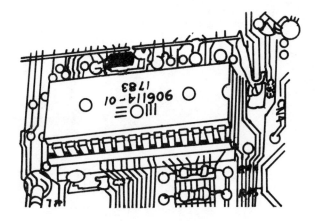

The Computer Board

RESISTORS, CAPACITORS, DIODES, BIPOLAR transistors, and FETs are cast in silicon chips or wired as discrete components onto a printed circuit board. Coils with inductance are not easily contained in a silicon chip but are wired discretely onto the board. Fuses, regulator components, male and female plugs, and copper traces are also laid out on the board. It is not difficult to place a complete computer on a print board not much bigger than this sheet of paper. This same computer twenty years ago would have filled a floor of offices in a building.

When you look down at the print board in Fig. 7-1, first glance reveals a complex mixture of electronic components arranged neatly from one end of the board to the other. It is something like approaching a city in an airplane. At first you are lost. What you need is a closer look and some information on landmarks.

On the print board, the first things you want to look for are the MPU and the RAM chips. They are the heart of the board. They could be anywhere on the board. As you take a closer look at the board, the landmarks begin to show up. First of all, a professional print board has printing on it. There are C numbers next to all the capacitors. R numbers are printed next to all the discrete resistors. An L number here and there indicates inductance coils. Next to each chip is a U number and so on for every component. Refer to Fig. 7-2.

The fuse in the power supply is quite obvious. The keyboard has a cable that connects near a large chip. The off-on switch is noticed, and all the port plugs are found easily residing at the rear and sides of the board. If there is an rf modulator in the circuit, it is in a metal case conspicuously at the back of the board. Another metal shield or two is also noticed. Beneath these shields are found groupings of chips that are obviously sensitive to external radio waves. The shield protects the chips from the external radio interference and also will stop any radiation these chips might inadvertently transmit on their own.

A close look at the chips arranged over the

Fig. 7-1. A single print board containing a complete computer appears as a neatly layed out group of many components. Particularly obvious are the fuse and the metal shields.

board reveals they are all marked with numbers, letters, and manufacturers logos. The numbers identify the chip, provide warranty dates, and let you know who made it. An even closer look shows the chips all have little inline legs arranged in two neat rows. There is a notch at the top of each chip that is the keyway indicating pin numbers 1 on the left and the last pin on the right. The pin numbers are counted counterclockwise. ALL chips are laid out in the same manner. The top of the chip points to the rear of the board. The larger chips are often socketed and the smaller ones soldered directly to connections on the print board.

The more you look, the more detail reveals itself. A very experienced technician is often able to read the print board in the same way a schematic diagram is read.

LOCATION GUIDE

In most pieces of electronic gear, manufacturers paste a location guide somewhere inside the case. The guide takes a lot of the mystery out of the way the components are placed on the print board. Years ago the guides were called tube location guides. Then they were changed to transistor location guides. Today, if they are available, they are chip location guides. These guides are the most used pieces of service information when they are available. Chips are tiny and packed tightly onto a board. It is a confusing, time consuming chore just to identify which chip is which.

Drawing Your Own

A chip location guide takes all the pain and strain out of the chip locating. Figure 7-3 is a Location Guide that I drew off one of the popular home computers. If your personal computer does not come with a chip location guide, it would be useful to draw one. The drawing exercise will also familiarize you with the print board in your machine.

The chip location guide is the first step in understanding the way the computer operates. The second step to understanding is a block diagram that is an outgrowth of the location guide. The third step is to learn to read the schematic diagram of the computer and relate it to the print board. Every C, R, L, U, and so on that is found on the print board is also on the schematic. Once you have the preceding under your fedora, then you'll be able to understand the theory of operation that your machine computes by.

On the location guide in Fig. 7-3, there are 32 chips, numbered U1 through U32. As extra features, there are two regulators in the power supply: a 7805 and a 7812. The 7805 regulates a +5 volt source and the 7812 a +12 volt source. The 32 chips are made up of four 40-pin chips, two 28-pin chips, three 24-pin chips and rest are 18, 16, 14 pin chips, and so on. Eight chips are in sockets and the rest are soldered in place.

Printed on the chips are all sorts of numbers, letters, and symbols. The most important number

Fig. 7-2. If you look closer, you'll find that printed on the print board are letters and numbers that are ID for all the components. The chips themselves are marked with numbers, letters, and logos.

is the generic chip number; for instance, 74LS74 or 4164. These numbers are the generic names of the chips. All manufacturers will refer to these numbers. The chip could be manufactured by a lot of companies. Each company will have its own particular name or number for the chip, but they all must use the generic number in the chip description.

If you look closely at a chip in Fig. 7-2, among the markings you can probably puzzle out the generic number. For instance, the 4164 chip I mentioned before could have the following markings on it.

M3764-20RS
OKI
41227

The generic number is keyed by the 64 in the top line. That tells the experienced tech that this is a 4164 RAM chip. OKI is the trademark logo of the oriental manufacturer of the chip. The other numbers could deal with the date of manufacturing and other internal notices. The important thing for you to find out is the generic name of the chip so you can locate it on the schematic diagram.

Chip Jobs

A chip location guide should mention the jobs of the chips. If you have an idea of how a computer works, the jobs the chips do will start forming a block diagram of the computer in your mind. On any location guide, the action takes place between the MPU and the residents of the memory map. The MPU for the computer in Fig. 7-3 is a form of 6502. It is U7. The RAM storehouse area is contained in eight 4164 chips. They are U9, U10, U11, U12, U21, U22, U23, and U24. They are all 16-pin DIPs and are arranged in two rows at the bottom left of the board.

If you'll notice the chips are numbered 0 through 7. Each chip contains one bit of each byte in the memory map. Chip #0 contains all the bit 0s stored in RAM, chip #1 contains all the bit 1s, chip #2 contains the bit 2s, etc. One line each of the data bus goes to its respective chip in the RAM set. The

chip set numbers tell you which is which.

Also in the memory map are the three ROM chips, U3, U4, and U5. they are all 24-pin chips. Their generic numbers are 2364 for two of them and 2332 for the third one. These permanently filled chips contain the operating system of the computer and other data sets that contribute constantly to the normal operation of the unit.

To the left of the ROM are the I/O chips in the memory map. They are called CIAs and provide access to the inside of the computer. They are U1 and U2. CIA#1 is used by the keyboard to get the highs and lows produced by keystrikes into the digital circuits. CIA#2 is used by other ports in the machine to input and output information to and from external devices. They both have the generic number, 6526. They have addresses in the memory map just as the RAM and ROM does.

Two other mapped chips are the video output chip, a 6567, designated as U19 and the audio output chip, a 6581, U18. The last mapped chip is a special small RAM, U6, a 2114. Those are the members of the memory map. The MPU is the originator of all the addresses. It is able to read and write to all nine of the RAM chips, read from the three ROM chips, read and write to the CIAs, read and write to the video chip and mostly write to the audio chip with a small amount of reading too. The rest of the chips in the machine are not read or written to since they do not have addresses.

Some of the chips though, do help the MPU with the addressing of the map residents. The 28-pin PLA chip, U17, is like a telephone substation. It helps the MPU locate main chips. The PLA connects to the ROMs, the CIAs, the video chip, the audio chip, and the little 2114 RAM device. The MPU sends addresses to the PLA and it in turn decodes the addresses and selects the desired chip out of the addressable group.

The two 74LS257 chips, U13 and U25, do a similar job for the MPU on the eight RAM chips. The MPU sends RAM addresses to the two 74LS257s, and they are able to choose a single address out of the 64K addresses contained in the RAM set.

The 74LS258, U14, joins with the U13 and U25

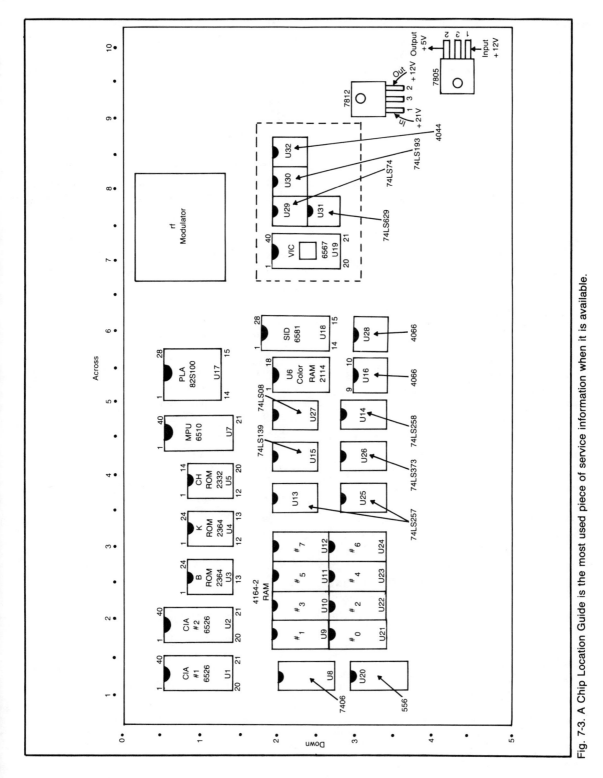

Fig. 7-3. A Chip Location Guide is the most used piece of service information when it is available.

in giving aid to the addressing chores. It works with U19, the video chip in the addressing of RAM. The 74LS139, U15, also is involved in the addressing mechanism. It gives the PLA, U17, additional address lines and helps select the video out, audio out, the 2114 RAM, and the CIAs. The 74LS373, U26, is still another address helpmate. It operates between the MPU address lines and the video chip address lines.

Under the metal shield and to the right of the video chip are four small chips in a clump. They are U29, U30, U31, and U32. They are the main parts of the system clock circuit. They all operate together around a crystal oscillator to produce the master frequency required.

That leaves a few support chips that contribute some logic to the operation. U8, a 7406, contains six NOT gates. They are inserted here and there in the computer to invert logic states as needed. U27, a 74LS08, has four AND gates in its internal circuits. These gates are distributed to four circuit spots and give those points a switching action that turns on when two highs are input to a gate. The two 4066 chips, U16 and U28, are each equipped with four electronic off-on switches. They are installed in places that need four electronic switches.

Lastly there is one 556 chip, U20. It contains two separate timer circuits. One of the circuits controls the reset network, and the other one responds to one of the keys on the keyboard.

The experienced tech, as he looks down on the print board and refers to the location guide, sizes up the computer in that way. You should be able to appraise your board in the same way. Different computers are built with entirely different details but the general approach is the same with them all. One computer is basically the same as another. They all have an MPU, RAM, ROM, and I/O chips like the CIAs. They all have a number of logic support circuits to control and transfer addresses and data bits from place to place.

BLOCK DIAGRAM

Once you have familiarized yourself with the actual physical layout of a board and you know the main landmarks and even where all the chips are, it is time to form a mental picture of the system arrangement and the routes that the computing takes. There are really three separate systems in a computer. First of all, there is the addressing complex. It operates on its own. It even has its very own clock. Secondly, there is the data transfer circuits. It too is an independent operation. The data workings has its own clock too. Thirdly, there are the various control circuits. These are a loose conglomeration of different circuits all grouped under the heading of control. They bind together the overall computer and help keep the addressing and data transferring in tight sync with each other.

Keyboard Inputs

The general block diagram of a computer usually shows the pathways the data takes to get processed. Figure 7-4 shows the example computer system I used before with the same U numbers. U7, the MPU, like ancient Rome, has all roads leading to it. When you strike the keyboard, one out of a possible 64 connections are shorted together. The 64 spots are the results of eight rows and eight columns wired so they intersect in 64 locations. Refer to Fig. 7-5. Each intersection generates a separate set of bits that are sent to U1 the CIA#1.

The CIA in turn transfers the bits to the MPU. The MPU decodes the bits, and addresses the ROM that contains the ASCII code for the character generated by the bits. The ROM sends the appropriate bit set back to the MPU. The MPU then sends one copy of the ASCII byte to a location in RAM that is called video RAM. The MPU sends a second copy of the byte to the video output chip.

Video Machinations

The ASCII byte in the video chip causes the video chip to do some addressing on its own. It addresses the character ROM, U5. At that address in U5, there is a set of eight bytes that forms a pattern of the character of the key that you struck. These eight bytes are returned to the video chip.

The video chip then outputs the bit patterns to the TV display. The character is then shown on the

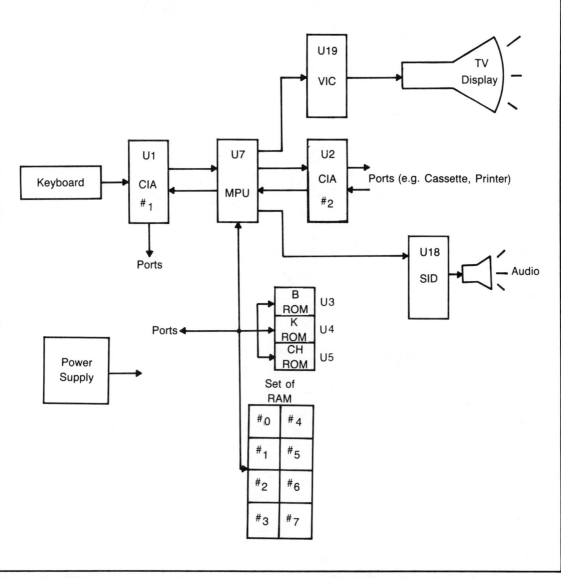

Fig. 7-4. The MPU sits in the center of its realm and communicates with all the residents of the memory map.

TV screen. Each high bit lights up a dot on the screen and each low bit extinguishes a dot on the screen. On the screen, the display is broken up into a number of smaller display blocks. In this computer, there are exactly 1000 tiny blocks on the screen. There are 40 blocks across and 25 down.

Each block contains a matrix of 8 × 8 dots. This matches up with the 64 bits in the eight bytes

that comprise the character pattern contained in the character ROM. There are 1000 byte locations assigned to RAM to match up with the 1000 spaces on the screen. These 1000 RAM locations are called video RAM. Each holds the ASCII code byte for the character displayed in the corresponding TV face location. This gives the character you strike a complicated maze to traverse before it shows

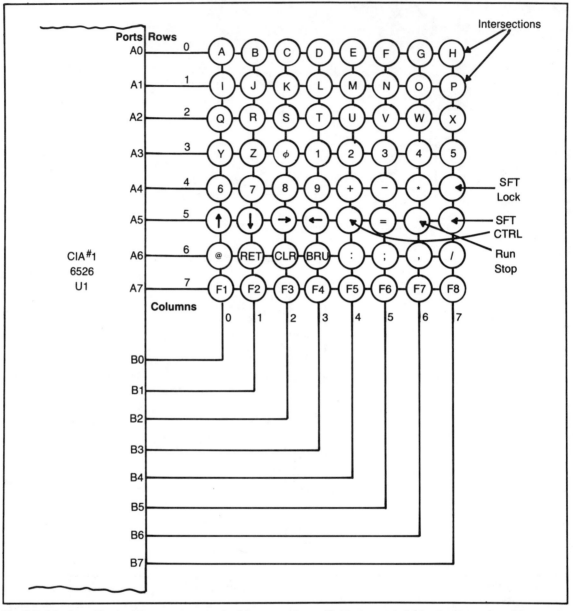

Fig. 7-5. A keyboard is wired so every row can short to every column. Eight rows and eight columns produce 64 separate short combinations.

on the screen. It also gets decoded, coded, and recoded. The entire process is discussed in more detail in Chapters 14 and 16.

Other Outputs

Besides getting the keyboard symbol up on the TV screen, the computer has other outputs. Refer to Fig. 7-4. First of all, it can output to a cassette. These same video RAM bytes can be sent to U2, the other CIA. U2 in turn outputs the bytes in serial form, one after another, to a digital-to-analog converter. There the bits are made into audio tones and sent directly to the cassette for tape recording.

Another output can go to a printer. The ASCII bytes are sent to other port pins on the CIA for the printer output. If the printer is arranged to receive serial inputs, only one port pin is needed. The ASCII bytes are sent out one at a time. The printer receives the ASCII bytes as single file bits. The printer is a digital computer in its own right. It takes the ASCII bytes and codes them into a form to drive the print head. The characters appear as hard copy on paper.

If the printer is to receive the bits in parallel, eight abreast, then eight pins of the CIA are needed to export the ASCII a byte at a time.

In this example computer, U18 is the audio output chip. The MPU deals with the audio output directly without any other port chips. The audio output can handle its own output. It receives specially conceived program bits that set the various registers for sound output. Then when the program is run, these registers change the bits into audio tones or blasts and outputs them to the TV display unit. The display will have an audio system to have the sound drive a speaker and be heard.

That, in general, is the way your computer is able to take keystrikes, joystick inputs, cassette inputs, disk signals and other forms of signals from the outside world into the digital world, process them and then output to the outside world once again. The outputs go to TV faces, cassettes, line printers, disk drives, loudspeakers and devices that require control. When you look down at the print board these ideas should be clear in your mind.

SCHEMATIC DIAGRAM

When you are looking at the print board you see directly all the copper wiring traces, the discrete capacitors and resistors, a large number of assorted chips and the usual electronic hardware and connections. On a professionally produced board, every discrete component and chip will have an identifying number. These have been mentioned often as the Cs, the Us, the Rs, and so on. If you have done a lot of electronic work on your board, you know which part is which and what job it is supposed to do. Should you not be familiar with the machine,

the board is colorful and interesting but not easily comprehended. That is where the schematic diagram enters the scene.

The schematic organizes the print board. However, the schematic uses electronic symbols to represent the components you are looking at. Figure 7-6 shows part of a computer sound circuit. You must be able to do a tricky, technical reading job before the schematic means anything to you. First of all, you have to be able to relate the drawn schematic symbol to the component it represents. The various symbols you will find on the schematic have been mentioned throughout the book. I'm sure you recognize most of the components on the schematic already.

The print board gives you additional help in this area. Sometimes a resistor will be built like a coil. When you look on the board and see one of those dual personality components, don't fret. Next to the component is a printed ID. Resistors will be an R number such as R34. Coils will show an L number like L4. All the components are marked on the board in that way.

In addition, it is conventional for the board markings to match up exactly with the component number on the schematic. This will help you relate the actual component with its position on the schematic. After awhile, if you do any appreciable electronic work on your computer, you will relate the board component to the schematic symbol without even realizing that one is a piece of hardware and the other printing on a piece of paper.

Pinouts

There is another confusion maker that comes about when chip drawings are consulted. There are two types of drawings. One is the symbol drawn on the schematic. It is usually a rectangle with leads sticking out. For example, the SID chip in Fig. 7-6 is a large rectangular layout on the schematic with 28 pins emerging from the chip. On the schematic, the pin arrangement seems to be completely without logic; however, the pins are drawn with thought. Usually the address pins are in one bunch, the data pins in a second group, and the control pins all over the place. The control pins are all over since the draftsman has tried to place them in the most easily recognized position in relation to the jobs they are to do and the aesthetic layout of the drawing. The end result is that the pin numbers seem to have no correlation to each other.

There is another way chips are drawn when no other components are on the same drawing. This is called the pinout. The SID chip in Fig. 7-7 is drawn as it is actually laid out physically. The rectangle is shown, the notched keyway is drawn, and the pin legs are arranged numerically. On the 28-pin SID, pin 1 is at the left of the notch, and pin 28 is

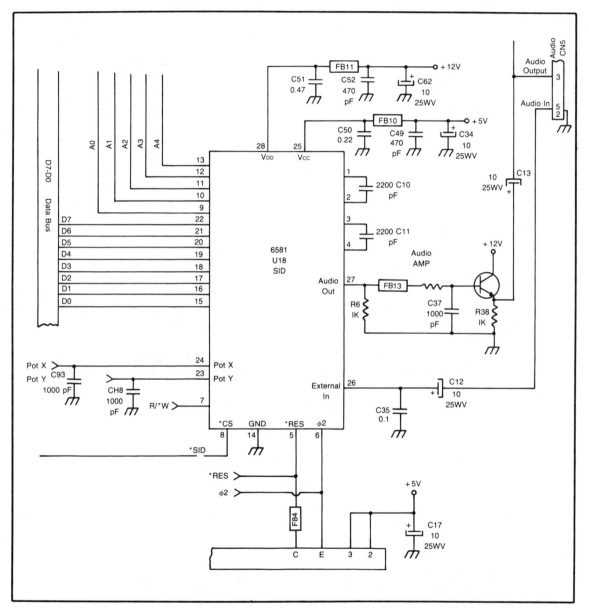

Fig. 7-6. This schematic diagram shows the data bus, D7-D0 and address lines, A0-A4 connected to the 6581 sound chip. The power sources, V_{DD} and V_{CC} as well as ground are easily located on the chip. A closer look reveals the $\phi2$, R/*W and *CS connections. The audio output pin connects to an npn audio output power transistor.

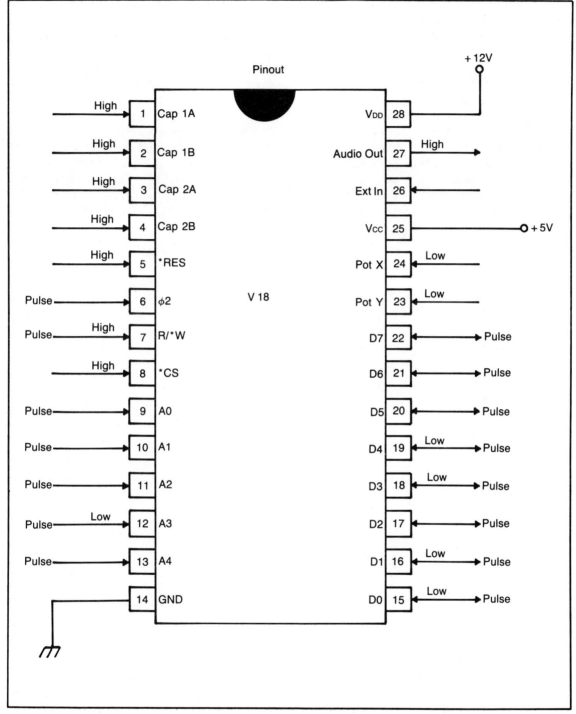

Fig. 7-7. The pinout is a layout of the chip showing the actual way the pins emerge from the body of the chips. This one also shows the highs, lows, and pulses that could be present when the chip is operating.

to the right. The rest of the pins are counted counterclockwise from pin 1 through 28. At the far end of pin 1 is pin 14, and at the far end of pin 28 is pin 15. The view in Fig. 7-7 is from the top.

Schematic Layout

When a schematic is drawn, some effort is made to lay it out to resemble the print board. Of course this is an impossible task but the finished product often does have the inputs and outputs entering the drawing in a way that resembles the board. The schematic though will layout in the same direction as the block diagram. The inputs are often on the left and the outputs on the right.

The data flow is usually shown traveling from chip to chip somewhat like the block diagram has it.

The clock is usually given its own section in the schematic. One of the top corners is typical. The power supply that powers all the chips is often drawn down near the bottom of schematic. The RAM set can be shown all in one group, and the ROM chips are shown in another group.

Computer schematics are extensive drawings. They present a formidable picture when viewed all at once. However each section is not too difficult to read. Typical schematic sections will be covered one by one, starting with the next Chapter, the Clock, and continuing throughout the book.

Chapter 8

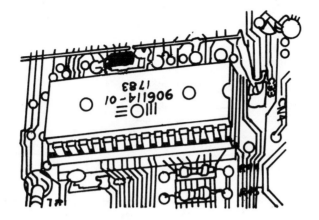

The Clock

THE COMPUTER CLOCK IS THE MOTOR OF THE machine. The clock is a crystal-controlled oscillator. It is tuned by the crystal to beat at a particular frequency. Different manufacturers cut their crystals to ring at particular frequencies. Just as a motor is made to rotate at some desired rpm and keep equipment operating, clocks are designed to run at a needed megahertz frequency and keep the computer working. The continuous energy from the clock moves the highs and lows from place to place in the digital circuits.

The crystal oscillator is an analog circuit and produces a continuous sine wave. The sine wave is useless in the digital circuits. It is therefore pumped into a circuit where the smooth ups and downs of the sine wave are converted into square-wave pulses with highs, lows, rising edges, and falling edges. Once the clock signal is a square wave, it can then be used to power the movement of the addresses and data that performs the computing.

In various computers, many different clock frequencies are used. Some computers have a basic frequency of 5 MHz and others 1 MHz. All the frequencies do the same type of jobs. The higher frequencies just do it faster.

A common crystal that is used in home computers is cut to oscillate at 14.31818 MHz. This is known as the master frequency. It is not useful at that high range, but it divides out into a number of important frequencies. These are shown in Fig. 8-1. If you divide the master by 16, the result is a frequency of 0.89 MHz. This is close to 1 MHz. In fact, it is close enough to 1 MHz that many small computers use the 0.89 MHz and call it 1 MHz. This is perfectly acceptable since the computer uses the 0.89 as 1 and never notices the difference.

If you divide the 14.31818 by 4, the result is 3.579545. This is an important frequency and must be accurate. It is the TV color oscillator frequency. In a color computer, this is called the video clock frequency. In the division circuit, an adjustable capacitor, called a trimmer, is usually installed. This trimmer is there to readjust the video clock in case it should drift off a bit. In order for the color com-

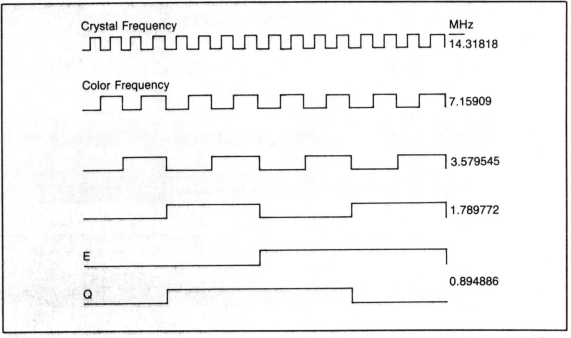

Fig. 8-1. The 14.31818 MHz, when divided can provide the 3.579545 MHz color TV frequency and the 0.89 MHz E and Q frequencies that run the MPU.

puter to produce a good color picture in the TV display, this frequency must be right on.

SINE WAVE TO SQUARE WAVE

Converting the sine wave to a squarewave is fairly easy to do. In lots of computers the sinewave is sim-ply injected into a large chip. In the chip, is a square-wave generator circuit that chops off the top and bottom of the sinewaves and straightens up the sides. In these cases, the squarewave generator is in the black box and requires little thought. Figure 8-2 shows the final square wave.

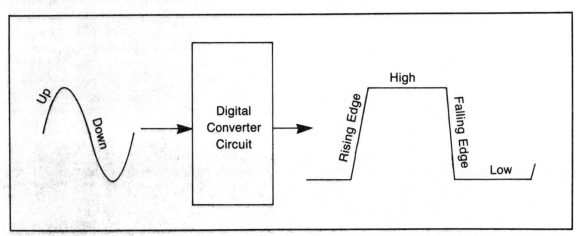

Fig. 8-2. The analog sine wave output is pumped into a digital converter circuit where it is made into a square wave. A square wave has a rising edge, a high, a falling edge, and a low.

In other circuits, the square-wave generator is out in the open. In the Heathkit H-89A circuit in Fig. 8-3, the crystal is cut to ring at 12.288 MHz. The crystal contains the inductance required for the oscillation. Across the crystal is a NOT gate. It is a bipolar transistor amplifier. The crystal is connected effectively between the input base and the output collector. Also across the crystal is a resistor-capacitor circuit that will help the crystal ring at its prescribed frequency.

When the circuit is turned on, the voltage on the crystal starts it up and the rest of the tuned circuit keeps it going. The output of the NOT gate inputs to the base of another NOT gate. This second gate acts as a NOT switch. The sine-wave output of the crystal turns the switch on and off as the sine wave goes up and down. The final output of the second NOT gate is a square wave.

Once the 12.288 MHz square wave is pro-

duced it is fed into a 7492 chip. The chip is called a 4-bit counter. As Fig. 8-4 shows, it consists of four J-K flip-flops. The flip-flops receive inputs at both the J and K entrances. The internal wiring is complex but of little consequence to you. If you check the chip on the board, only the pins shown on the schematic in Fig. 8-3 are wired up. The rest of the pins have no connection.

The square wave enters at pin 1. It exits at pin 8. Inside the chip, the square wave is divided by six. The division is accomplished by electronic manipulation as the four bits count from 0 to 15. Out of pin 8, the 2.048 MHz frequency is coupled into the clock input of the Z-80 MPU. The MPU takes the frequency from there.

MPU TIMING

Once into the Z-80, the steady stream of highs and lows runs the computer on a TTL clock of about

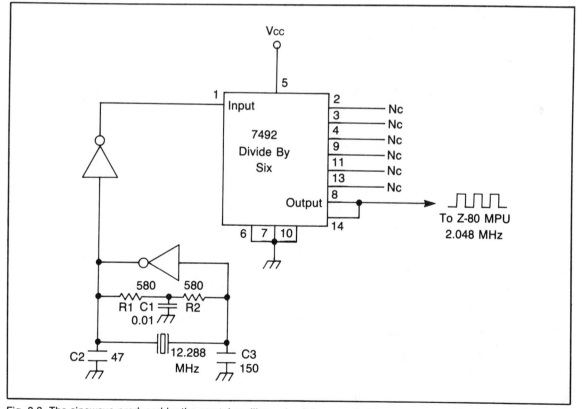

Fig. 8-3. The sinewave produced by the crystal oscillator circuit is converted to a square wave by the two NOT gates.

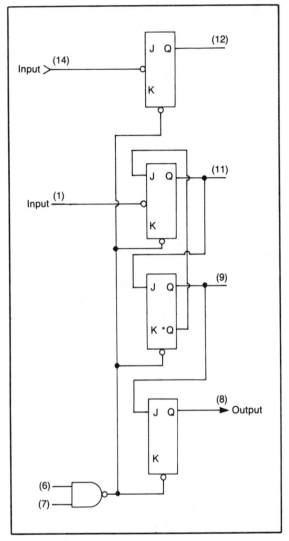

Fig. 8-4. The 7492 4-bit counter is wired to divide the incoming frequency by six.

2 MHz. This is known as a single phase ϕ clock. There is only one stream of signals needed in this Z-80 MPU.

Each full square wave, beginning at a low, rising to a high, and returning to the same place in the next low is a clock period. The clock drives the MPU to perform fetches, memory map reads, and memory map writes. Each of these primary operations are called machine cycles. The machine cycles can each be completed in a minimum of three to

a maximum of six clock periods. The timing diagram in Fig. 8-5 illustrates these ideas.

Op-Code Fetch

As the steady stream of highs and lows enter this Z-80, they have a frequency of about 2 MHz. The signal is dubbed ϕ (phase). This is going to be the basic running speed of the computer. The signals find a number of paths open and awaiting the voltage energy. The Z-80, by means of its internal circuits, carefully counts the incoming clock periods. The first four periods, each containing a high and a low, are all entered simultaneously to a half dozen or so circuits. These four periods are designated as one machine cycle. This cycle is the op-code fetch cycle. Figure 8-6 illustrates it in detail.

In a program that is stored in RAM or ROM, there are a series of machine-language lines. Each line is one byte long and occupies one byte-sized address. The programs consist of op codes from the Instruction Set and data for the op codes to work on. The MPU is built to automatically read program line after program line as the clock is running. These first four clock periods trigger the Z-80 to fetch a byte sized line of op code from memory.

The clock periods themselves do not fetch the op code. They provide the drive energy to the MPU registers and circuits that do the job. For instance, the first rising edge of the first clock period in the machine cycle triggers the program counter in the Z-80 to place its contents onto the address bus. The falling edge of the same period triggers a memory request signal (*MREQ) to output a low to enable the memory chips. The same falling edge also triggers a read signal, *RD to the memory to cause a read to take place.

A sample of the op code enters the data bus as a result of these signals activating the memory location. The data enters the bus and stabilizes during the second clock period. As the rising edge of the third period occurs, the MPU absorbs the contents of the data bus. The same rising edge also turns off the *MREQ and *RD signals.

These first four clock periods, then, are there expressly to fetch op codes. They do the job easily

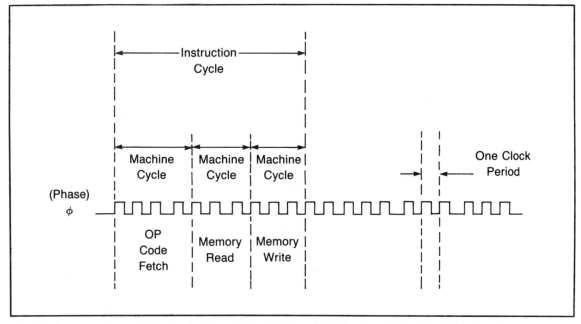

Fig. 8-5. The square wavetrain is called φ (phase). Each individual high-low is called a clock period. One instruction cycle takes about a dozen clock periods. The instruction cycle consists of three machine cycles. They are the op code fetch, the memory read, and the memory write.

by triggering circuits on and off as the edges of the periods rise and fall. Once the op code has reached the Z-80, the MPU is ready to do something with data.

Data Movement

Once the first four clock periods, the first full machine cycle, is completed and an instruction is fetched, the next machine cycle, consisting of three clock periods arrives. This machine cycle could be four or five cycles long, but we'll use three for our example. Remember, this action is fast. All this is happening at a rate of two clock periods to a millionth of a second.

When you are reading data, it is a fetch operation and very similar to the op-code fetch. Upon the rise of the first clock, the address of the memory location is placed on the address bus by the program counter. As the first clock falls, the signal *MREQ is activated and outputs a low. At the same time, *RD also becomes active and outputs a low.

The main difference between the op-code read and the data fetch is when the data is valid and reliable in the data bus. If you look at the op code read in Fig. 8-6, notice the data exhibits a straight line over most of the time the four clock periods take place. Only under the rise of the third clock does the graph show a container with the word *op code*.

The container has a high and a low. This represents the highs and lows of the op code in the eight data bus lines, D7-D0. As the third clock begins and the edge is rising, the graph shows the clock makes the MPU absorb that container of highs and lows called op codes.

In contrast, when the clock is doing a data read, the timing diagram shows the data not under the rise of the third clock. The data container is under the falling edge of the third clock.

Immediately following the data-read machine cycle is the data-write machine cycle. Like the read it too is typically three clock periods, but it can actually use more clock periods. The write operation is, of course, the act of sending data from the MPU to the memory and is not a read. The clock periods though are quite alike.

ϕ has the typical three clocks. Upon the rise of the write's first clock, the 16 bits of the program counter place the address where the data from the MPU is to be stored. As the first clock has its falling edge, the low from pin 19, *MREQ, is triggered. *RD is not activated since it only plays a part in the read operations.

With the address bus and the *MREQ on, the memory location opens up, and it is ready to receive data. The MPU meanwhile lets the data bleed out into the data bus lines where it assumes its high and low states. The data thus becomes very stable in the data bus. Then during the fall of the second write clock a low out of pin 22, (*WR, the write pin) occurs. Refer to Fig. 8-7. This low strobes the data on the bus into the memory chips and into the addressed location.

That is the way the clock used to drive a Z-80 MPU computer performs. It is a single-phase clock. There is only one motor perking along. The crystal

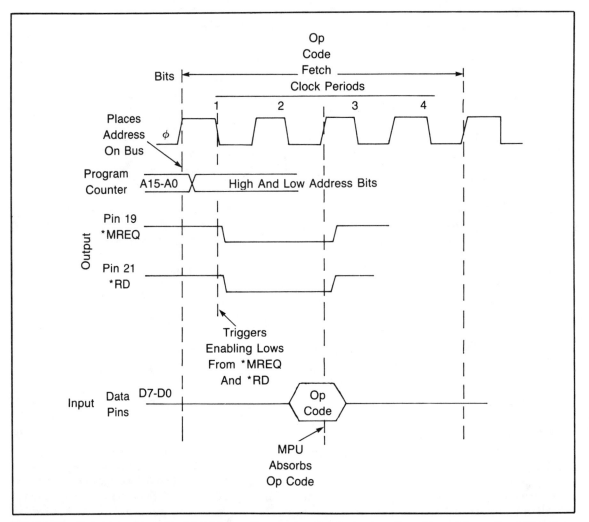

Fig. 8-6. The first rising edge of the fetch triggers the program counter to place the address bits on the address bus. The first falling edge triggers *MREQ to enable the memory chips and enables the *RD signal to cause a read. The op code enters the data bus. The third rising edge strobes the op code, from the data bus, into the MPU. The third rising edge also turns off *MREQ and *RD.

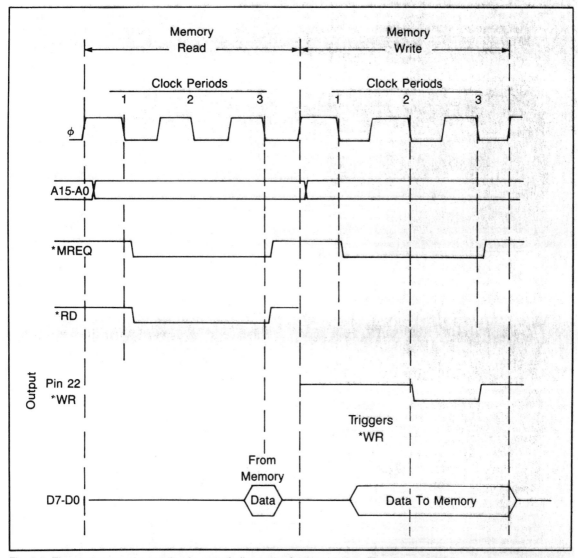

Fig. 8-7. The memory read operation is very similar to the fetch operation. The rising edge places the address on the bus. The falling edge triggers *MREQ and *RD. The falling edge of the third clock strobes the data into the MPU. The memory write operation has a difference. The addressing is the same, takes place during the rise of the first write clock, and *MREQ is enabled at the fall of the first clock. *RD is not used, *WR is. Data enters the data bus and stabilizes. At the fall of the second write clock, *WR strobes the data into the memory location.

starts vibrating mechanically at a resonant frequency as voltage is impressed onto its crystalline structure. This vibration is converted into the clock periods. A certain number of clocks becomes the machine cycles that perform the addressing, op code fetching, control triggering, reads and writes.

There are some other basic duties the clock has

to energize. There is reading and writing to I/O devices and the refreshing of dynamic RAM memories. These operations are covered in more detail in later chapters.

DUAL-PHASE CLOCKS

The Z-80 uses a single-phase clock. Other MPUs,

such as the 6800 and the 6502, use a dual-phase clock. These MPUs take the single output of the crystal-oscillator circuit, pass it through a phase detector network, and end up with two separate frequencies.

In the illustration in Fig. 8-8 a frequency of 14.31818 MHz is developed in the crystal. The sine wave is sent to a large chip called SAM, and in the chip the sine wave is changed to a square wave and then inserted, still in SAM, into a split-output phase inverter.

The inverter receives the single frequency and feeds it to a pair of direct-coupled transistors, shown in Fig. 8-9. The two circuits both amplify the frequency, but each outputs a different phased version of the other. While one of the amps is outputting a high, the other one outputs a low. This makes the two frequencies the opposite state of each other. The two different phases are then fed to different output pins of the SAM chip. The two outputs are inserted into two different input pins of the MPU. It is as if they came from two different oscillators.

The two phases are typically called $\phi1$ and $\phi2$. In the 6800-type MPUs they perform the following jobs, which are different than the single-phase operation shown in the Z-80. Figure 8-10 shows one full clock of $\phi1$ and $\phi2$. $\phi1$ has a high pulse in the middle of the cycle, and then it goes low. $\phi2$ is shown at first with a low and then it goes to a high. If the 14.31818 MHz crystal frequency has been divided by 16, then the 0.89 MHz basic frequency for each phase is developed. Both ϕs are then running at 0.89 MHz. They are just out of step with each other.

In the single-phase clock of the Z-80, the single motor has to drive all of the addressing registers, the data registers and the control lines. The dual-phase clock of the 6800 and 6502 types are able to split up the duties between the two phases. $\phi1$ is given the job of handling the addressing with the program counter and the address bus. $\phi2$ has the chore of moving the data, either during a read or a write.

In this example, the basic frequency of the computer is 0.89 MHz. That is close enough to 1 MHz

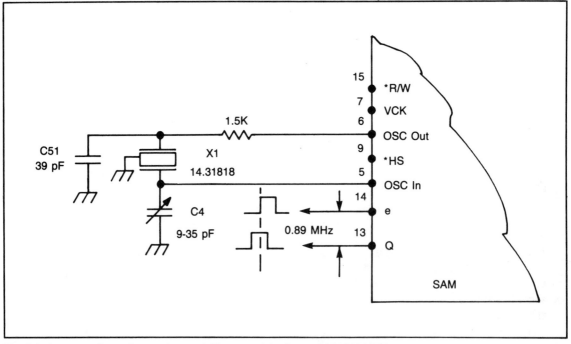

Fig. 8-8. A commonly used computer crystal is one cut to ring at 14.31818 MHZ.

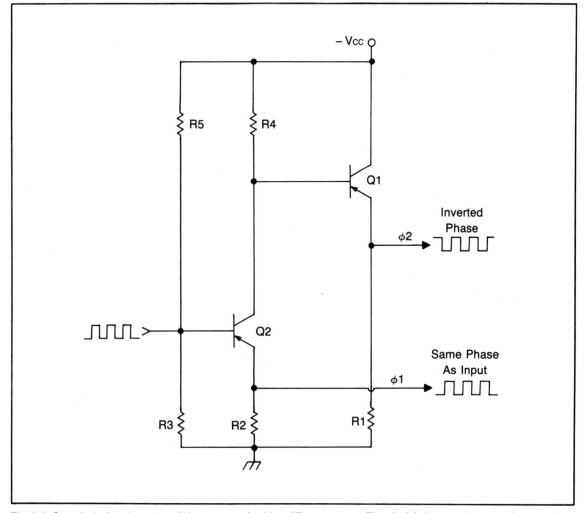

Fig. 8-9. One clock signal can be split into two, each with a different phase. The clock is input to the base of an amplifier. The input is output directly from both the emitter and collector. The collector output is then delayed in a second amplifier changing the phase to a new prescribed time.

so that I can round off the frequency and consider it as a 1 MHz. This means one million clocks a second. There are 1000 nanoseconds in a millionth of a second so there are 1000 nanoseconds in one clock period at this frequency. A clock period is usually described in nanoseconds.

A $\phi 1$, therefore, takes place in 1000 nanoseconds. During that time the high can be thought of as taking place in 475 ns, the low in 475 ns, and the rise and fall of the edges in 25 ns each. As $\phi 1$ proceeds, the first event that occurs is the

rising edge of 25 ns. At this time, the MPU is forced to take the 16 bits in the program counter and place them into the address bus.

$\phi 2$ at that point in time is low. The fact that it is low renders it impotent. $\phi 1$ is in control. $\phi 1$ then experiences its high and reaches the end of the high. $\phi 1$ then falls. The falling edge triggers the program counter and causes it to increment. $\phi 1$ then goes low and becomes helpless.

Meanwhile $\phi 2$ goes onto its rising edge. The rise in voltage opens up the data bus, either for

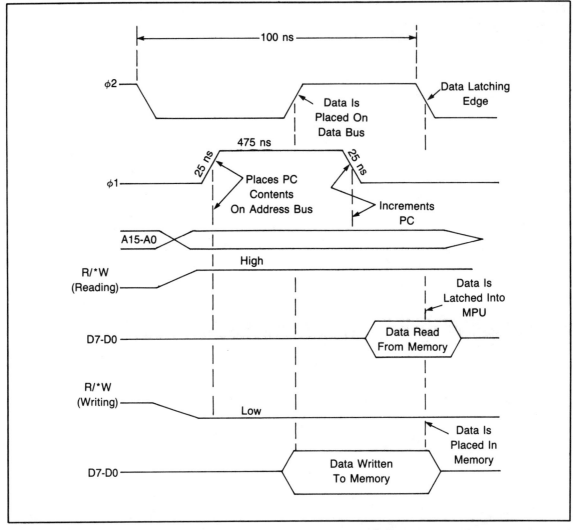

Fig. 8-10. φ1 does the addressing. φ2 takes care of the data movement. A high is roughly 475 nanoseconds while the edges take about 25 ns. The rising edge of φ1 places the program counter bits onto the address bus. The R/*W line, also during the rise of φ1 either goes high for a read or low for a write. The falling edge of φ1 increments the program counter. The rising edge of φ2 places data on the data bus from the source register either in memory or from the MPU. The falling edge of φ2 then latches the data into it's destination register.

some data from the memory to be read by the MPU or data from the MPU to be written to the memory.

φ2 then goes into its high state. The data bleeds into the data bus and stabilizes. Once it is stable, the falling edge of φ2 arrives. It latches the data into the MPU during a read or into the memory if the operation is a write.

In the 6800 and the 6502 type MPUs, the read

and write operations are aided by one read/write line (R/*W). In the Z-80, there were separate read (*RD) and write (*WR) lines. The dual-phase MPUs use one R/*W line. During a read operation, the R/*W line of the 6800 is forced to a high as φ1 goes high. This high tells the memory that a read operation is taking place. The addressed location is further told to place a copy of its contents onto the data bus so the MPU can read it.

If a write operation is taking place, the R/*W line is forced to go low during the high of $\phi 1$. The low instructs the memory location that a write is going on. It further tells the location to get ready for delivery of data over data bus from the MPU.

There is a lot more to the timing of the operations between the MPU and the residents of the memory map. The next chapter on microprocessors goes into more of the details.

Chapter 9

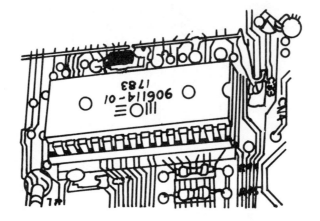

The Hard-Working Microprocessor

S OMEWHERE IN ELEMENTARY SCHOOL YOU learned arithmetic. The ability to add, subtract, multiply, and divide has been with you ever since. It is an ability that you must use on a daily basis. Without arithmetic, you would be seriously handicapped and not be able to do practically any type of responsible job.

The digital computer started out many years ago as an Arithmetic Unit. It was built out of vacuum tubes, resistors, capacitors, and other electronic parts. It is the very core of any computer. Without it, the computer could not exist. In today's microcomputers, the Arithmetic Unit is a set of registers buried deep in the microprocessor. All MPUs have these units.

In addition to the arithmetic, the ability to perform logic is also bestowed on the unit. As a result, it is known as the Arithmetic Logic Unit or ALU.

ARITHMETIC LOGIC UNIT

In an 8-bit MPU, the ALU can be thought of as being built out of three 8-bit registers. There are two

sets of eight flip-flops used as the two input registers and one 8-bit output register. Between the input and output registers are a bunch of circuits. These circuits take care of the jobs the registers are assigned to perform.

The ALU is quite the same electronically as any calculator. You can use your computer directly as a calculator, if you so desire. However the real power of the computer is its use with programs. Instead of only responding to you punching buttons on the calculator, the ALU is able to go to work on data stored in memory and follow the instructions also stored in memory. Once the program and data is in memory, the computer is able to run the program automatically and at blinding speed.

The ALU really can't do that many things. However, the things it can do are among the most important basic abilities that control our civilization and nature. Refer to Fig. 9-1. The ALU is able to add. The ALU is able to subtract, even if it is really addition of complements. The ALU is able to multiply. It multiplies by repeated addition and

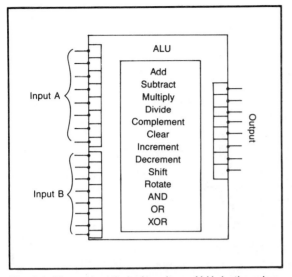

Fig. 9-1. The arithmetic logic unit, or ALU, in the micro-processor can be thought of as two input registers that outputs results to a single register. It performs the listed jobs.

its talent of being a shift register. The ALU can do division by repeated subtraction and doing some more shift register tricks.

The ALU with the aid of some logic gates between the inputs and the output is able to AND, OR, and NOT the two input register contents. With these three types of gates in place, an ALU can conceivably do all the other logic jobs such as EOR, NAND, NOR, and ENOR.

The ALU can complement an input, that is change all the highs to lows and lows to highs. It can also clear an input or make all eight of the bits into lows no matter what they were input as. Then the ALU can also increment and decrement the inputs to obtain desired outputs.

The ALU works with another register in the MPU called the Condition Code Register. It helps the ALU make all sorts of decisions. This will be discussed later in the chapter.

Another tricky job the ALU does is distinguishing between positive and negative numbers. When a number is positive, the ALU responds in one way. If a number is negative, the ALU must do a different form of job. If the remainder turns out to be zero then care must be taken. Especially if the remainder is supposed to be divided into a number. The computer cannot divide by zero and arrive at infinity.

ACCUMULATOR

The ALU is buried deep in the internals of the microprocessor. Between it and the pin connections of the chip are many circuits and other registers. In order for data to be input to the ALU and then be output to the rest of the computer, the data must traverse these other circuits.

In an 8-bit computer, these circuits are typically forms of 8-bit registers. A 16-bit computer uses 16-bit registers in these ALU related circuits. These bit sizes are the reason to designate a computer as an 8-bit type or a 16-bit kind.

These circuits consist of multiplexers, storage registers, and registers that are able to add like the ALU. These circuits and the ALU itself are loosely referred to as the accumulator. The accumulator is thought of by programmers as an 8-bit register. The accumulator is thought of by technicians as one of the registers connected to the eight data pins of the MPU. The pins are called D7-D0.

The accumulator circuit group in Fig. 9-2 receives two main inputs. One is an input from the instruction register and decoder. Secondly, the accumulator has an input coming from the data bus, D7-D0. As to be expected the input from the IR is an instruction or op code and the data bus input is data.

Once the inputs are received the accumulator processes the data according to instructions. It then outputs the finished data back out over the two-way data bus. Sometimes the instruction deals with addressing and not data. In those cases, the accumulator outputs to addressing circuits, which I will discuss later in this chapter.

The Accumulator and the IR

Inside the MPU is an internal data bus. It connects to pins D7-D0 and then to the system data bus that runs around the print board to all memory and I/O chips. The data bus is bidirectional.

All of the internal registry connects to the MPU internal data bus. All of the registers make

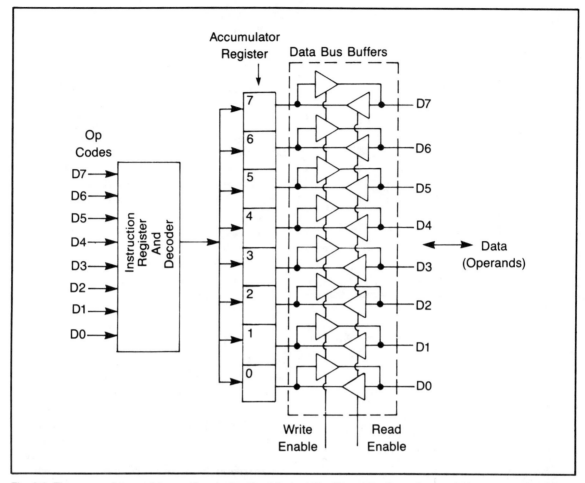

Fig. 9-2. The accumulator register receives instruction bits from the IR and D. It receives and also outputs data bits to and from the data bus. The data bus buffers control the direction of the data bus flow.

good use of the two-way characteristics of the data bus except for the instruction register. The IR only requires a data bus input. It does not output to the bus. Copies of the op codes that are stored in memory in the program locations only have to be fetched. They are never sent back into memory from the IR. For example; during a Z-80 op-code fetch, the instruction is read out of memory during the first four clocks of the ϕ signal. There aren't any clocks needed to write the op code back to memory.

During the op code fetch, the instruction is filed into the IR and is decoded by the circuits of the IR. The output of the IR is then injected into the ac-

cumulator. In the accumulator, the bits of the op code readies the circuits for data processing. The IR then shuts its entrances so no data can enter the IR. The IR is only interested in incoming op codes. The data, known as operands, that will be moved over the data bus next, is not allowed to get into the IR.

The Accumulator and the Data Bus

In a program after an op code byte, there are bytes of operands. The first four clocks of ϕ (Fig. 8-6) reads the op code into the IR over the data bus. If the op code is a read type instruction, the next three clocks are placed into action (Fig. 8-7). Their

152

energy causes the addresssed location to place its operand byte onto the data bus. The byte travels the bus to the MPU pins D7-D0. The byte enters the MPU.

Inside the MPU, the operand finds two pathways. One goes to the IR, but the IR is closed. The operand can't take that route. The second path is to a set of enabled input buffers. The operand passes quickly through the buffers and arrives at the awaiting accumulator registers. The accumulator then receives and processes the data according to the op code instruction that had arrived courtesy of the four previous clock periods.

When the operation is a write type operation, a similar event takes place, but the operand goes the other way. The write op code will arrive at the IR the same way the read op code got there. The first four clocks of ϕ still read the op code out of the program location. The next three clocks are the op-code read clocks, but they do not do anything during a write operation except pulse past. The last three clocks in the series are the ones that power the write operation (Fig. 8-7).

As the three write clocks occur, they first cause the data bus buffers in Fig. 9-2 to reverse their direction. Next, they output the contents of the accumulator onto the data bus. Lastly, they install the operand that was in the accumulator into the memory location it is supposed to be stored at.

PROGRAM COUNTER

The program counter deals in addresses. In an 8-bit computer the program counter is a register with 16 bits. In a 16-bit computer, the program counter can have up to 32 bits but for practical purposes only uses 24 bits at a maximum. Down the road, there might be some needs for 32 bits but presently 24 bits is more than enough.

The register is given its name because it is built to start counting at 0 in decimal and continue unabated, as long as the clock is pulsing, to its last possible combination of bits. In the 8-bit computer, the 16 bits of the counter can count from 0 to 65,535. In the 16 bit computer, the 24 bits of the counter can count from 0 through 16,777,215. If a 32 bit counter should be employed, it could count

up to 4,294,967,296 or 4 gigabytes.

In the typical 8-bit computer, there are 16 lines in the address bus, A15-A0. The 16 bits of the PC connect to the address bus through 16 buffers. Figure 9-3 shows these connections. The buffers are one way out from the MPU to the residents of the memory map. There are no address lines returning from the memory to the MPU.

The program counter is built to automatically start at LLLL LLLL LLLL LLLL, which is decimal 0, and count in sequence once every machine cycle till it reaches the last possible bit combination, HHHH HHHH HHHH HHHH, which is decimal 65,535. There are about a half dozen instructions though that can make the PC stop its normal sequencing and branch or jump to a different address out of sequence. These instructions trigger another MPU register to accomplish that end. This is covered in the next section.

The addressing and the data moving are a coordinated activity. In the Z-80, the addressing is triggered at the beginning of each machine cycle. The data read or write signal is triggered later in the cycle. In a 6502 or 6800, the addressing is accomplished with $\phi1$ and data movement is made with $\phi2$ (Fig. 8-10). The timings are critical and cannot be tampered with or the computing will be stopped.

In the dual-phase MPUs, the PC places its address on A15-A0 as the high of $\phi1$ experiences its rising edge. The PC increments by one automatically as $\phi1$ has its falling edge. The addressed location is opened up during the high between the rising and falling edges. $\phi1$ keeps addressing location after location unless some event occurs to force the PC to make a change of address.

Change of Address

While there are some rare programs that can be run off and never change an address and sequence from the first byte to the last, practically all software has constant switching around of addresses. The address changing is made with the help of some other MPU registers. These other registers force the PC to suddenly stop sequencing and place a newly calculated address onto the address bus. The address bus has no trouble with

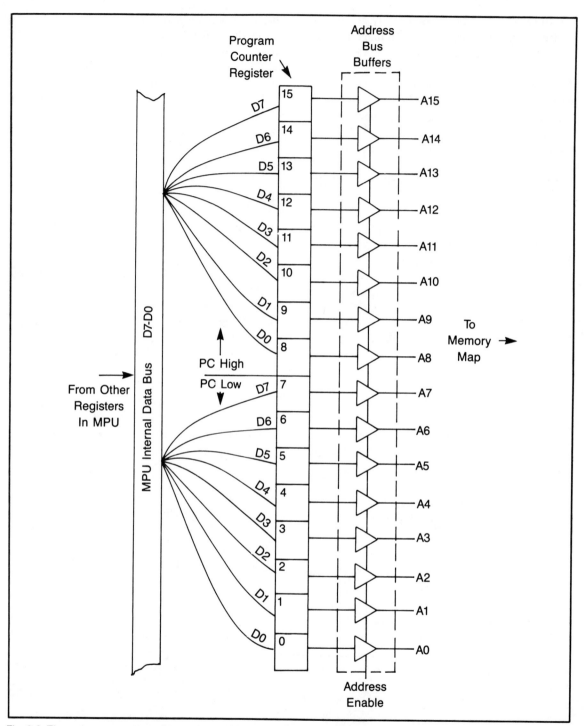

Fig. 9-3. The program counter register outputs address bits onto the address bus. The PC increments automatically from address to address. It also can receive addressing type bytes from other registers in the MPU to make change of addresses.

a different set of bits. It will quickly activate any address that is placed onto its 16 lines no matter what it is, as long as the address exists in the computer.

It was mentioned earlier that there is a small group of instructions that will cause a change of address. If one of these op codes finds its way to the IR, the following situation takes place. Normally, when instructions arrive at the IR and they are one of the data processing op codes, the IR sends them directly to the accumulator. However, when the instruction is one of the change of address op codes, the IR could bypass the accumulator and send the bits to the PC circuits. There the PC has numbers added or subtracted from its register bits

or the register contents could be changed altogether. The altered states of the PC are then placed on the address bus and a change of address takes place.

The change of address op codes can cause the PC to jump, branch, call, return, or halt altogether.

Jump and Branch

The Jump and Branch instructions are somewhat alike. (In some computers, they are exactly alike.) In general, though, they have a difference. When a Jump op code arrives at the IR, the PC is stopped from automatically sequencing. As Fig. 9-4 shows, the Jump instruction is followed

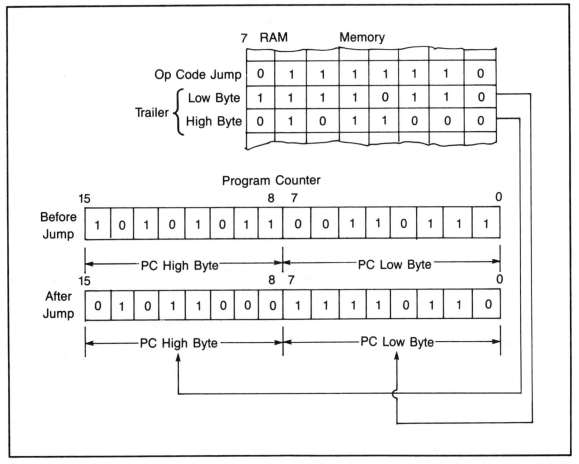

Fig. 9-4. When a Jump op code arrives at the IR, the next two bytes are a new address. The bytes are installed in the PC and the change of address is placed onto the address bus.

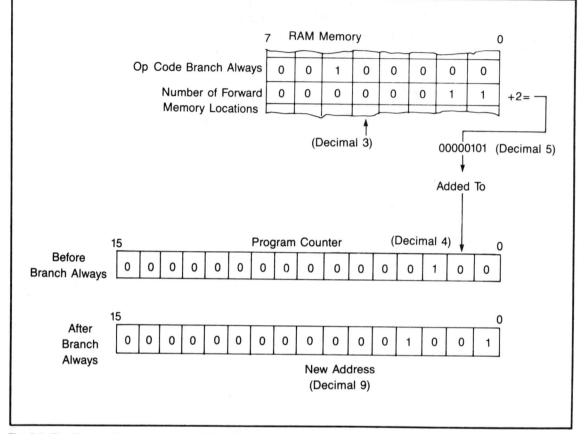

Fig. 9-5. The Branch Always op code is followed by a number +2 that is to be added to the contents of the PC. The number here is binary 00000011 which is decimal 3. 3 + 2 = 5, binary 00000101. This is added to the PC contents, decimal 4, 0000000000000100. The results of the binary addition is 0000000000001001, which is decimal 9. The PC thus branches ahead from decimal 3 to 9.

by a new complete address. The byte or bytes that trail the op code are placed into the PC as they are. The PC then places them on the address bus and they are activated. The PC therefore jumps to the new address.

The Branch Always instruction in Fig. 9-5, is trailed by a byte or bytes that is not a new address. It is a + or − number that is to be added or subtracted from the current address in the sequence, plus 2. When the Branch op code arrives at the IR, the next byte or bytes plus 2 is added or subtracted to the existing contents of the PC. The resultant set of 16 bits is then placed on the address bus and the location accessed.

There can be many Branch instructions in an MPU Instruction Set. The Branch Always just mentioned is only one of many. The rest of the Branch instructions have conditions attached to them. The Branch Always, as the name implies has no strings attached. When it arrives at the IR, the IR forces the trailer byte or bytes into the PC register and the address gets changed. With the rest of the Branch instructions, the IR checks with the condition code register to see if the conditions are correct for the branch to take place. If the conditions are not met, the PC is allowed to sequence on to the next address. The condition code register is discussed in the next section.

The Call and Return instructions deal in subroutines. A subroutine is a separate little program installed way off in memory somewhere that is there to do a special job. For instance, most ALUs can't really multiply. You could perform multiplication by repeated addition. For small multiplication tasks repeated addition is fine. However, if there is going to be a lot of extensive mathematics, it is a good idea to simply write a multiplication program and install it deep in memory. Then when it is time to perform some multiplication, you can Call the little subroutine, do the multiplication, and then Return from the subroutine back to the main program.

The Call op code changes the PC to the subroutine address in the same way that the Jump op code does. Then the PC sequences automatically through the subroutine multiplying your number. Once the operation is run, the last op code in the subroutine is encountered. It is the Return instruction. This changes the PC back to the main program address. The program then continues on where it had left off before it was called to multiply.

The Halt instruction is just that. It stops the PC from the automatic incrementing. A Halt op code is often used as a form of Stop in the middle of programs. This is different than an End op code that is mostly found at the very end of programs.

CONDITION CODE REGISTER

In an 8-bit MPU there are eight bits in the CCR. a 16-bit MPU makes room for a 16 bit CCR. The CCR is typically connected between the PC and the accumulator circuit complex as Fig. 9-6 shows. There is a two-way bus line between the CCR and the accumulator. There is only a one-way connection from the CCR to the PC. The CCR needs to output to the PC, but there is no reason for the PC to respond back to the CCR.

As a program is run, the accumulator and the CCR keep up a steady communication with each other. They are constantly checking each program byte to see if a byte contains a signal that might want the PC to output a change of address.

The CCR in Fig. 9-7 is a register of individual flip-flops. It is really eight separate 1-bit registers. Each bit is called a flag. The flags can be set with

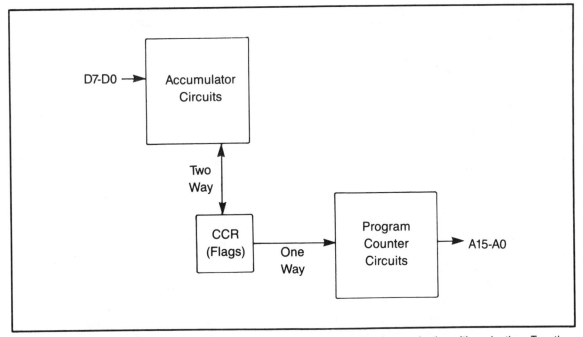

Fig. 9-6. As a program is run, the CCR and the accumulator keep up a steady communication with each other. Together, they check every byte being processed to see if a branch type change of address is called for.

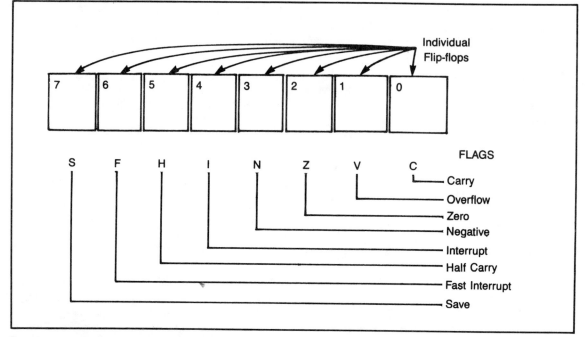

Fig. 9-7. The CCR is a collection of single bit registers. Each bit is an individual flag. As the flags are set or cleared, various branch instructions and interrupts are enabled or disabled.

a high or cleared with a low. Most of the op codes that the MPU obtains instructions from can cause one or more of the flags to be set or cleared. The flags in turn can produce all sorts of changes in the PC and the accumulator.

Typical names of the flags are carry, overflow, zero, negative, interrupt, halfcarry, fast interrupt, and save. These flags are off-on switches for some of the most important functions of the MPU. A good assembly-language programmer must be able to use the flags with dexterity.

Carry

The C flag (for carry) works with the 8-bit accumulator register. Refer to Fig. 9-8. It becomes the ninth bit of the accumulator. In some computations, the binary number might get larger than eight bits. The C flag can then be used to store the carry as a ninth bit. In other cases, where the accumulator performs a shift or rotate operation one of the end bits could fall out. The C flag could be used to store the loose bits.

The op code of the instruction will set or clear the carry bit as a result of the operation. Carry is normally clear until it receives a carry instruction.

Negative

The N flag is called negative. The accumulator register is capable of containing a negative number. It uses bit 7 to designate the number. When bit 7 is an L or 0, bits 6-0 is binary for a positive number. If bit 7 is an H or 1, then the accumulator holds a negative binary number. Refer to Fig. 9-9.

Bit 7 only is used to indicate a + or − number when it is necessary to go plus and minus during the computation. At that time, it is said that the accumulator is working with signed numbers. The signs, of course, are the + and −, indicated in bit 7 by a 0 or 1.

The signed numbers are in contrast to the unsigned numbers. These are usually the positive numbers needed in routine computations.

When signed numbers are used, the most significant bit, bit 7 is occupied indicating the sign.

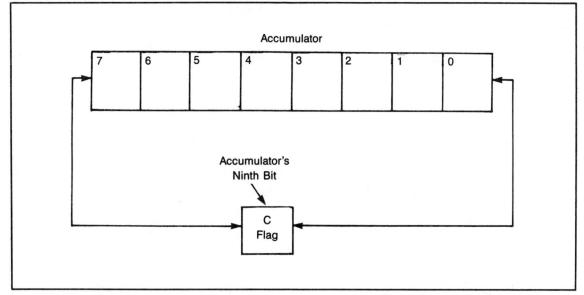

Fig. 9-8. The carry flag can act as the accumulator's ninth bit. It can store an extra bit during adding, shifting, and rotating.

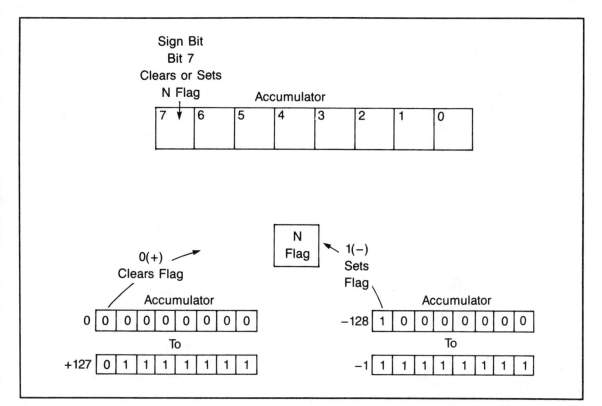

Fig. 9-9. The sign bit of the accumulator is bit 7, A 0 is a + and A1 is a −. When bit 7 is 0, the negative flag is cleared. If bit 7 is a 1 the N flag is set.

This means that there are only seven bits left to code the decimal. With only seven bits there are only 128 possible combinations of bits. That means the bits can only code the decimal numbers from 0 to +127. That would be binary 0000 0000 to 0111 1111.

At that point, the accumulator, if counting, would become binary 1000 0000. This is recognized as –128. The next number is binary 1000 0001. This is –127, If the count continues, the accumulator will cycle on to 1111 1111. This is –1 in signed numbers. The signed number chart in Table 9-1 shows the possibilities of an 8-bit accumulator register. It can count from 0 to +127, switch signs as bit 7 becomes a 1. Then it counts from –128 back to –1.

The N flag signals when the sign changes. The N flag is cleared as long as bit 7 of the accumulator is positive and is showing a 0. Should bit 7 go negative by getting set to a 1, the N flag in turn also gets set and becomes a 1. This signals the ALU and the PC that bit 7 has a 1. They act accordingly to the dictates of the program.

Table 9-1. Signed Decimal, Binary, and Hex Number Comparison.

Decimal	Binary	Hex
+127	01111111	7F
+126	01111110	7E
+125	01111101	7D
+124	01111100	7C
↑	↑	↑
+5	00000101	05
+4	00000100	04
+3	00000011	03
+2	00000010	02
+1	00000001	01
0	00000000	00
–1	11111111	FF
–2	11111110	FE
–3	11111101	FD
–4	11111100	FC
–5	11111011	FB
↓	↓	↓
–124	10000100	84
–125	10000011	83
–126	10000010	82
–127	10000001	81
–128	10000000	80

Overflow

Another flag is V, the overflow. It is the assistant of the N flag. The N flag is busy watching bit 7 of the accumulator. If bit 7 is a 0 then the N flag is 0. Should bit 7 go to a 1 then the N flag goes 1. These movements of bit 7 can in some situations designate a signed number. Bit 7 in other programs can simply be the MSB of an unsigned number.

The programming can get sticky if the accumulator computations accidentally spill over a carry from bit 6 to bit 7. The sign could accidentally get changed and a program could crash.

The V flag keeps a watch on this potential overflow from bit 6 or bit 7. Refer to Fig. 9-10. During computation, the V flag monitors the overflow. If there is an overflow and bit 7 is set to a 1, then the V flag will also set itself to a 1. Should an overflow occur and bit 7 is cleared to a 0, then the V flag also clears to a 0. The overflow occurs when the result of an operation places a number larger than the –128 to +127 7-bit range.

Zero

The Z flag, zero, is common. The Z flag gets set to a 1 whenever the accumulator becomes 0000 0000. Refer to Fig. 9-11. If the accumulator has any other set of bits the Z flag is clear. The Z flag is handy during a countdown. The program can be written to have a countdown and bring the program can be written to have a countdown and bring the program to a halt when the accumulator becomes 0000 0000. The Z flag is attached to the program counter. as the end arrives and the accumulator becomes zero, the Z flag is thrown and the PC is halted. The Z flag has many uses.

Half-Carry

There is an H flag, which stands for half-carry. This flag keeps an eye on bits 3 and 4 of the accumulator. Refer to Fig. 9-12. Between bits 3 and 4 is the separation of the two nybbles in the accumulator register. Bits 3-0 holds the binary for the least significant nymbble, and bits 7-4 hold the most significant nybble. The 4-bit nybble, of course, is the code for a single hex or decimal number.

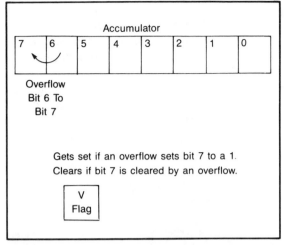

Fig. 9-10. The overflow flag keeps track of the potential overflow from bit 6 to bit 7. If there is an accidental overflow, the sign flag could change when it should not. If there is an overflow, the V flag will be affected and warn of the change. It gets set when the overflow causes bit 7 to be a 1 or gets cleared if the overflow makes bit 7 a 0.

When the accumulator register is performing arithmetic such as addition, it is actually adding one nybble to the next. If there is a carry from bit 3 to bit 4 the carry is taking place from the LS nybble

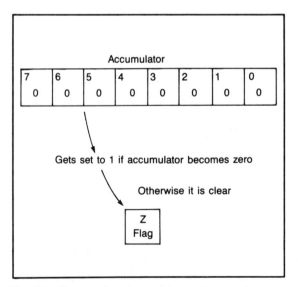

Fig. 9-11. The zero flag, is clear except if the accumulator becomes 00000000. When the accumulator becomes all zeros, then the Z flag is set.

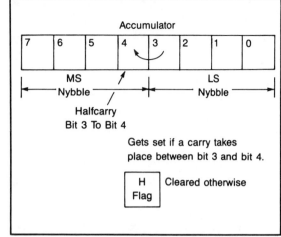

Fig. 9-12. The half carry flag watches over the carry between bits 3 and 4 of the accumulator. These bits are the separation place between the two nybbles the accumulator byte is made of. Often during addition, it is necessary to make note of the carry between the nybbles. The H flag gets set when there is a carry and stays clear when no carry has taken place.

to the MS nybble. This is a special carry unlike carries that take place inside a nybble. In certain cases, the carry from nybble to nybble must be taken into consideration during programming.

The H flag monitors the nybble-to-nybble carry, which is appropriately called halfcarry, since it is the halfway bits of the register. When a halfcarry takes place, the H flag is thrown and will hold a 1. If no carry takes place during an addition op code execution, then the H flag is cleared and holds a 0. The H flag normally remains clear until a halfcarry sets it.

INTERRUPTS

One of the abilities of a computer that makes it seem almost a living entity is an interrupt. During the running of a program certain electronics can step in and interrupt the proceedings. The MPU then finishes out the machine cycle it is in the middle of and stops to service the interrupt. The first servicing step consists of storing all the contents of the MPU registers in a safe place in memory. That place is called the stack, which will be discussed later in this chapter.

During the interrupt the MPU switches to addresses that contain a vector. The vector, which is a two byte address, is then loaded into the program counter. The PC places the vector address on the address bus. The address that the vector points out is a service program. The MPU then sequences through the service program. Once the interrupt is serviced, the MPU reloads its registers from the stack and continues what it was doing before it was so rudely interrupted.

In the group of flags, there are usually one or more to help out with the interrupt activity. They are I type flags. They play the part of a *mask* during the interrupt. A mask in an I bit stops up or masks the interrupt input of the MPU. The mask operates when it is set to a 1. Once an interrupt sequence is begun the I bit is set. The reason for the masking is to stop any additional interrupts from interrupting the interrupt that is in progress. The MPU can only handle one interrupt at a time. Any other interrupts that try to stop the MPU are masked off.

The I bit will mask off most interrupts when it is set. However, there is one type of interrupt called a *nonmaskable* interrupt. When one of these special interrupts arrives at its own special pin on the MPU, it will cause an interrupt whether the I bit is set or not. The nonmaskable interrupts happen only when the computer is in dire straits. For instance, there could be a nonmaskable interrupt if the computer senses there is an impending power failure. An interrupt of this nature goes right through any I-bit mask settings.

CCR AND BRANCH OP CODES

The many Branch instructions are very dependent on the flags in the CCR. The branch instructions except for Branch Always have a decision to make. Branch Always has no decision. When the Branch Always op code bits arrive at the IR, the branch is made. The operand trailers are added or subtracted to the contents of the PC and a new address is accessed.

Not so with the rest of the branch instructions. When their code bits reach the IR, the CCR is checked first before the branch is permitted. For

instance, the instruction, Branch if the Accumulator is Zero, could arrive at the IR. When the accumulator is zero, then the Z flag gets set. Should the accumulator be any other binary value but 0000 0000, then the Z flag is cleared.

The IR checks the Z flag. If the Z flag is set then the IR will cause the branch to be made. The operand trailers will be added to the PC and a new address accessed. Should the Z flag be clear however, then nothing will happen. The branch instruction and its trailing operands will be ignored and the PC will address the next program line instead.

The CCR and its flag collection are wired internally between the accumulator and the program counter. The instructions, as they are executed, set and clear the flags continually. The assembly-or machine-language programmer must be aware and adapt at knowing what instructions under what circumstances set and clear the flags in his machine. Then when a flag is thrown, the programmer must know how the program is affected. Flag control is a vital ingredient in good programming technique.

Most of the instructions affect one or more flags during a program run. If lights were attached to the flags, they would be flashing continually as programs were run.

STACK POINTER

In MPUs, there are one or more registers called the stack pointer. As mentioned, the *stack* in computerese is a term for a safe storage place somewhere in RAM. The stack, illustrated in Fig. 9-13, must be in a place where bytes can be stored and not be affected in any manner by a busy program run.

All the word *pointer* means is address. A stack pointer is the address of the first byte of the stack area in RAM. Even though the address only points to an 8-bit location in RAM, the address must still be a 16-bit collection. Therefore, a typical stack pointer is a 16-bit register. In a larger 16-bit microprocessor the stack pointer could have 32 bits if it had to address a four byte address.

The stack pointer is wired in parallel with the program counter. It can place 16 bits on the address bus in the same way the PC can. When it points

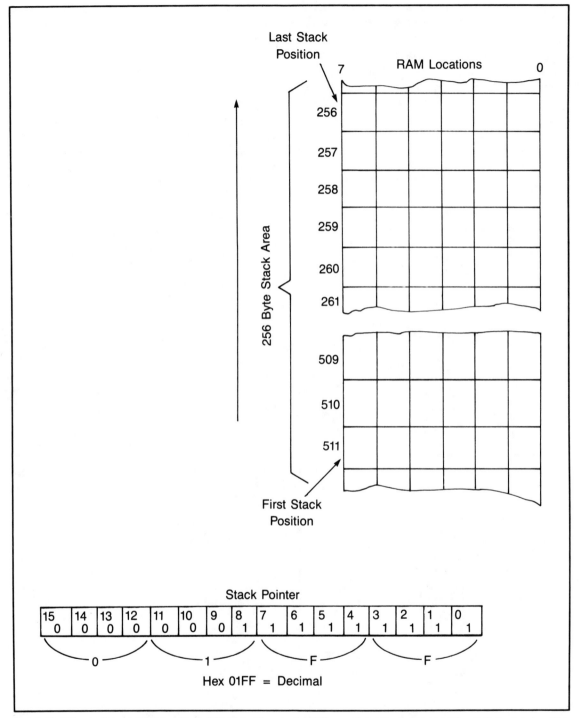

Fig. 9-13. This stack is at RAM locations 256-511. The stack pointer contains the address of the first stack byte, 511, hex 01FF, binary 0000 0001 1111 1111.

to the stack, that is just what it does.

It was mentioned that the stack points to the beginning address of the stack. When an interrupt occurs and the MPU must store the contents of its registers into RAM. For the example, in a typical MPU there are nine 8-bit programming register segments. There are eight bits in each of the blocks in Fig. 9-14.

Accumulator A
Accumulator B
PC High
PC Low
Stack Pointer High
Stack Pointer Low
Index Register High
Index Register Low
Condition Code Register

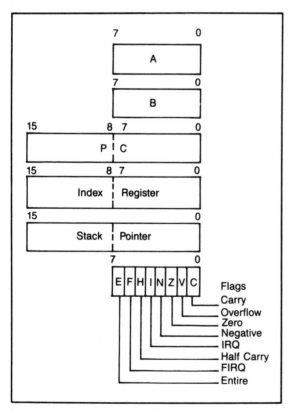

Fig. 9-14. This programmer's diagram shows the bit sizes of the MPU registers. There are nine, 8 bit register segments to consider.

During a program run, at any beat of the clock, these registers will all have a specific set of bits. When an interrupt occurs and is acceptable for servicing, the MPU is going to stop the program and service the interrupt. The interrupt routine will need the use of the registers in the MPU. Unless measures are taken, the existing set of bits will be destroyed. This cannot be allowed to happen, so a copy of the contents of the registers are stored in the stack. For these nine bytes in the MPU seven bytes are saved in the stack in RAM. The stack pointer will contain the beginning address of the stack.

The reason only seven stack locations are necessary is because the stack pointer itself does not need saving. Its contents are not destroyed as the interrupt routine is run off. There are two bytes in the pointer and that leaves only the remaining seven register bytes to be saved.

Before the interrupt is allowed to run the MPU, the register contents are loaded into the stack. The stack pointer places its pointer on the address bus and the CCR bits are written to the beginning address. Then the stack pointer is decremented and the contents of accumulator B is written to that address.

Next in line is the contents of the accumulator A followed by the index register high. Continuing on and decrementing the stack pointer each time, the contents of index register low and then PC High is stored. Lastly the PC low is placed in the stack. The stack now looks like the following.

Stack Address	Contents
505	PC Low
506	PC High
507	Index Low
508	Index High
509	Accumulator A
510	Accumulator B
511	CCR

The CCR was the first byte stored and it is at the highest address of the stack. The PC low was the last byte stored and it is at the lowest address of the stack. The stack pointer in the MPU at this stage contains the last address stored, the PC low, address 505 of the seven bytes stored.

After the interrupt when the MPU wants to get back to the program it had been running, it starts reading back the contents of the stack. The stack pointer holds the address of the last register stored, the PC low. The last one in, is the first one out from the stack address 505. Then the stack pointer increments to address 506 and reads the PC high bits out of the location. It keeps incrementing till it reads all seven bytes back into the registers from where they originated.

During a program run, the register bits keep getting stacked and retrieved many, many times. During the stacking and retrieving the stack pointer operates just as if it was the program counter. The PC at those times takes a rest.

INDEX REGISTER

The index register can also be wired in parallel with the program counter. Indexing is a valuable technique that programmers have been using for many years before micros were even dreamed of. Indexing is another way you can get the addressing to stop sequencing and go to another method, namely indexing.

Index registers are usually 16 bits in the 8-bit computers and 32 bits wide in a 16-bit computer. It is the same size as the PC. The index register starts its operation when a specific index type op code arrives at the instruction register. While the index register is doing the addressing, the PC takes another rest. If both were in operation at the same time, there would be an addressing conflict.

Indexing is one of the important addressing-mode techniques. This was discussed in Chapter 2. The IR is able to recognize an instruction that enters in the index addressing mode. The op code specifies that the index register is to be used to form the address where needed data is stored in memory. After the op code trails an operand. This operand is added to the specified index register. The contents of the index register plus the operand form a 16-bit address. At this address is the needed data. The index register places the formed address

on the address bus and the MPU is able to access the address.

Not all computers have index registers. When there aren't any, other addressing means must be used. However, for certain applications, like looking up values in a table, indexing is usually the best way to go.

INSTRUCTION REGISTER

The IR is thought of as both the input register and the instruction decoder. The input register is connected directly to the system data bus. The register is an input only; nothing can go back out to the data bus. This is in contrast to the data input/output buffers also connected to the same data bus.

The IR is the place where the op codes for the instructions arrive. The other data bus connection, the input/output buffers, deals with the data operands. It can receive the operand or transmit an operand back out on the data bus.

The buffers are three-state as well as the IR. The reason is as follows. In a program line, the op code comes first and the operands trail next. That's why operands are referred to as trailers. The program line is stored in bytes of memory in the same way. The op codes are stored in RAM bytes and the operands are stored in the following RAM bytes. When ROM is used, the op codes are burnt into ROM bytes, and the operands are burnt in to the following ROM bytes. As far as the MPU goes, the RAM or the ROM storage is the same to it. All it wants is a copy of what is in the location.

As the clock beats, the three entrances are turned off and on. During the time the op code travels the data bus, the IR entrance is turned on. Then when data is to be on the bus, the IR doorway is slammed shut. If the data is moving from memory to MPU as during a read, then the eight buffers that can accept the operand are opened and the eight buffers that are wired in the opposite direction are put into a three-state condition. Should the data be moving from MPU to memory as during a write, the read buffers are three-stated and the write buffers are enabled.

The IR only deals with the op codes. The operands are sent to all the other registers. The op codes are codes from the Instruction Set. The operands are simply data that needs to be worked on. The op codes tells the ALU and other registers what sort of work the data is to be subjected to.

Op codes in the 8-bit computer are usually one byte in size. In eight bits, there can be 255 combinations. That means an 8-bit computer can have a possible 256 different op codes. There is really no need to have that many codes. A total near 75 is plenty to do the computing. Actually a lot of the codes do the same jobs but with different registers and with assorted addressing modes. There are less than two dozen different basic jobs that the computer does. The rest of the instruction set consists of variations of the same basic jobs.

INSTRUCTION SET

The MPU is able to perform three general types of jobs. First, it can move data around the computer. That is, it can fetch op codes, fetch operands, and write operands to memory and I/O devices. This moving job requires a few instructions. The instructions in general, are called Move, Load, Store, and Transfer. There are many chips and registers in the MPU and memory map and each particular movement of bytes between them requires a separate op code. Therefore, you'll find a lot of data movement op codes in the Instruction Set. Essentially though they are really only one of the above types. The moving instructions are the most used of all in the set. They represent about 75% of all the op codes you'll find in a program.

The second sort of instructions are the ones that run the ALU: arithmetic, logic, and register bit manipulators such as Shift, Increment, Clear, and Complement instructions. They are the calculator instructions of the MPU.

The third type of instructions do not have much to do with the op codes and operands. They deal with the addressing mechanism of the MPU. They are the Jump, Branch, Call, Return, and Halt instructions. They and the automatic incrementing of the program counter keep the MPU accessing the correct locations in the memory map.

In an 8-bit MPU there can be about 75 of these instructions. That leaves about 175 unused bit com-binations that could be installed in future MPUs of the same type. No doubt there will be many more variations of these instructions and even many new ones as time goes by and additional needs are conceived. Table 9-2 lists the Instructions Set for the 6800 MPU. The hexadecimal code for each instruction is listed.

MPU ROM

Have you wondered where the electronics that implement these instructions are located? The wiring is in the Instruction Decoder circuitry. The decoder works with a control unit. They decode the incoming bytes and cause the instructions to be executed. One such method is the following.

Deep down in the decoder circuit area are ROM circuits. They are somewhat like the ROM chips that operate the rest of the computer, but they are buried in the MPU. On these miniscule ROMs are built in little programs for each instruction in the set. When these programs are activated, they send bits to the indicated MPU registers and the registers perform the specified instruction.

These ROMs contain microprograms. The microprograms, are not available to you. They are permanently installed in the MPU. Future versions of the same number MPU will no doubt have updated microprograms. Meanwhile, the microprogram in your MPU will respond to the op code for a particular instruction.

For example, suppose you want to LOAD accumulator A with 11111111. If you enter the op code 10000110 (hex 86) into the IR, the following will happen. To the beat of the clock, the bits will address the microprogram that is wired to open up the A accumulator. Then the operand 11111111 enters through the data bus buffers. The clock energy then pushes 11111111 into the accumulator. The operation took place as a few lines of the microprogram was executed inside the MPU. It all happened in response to the op code 10000110 that arrived from the main program stored in the memory.

Each and every one of the 75 or so, op codes in an instruction set can trigger off its very own little section of the MPU microprogram. As this

Table 9-2. 6800 Instruction Set .

1 LOAD ACCUMULATOR A

86	IMMEDIATE
96	DIRECT
B6	EXTENDED
A6	INDEXED

2 LOAD ACCUMULATOR B

C6	IMMEDIATE
D6	DIRECT
F6	EXTENDED
E6	INDEXED

Flags affected, N. Z. Flag cleared, V.

3 LOAD STACK POINTER

8E	IMMEDIATE
9E	DIRECT
BE	EXTENDED
AE	INDEXED

Flags affected, N. Z. Flag cleared, V.

4 LOAD INDEX REGISTER

CE	IMMEDIATE
DE	DIRECT
FE	EXTENDED
EE	INDEXED

Flags affected, N. Z. Flag cleared, V.

5 STORE ACCUMULATOR A

97	DIRECT
B7	EXTENDED
A7	INDEXED

6 STORE ACCUMULATOR B

D7	DIRECT
F7	EXTENDED
E7	INDEXED

Flags affected, N. Z. Flag cleared, V.

7 STORE STACK POINTER

9F	DIRECT
BF	EXTENDED
AF	INDEXED

Flags affected, N. Z. Flag cleared, V.

8 STORE INDEX REGISTER

DF	DIRECT
FF	EXTENDED
EF	INDEXED

Flags affected, N. Z. Flag cleared, V.

9 PUSH DATA onto STACK

36	(Push accumulator A onto stack)
37	(Push accumulator b onto stack)

No flags are affected by these instructions.

10 PULL DATA from STACK

32	(Load the A accumulator from stack)
33	(load the B accumulator from stack)

No flags are affected by these instructions

11 TRANSFER from ACCUMULATOR A to ACCUMU-LATOR B

16

12 TRANSFER from ACCUMULATOR B to ACCUMU-LATOR A

17

Flags affected, N. Z. Flag cleared, V.

13 TRANSFER from INDEX REGISTER to STACK POINTER

35

14 TRANSFER from STACK POINTER to INDEX REGISTER

30

No flags are affected by these instructions.

15 TRANSFER from ACCUMULATOR A to CONDITION CODE REGISTER

06

16 TRANSFER from CONDITION CODE REGISTER to ACCUMULATOR A

07

Flags are affected when accumulator A transfers contents into CCR. Whatever was in the accumulator register bits 0-5 will be in bits 0-5 of the CCR.

17 INCREMENT

4C	ACCUMULATOR A
5C	ACCUMULATOR B
7C	EXTENDED ADDRESS
6C	INDEXED ADDRESS

Flags affected are N, Z, V.

18 INCREMENT STACK POINTER

31

No flags affected

19 INCREMENT INDEX REGISTER

08

The Z flag is set if all 16 bits are cleared.

20 DECREMENT

4A	ACCUMULATOR A
5A	ACCUMULATOR B
7A	EXTENDED ADDRESS
6A	INDEXED ADDRESS

Flags affected are N, Z, V.

21 DECREMENT STACK POINTER
34

No flags are affected.

22 DECREMENT INDEX REGISTER
09

The Z flag can be affected.

23 CLEAR

4F	ACCUMULATOR A
5F	ACCUMULATOR B
7F	EXTENDED ADDRESS
6F	INDEXED ADDRESS

The Z flag is set. The N, V, and C flags are cleared.

24 CLEAR 2'S COMPLEMENT OVERFLOW BIT

0A

The V flag is cleared.

25 CLEAR CARRY

0C

The C flag is cleared.

26 CLEAR INTERRUPT MASK

0E

The I flag is cleared.

27 SET 2'S COMPLEMENT OVERFLOW BIT

0B

The V flag is set to 1.

28 SET INTERRUPT MASK

0F

The I flag is set to 1.

29 SET CARRY

0D

The C flag is set to 1.

30 TEST N or Z

4D	ACCUMULATOR A
5D	ACCUMULATOR B
7D	EXTENDED ADDRESS
6D	INDEXED ADDRESS

Flags affected, N, Z. The V flag is cleared.

31 LOGICAL SHIFT RIGHT

44	ACCUMULATOR A
54	ACCUMULATOR B
74	EXTENDED ADDRESS
64	INDEXED ADDRESS

Flags that can be affected, Z, V, C. The N flag is cleared.

32 ROTATE LEFT

49	ACCUMULATOR A
59	ACCUMULATOR B
79	EXTENDED ADDRESS
69	INDEXED ADDRESS

Flags that can be affected, N, Z, C, V.

33 ROTATE RIGHT

46	ACCUMULATOR A
56	ACCUMULATOR B
76	EXTENDED ADDRESS
66	INDEXED ADDRESS

Flags that can be affected, N, Z, C, V.

34 ARITHMETIC SHIFT RIGHT

47	ACCUMULATOR A
57	ACCUMULATOR B
77	EXTENDED ADDRESS
67	INDEXED ADDRESS

Flags that can be affected, N, Z, V, C.

35 ARITHMETIC SHIFT LEFT

48	ACCUMULATOR A
58	ACCUMULATOR B
78	EXTENDED ADDRESS
68	INDEXED ADDRESS

Flags that can be affected, N, Z, V, C.

36 COMPLEMENT

43	ACCUMULATOR A
53	ACCUMULATOR B
73	EXTENDED ADDRESS
63	INDEXED ADDRESS

Flags that can be affected, N, Z. C is set to 1.
V is cleared.

37 NEGATE

40	ACCUMULATOR A
50	ACCUMULATOR B
70	EXTENDED ADDRESS
60	INDEXED ADDRESS

Flags that can be affected, N, Z, V, C.

38 ADD ACCUMULATOR A TO ACCUMULATOR B

1B

Flags that can be affected, N, Z, V, C, H.

39 SUBTRACT ACCUMULATORS

10

Flags that can be affected,N, Z, V, C.

40 ADD WITH CARRY IN ACCUMULATOR A

89	IMMEDIATE
99	DIRECT
B9	EXTENDED
A9	INDEXED

Flags affected are, N, Z, V, C, H.

41 ADD WITH CARRY IN ACCUMULATOR B

C9	IMMEDIATE
D9	DIRECT
F9	EXTENDED
E9	INDEXED

Flags affected are, N, Z, V, C.

42 ADD WITHOUT CARRY IN ACCUMULATOR A

8B	IMMEDIATE
9B	DIRECT
BB	EXTENDED
AB	INDEXED

Flags affected are, N, Z, V, C, H.

43 ADD WITHOUT CARRY IN ACCUMULATOR B

CB	IMMEDIATE
DB	DIRECT
FB	EXTENDED
EB	INDEXED

Flags affected are, N, Z, V, C, H.

44 SUBTRACT WITH CARRY IN ACCUMULATOR A

82	IMMEDIATE
92	DIRECT
B2	EXTENDED
A2	INDEXED

Flags that can be affected are, N, Z, V, C.

45 SUBTRACT WITH CARRY IN ACCUMULATOR B

C2	IMMEDIATE
D2	DIRECT
F2	EXTENDED
E2	INDEXED

Flags that can be affected are, N, Z, V, C.

46 SUBTRACT (memory byte from ACCUMULATOR A)

80	IMMEDIATE
90	DIRECT
B0	EXTENDED
A0	INDEXED

Flags that can be affected, N, Z, V, C.

47 SUBTRACT (memory byte from ACCUMULATOR B)

C0	IMMEDIATE
D0	DIRECT
F0	EXTENDED
E0	INDEXED

Flags that can be affected, N, Z, V, C.

48 DECIMAL ADJUST the A ACCUMULATOR

Flags that can be affected are N. Z. C.

49 LOGICAL AND ACCUMULATOR A

84	IMMEDIATE
94	DIRECT
B4	EXTENDED
A4	INDEXED

Flags that can be affected, N, Z. The V flag is cleared.

50 LOGICAL AND ACCUMULATOR B

C4	IMMEDIATE
D4	DIRECT
F4	EXTENDED
E4	INDEXED

Flags that can be affected, N, Z. The V is cleared.

51 INCLUSIVE OR (Logical OR) ACCUMULATOR A

8A	IMMEDIATE
9A	DIRECT
BA	EXTENDED
AA	INDEXED

Flags that can be affected, N, Z. The V flag is cleared.

52 INCLUSIVE OR (LOGICAL OR) ACCUMULATOR B

CA	IMMEDIATE
DA	DIRECT
FA	EXTENDED
EA	INDEXED

Flags that can be affected, N, Z. The V flag is cleared.

53 EXCLUSIVE OR ACCUMULATOR A

88	IMMEDIATE
98	DIRECT
B8	EXTENDED
A8	INDEXED

Flags that can be affected, N, Z. The V flag is cleared.

54 EXCLUSIVE OR ACCUMULATOR B

C8	IMMEDIATE
D8	DIRECT
F8	EXTENDED
E8	INDEX

Flags that can be affected, N, Z. The V flag is cleared.

55 BRANCH ALWAYS

20	Unconditional

56 BRANCH to SUBROUTINE

8D	Unconditional

57 RETURN from SUBROUTINE

39

58 BRANCH if CARRY SET

25	Conditional, C is set to 1.

59 BRANCH if CARRY CLEAR

24	Conditional, C is cleared to 0.

60 BRANCH if OVERFLOW SET

29	Conditional, V is set to 1.

61 BRANCH if OVERFLOW CLEAR

28	Conditional, V is cleared to 0.

62 BRANCH if ZERO SET

27	Conditional, Z is set to 1.

63 BRANCH if ZERO CLEAR

26	Conditional, Z is cleared to 0.

64 BRANCH if NEGATIVE SET

    28   Conditional, N is set to 1.

65 BRANCH if NEGATIVE CLEAR

    2A   Conditional, N is cleared to 0.

66 BRANCH if HIGHER

    22   Conditional, C or Z is cleared to 0.

67 BRANCH if LOWER or SAME

    23   Conditional, C or Z is set to 1.

68 BRANCH is LESS THAN ZERO

    2D   Conditional, N is set to 1 and V is cleared to 0, or N is cleared to 0 and V is set to 1.

69 BRANCH if LESS THAN or EQUAL TO ZERO

    2F   Conditional, Z is set to 1, N is set to 1 and V is cleared to 0, or, Z is set to 1, N is cleared to 0 and V is set to 1.

70 BRANCH if GREATER THAN ZERO

    2E   Conditional, z is cleared to 0, N is set to 1 and V is set to 1. Or Z is cleared to 0. N is cleared to 0 and V is cleared to 0.

71 BRANCH if GREATER THAN or EQUAL TO ZERO

    2C   Conditional, N and V are set to 1, or, N and V are cleared to 0.

72 JUMP

    7E   EXTENDED ADDRESS
    6E   INDEXED ADDRESS

73 JUMP to SUBROUTINE

    DB   EXTENDED ADDRESS
    AD   INDEXED ADDRESS

74 RETURN from SUBROUTINE
    39

75 NO OPERATION
    01

76 COMPARE ACCUMULATORS
    11

    Flags that could be affected, N, Z, V, C.

77 COMPARE ACCUMULATOR A

    81   IMMEDIATE
    91   DIRECT
    B1   EXTENDED
    A1   INDEXED

    Flags that could be affected, N, Z, V, C.

78 COMPARE ACCUMULATOR B

    C1   IMMEDIATE
    D1   DIRECT
    F1   EXTENDED
    E1   INDEXED

    Flags that could be affected, N, Z, V, C.

79 COMPARE INDEX REGISTER

    8C   IMMEDIATE
    9C   DIRECT
    BC   EXTENDED
    AC   INDEXED

    Flags that could be affected, N, Z, V.

80 RETURN from INTERRUPT

    3B

81 SOFTWARE INTERRUPT

    3F

    The I flag is set to 1.

82 WAIT for INTERRUPT

    3F

    The I flag can be affected.

portion of the microprogram is forced to run by the op code, the registers and gates in the MPU follow the microprogram orders. The Instruction Set causes the MPU internal components to address the memory map in different modes, move data from place to place and process the data through the ALU.

In the next chapter the various types of ROM chips are discussed. The ROM in the MPU is usually different in makeup than the ROMs external to the MPU. The MPU's ROMs are often made up of a type called Programmable Logic Arrays, or PLAs. A PLA is a combination of two kinds of ROM: AND gate ROMs and OR gate ROMs. These are in contrast to the external ROMs that are made from rows of diodes or transistors.

When you configure a group of AND and OR gates together as in Fig. 9-15, they are capable of encoding and decoding logic signals. The PLAs use a set of AND gates as the ROM inputs and another set of OR gates as the ROM output. If you wire them up with thought you can input a set of op code bits and output a predictable set of bits that will control a circuit.

In the digital circuit, all activity is nothing more than inputting a series of highs and lows that cause certain switches to turn off and on. These switch actions then produce the addressing, data movement, and data manipulation. If you wire up a group of AND gates, they will receive the highs and lows and output a logical group of highs and lows according to the AND logic. The AND gates can accept one or more inputs.

If the AND outputs are then passed through a group of OR gates, the final outputs will then reflect the OR logic. Should strategic NOT gates be placed throughout the AND-OR configurations, ever sort of logical manipulation can be produced. In other words, if you have 75 different op-code bit combinations entered into the AND in out of the PLA, you can make the PLA OR output produce whatever control bits are needed to run the computer.

Microinstructions

In the computer's memory map, programs are stored in RAM locations in sequence. The program counter addresses the first program location and then automatically increments to address location after location, unless instructed otherwise. The automatic incrementing, driven by the clock, runs the program. The instructions of the program in RAM are often called op codes.

When the op codes of the main program arrive at the Instruction Register-Decoder of the MPU, the bits of the op code are directed to particular inputs of the decoder. For example, in Fig. 1-5, a Load Register A instruction was shown. Bit 6 is sent to a circuit that is able to open up either register A or register B. A high opens B and a low in bit 6 will enable A.

Bits 5 and 4 are sent to logic circuits that choose the addressing mode. Since there are two bits to choose with, one of four modes can be activated. Bits 3-0 are logically sent to the ALU whereby one of 16 possible ALU operations are forced to take place.

These logical actions are broken down into a series of basic steps. Each step is known as a *microoperation* in a *microinstruction*. There is no program counter to step the microprogram from one microinstruction to the next. The steps in the microprogram use logic to find the next microinstruction. Then once the logic finds the microinstruction the microoperations in the instruction can take place.

In the PLA type of ROM, Fig. 9-16, the microinstructions are stored in a wired matrix of rows and columns. Each column is reserved for one microoperation. The columns connect to the register or gates that are to be controlled. Each row then, is connected to the microoperations that will fulfill a specific microinstruction. Different combinations of microoperations will perform the specific fetching, decoding, and executing of the microinstruction assigned to the rows.

When rows are selected by the decoder, those microoperations on those rows are energized and the microinstruction takes place. For example, in Fig. 9-16, there are six input rows. There are eight columns connected to the rows. Each combination of rows shown will cause one microinstruction to take place. That means this setup has three

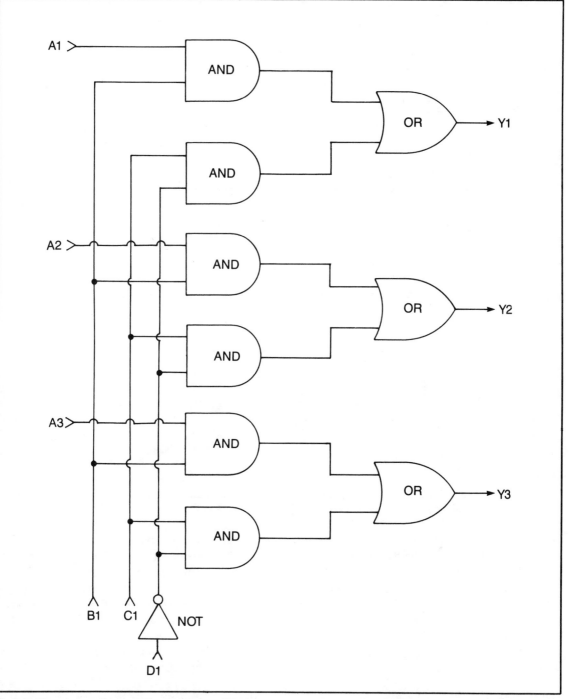

Fig.9-15. When you configure AND gate inputs to OR gate outputs and throw in some NOT gates, logic can be manipulated in many ways to encode and decode signals. This is the basis of PLA control programs built into the instruction and decoder registers in the MPU.

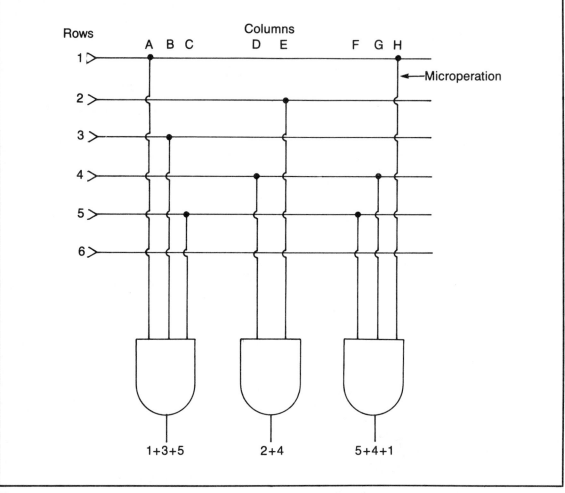

Fig. 9-16. In order for one for the AND gates to turn on, all inputs must be enabled.

microinstructions possible. All that is needed to get an operation underway is to activate the rows that the columns are connected to.

On the six rows, there are different operations connected, except for row 6 which has no connections. If row 6 is activated nothing will happen. Should row 1 be energized, then columns A and H are turned on. If row 2 is activated then column E will go on, etc.

Microaddressing

The logical addressing of the next microinstruction is accomplished in a similar way. Again there is a matrix of rows and columns, as in Fig. 9-17. The columns connect to an address register. Any microaddressing columns that are energized send a bit to its respective bit holder in the address register. For instance, there could be three columns. Three bits can address a possible eight different addresses.

The address rows are nothing more than an extension of the microinstruction rows. When a microinstruction row is activated, the address bits at the far end of the row are also turned on. Not only is the microinstruction fetched, decoded, and executed, but the next address, at the far end of the row is also sent to a microaddress register. The next address is thus part of the preceding microinstruction.

In addition to this automatic addressing mechanism, additional connections can be made to the rows from the flag bits. The highs and lows from the flags could alter the address when specific flags are thrown.

The microaddress register is in turn connected back to the decoder that is choosing the rows. The clock is also connected to the decoder. As the clock beats, the contents of the microaddress register is fed to the decoder which chooses the address of the desired row. The activated row then energizes the microoperations that it is connected to that comprise a microinstruction. The microoperations then enable or disable the registers and gates it is connected to. The microoperation thus is executed.

Attached to the far end of the enabled row is the collection of columns that represent the next microaddress. These bits go directly to the microaddress register which is connected to the decoder. The decoder then turns on the next addressed row. The procedure goes on and on till the microprogram executes the dictates of machine op code.

The preceding is a typical way that an MPU can control its own registers and gates, which in turn controls the rest of the chips in the computer. Let's examine the way a specific MPU, the Z-80 is able to perform its controlling.

Z-80 MPU

The Z-80 is a 40-pin DIP with pin 11 receiving a well regulated +5 volts from a power supply and pin 29 the ground connection. A single-phase

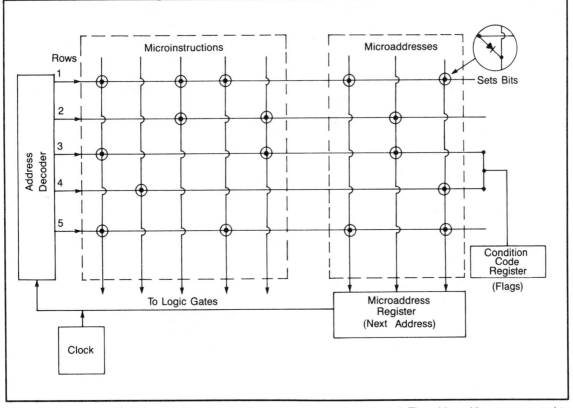

Fig. 9-17. The microaddress for the next microinstruction is automatically activated. The address bits are connected to the end of the same row as the instruction. The next address is part of the preceding instruction.

square-wave clock signal is input at pin 6. Figure 9-18 shows the pinout.

The internal address bus exits the Z-80 out of 16 pins, A15-A0. Pins 30-40 are the connections for A0-A10, and pins 1-5 permit A11-15 to let their bits out.

Each address bit has its own three-state buffer. The three-state connections are all wired together. That way the address bus can be turned off and on by the control circuitry during normal operation.

The 16 bits of the bus can form 64K different address combinations. This allows the memory map to have 64K bytes of addressable locations. The locations can consist of chips such as RAM, ROM, and I/O ports.

The Z-80 has some special I/O instructions in its Instruction Set. These instructions use address lines A7-A0 to address I/O ports. The eight bits permit you to directly address an external device with these bits. That means 1 out of 256 devices can be addressed.

The lower seven bits are able to provide one

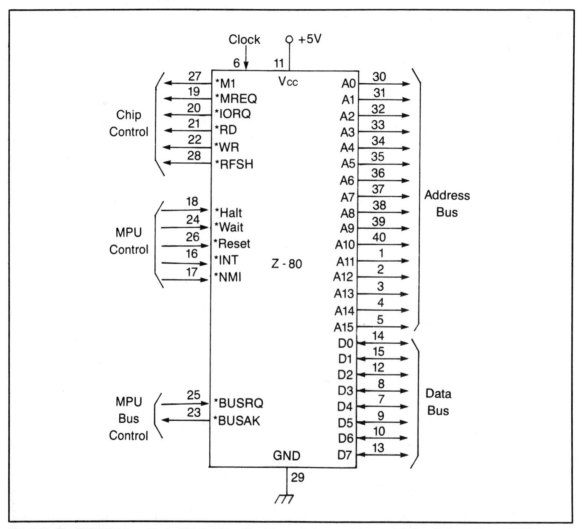

Fig. 9-18. The Z80 MPU is a 40-pin DIP that has 16 address, 8 data, and 13 control pins. Featured is a *RFSH output that permits the use of dynamic RAM without special circuits.

more duty called refreshing. If the RAM in the machine is dynamic, it needs refreshing. This is covered in Chapter 11.

The data bus, D7-D0 emerges from pins 13, 10, 9, 7, 8, 12, 15, and 14. The data bus is a two-way street and also is wired so the MPU can have three-state control. There are two buffers for each data bus line so the direction of the data flow can be controlled in addition to the three-state control.

There are six control lines that output to the rest of the computer. Pin 19 output the signal called *MREQ. This is the memory request line. When it is active, it tells the device being addressed that the address bus contains a set of bits that is valid. Note the asterisk in the front of the name. This is a notation to tell you that the line is active low. If the active signal was to be a high, then the MREQ would not have the asterisk. On some schematics, the asterisk could be replaced with a line over the MREQ. Either way, when the asterisk or line is present, the pin is typically held high when inactive and forced low when it is signalling the validity of the address bits.

Pin 20 is another three-state request line called *IORQ. It is the I/O request. It too is active when in a low state. When pin 20 is high, the line is dead.

As mentioned, the address bus is able to address a total of 256 external devices. The lower eight bits of the address bus, A7-A0, does the job. *IORQ is the line that indicates the address bus contains a valid I/O address. *IORQ goes low to give the validity signal for both reads and writes of the I/O operation.

Pin 27 is called *M1. M1 is the name of the first machine cycle in the Z-80 instruction cycle, as shown earlier in Fig. 8-6. M1 is composed of the four clock periods that drives the op code from its location in the memory map to the MPU. While this op code fetch cycle is taking place, *M1 goes low. The low can enable other circuits to concide and work with the op code fetch.

*M1 will also go low when *IORQ goes low. This *M1 low gives an interrupt signal the ability to place an interrupt vector on the data bus so an interrupt can be serviced.

Pin 21 is *RD, the three-state read line. It goes low when the MPU wants to have the memory or I/O device place the addressed data onto the data bus. Pin 22 is *WR the three-state write line. It goes low when the Z-80 puts data that it wants stored in memory or an I/O device onto the data bus.

Pin 28 is *RFSH. This line is only used with dynamic memories. Dynamic memories, you'll recall, stores highs and lows as capacitance charges. The charges however are not stable as a flip-flop state is. The charges will leak off in a few milliseconds unless they are recharged.

The recharging, or refreshing as it is called is easily done. All that is needed is to read the address. The reading refreshes the stored voltage state. *RFSH is the output signal that causes the recharging. When *RFSH goes low it signals that the lower seven bits of the address bus contains the correct refresh address and *MREQ should go low and cause the addressing to take place. There will be more about this in Chapter 11.

The last six signals all dealt with controlling the chips in the memory map that the Z-80 works with. The next five pins hold signals that control the Z-80 itself. First of all there is pin 18 *HALT. It is an output pin and performs the halt job when it goes low. When it is low, it means the Z-80 has ceased computing and is in a hold configuration. The Z-80 is performing a no operation op code. This keeps the clock working and the Z-80 in a hold pattern ready to go back to work at any time. The MPU will resume when an appropriate interrupt signal arrives.

Pin 24 is an input signal named *WAIT. When *WAIT enters the MPU with a low, it tells the MPU that the addressed location is not ready and is out of sync with the clock. The MPU will then wait till synchronization does take place and the low on *WAIT goes high.

Pin 26 is the input *RESET. When it goes low, the Z-80 stops execution. In addition, the command initializes the program counter. It goes to decimal zero. There is often a reset button on a computer that causes the low. Other computers can do without the manual reset and have an automatic circuit that will produce the low. Either way the *RESET pin will go into the reset routine when a low is input there.

The Z-80 is endowed with two interrupts. Pin 16 is *INT, and pin 17 is *NMI. The *INT is maskable. If the I flag is set, the Z-80 will not respond if a low appears on *INT. *NMI is the non-maskable interrupt. When a low arrives at pin 17, the Z-80 will go into its interrupt routine regardless of the status of the interrupt flip-flop.

The *INT low is produced by I/O devices. The Z-80 will respond to a *INT at the end of the instruction in progress if the interrupt flip-flop is clear. In addition, pin 25, the *BUSRQ, must be high. When the *INT is accepted, at the beginning of the next instruction cycle, during M1, a *IORQ low is sent out. This acknowledges the interrupt and the computing to be accomplished during the interrupt is begun.

The *NMI is always paid attention to at the end of the instruction in progress. It ignores the status of the I flip-flop. The *NMI then places the address hex 0066 on the address bus. The address that was on the program counter when the interrupt occurred is placed in the stack. That way the MPU can go back to the program that was interrupted.

The last two pins on the Z-80 are pin 25, *BUSRQ, and pin 23, *BUSAK (bus request and bus acknowledge). These are pins used when the system is being tested. *BUSRQ is an input that is normally held high. Typically it is connected to a pullup resistor from +5 volts. While it is high, it is inoperative. However, during a test it can be forced low. When it goes low, it turns off the Z-80. The address, data, and all the control lines than can go into a three-state mode. When that happens, the signal on pin 23 *BUSAK will output a low acknowledgeing that the MPU is indeed three-stating.

It was mentioned before that pin 17, *NMI, is a nonmaskable interrupt. When a low arrives at pin 17 the interrupt will take place no matter what. It can't be masked by any type of I flip-flop in the MPU. While the *NMI cannot be stopped by a mask bit, it can be overridden. If you force a low

into *BURSQ, it will have more priority than *NMI and cancel out any *NMIs that might occur during the *BUSRQ low.

Besides the clock and power inputs and the test pins, the MPU connects to the residents of memory map. At these addresses, there are only three types of devices: ROM, RAM, and I/O ports. These chips must be the types that can work with the MPU. For example, the chips that work with the Z-80 must have the following characteristics. The Z-80 has eight data lines, each able to transport a bit. Therefore, the chips connected to the data bus must have locations eight bits wide. The Z-80 has 16 address lines. There are 65,536 possible combinations of bits in 16 lines. Therefore, the chips in the system must have no more than a total of the 64K possible addresses.

When a program is stored in the locations, each byte must be arranged so that the bits are meticulously placed in their correct D7-D0 setup. D7 must hold the most significant bit and D0 the least significant bit, with the inbetween bits arranged in their correct order. Any mixup in the bit layout could ruin a program run.

When the bytes are placed into locations, the Z-80 dictates that they must be placed in the exact right order. The microprogram in the instruction decoder register will decode only correctly delivered bytes. The Z-80 is able to recognize and handle single, double, triple, and quadruple byte instructions. An instruction takes place during an instruction cycle and consists of op codes and data.

A single-byte instruction is simply eight bits of op code. A two-byte instruction is made up of eight bits of op code followed by a byte of data. The data, according to the addressing mode, can be either pure data or an address between 0 to 255.

A three-byte instruction is one byte of op code followed by two bytes of data or a two-byte address. A two-byte address is able to address the entire 64K map. The four-byte instruction consists of a two-byte op code and a two-byte data or address combination.

Chapter 10

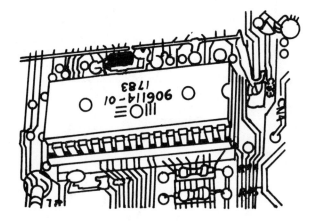

The ROM Pulls the Strings

THE MICROPROGRAM IN THE CONTROL SEC-tion of the MPU that I discussed in the last chapter is a form of ROM. The program is held in a matrix of rows and columns. Each row contains a number of diode connections to some of the columns. When an op code off the data bus is decoded by the layout of AND and OR gates the microprogram is made to run. A row is energized and the columns output a high voltage or a low voltage to gates and registers. The columns that connect to the row output are highs, and the columns that do not connect to the row output are a low. That way each row can be designed to output a particular pattern of bits that will cause the registers and gates to turn off and on in a prescribed fashion.

Each microprogram row has two connection areas (as Fig. 9-18 showed). One is an output to the data gates and registers. These connections produce the microoperations. The second connection area outputs to an address register that forms the address of the next row in the microprogram to be energized. This second area then, as part of the row

is also the addressor of the next microoperation.

The microprogram ROM therefore is continually read by the data gates and registers as well as the address register in the instruction decoder system deep in the MPU. It is a read only operation. There is no writing that takes place from any register to the stored microprogram. That is why it is called a ROM.

The other ROMs in the computer are also built around a matrix of rows and columns. Each row is also the owner of an address. Each column is also the medium by which the highs and lows are output. The difference is in the format of these individual chip ROMs. While the microprogram ROM row contains one group of bits that are microoperations and a second group of bits that are the next address to be energized, ROM chips have rows that are simply one byte wide.

The ROM chips come in many lengths though. The length is the number of byte-sized locations. The lengths are usually numbered in Ks or portions of Ks. For instance, there can be a 1K, 2K, 4K, 8K, or even a 1/4K such as 256 locations. In any case, ordinary ROMs have the same width; one byte per location.

A TYPICAL ROM

Figure 10-1 is a typical example of a 1K ROM. The internal addresses in the matrix are 0-1023. This is a matrix of 1024 rows each eight bits wide. It is said that it is organized as a 1024 × 8. It is built on a 24-pin DIP.

When this ROM begins life, it has diodes mounted on every row to every column bit position. If, at this time, any of the rows are addressed, the

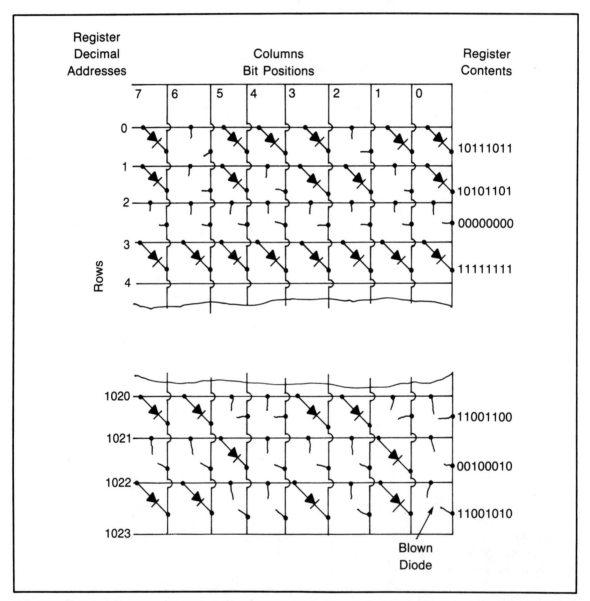

Fig. 10-1. When a program is burnt into a diode matrix, the bit positions that are to hold 0s have their diodes blown out. The position still containing diodes can output a 1.

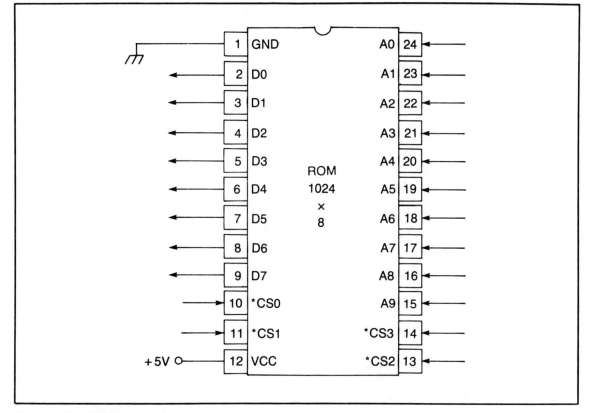

Fig. 10-2. This ROM has ten address pins to choose the internal bytes. The four CB pins also address pins, but they select the chip.

row will output 11111111, as every diode in the row will conduct.

Should you decide to install a program into the ROM, you set up your equipment and start blowing out diodes. Every position of every diode that you blow has its logic state changed from 1 to a 0. Note how the presence of a diode indicates the location of the 1s in Fig. 10-1.

Actually this type of bit-by-bit program installation is reserved for experimenters and hobbiests. In a computer factory, ROMs must be custom programmed to become operating systems, BASIC interpreters, character ROMs, and many other jobs. The manufacturer will produce a special mask for the program. Then he builds a custom chip. There will be a diode-like connection at every position that holds a 1 and no connection for the 0 positions.

The final ROM result is a chip that is connected to the address bus to receive bits that will energize a row. The chip is also connected to the data bus so that the highs and lows that are freed by the addressing can leave the ROM and travel to the MPU to perform its job.

ROM Pinout

The ROM in Fig. 10-2, has 24 pins. Ten of them are address pins. In a pattern of ten bits, the 1024 possible bit combinations will locate the desired byte. The ten bits, A9-A0 enter an internal decoder in the chip and the decoder routes the bit results to the desired matrix address.

Once the row is energized, the eight bits are sent to a three-state buffer and leave the chip by way of eight more pins. This uses up 18 pins. Two more are needed for the +5 volt source and the ground connection. That leaves four pins on the DIP. These pins are used by the chip select.

Chip Select

The memory map of a computer can contain many chips. The chip in Fig. 10-2 is a 1K type, and the ordinary 8-bit MPU is able to address 64K. This chip is going to be one of many. Also if you consider the internal addresses of this chip, it ranges from 0 to 1024. It requires ten address lines to access all the rows. The rest of the chips in the machine also have identical addresses going from zero on up. They can use the same ten address lines that this ROM does. If you address a row in this chip, unless you take measures, you could energize the same number row in a lot of other chips at the same time. This, of course, must not happen. That is why the chip select pins are there. They have to be wired so that only one row of one byte, a single address, is contacted.

The four pins in the chip select group in Fig. 10-3 are numbered *CS0, *CS1, *CS2, and *CS3. The asterisks mean that they will be enabled if a low is received by that pin. On the inside of the chip, the four pins are connected to an AND gate. Between each gate connection and the pins are NOT circles. Therefore, if four lows enter the pins, the NOT circles will invert them to four highs. The four highs into the AND gate logically produces an output high.

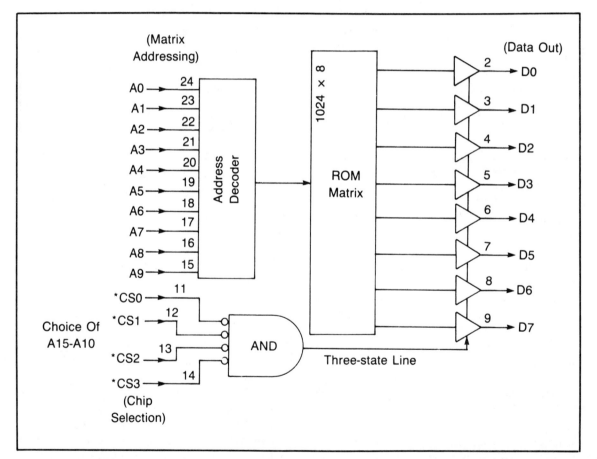

Fig. 10-3. The ten address pins connect to the address decoder that leads to the ROM's matrix. The four chip select pins are input to an AND gate. The gate turns the output buffers on and off. When the buffers are turned on, the chip is selected. If the buffers are turned off, the chip is not selected.

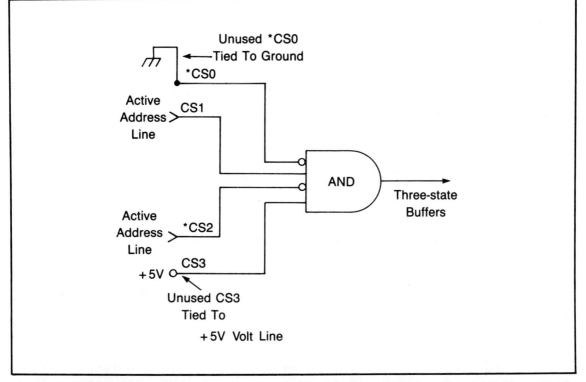

Fig. 10-4. An unused *CS pin can be connected to ground so that it is always enabled and does not interfere with chip selection. An unused CS pin can be attached to +5 volts to keep it always enabled. The chip select pins connected to address lines will then choose the chip to be accessed.

The output of the AND gate connects to the eight three-state output buffers. When the high appears from the AND gate, the buffers turn on. The chip is the chosen one. Should the AND gate output a low, the buffers will three-state and the chip remains inert.

Therefore, the four lows at the input pins will chose the chip. Any other combination of the four bits will not choose the chip. The four bits are able to choose from among 16 chips with this arrangement.

These four bits are coming from the address bus. They could possibly be any of the remaining bus lines, from A15-A10, not otherwise attached to the ROM.

If a chip select line does not have an asterisk then it is a positive CS. It will need a high in order to be enabled. When excess chip select lines are not needed in a system but are present on a chip,

they cannot be ignored. They must be rendered helpless. Figure 10-4 shows how this can be done. Positive CS lines are connected to +5 volts. This keeps the line on continually. In the same way, when a negative *CS line is not used, it is connected to a low or ground. That way it is kept on all the time and won't get in the way.

ROM Programs

The ROM program is wired in. It is part of the chip. Under most circumstances it cannot be changed. The most obvious use of the ROM is to give the computer some intelligence when you first turn it on. Otherwise, the computer is helpless. It must have enough brains to be able to either allow you to load memory from the keyboard or a storage area like the cassette.

The MPU, RAM, and I/O chips are poor, dumb brutes that can only respond to intelligently

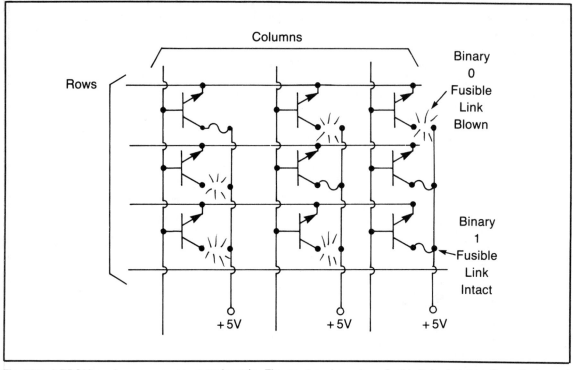

Columns

Rows

Binary
0
Fusible
Link
Blown

Binary
1
Fusible
Link
Intact

+5V   +5V   +5V

Fig. 10-5. A PROM can have an npn connected matrix. The npn transistors have fusible links between the collector and the +5 volt source. When the link is attached, the npn can conduct and output a 1 from that column. If the link is blown, the npn is open and outputs a 0.

directed high and low voltages. It is up to humans to deliver up the voltages to run the computer. Humans write the programs of bytes. The first program the computer needs is a *bootstrap*. The bootstrap is a program that will arrange the computer's chips so that a larger monitor program that can really take over control of the computing can be loaded into RAM. A typical bootstrap will have just enough bytes so that a cassette tape can be loaded. Once the cassette tape program is in RAM, the computing can get underway.

Lots of computers use a ROM as a bootstrap. The ROM can be as limited as 64 bytes. The ROM must be wired so that it runs immediately after the computer is powered up. It can execute as a result of the incoming voltage rise from zero to +5 volts, or it can be activated by pressing a button like the reset. Either way, the bootstrap will start working and either arrange a keyboard loading ability or a cassette tape load facility. That way, you can get

a monitor into RAM so you can start computing.

A better way, with a bit more expense, is to use a mask-programmable ROM that is manufactured for the computer. This is a ROM that is made by the computer manufacturer expressly for its own product. It is made in quantity just like any other chip. It will contain the bootstrap program and the monitor. In the machine, it runs automatically when you turn on the computer. It quickly takes over and allows you to start right off with computing and not give the housekeeping details a thought.

ROMS, PROMS, AND EPROMS

The ROM is usually thought of as memory chip that is produced in production for a particular computer. They are built in the same permanent way the MPU or any dedicated chip is. The program, while laid out with rows and columns, can only be read out of the chip. It cannot be written to because there are no storage facilities such as flip-flops or handy capacitances. If a diode matrix is used, diodes are built in where the bit position calls for a 1. The bit position for the 0 is left open. There is no need to bother installing diodes and then going to the trouble of blowing them out. A mask is used to construct and program the ROM. The finished product cannot be altered.

The PROM, programmable read only memory, is a chip that you can program. If you write a machine-language program in hex it is easy to convert it into binary, one hex character per four binary bits. Once you have your finished program in bytes, they can be installed onto a PROM. However, once installed that is it. The PROM can only be written once and it becomes permanent.

A typical PROM uses bipolar transistors to connect the rows to the columns. This arrangement is shown in Fig. 10-5. The transistors are built with a fusible link. When you install your program, you blow out the fusible link with an electric pulse at every bit position that you want a 0 to reside. The

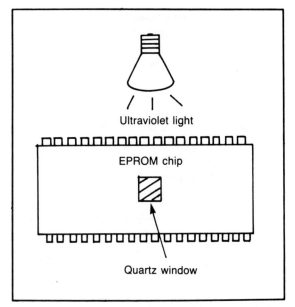

Fig. 10-6. If ultraviolet light shines through a quartz window onto charged FET bit positions, the charge will gradually leak off.

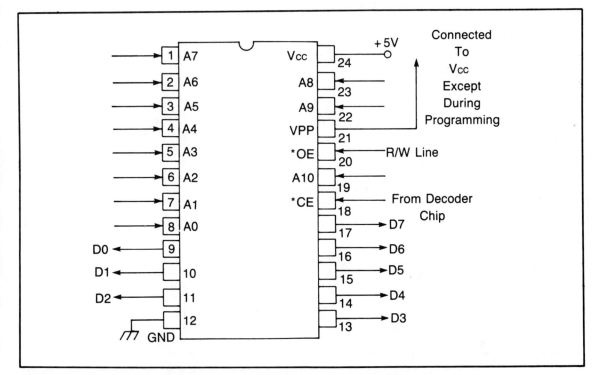

Fig. 10-7. The 2716 UV Erasable PROM only has one chip select pin, *CE. In order to select this chip from among many chips, a decoder chip must handle the chip selection. A low from the decoder will turn on the 2716.

transistor connection automatically provides a 1 at the bit positions that are intact.

The PROM is strictly a ROM that is programmed by the user. Once it is made, it becomes a permanent chip. If a mistake is made in the programming there is no way to correct it.

The EPROM is the erasable-programmable read only memory. It is like the PROM except for the feature of erasing. It can be used over and over again. It arrives without any program on it. The common EPROM uses p-channel FETs in the bit positions. The gate glassy insulator is built to com-pletely encase the gate electrode. This makes the gate without any direct connection and it is said to be floating. In fact these EPROMS are called, floating-gate avalanche injection MOS storage devices.

If you apply a 25 volt charge on a bit position where a gate resides, the gate will charge up. When the gate charges, it will then hold that charge for years. If a gate is charged, it is said to be in one logic state, and if uncharged it is in the opposite state. The 1s and 0s are derived from the two different states.

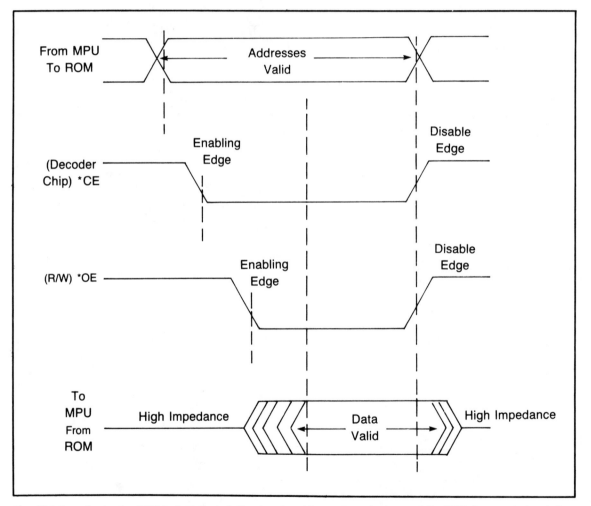

Fig. 10-8. In order for the 2716 to be selected, the decoder chip must send a low and the R/W line must also deliver a low. Then the address bits in the bus will be valid for the 2716. Valid data will then emerge from the addressed location and proceed to the MPU.

To erase the program, the chip is exposed to concentrated ultraviolet light. Refer to Fig. 10-6. A quartz window is built directly over the chip. The light passes through the window and lands on the bit positions. Those with a charge gradually discharge through the silicon dioxide insulator. The program then disappears and the chip can be used again.

READING A ROM

Whether a ROM is loaded with data by a mask process in the factory, by having fusible links blown, or by having FET gates charged up, it is still a read-only type memory chip, and the MPU reads them all in the same way. For an example ROM, I have chosen the 2716 EPROM. It is a 24-pin DIP.

The pinout shows 11 address inputs, A10-A0. They are connected to A10-A0 of the address bus. Eleven address lines can form 2048 combinations of bits. The lines are able to address 2K bytes. It is a 2K byte ROM. Incidentally, the 2048 bytes consists of 16,384 individual bits. As a result, the chip is sometimes called a 16K. When it is, the bits are being referred to, not the bytes.

There are two chip select pins on the chip. One is called *CE for chip enable. The second is *OE, for output enable. As the asterisk indicates, both enables must be low in order for the chip to place the addressed data onto the data bus.

The *CE pin can be tied into one or more of the higher address lines. If the MPU has to select from among a number of chips, the *CE pin will be connected to the output of a decoder chip that is connected to a number of the higher address lines as Fig. 10-7 shows.

*OE is not usually connected to an address line. It is often enabled by a read/write-type line. A 6800 type MPU will connect *OE to its R/W line. When the 6800 is in a read mode, *OE is brought low. Otherwise, it stays high. With a Z-80, *OE is connected to the *RD line. In those ways, the 2716 will not be selected unless both *CE and *OE are both forced low.

The 2716 is built in a few different models. The main reason for the variety is the access timings. A fast 2716 can be accessed in 350 ns. A slow one takes 650 ns. The complete read access must take place during the read cycle of the MPU.

The first signals that the MPU sends out over the bus lines are the address bits. The bits arrive at all the chips in the memory map. When the MPU is reading the 2716 specifically, the higher address bits are decoded and a low arrives at *CE from the decoder. Immediately after the low connects to *CE, a second low arrives at *OE over the read/write line.

The 2716 is activated by the two chip-select lows and allows the 11 address bits into the decoder inside the 2716. The decoder chooses the correct location that is to be read. Refer again to Fig. 10-3. The byte of data is then sent to the output buffers and placed onto the data bus.

The data is valid from just after the time *OE is enabled until *CE, *OE, and the address bits are disabled as their signals change states. The data inputs at the D7-D0 pins of the MPU.

During write operations the 2716 is shut down by the prevailing highs that are kept at the *CE and *OE pins. The 2716 therefore can only be read and never written to.

Chapter 11

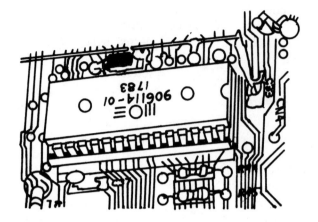

The RAM Storage Areas

T HE NAME RAM WHICH STANDS FOR RANDOM access memory is misleading since ROM also can be accessed in a random fashion. A more descriptive title is read/write memory in contrast to ROM which is read only memory.

RAM is temporary storage for bits and bytes of op codes and data. Ordinary RAM can only store bits when it is powered. As soon as power is stopped, the bits in storage evaporate. It doesn't take long either, as you have probably learned to your dismay. A flicker of the lights and your RAM can be emptied of all data.

RAM typically is made of one of two circuits. First there is the so called *static RAM* which consists of rows and rows of flip-flops connected together. The FFs are quite stable and will store highs or lows as long as the dc voltage is applied at the voltage pin.

The FF type RAM is useful in applications where small amounts of memory are required by the computer. The circuitry takes up relatively large amounts of chip area. If a lot of memory is

needed the static RAM becomes prohibitively expensive.

The *dynamic RAM* does not resemble static hardly at all. The high or low bits are held in a capacitance that is formed between the gate and substrate of a FET. The highs are difficult to store. The charge continually leaks out of the capacitance. The charge becomes worthless after a couple milliseconds or so. The highs must be continually recharged faster than it can leak off. Fortunately all that is needed to refresh the highs is for the MPU to read the addresses in RAM. This refreshing is discussed in more detail later in the chapter.

STATIC RAM

A typical small static RAM chip is layed out quite like a ROM. The chip is read almost exactly the same way that a ROM is read. The major difference, of course, is the RAM can also be written to. A read/write control line is used for that end.

The R/W line originates at the MPU and is input to a pin on the RAM chip.

On the 24-pin DIP chip in Fig. 11-1, there are the usual +5 volt and ground lines, the eight connections to the data bus, D7-D0, the address lines, and the chip select pins. This chip has a matrix of 128 × 8 so only seven address lines are needed. Seven lines are able to form 128 bit combinations to address any byte in the matrix.

There are six chip select pins: two positive and four negative. The two positive pins, CS0 and CS3 will be enabled only with highs. The remaining four negative *CS pins must have lows to turn on.

The block diagram in Fig. 11-2 shows that inside the chip the circuits resemble a ROM with a few changes. The address lines are still one way in and arrive at the RAMs decoder. The seven lines are decoded into a single matrix address from 0 to 127 and are fed to the matrix.

Meanwhile, down at the chip select entrances, the six chip select voltages are input. They all lead to a six input AND gate. For the chip to be selected, all six inputs must be made correctly. Note the six

NOT circles at the AND inputs. They will invert all the inputs. Therefore if six lows are input to the NOT circles they will be inverted, become highs and cause the AND to output a high.

Four of the chip select are *CS, so lows at those inputs will properly do their part to select the chip. However, two pins CS0 and CS3 are positive inputs. They indicate that they must receive highs to aid in the chip select. Note that both CS0 and CS3 inputs to the AND gate have two full-fledged NOT gates. They are the means by which a high at the positive inputs are able to be inverted to become a low at the NOT circle. They invert again to be a high and enable the AND gate.

Read/Write Control

If you'll notice, the memory matrix has two-way lines connecting it to the three-state buffers that connect to the two-way data bus. Both the matrix and the buffers are able to send data either out to the bus or receive data from the bus. They are controlled by a special control circuit.

The control circuit has one input from the chip

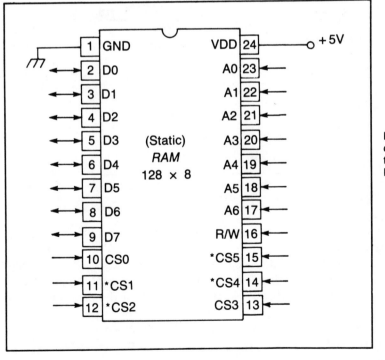

Fig. 11-1. A typical static RAM chip looks quite like the ROM, except it can be written to as well as being read. Note the R/W line.

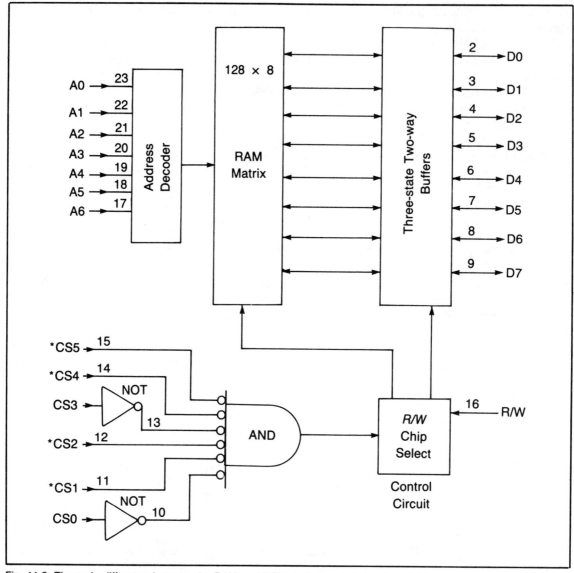

Fig. 11-2. The main difference between the RAM and ROM is the control circuit and the two-way buffers. The control circuit not only controls the buffers, but it also changes the data flow direction with the aid of the R/W line.

select AND gate. The circuit has a second input from the R/W line. When the RAM is addressed and the six chip select lines all have the correct state, the matrix is addressed and the AND gate outputs a high. The AND high is input to the control circuits.

If the MPU wants a read of the RAM, it sends a high out over the R/W line. The two highs into

the control circuit sends a signal to buffers in both the matrix area and the three-state lines. The two highs enable the output sections. A copy of whatever eight bits are in the addressed location will exit the RAM and be placed on the data bus. From there, it speeds to the MPU.

Should the MPU want to write to the RAM the addressing and chip selection takes place in the same way. Only the R/W signal is changed. The MPU sends a low to the RAM. The low finds its way to the control circuit. The control thus still has a high from the AND gate but now has a low from the R/W line. This change in signal changes the output of the control circuit. The high and the low cause the matrix buffers and the three-state buffers to change direction.

Meanwhile the MPU has placed bits on the data bus. When the RAM buffers open to the data bus, the bits swiftly enter and file into the addressed location in the matrix.

The only other thing that can happen to the RAM chip is at the times when it is not addressed. When that happens, the buffers three-state, and the chip lies still in a high impedance state.

2114 RAM

The preceding example RAM with only 128 bytes of storage is used in some dedicated applications but not usually in a more general-type computer. One static RAM with more memory capacity is the 2114L chip. It has 4096 static bits but is organized in a 1024 × 4 bit layout. Four bits are a nybble and usually bytes are needed for convenient computing. Designers therefore will take two

2114Ls and wire them together to form a 1024 × 8 arrangement.

The 2114L shown in Fig. 11-3 is an 18-pin DIP. It has ten address lines, A9-A0. They can address the 1024 byte-size locations on the two chips. There is one chip select and a read/write input. Note the four two-directional data pins on each chip. They are I/O1 through I/O4.

These are the pins that connect to the data bus, D7-D0. Since two nybble chips are going to form one byte location, one of the chips has its I/O1-I/O4 connected to data bus lines D0-D3, and the second chip connects its I/O1-I/O4 pins to bus lines D4-D7. That way, a byte at a time can be sent to the chips or received from them. Figure 10-4 shows how two 2114s would be wired together.

The rest of the pins, the address, chip select, R/W and power are all connected in parallel. When the chip pair is addressed, the same location on both chips must be opened up at the same time. Both chips must be selected together. They must simultaneously receive a read or write. The two chips are wired as one except for the I/O lines.

Timing

There are separate timing sequences for both the read and the write accessing of the chip. Figure 11-5 illustrates them. All of the signals are coming from the MPU. All the 2114L does is respond to the incoming signals. Both the read and write cycle times for the chip are 450 ns each. This must be the addressing time from the MPU.

During a read, the first signal that arrives at the chip is the 10 address bits A9-A0 to locate the desired address number. Immediately after the address bits show up, the *CS line goes low. It is held low for a period of 120 ns. *WE is held high by the R/W line. This causes the three-state output buffers to go on and open up the connections to the data bus.

The data in the addressed location then sends a copy of itself out over the data bus. *CS then goes high and the address changes in preparation for the next operation. The data, which is safe in the data bus, flashes over to the input at the MPU.

For the write operation, the accessing again

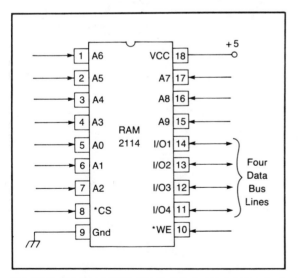

Fig. 11-3. The 2114 RAM chip is able to store and output a nybble of data. Note the four I/O lines. They connect to four of the data bus lines.

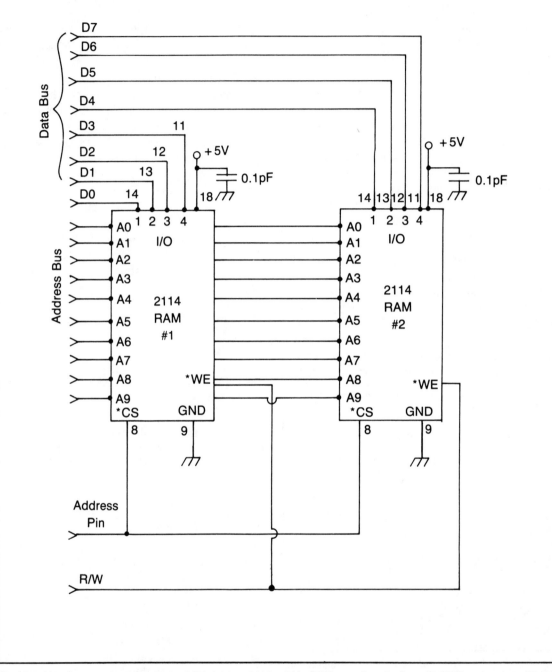

Fig. 11-4. In order to store and output a full byte, two 2114 nybble RAMs can be wired up. #1 RAM connects to D3-D0 and #2 RAM to D7-D4 data bus lines.

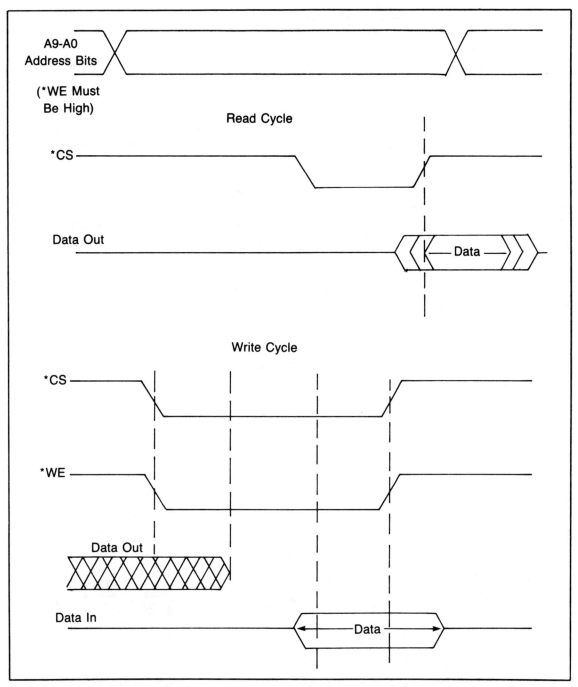

Fig. 11-5. The 2114 has timing requirements for both reads and writes. When it is being read, the *CS line is made to go low. While *CS is low, the *WE line must remain held high. The address bits A9-A0 will then locate the needed nybble and place the data onto the data bus. When the 2114 is begin written to, *CS again goes low. However, *WE, which is controlled by the R/W line from the MPU, is also forced low. Then as the address bits energize the nybble location, the bits from the data bus can enter and take up their logic positions.

begins as the address bits A9-A0 becomes stable. Shortly thereafter, *CS and *WE are both forced low. They must be held low for 200 ns. During that time, they cause the output buffers to go on, but the data direction is changed. Data will be coming from the MPU to be stored in the location that is accessed.

The data arrives over the data bus sometime in the middle of *CS and *WE low periods. The data enters the chip, passes through the buffers, and is stored in the accessed address.

When the data bits take up residence in the flip-flops, they are stored in a very stable fashion. The FFs will maintain the logic state as long as the power stays on. Refer to Fig. 11-6. The only way the state of the bits in the location can be changed is if you write different bits into the location. Then the old bits will be destroyed and the new ones take up occupancy. When you read a location the bits

remain intact. The read results are only a copy of what is in the bit holders.

DYNAMIC RAM

The static RAM just covered are MOS chips. They have n-channel FETs that are wired up as flip-flops as shown in Fig. 11-6. They are directly compatible with TTL bipolar chips though, so there is no concern about the construction. The dynamic RAM are also n-channel MOS chips. They also use FETs, but the result is not FFs.

Figure 11-7 shows a couple of typical dynamic RAM bit holders. The clock is two phase on the order of the ones used in a 6800 or 6502 MPU. The $\phi1$ clock connects to the tied together gates of the first stage. The $\phi2$ clock is attached to the connected gates of the second stage. $-VDD$ powers both stages through the drains of the top FETs.

These stages are each an inverter and a coupler

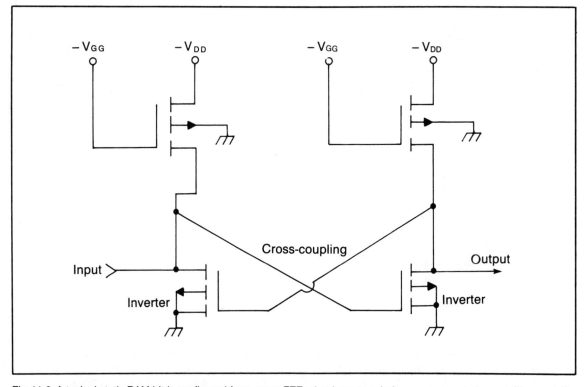

Fig. 11-6. A typical static RAM bit is configured from some FETs that have two drains cross-coupled over to the opposite gates. It will store a logic state as one FET will saturate and the other FET will cut off. If is able to flip-flop when appropriate states are input.

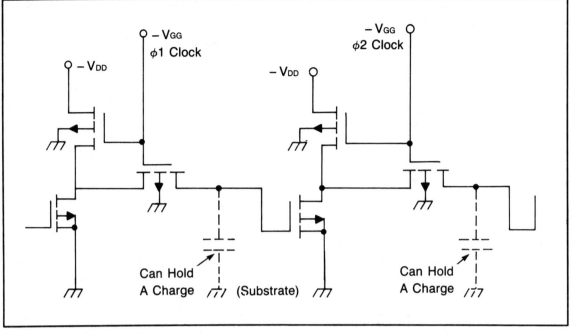

Fig. 11-7. A dynamic RAM bit is an FET signal coupling circuit that has a built in capacitance between the gate and substrate. When the capacitance is charged, the logic state produced is a 1. If the capacitance does not get charged, the logic state is a 0. A problem exists because the charge leaks out of the capacitance quickly, unless it is refreshed.

to the next stage. The gates of the inverters have a certain amount of capacitance from the gate to the substrate. The glassy insulator is installed there and acts as a dielectric. This capacitance is able to store a charge.

This charge can be read as a high or low. The charge can be shifted to the next stage. The charge can be replaced by another charge if it is written to. In short, it is a bit holder and a shift register. These are the qualities a RAM bit must possess.

The only problem is that the bits must be operated with a clock frequency. The capacitances leak and the charge will be lost if not refreshed. Other than the problem, the dynamic forms of RAM are far superior to static. The dynamic bit holders are much smaller than their static counterparts and many, many more bits can be placed on the dynamic chips. When large quantities of memory are required, the dynamic chips are usually first choice.

The 4116 chip has been the standard dynamic RAM chip for a number of years. A set of eight

chips produces 16K bytes of RAM. In the last couple of years, the 4164 chip has been replacing the 4116. As the numbers in the name indicates, a set of eight 4164s will produce 64K bytes of memory. Recently, the 41256 chips have been readily available for sale by suppliers. Eight 41256 chips will provide 256K of memory. A set of eight 411024 chips will provide a computer with 1024K bytes of RAM.

All of these chips use a similar layout for their matrix. The bit holders in a 4116 are placed into a square on the silicon. There are 128 rows of bits and 128 columns in the rows. Refer to Fig. 11-8. 128 × 128 totals 16,384 bits on a chip. A set of eight chips will provide 16,384 bytes of RAM, or 16K bytes of RAM. They can be obtained with access times of 150 ns, 200 ns, and 300 ns.

Once manufacturers solved the problem of producing the 4116 chips, they went after a chip with more bit density. They devised a new layout of 256 × 256 bits on the chip. This doubling of the rows and columns quadrupled the number of bits (256

× 256 = 65,536 bits in density). From there, they went after even more density. They doubled the row and column once again to 512 (512 × 512 bits totals 262,144 or 256K). The next obvious step is to double the rows and columns once again to 1024 × 1024 on the chip. This result is 1,048,576 bits or 1024K. This is the million bit chip.

All of these chips operate in a similar way. Let's examine a 16K chip set that provides 16K bytes of RAM for a computer.

Matrix or Memory Array

The 4116 chip is organized as 16,384 × 1. Each of the 16K bits has its own individual address. That way a set of eight chips all have the same 16K addresses. Each byte of memory has the bits that make up the byte spread out over eight chips. Each chip is designated a number in the set. The chips are numbered from #7 to #0. In the bytes, all of the bit-position 7s are on chip #7. All number 6 bits are on chip #6, and so on. Refer to Fig. 11-9.

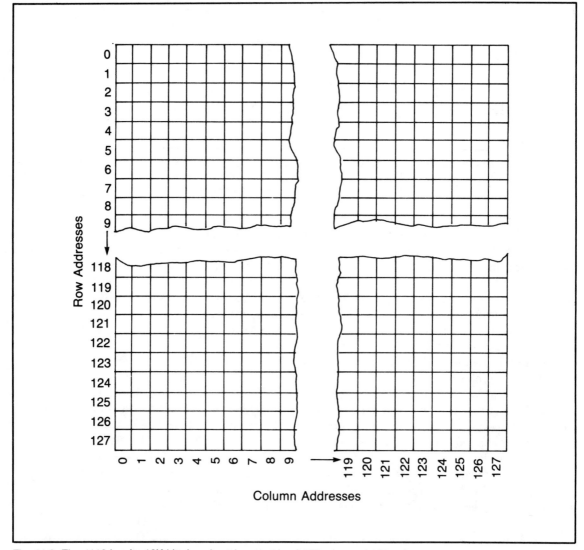

Fig. 11-8. The 4116 has its 16K bits layed out in a matrix of 128 rows and 128 columns.

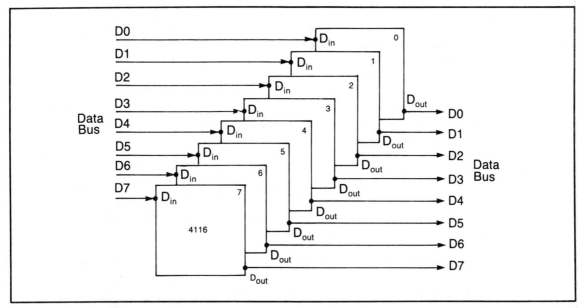

Fig. 11-9. Since the dynamic RAM is organized in bits, it only needs to input and output one bit at a time. Each RAM chip in a set of eight is connected to one of the eight data bus lines.

Each chip has one input pin, D_{in}, and one output pin, D_{out}. Typically the pins are tied together and connected to one data bus line. Chip #7 is connected to D7, chip #6 to D6, and so on till chip #0 attaches to D0. When a location is addressed, eight bits on eight chips are simultaneously addressed. If the operation is a read, then one bit from each chip, which comprises a byte, leaves the RAM set and goes to the MPU. During a write, eight bits from the MPU traverse the data bus. The eight bits are distributed, one bit to a chip, each bit going to its respective position.

Block Diagram

The 4116 is a 16-pin DIP. A pinout appears in Fig. 11-10. There are FETs in the memory array. They require their own power. Pins 8 and 16 provide VDD and VSS. Bipolar transistors are used in the control circuits. Pins 9 and 1 provide VCC and VBB. That leaves a dozen pins. Pin 2 D_{in}, and pin 14 is D_{out}.

The remaining ten pins use seven for addressing, two for strobes, and one as a read/write line. They are tricky.

First of all there are only seven address lines. To address 16K locations, 14 address lines are required. This situation is handled by splitting the address chore into two sections. Refer to Fig. 11-11.

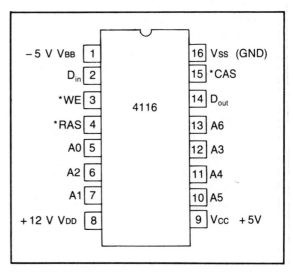

Fig. 11-10. The 4116 dynamic RAM chip has been the standard for a number of the early microcomputer years. Typically, they are arranged in sets of eight to produce a bank of 16K bytes.

197

This is called *multiplexing*. The seven address lines are going to address each chip in two segments. First the lines are going to carry address bits A7-A0. Then after these lower seven bits are delivered, the lines will then conduct bits A13-A8. The timing is very precise as the timing diagram in Fig. 11-12 shows. The gating for the *RAS, *CAS, and *WE is shown in Fig. 11-13.

Pin 3, the *WE line, performs the read/write job. *WE holds high as long as read operations are taking place. It goes low for the write operation. The *WE line connects internally to the Data In latch. A high on the line keeps the latch shut so the MPU can read the chips without any interruptions. A low into the latch opens it up so the MPU may write data into the memory locations.

The two signals *RAS and *CAS do the following. When the A6-A0 bits arrive at the address pins of the chip, *RAS goes low. *RAS is in control of a latch called the row address latch. This latch is the first circuit the low address pins run into. When *RAS goes low, it opens up the latch. The address bits are allowed to pass and are then ushered into a row address decoder.

Shortly thereafter, the lower address bits arrive at their decoder, and the higher bits, A13-A7, arrive on the multiplexed address lines. They run into a circuit called the column address latch. At that instant, the *CAS line goes low. It controls the column address latch. The latch opens and the

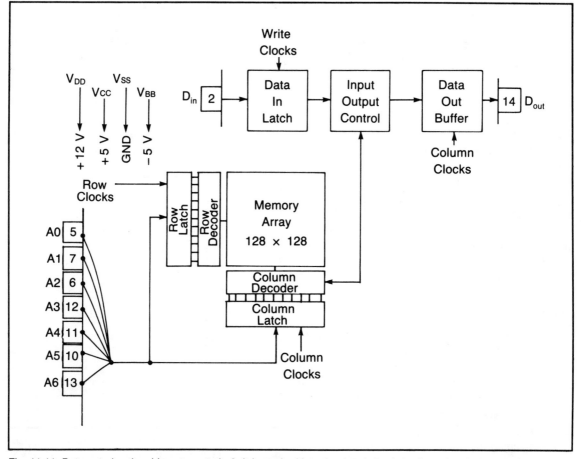

Fig. 11-11. Data entering the chip enters at pin 2. It is strobed into the data in latch by the write clock. Data leaving the chip exists at pin 14 through the data out buffer.

198

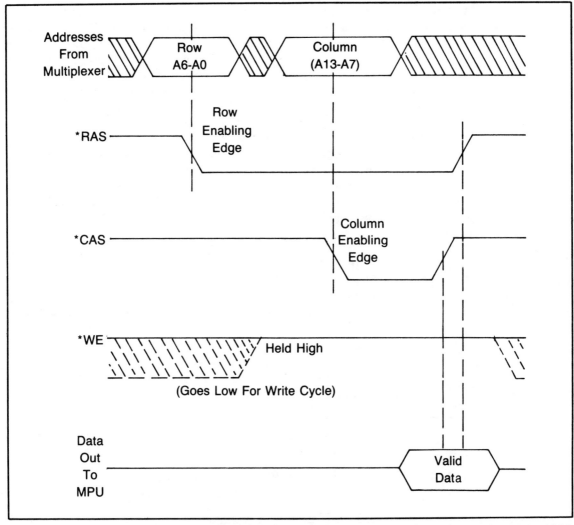

Fig. 11-12. During a 4116 Read Cycle, *RAS goes low and strobes the row addresses into the chip first. Next, *CAS goes low and strobes the column addresses into the same pins *RAS has just passed through. In the matrix, the addressed row and column intersect and output a copy of the contents of the bit selected.

higher bits pass through the latch into the column decoder.

From the row decoder the seven lower bits then address the 128 rows in the matrix. They choose one of the 128 rows and turn it on. Shortly thereafter, the seven higher bits from the column decoder address the 128 columns in the matrix. They choose one of the 128 columns and turn it on.

With one row on and one column on, they coincide at one location. This is the single bit out of the entire 16K that the address wants to open up. The same set of circumstances takes place in all eight chips in the set at the same time. As a result, a complete byte of bits has been contacted.

If the MPU is reading the RAM location, then *WE will be high. The D_{in} pin will be disabled. The D_{out} pin receives a copy of the addressed bit through the output buffer. *RAS and *CAS remain low till the data state clears the buffer stage and is out on the data bus line.

199

When the MPU is writing data to RAM, the *WE is made to go low. This opens up the D_{in} latch and the bit is stored into a memory location.

Refreshments

When a location is read by the intersecting of the row and column addressing, the capacitance holding the charge is rocked somewhat. The read operation lowers the stored charge. During a read the charge is not supposed to be lost, so measures must be taken so the charge will return to normal. In addition, the charge will simply leak out of the capacitance over time even if it isn't read. All the bits in all the chips, therefore, must be continually recharged. At first glance, it looks like a very trying job.

The charge will leak out of the 4116 in about two milliseconds. In newer higher density chips, that timing has been delayed, so it is easier. In 4164 chips, the leaking of the charge takes about three and a half milliseconds, almost twice as much. However the leaking situation must be handled or else it will ruin the computing.

In a 4116 RAM set, there are 16K locations. The locations are found by addressing rows and col-umns. It works out that you can refresh any location by simply addressing its row. The columns can be ignored. If you address any row you will automatically refresh all 128 columns on that row. In addition, if you address the 128 rows on one chip, all eight chips will be refreshed at the same time. The addresses on all eight chips are identical and are simultaneously contacted when a byte is read or written to.

Therefore, it is not necessary to address all 16K of addresses every two milliseconds. The requirement is only 128 row locations every two ms. There are 1000 microseconds in each millisecond. There are 1000 nanoseconds in each microsecond. A typical MPU running at 1 MHz can address one location in one microsecond. As you can see, there is plenty of time to address 128 rows before the charge on the capacitors leak off.

The 4116 is easily recharged with one location addressed every 16 microseconds. The refresh addresses are distributed throughout the two millisecond period. When seven bits are placed on the address bus and the *RAS signal (row address strobe) is brought low, one out of 128 rows is addressed and recharged. All 128 columns on that row

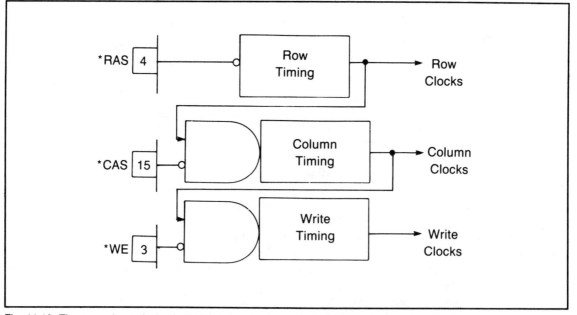

Fig. 11-13. There are three clocks that drive a dynamic RAM chip: *RAS, *CAS, and *WE.

200

on all eight chips receive the refreshment at the same time.

This row refreshing must not take place in such a way that any locations are actually accessed. The performance is only to refresh and nothing else. In addition, the refreshing must not take place while actual accessing is going on. As a result, refreshing operations are timed to take place while the processor is doing other jobs and not while it is addressing locations.

In the Z-80, the op-code fetch cycle takes four clock periods to make the fetch. The address of the location that is being accessed is placed on the address bus by the program counter during the first two clocks. Then the *MREQ, and *RD, and the *M1 signals are brought low. The op code in the location then emerges onto the data bus and heads toward the MPU.

As the third clock takes place, all those signals go high and shut down. The *RFSH signal that had been held high during the first two clocks then goes low. Refer to Fig. 11-14. At the same time, a refresh register (a special register in the Z-80) outputs a 7-bit address onto the address bus. The address takes place during the third and fourth clock of the op code fetch. The signal, along with the low from *RFSH, is sent to the dynamic RAM and recharges one of the 128 rows.

The Z-80 has a special memory refresh register that has no other job but to supply refresh addresses during the third and fourth clocks of the

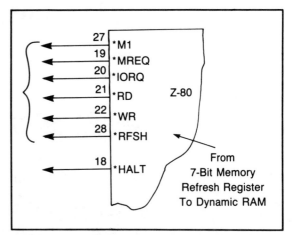

Fig. 11-14. The Z80 has a special memory refresh register that does nothing else but supply row refresh addresses during the third and fourth clocks of the op code fetch cycle.

op code fetch cycle. The register automatically increments after every op code fetch cycle. That way it keeps counting from 0 through 127 and continually steps through the 128 row addresses.

The Z-80 is the only common MPU that has a special refresh circuit. Others, like the 6502 and 6800, do not. When MPUs without refreshing circuits use dynamic memory, a refresh circuit must be supplied in the computer. This can be an expense. However the advantages of the dynamic RAM over static RAM when large amounts of memory are needed far outweighs the refresh inconvenience and cost.

Chapter 12

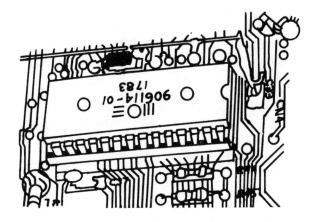

Digital Portholes

I N CHAPTER 5, THE DIGITAL-TO-ANALOG AND analog-to-digital circuits were discussed. They took analog signals from the outside world and gave them digital stature. They also took digital signals from inside the computer and converted them back to analog. All that is well and good, but what about the digital signals in the outside world that are to be placed into the digital world and the processed digital signals that have to be sent back out the outside world and still retain their digital characteristics.

For example, the keyboard is a digital device. A key is either struck or it is not. There are no in-betweens. It either shorts its row-column position, or it leaves the position open. This digital signal must be input to the digital circuits. How about the ASCII signal from memory that must be output to a printer? The ASCII bits are digital and the printer accepts them in that way. It translates the ASCII to the physical printing, but that is another matter. The computer to printer transmission is digital-to-digital. These types of digital-to-digital inputs and

outputs all must pass through special ports in order to do their job. Refer to Fig. 12-1.

Typically there are two kinds of interfaces that act as digital-to-digital ports. One is serial, and the other is parallel. Each type has its advantages and disadvantages.

SERIAL DATA MOVEMENT

The digital action between the MPU and memory is mostly done with parallel bus lines. The address bus in the 8-bit computer uses 16 lines to carry 16 bits simultaneously. The data bus sends the data back and forth eight bits abreast. Only the control lines move one high or low to enable or disable a chip function.

The data, though, is the only bit set that comes from outside or leaves the computer to the outside. The address bits and control signals never leave the computer.

The data, then, is always in parallel form inside the computer. In order to enter or leave serially, it follows that the data must be converted. Serial

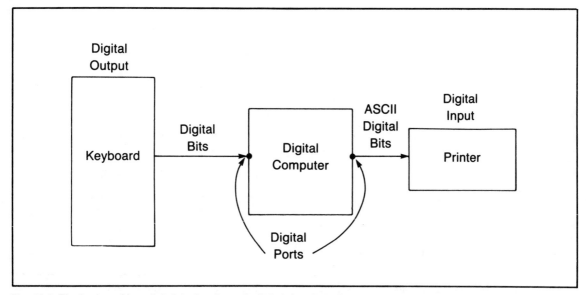

Fig. 12-1. The keyboard is a digital device. It sends digital signals to the computer through a digital port. After the computer processes the input, it in turn, sends digital code out to the external printer through a digital port.

inputs have to be converted to parallel form and parallel outputs must be lined up serially. There are two types of chips that specialize in converting serial to parallel and parallel to serial for input/output jobs. One is called an ACIA for asynchronous communications interface adapter. The other is the UART, for universal asynchronous receiver transmitter. They are both large chips. The ACIA is often packaged with 24 pins, and the UART can have 40 pins. They connect to the data bus and are addressed and controlled by the MPU.

The advantage of transmitting data outside of the computer over a single line rather than eight is obvious. Inside the machine the distance between any two chips cannot be further than the length of the print board. Outside the computer, data might have to travel 30 feet across the room, or even to the moon and planets. It is much easier to send the data over one line than eight.

When serial data is input to the computer it is sent bit-by-bit to the adapter chip. Generally, the adapter accepts the bits in a shift register as in Fig. 12-2. The bits are marching in a line in groups of bytes. Bit 0 enters the register at bit position 7. Next bit 1 enters and the register shifts bit 0 to bit position 6. Then bit 2 enters and the register shifts

bits 0 and 1 to positions 5 and 6. The input of the byte continues until the complete byte has entered the register, the shifting finally put bit 0 into position 0, bit 1 into position 1, and so on until bit 7 is in position 7.

Once the full byte is in the register, the chip output can take place. While the register has one input into bit position 7, it has eight outputs into the data bus D7-D0. The input is serial but the output is parallel. The register then outputs the entire byte at one time onto the data bus. That is the serial-to-parallel conversion technique.

To accomplish the parallel-to-serial conversion, opposite events take place. The MPU places the parallel data onto D7-D0, and it is written into an output shift register as in Fig. 12-3. The register then outputs the bits one at a time from bit position 0. The bits are all shifted out into the single serial line to the external device.

Asynchronous Data Transfer

If you'll notice, the ACIA and the UART have the word asynchronous common in their names. This is in contrast to the word synchronous. These terms deal with the way the data is timed in reference to a clock. The movement of data

203

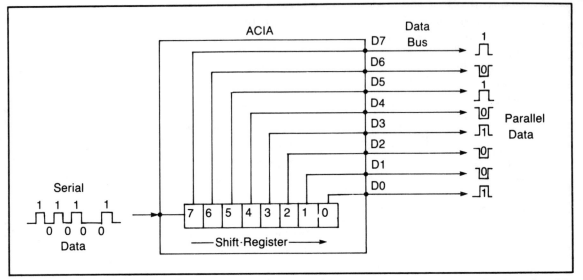

Fig. 12-2. When serial data is input to a shift register, it can be quickly converted to parallel data. The incoming data enters the register at bit position 7. It is shifted over bit by bit till it fills the register. Then all eight bits are placed onto the data bus simultaneously.

between the MPU and RAM or ROM is synchronous. The data transfers take place only to the beat of the system clock circuit. The strict timing as shown in timing diagrams must be tightly synced or else the transfer won't take place.

Asynchronous transmission has little to do with the clock rate. The data is moved in response to additional bits that are installed around the byte. At the beginning of the byte before bit 0, a *start bit* is installed. At the conclusion of the byte after

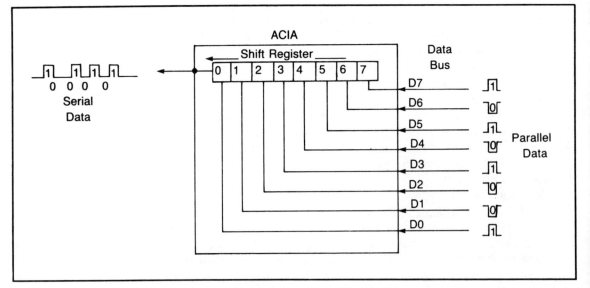

Fig. 12-3. When parallel data is input to a shift register, it can be quickly converted to serial. The incoming data enters all eight bits at the same time. The data is then shifted out bit by bit from position 0.

bit 7, *stop bits* are placed. Figure 12-4 shows what such a byte would look like.

If you consider an input device like a keyboard as a transmitter and the converter chip as a receiver, the following happens. The transmitter prepares a byte complete with the start and stop bits. The connection from the keyboard to the input of the line in the converter is meanwhile held high.

When the key is struck the byte being prepared by the keyboard is loaded with the ASCII code of the character on the key. The byte is launched and the start bit is a low. The connecting line thus is forced low. The start bit is one clock period long. The converter has been sitting and waiting for the start bit. It knows that a byte is following the start bit. The start bit ties the signal into sync with the system clock.

The byte follows on the heels of the start bit and is clocked into the shift register. One bit is clocked into place with every beat of the clock. At the end of the byte, the stop bit takes place. This lets the receiver know that the byte of data is in place.

Once the serial input is in place, the MPU reads the byte in the same way it reads any addressable location. The receiver chip then sits and waits for the next start bit. The asynchronous part of the operation takes place after the stop bit and while the receiver waits for the next start bit. Once the byte is in the shift register, it is synced as the MPU reads it.

Typically the start bit is a low to enable the receiver chip and the stop bit is a high to put the chip back into a waiting posture for the next start low bit. With different systems there could be more than one start bit and more than one stop bit. In addition some transmitting devices could add a parity bit or two. The parity bit is placed at the end of the byte but before the stop bit. Refer to Fig. 12-4.

Parity

The word parity means equal. In computerese, it refers to a code that is added to either the 1s or 0s in a group of bits like a byte, to make the total of the selected state always an odd or always an even number. For example, if you want to code the bytes in a transmitted data message as *odd parity* you would have every byte that passes over the serial line contain an odd number of 1s.

The transmitter, then, as it prepares the byte in serial format, counts the 1s in the byte. If there is an odd number of 1s like three 1s, it will place a 0 in the parity bit. That way the byte will have a total of three 1s, which is an odd amount. If the byte has an even number of 1s such as four, then the transmitter will place a 1 in the parity position.

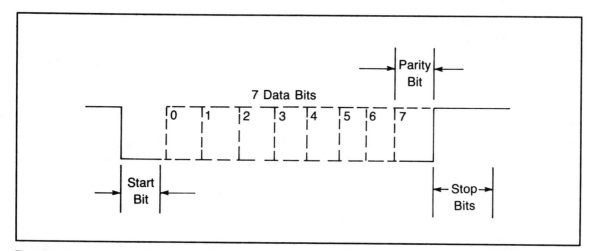

Fig. 12-4. A serial byte must be packaged with some control and test bits. Typical are start, stop, and parity bits. The start and stop signal the beginning and end of the byte while the parity checks the accuracy.

Then the total byte will have five 1s, which is still an odd number.

Should the system be designed to have an even parity, the transmitter will do the same thing to effect an even total in every byte. If there is an odd number of 1s in the byte then the transmitter will place a 1 in the parity it to make the total even. Should the byte contain an even number, then a 0 is placed in parity.

When the byte arrives at the receiver chip in the computer, the receiver checks the parity. The receiver is set to check for an odd or even parity to coincide with the transmitter. The parity must match. If it doesn't the receiver will not be enabled to receive the data.

The parity check is vital for converting serial to parallel and back. Inside the computer, faulty data transmission is not a serious problem in properly designed equipment. When you must transmit data over external lines or over the air though, it is not too difficult to lose a bit. Should a single bit be lost the parity check will detect it and measures can be taken.

While parity bit checking is vital, it can, under certain circumstances, fail to detect lost bits. That is when there are an even number of bits that are lost and never arrive at the receiver. The parity check only checks odd or even. If an even number of bits are lost, for instance two, the parity check will come out correct since the odd or even test measure won't be affected.

Data Rate

The term *baud* is familiar to computer people.

It is sometimes mixed up with bits per second, or bps. There is a difference. The baud rate of data moving along a serial line is the rate of the bits per second, but it includes the start, stop, and parity bits. The bits per second by itself is thought of as only the number of data bits in the total, excluding the stop, start, and parity bits. The baud rate is the commonly used term with the bits per second only needed during special type calculations.

For example, a baud rate of 300 only has 218.6 data bits per second transmitted. The other 81.4 bits every second are one start bit, two stop bits, and one parity bit surrounding every byte.

Keyboard

When you strike a key on an encoded keyboard, the row and column shorting enables the encoder to produce a character word. If the encoder gives even parity and has one start and two stops the finished square wave looks like Fig. 12-5 if you strike an M.

The wave begins from the high that the line was held at. The first clock period is the start bit. It drives the line low. The next seven clocks are the ASCII seven bit code for M. The line goes high, low, low, high, high, low, and high.

Following the M is a low for the even parity. In the M ASCII code are four 1s. With a low, the parity bit is a 0 and the total of the 1s therefore is four, which is an even number. This is correct and shows even parity. Bringing up the rear are two highs, the two stop bits. They place the serial line back into a high-hold position. The line then relaxes and waits for the next keyboard strike.

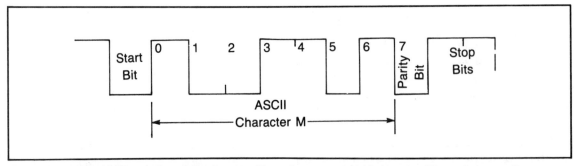

Fig. 12-5. A typical ASCII encoding of the character M can have one start bit, two stop bits, and even parity.

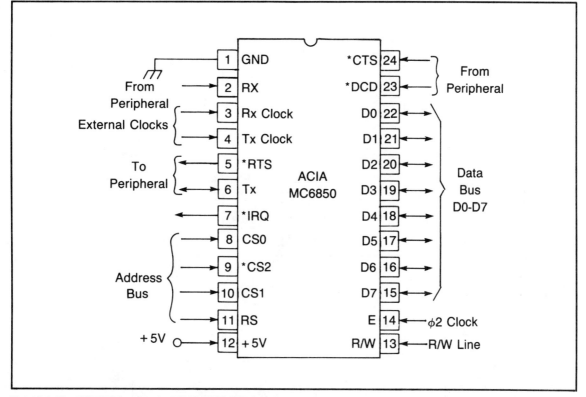

Fig. 12-6. The MC6850 is a 24-pin ACIA NMOS DIP. It has serial input and output communication capability with an external device. It connects to the system data bus and has four addressable registers.

6850 ACIA

An actual ACIA that is used with 6800 family chips is the MC6850. This 24-pin NMOS chip shown in Fig. 12-6 is packaged dual inline. It is arranged to handle up to eight bits of data in one character period. This means both the ability to receive the byte-sized information from an external device as well as transmit byte-sized information to it.

The chip has four addressable 8-bit registers that can take up residence on the memory map. Two of the registers take care of the transmitting and receiving. The other two are a control register and a status register. Figure 12-7 contains a block diagram of the MC6850.

Pins 15-22 are the D7-D0 connections to the data bus. They are two-way streets and can take data from the internal receive register to the MPU or carry data from the MPU to the transmit register. The receive register in the ACIA accepts the

serial data from the external device at pin 2 and latches the bits. The MPU then reads the register to obtain the data. The receive register is only read and never written to. In fact it is not wired for writing, it is a read only register.

When the MPU is transmitting, it writes the data to the transmit register. The byte from the MPU enters the register through the data pins and is latched into the bit positions. The data is then output serially from pin 6 to the peripheral. The transmit register can only be written to. It is not wired to be read.

The chip is controlled to read or write at pin 13. The MPU provides the control with its R/W line. A high on the R/W line reads the receive register and a low permits writing to the transmit register.

There is one register select at pin 11, RS. This is the only address line needed to choose among the

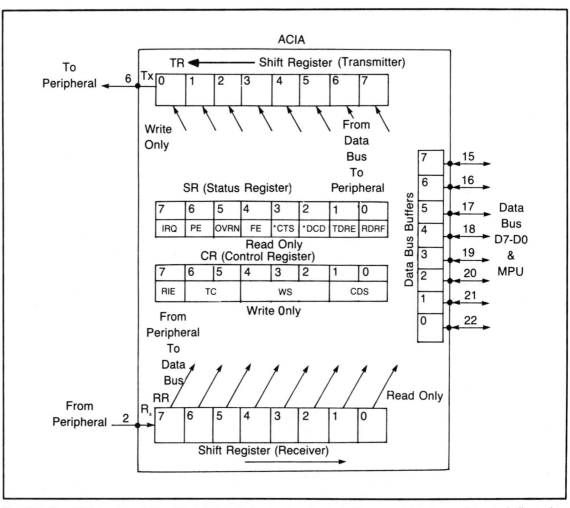

Fig. 12-7. The ACIA has two shift registers to handle the input and output. There are two other registers to indicate the status and effect control of the signal movement through the chip.

four addressable registers. A high addresses both the receive and the transmit registers at the same time. However, since the receive register can only be read and the transmit register can only be written to, the R/W line finishes the addressing by choosing which function is to take place. A read chooses the receiver and a write picks the transmitter.

The same situation exists with the control and status registers. A low at RS selects the pair, and the R/W line chooses the specific one. The control register is a write only and the status register is a read only.

Pins 8, 9, and 10 are the three chip selects, CS0, *CS2 and CS1. They are tied to the address lines too. They select the chip, and then the RS is able to select a pair of registers. Pin 14, E (for enable), works with the addressing in that the chip is three-state and there are buffers in the input and the output. E turns the buffers on and off. When the buffers are off data can not move. E usually receives a $\phi2$ signal. As $\phi2$ goes high, it enables the buffers, and data is able, at the $\phi2$ high, to move to or from the MPU.

Pin 7 is *IRQ. It connects to the *IRQ pin of the MPU. This interrupt will occur if bit 7 of the status register goes high. When it does, it causes the *IRQ line to go low and interrupt the MPU. The MPU then goes into its *IRQ service sequence.

This interrupt can be cleared by reading or writing to particular registers as discussed later in this chapter. As long as bit 7 of the status register remains in a dormant low state, the *IRQ pin is held high and no interrupt is generated.

Peripheral Connection

As you just saw, the ACIA deals with the MPU in much the same manner that any addressable chip does. It can be selected and one of its registers accessed over the system address, data, and control lines. In most cases, the MPU views the chip as a form of memory read/write equipment. It only sees the inside of the port.

The other side of the port connects to the peripheral. A typical two-way peripheral that needs a serial connection is a telephone modem. In Fig. 12-8, the modem is able to take the serial square wave, transform it into a form of audio, and send it out over a telephone line. It also is able to receive an audio signal, change it to a serial digital signal, and input the wave train into the ACIA.

It was mentioned that pin 2 in Fig. 12-6 is the receiver of the serial signal, and pin 6 transmits the signal to the peripheral. In addition, there are three more pins on the ACIA that aid in the transmission-reception procedures.

Pin 24 is *CTS, an input from the peripheral, for instance a modem, *CTS, Clear To Send, connects to bit 3 of the status register. It controls the status of bit 1. The way the register works is discussed shortly, and this control is covered in more detail.

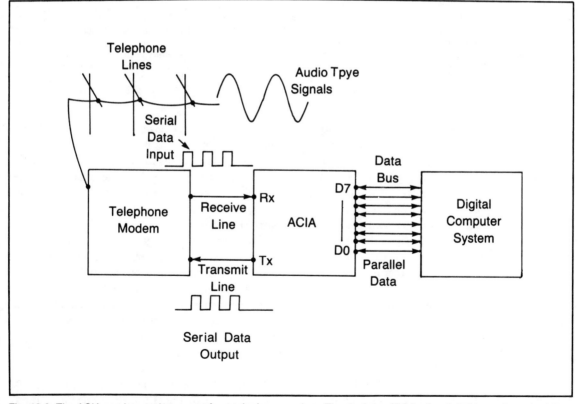

Fig. 12-8. The ACIA can be used as a port for a telephone modem. The modem will take the digital input from the ACIA, convert it to audio frequencies, and then send it out over the telephone lines. The modem will also accept the audio type signal from the telephone and convert it into a digital input for the ACIA.

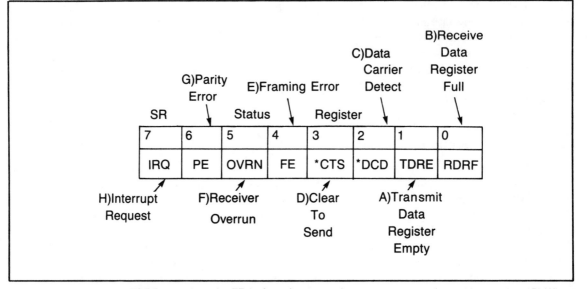

Fig. 12-9. A) When bit 1, TDRE, goes low, the TR is forced to empty its contents out to the waiting modem. B) When bit 0, RDRF, goes high, the MPU is signaled that the RR is full of the wanted data. C) If bit 2, *DCD, goes high, the carrier from the modem is not present. A low indicates it is there. D) When bit 3, *CTS, is high, the modem is not ready for data. A low means it is waiting for data. E) When bit 4, FE (framing error), is high, that means the received character from the modem is not packaged correctly by the start and stop bits. The error flag is set. When the bit is low, the character framing is ok. F) Should bit 5, OVRN (receiver overrun), be high, it means some characters in the wave train have been lost. A low means the data is being processed correctly. G) Bit 6, PE (parity error), is high when the flag is set. If the bit is low, the parity is not in error. H) Bit 7, IRQ, is the interrupt request. When the bit is high, the *IRQ pin of the ACIA goes low which will interrupt the MPU. As long as bit 7 itself stays low, the interrupt will not be triggered.

Pin 5 is *RTS, Request To Send, an output signal to the modem. This pin reflects the state of bits 5 and 6 of the control register. Their states can be altered by the MPU over the data bus. Through them, the MPU can take control of the modem.

Pin 23 is *DCD, Data Carrier Detect, another input from the modem. It provides control over the receiver by means of a signal from the modem.

Pins 3 and 4 are inputs for external clock signals to be applied to the receiver and transmitter. Pin 3, the receiver's clock input, is used to sync incoming data. Pin 4, the transmitters clock input, syncs the outgoing data.

ACIA Registers

There are two separate operations that the ACIA port performs. First, it can transmit data from the MPU to the modem, and second, it can receive data back from the modem. Two entirely separate circuits could be used for the operation if there were two data buses in the machine. However the two operations must share the same bus even though traffic has to move in two directions. In order to properly conduct the operations, the transmitter and receiver also must share the controlling registers, the status register (SR) and the control register (CR).

The transmitting register (TR) is a combination latch and shift register. It is used to take the parallel byte from the data bus and hold it till it can transmit it to the modem in serial form. When the chip selects are enabled by the address bus the data is latched into the register on the falling edge of the E signal from the $\phi 2$ clock. At that instant, the register select pin must be high and the R/W line low.

As the TR register fills, the status register is affected. Refer to Fig. 12-9. Bit 1 goes low. Bit 1 is the Transmit Data Register Empty, signal. This causes the TR to empty the data, in a serial form, from pin 6 to the modem. Once the modem receives the data, bit 1 goes high again.

The SR is the register that notes and acts upon the status of the ACIA operations. It is a register that is read by the MPU. In fact, the register is a read-only type. It cannot be written to. Bits 7, 3, 2 have already been mentioned.

The Receive Register, RR, is a shift register and latch. It is used to receive the packaged data from the modem. As the data with its start, stop, and parity bits enter the ACIA, the control bits are stripped away and the actual data is inserted into the shift register. The RR then latches the data until a signal can be given to send the data to the MPU over the data bus.

As the data files into the RR, bit 0 of the SR goes high. Refer to Fig. 12-9. This tells the MPU that the RR contains the wanted data. The MPU then selects the chip. It sets the register select to a high and sets the R/W line to a high. A copy of the data is then able to emerge from the RR, travel the data bus, and arrive at the MPU. Once the data arrives at the MPU, bit 0 goes low again.

Meanwhile, the Control Register, CR, has to be configured so the transmitting and receiving can proceed in a correct manner. The MPU is able to write to the CR to install the correct highs and lows to run the ACIA. There is no reason to read the CR, so the CR is wired as a write only register.

To address the CR, the MPU must select the chip with the CS pins, send a low to the register select, and transmit a low to the R/W line. This addresses the CR, and the MPU can then write the control bits into the register. Figure 12-10 shows the CR and the bits. Of especial interest are bits 2, 3, and 4. They are able to pick from an assortment of eight choices: number of data bits, number of stop bits, and parity for both transmission and reception.

PARALLEL DATA MOVEMENT

There are many external devices that do not need the parallel data in the computer to be changed into a serial stream before they can handle the data. Instead of having one transmission line to these devices, the computer can connect with the full eight data bus lines. The data that is sent out in parallel form does not require all the extra start, stop, and parity bits that the serial data transfer needed. Also sending out eight bits abreast is faster than one at a time.

A typical device that can receive parallel data is a printer. Printers often have both a serial and parallel plug to accommodate both a serial input, or the output of a parallel interface chip.

6821 PIA

There are a number of parallel interface chips that are used in computers. A common chip that is in the 6800 family is the 6821 Peripheral Interface Adapter, known as the PIA. It is a 40-pin DIP composed of NMOS materials.

The 6821 is addressable and needs to be configured by the MPU in order to operate. The MPU usually programs the PIA at the start of a day's work on the computer. There are four addresses that can contact the registers.

PIA Registers

The PIA has two sides, A and B. They are illustrated in Fig. 12-11. Each side contains three 8-bit registers. They are called the peripheral data register (PDR), the data direction register (DDR), and the control register (CR). The registers in the two sides are almost identical. For the most part, side A and side B operate in the same way.

The chip has eight data pins that connect internally to the data bus D7-D0. Data is able to travel into the PIA from the MPU or from the PIA to the MPU in the same way that RAM is written to or read from.

D7-D0 connects inside the PIA to both the A and B sides. When the chip is addressed, a register is selected. The selected register becomes the one accessed by the MPU to be read or written to.

Each side of the PIA has its very own pin set that connects to the peripheral. Side A has pins PA7-PA0, and side B has pins PB7-PB0. These pins are all two way and can be programmed to act as either input or output lines.

D

Receiver Interrupt Enable (RIE)	Tramsmiter Control Bits 6	Tramsmiter Control Bits 5	Pin 5 RTS	Communications Channel (TDRE)	
0	0	0	L	REquest For Set Up	**C**
1	0	1	L	Set Up	
	1	0	H	Knock Down	
	1	1	L	Interrupt	

A

External Clock Settings

Bits 1	Bits 0	Modes
0	0	÷ 1
0	1	÷ 16
1	0	÷ 64
1	1	Master Reset

Control Register

	7	6	5	4	3	2	1	0
CR	RIE	Transmitter Control		Word Select			Counter Divide Select	

(Write Only)

B

Word Select Bits 4	Word Select Bits 3	Word Select Bits 2	Number Of Data Bits	Parity	Stop Bits
0	0	0	7	Even	2
0	0	1	7	Odd	2
0	1	0	7	Even	1
0	1	1	7	Odd	1
1	0	0	8	No Parity Bit	2
1	0	1	8	No Parity Bit	1
1	1	0	8	Even	1
1	1	1	8	Odd	1

Fig. 12-10. A) Bits 0 and 1, CDS (counter divide select), are able to assume four states. Three of the states set the baud rate the ACIA is able to receive from an external clock. It can handle the same rate, mode − 1, 16 times the MPU's rate, − 16, and 64 times the rate, − 64. The different rates are used to detect noise errors. The fourth state is used as a reset to clear the flags in the status register. B) Bits 2, 3, and 4, WS (word select), have eight possible states. They choose the number of data bits, stop bits, and type of parity to be used. C) Bits 5 and 6, TC (transmitter control), has four possible states. They put lows or a high out on pin 5 *RTS (request to send), of the chip. The bits then set up, knock down or interrupt the communications channel from TDRE. D) When bit 7, RIE (receiver interrupt enable), is high, it enables interrupts that occur when RDRF or *DCD go high. If RIE is low, it masks the interrupts that might happen due to RDRF or *DCD.

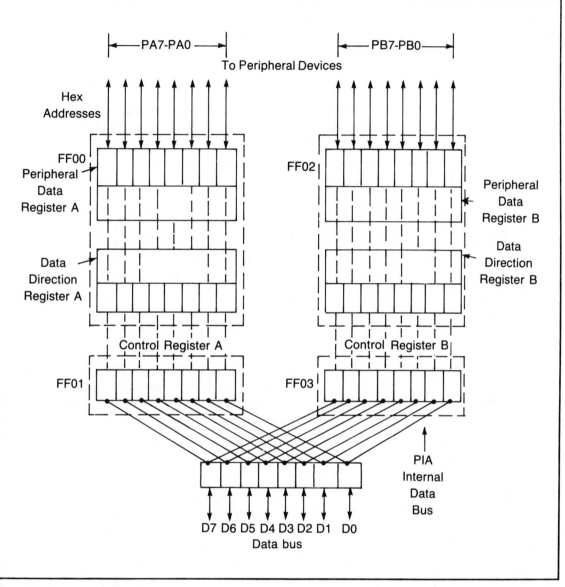

Fig. 12-11. The 6821 Peripheral Interface Adapter is a 40-pin DIP made out of NMOS materials.

6821 Pinout

The pinout for the PIA is shown in Fig. 12-12. D7-D0 at pins 26-33, PA7-PA0 at pins 9-12, and PB7-PB0 at pins 17-10 take up 24 of the total 40 pins. Pin 20 and pin 1 are the +5 volts and ground. Pins 22, 23, and 24 are the chip selects, CS0, *CS2, and CS1. Pins 36 and 35 are the register selects, RS0 and RS1.

The PIA is able to generate two interrupts from pins 36 and 37, *IRQA and *IRQB, one for each side. They go directly to the MPU and are essential in certain types of I/O activity like *handshaking*, which is covered later in the chapter.

A reset in the computer sends a low to pin 34, *RESET, and will reset the register according to design. There is a read/write input at pin 21. This

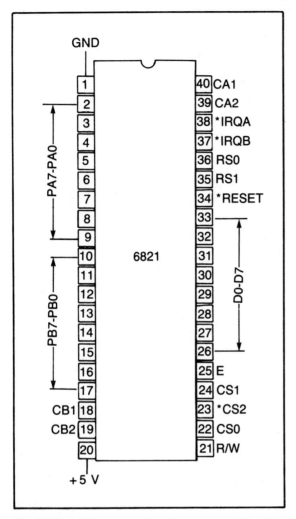

Fig. 12-12. A PIA has two sides that are almost identical. Each side contains three 8-bit registers. The data bus connects to both sides. Each side has eight I/O pins.

allows the MPU to access the PIA properly. Also an enable line, E allows the MPU to send a φ2 clock signal to the PIA to sync it in step. Lastly there are four control lines: an input and output to and from the MPU for each side. These are discussed in more detail later in the chapter. The control lines, CA1 and CA2 are at pins 40 and 39. CB1 and CB2 are at pins 18 and 19.

PIA Addressing

Transferring parallel data to a host of possible external devices gets complicated. The PIA is able to perform these complicated data manuevers. Since each side is almost identical, side A will be discussed with the idea that side B acts in the same way.

The first step is addressing the registers. There are three registers in side A that are located with two addresses. The control register has one of the addresses for itself. The DDRA and the PDRA share the second address. Refer to the hex addresses in Fig. 12-11. The DDRA is addressed as you start computing.

The data direction register A, as the name implies decides which direction the data is going to move. Refer to Fig. 12-13. The DDRA is connected to the data bus. The MPU accesses it and writes a few program lines that fills the DDRA with bits. If a bit position receives a high, then data is going to travel from the MPU to the peripheral over that data line. Should a bit position receive a low, then that corresponding data line is going to carry data from the peripheral to the MPU.

Once the DDRA receives its direction orders, it steps into the background and turns the address over to the PDRA. From then on during the program run, any accessing of the DDRA-PDRA results in the PDRA being addressed and not the DDRA. The DDRA does its job at the start of the proceedings and is not heard from again. This shutting down of the DDRA and giving preference to the PDRA is accomplished by bit 2 of the CRA. Refer to Fig. 12-14. When bit 2 of the CRA is low, then the DDRA is addressed. If bit 2 is then forced high, the DDRA relinquishes its addressablility and turns it over to the PDRA.

This procedure is part of the beginning of the program that is going to be run. It is some of the initialization that has to be done. The program step-by-step does the following. First of all the PIA must be accessed. An address is written that will apply highs to CS0 and CS1, and a low to *CS2. This enabling is done with high address lines. The two lowest address lines are used to select the DDRA. A low in bit position 2 of the CRA works with RS0 and RS1 to select DDRA.

Next, DDRA is configured with eight bits that

are written to it from the MPU. For instance if the MPU writes 00001111 to the DDRA, then bits 7-4 will be inputs and bits 3-0 will be outputs. Then the MPU loads a high into bit 2 of the CRA. The DDRA is taken out of the play, and the PDRA becomes the addressable register. The corresponding bits in the PDRA become the actual input and output bits. Positions 7-4 in the PDRA are inputs that will accept data from a peripheral while 3-0 are output bits that can send data to the peripheral.

If you had written 00000000 to the DDRA originally, then all the PDRA bits would be inputs.

Should 11111111 had been written all the PDRA bits would be outputs.

Control Register

Figure 12-14 shows CRA. It is an 8-bit register that runs the activity in the PIA once the PDRA bits are assigned their input or output condition. Bits 7 and 6 are both interrupt flags that control an output low or high from pin 38, the *IRQA output. Bits 5, 4, and 3 are the bits that decide what pin 39, the CA2 input/output line, is going to do.

Bit 2, as mentioned earlier, is the third bit

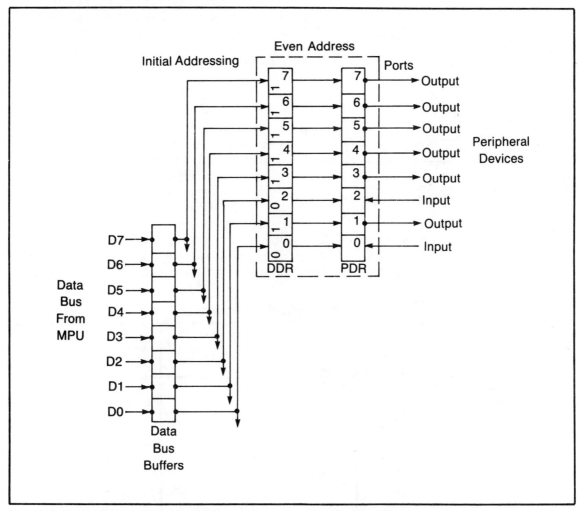

Fig. 12-13. The DDR and PDR registers both share the same address on the memory map. The DDR is addressed when you turn the computer on. Then after some configuring, it turns the address over to the PDR.

215

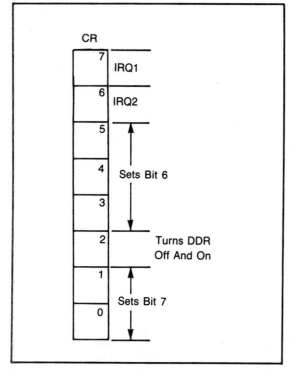

CR

7 IRQ1

6 IRQ2

5 ↑

4 Sets Bit 6

3 ↓

2 Turns DDR Off And On

1 ↑

0 Sets Bit 7 ↓

Fig. 12-14. When you turn the computer on, bit 2 of the CR is low and DDR is addressed. After configuration, bit 2 of the CR is made high, and the PDR takes over their common address.

needed to select one of the six registers in the PIA. The two register select lines from the MPU are only able to select from four possible registers. The additional CRA bit gives the RS bits two more

possibilities so all six registers can be addressed.

Bits 1 and 0 perform according to what signal enters pin 40, the CA1 input. The bits in turn connect to bit 7, the IRQA1. They decide whether to set bit 7 or clear it.

Pin 40, the CA1 control line, is an input from the peripheral being worked to the PIA. When the peripheral wants to contact the MPU and send along some data, it sends a signal over CA1 that is intended to set bit 7, IRQA1. IRQA1 is an interrupt bit for the line *IRQA, pin 38, that goes to the MPU. If bit 7 is low, the masking is on and the signal at CA1 will have not effect. However, if bit 7 is set with a high, the interrupt could take place and the MPU will get ready to receive the data.

Bit 7 can only be set if all of the following conditions take place. The first condition is bit 1 of the CRA is low and a low comes in from the peripheral over CA1. An alternative condition is bit 1 of the CRA is high and a high comes in over CA1. Then besides meeting one of those conditions, bit 0 must not mask the interrupt. When these conditions are all in place, then, and only then, bit 7 will get set and create the interrupt. Table 12-1 outlines the interrupt requirements whereby the peripheral can contact the MPU.

CA2 at pin 39 can also be used by the peripheral to interrupt the MPU and alert it that data is on the way. In addition, it can also be used by the MPU to output signals to the peripheral. CA1 is not that versatile. It can only act as an

Table 12-1. Status of the IRQA1 Bit.

CA1 Edge	CRA Control Bits Pin Number		Bit 7 IRQA1	*IRQA Pin 38
	1	0 (mask)		
Falling	0	0	1	Masked off
Falling	0	1	1	Interrupt
Rising	1	0	1	Masked off
Rising	1	1	1	Interrupt
Falling	1	-	0	Masked off
Rising	0	-	0	Masked off

Table 12-2. Status of the IRQA2 Bit.

CA2 Edge	CRA Control Bits Pin Number			Bit 6 IRQA2	*IRQA Pin 38
	5 I/O	4	3 (mask)		
Falling	0	0	0	1	Masked off
Falling	0	0	1	1	Interrupt
Rising	0	1	0	1	Masked off
Rising	0	1	1	1	Interrupt
Falling	0	1	-	0	Masked off
Rising	0	0	-	0	Masked off

input interrupt and not as an output.

Bit 5 of the CRA decides if CA2 is an MPU interrupter or a signal output line. If bit 5 is low, then CA2 is an interrupt. When bit 5 is high, it is an output.

When CA2 is in the interrupt mode, bit 5 is low, bits 3 and 4 control IRQA2 bit 6. IRQA2 is also an interrupt flag like IRQA1. If IRQA2 is set to a high, then the interrupt can go out to the MPU over *IRQA, pin 38. Bit 6 is permitted to go high only if the following conditions are met. One way is if bit 4 is low and a low enters on the CA2 line. The second way is if bit 4 is high and a high enters CA2. Table 12-2 shows the possible conditions and results.

Side A Handshake

When bit 5 of the CRA is high, then the CA2 line becomes a signal output line. In this mode, the PIA acts as the intermediary as the peripheral and the MPU conduct the data transfer procedure know as *handshaking*. The 6821 goes into the handshake posture when bit 5 is high and bits 4 and 3 or the CRA are low. The handshake takes place with three signals. Refer to Fig. 12-15 for this discussion. First, the peripheral signals the MPU that it has data. Second, the MPU signals back to the peripheral that it should send the data. Lastly, the data is sent, and the MPU sends a third signal letting the peripheral know that the data has arrived safely and that it is ready to receive more.

The signals start off with the peripheral sending a signal over CA1. The correct signal causes IRQA1, bit 7 of the CRA to get set to a high. This causes the *IRQA to interrupt the MPU with the message, "This is the peripheral calling. I have data for you."

As bit 7 sets to a high, it in turn sets the CA2 line high. The peripheral interprets the high from CA2 to be a message from the MPU saying "Message received, send the data." The data leaves the peripheral into the PA7-PA0 lines and is latched into the PDRA. The MPU then reads the PDRA.

As the MPU performs the read, it causes CA2 to go low. The low on CA2 has the effect of the MPU telling the peripheral, "I have read the data and you can send me more."

That is the way the peripheral contacts the MPU, the MPU acknowledges the contact, data flows from peripheral to MPU, and the MPU gives receipt to the data and asks for more. In other words the peripheral and the MPU conduct a handshake peripheral to MPU data movement. Side A specializes in this complex movement of data from peripheral to MPU.

Side B Handshake

What about the movement of data from the MPU to the peripheral? Side B is the group of registers that performs those honors. That is the primary difference between side A and side B.

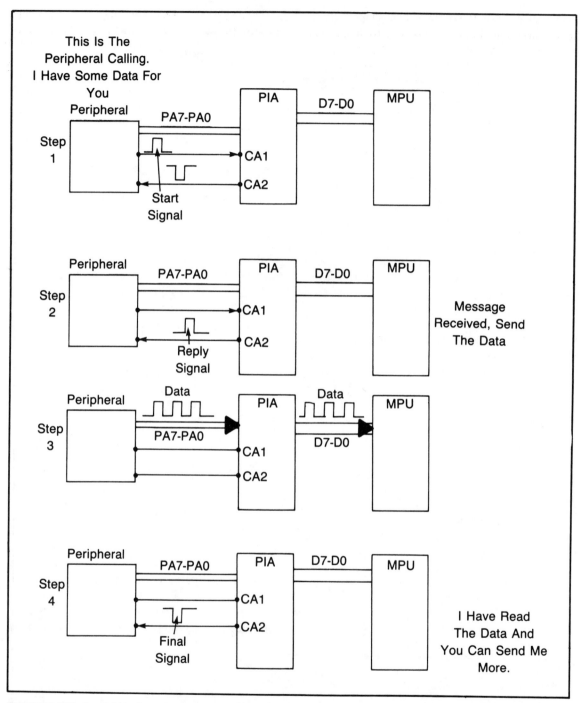

Fig. 12-15. This handshake from the peripheral to the PIA takes place on the A side. Control pins CA1 and CA2 are the lines that do the job. CA1 receives a high from the peripheral. CA2 sends a high back to the peripheral when the MPU is ready. Next, the data is sent from the peripheral to the MPU through the PIA. When the data has been received and the MPU is ready for more, a low is sent over CA2 to the peripheral.

They each perform the complex handshake in a particular direction. They also are able to do another less complicated data movement called pulse that is covered later in the chapter.

Moving data from the MPU to the peripheral in the handshake mode is quite like the side A procedure except for the fact that the data is going the other way. When side A is performing, the peripheral initiates the action. It tells the MPU, through the side A channels, that it has data for it. It conveys the message through a signal over CA1.

When side B is to perform, the peripheral again initiates the action. Refer to Fig. 12-16 for the following discussion. It sends a signal over CB1. The signal in effect says, "This is the peripheral calling, I need some data." The MPU understands the message as the signal over CB1 sets the bit 7 flag in the CRB to a high.

As IRQB1 gets set, the CB2 line back to the peripheral goes high. This high is interpreted by the peripheral as a message from the MPU, "Message received. I'll send you some data." The

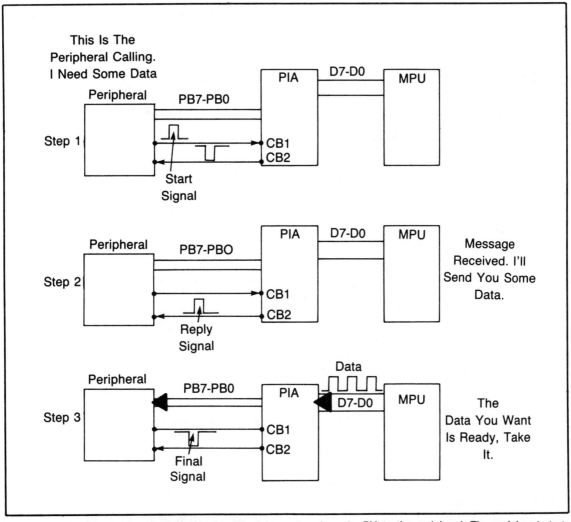

Fig. 12-16. Side B handles the handshake when the data must go from the PIA to the peripheral. The peripheral starts the operation by sending a high over CB1 to the PIA, letting it know it wants data. The PIA acknowledges the request by sending a high back over CB2. Then CB2 goes low and sends the data out over the eight B side data output pins.

219

MPU then writes the data to the PDRB, and it is latched into the PDRB.

Once the data is in the PDRB, the CB2 line goes low. The low tells the peripheral, "The data you want is ready, take it." The peripheral calls for more data and the handshake continues.

Pulse Modes

The pulse mode is a curt form of handshake. It is used when a full handshake is not needed. The pulse mode leaves the CA1 and CB1 lines out of the activity. It only needs CA2 and CB2 for the data transfer. When data is moved from the peripheral to the MPU with side A, all the peripheral needs to know in this mode is when the MPU takes delivery of the data. That message can be conveyed via CA2.

When the data is moved from the MPU to the peripheral, all the peripheral needs to know is when the data is latched into the PDRB. CB2 is able to deliver that message.

To get the pulse modes in operation, bits 5, 4, and 3 of CRA or CRB must be set accordingly. If you recall, to get the handshake mode operative bits 5, 4, and 3 of the CRs were installed with a high, low, low, or 100. To setup the pulse mode those bits receive high, low, high, or 101.

In side A, the activity begins when the MPU executes a Read the PDRA instruction. The instruction causes the peripheral to send data in a parallel fashion to the PDRA. The MPU, without further ado, reads it.

The CA2 line is usually held high. When the read of PDRA takes place, the CA2 line is forced low, as Fig. 12-17A shows. This tells the peripheral, "This is the MPU. I just read your data." After the message, the CA2 line goes high again till after the next read instruction is executed.

A similar procedure goes on in the B side for data moving in the other direction. CB2 is normally held high. When the MPU executes a Store Data in PDRB, it goes low, as in Fig. 12-17B. The low on CB2 tells the peripheral, "This is the MPU calling. I just latched data in the PDRB. You are free to take it."

The data then flows over the parallel lines into the peripheral. CB2 then goes back to its high position until the next store instruction.

Lock Modes

CA2 and CB2 are two directional lines that attach to peripherals. They can be used as an interrupt from the peripheral to the MPU in some applications, or an output to the peripheral in other cases. There are still other times when they must either be held high no matter what or held low without changing. There are two lock modes that will lock them either high or low.

To lock either in a constant high, bits 5, 4, and 3 of their respective CR are arranged with all highs, or 111. For a steady low to be on the CA2 or CB2 lines, its corresponding CR should have high, high, low or 110 in those control bits.

Preparing a PIA Port

The PIA is a tricky chip, but once set up properly, it will act in an automatic manner to transfer parallel data to and from peripherals. It is also able to transfer serial data to and from the parallel ports A and B.

The PIA is contacted by the MPU through the address bits. The chip selects are enabled with high address bits and the register selects with bits 0 and 1 of the address bus. There are four separate addresses, two for side A and two for side B. The first registers addressed are the two data direction registers, the DDRs.

The DDRs are then loaded with logical 1s and 0s. A logic 1 makes the bit position an output to a peripheral and a 0 makes the position an input from the peripheral. If all eight positions are given the same logic, then the register is able to transfer a full byte of parallel data. Should a mixture of bits be installed in the DDR, those 1s will be output and the 0s inputs. That way the register can act as either a parallel or a serial port. The PIA is indeed versatile.

Once the DDR is programmed, a 1 is loaded into bit 2 of both CRA and CRB. Each DDR and PDR share the same address. When bit 2 of its CR

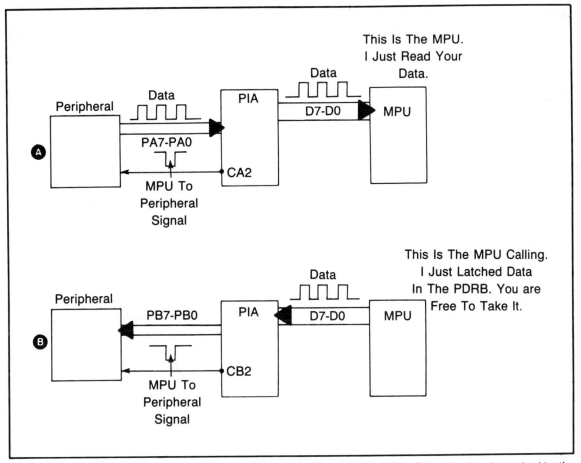

Fig. 12-17. A) Side A conducts the movement of data from the peripheral to the MPU. When the data is received by the MPU, a low is sent over CA2 to the peripheral. This lets the peripheral know the data has arrived. B) Side B conducts the movement of data from the MPU to the peripheral. When the MPU latches data into the PDRB for the peripheral, it sends a low over CB2.

has a 0, then the DDR is the one that will be addressed. As a 1 is loaded into bit 2, then the DDR is forced to step aside and relinquish the address to the PDR. At this point, the DDRs are no longer of any use. The PDRs are the portholes and are configured for input and output duty.

The control registers, CRA and CRB, take over. They have complete control over the control lines to the peripheral, CA1, CA2, CB1, and CB2. Bits 1 and 0 of the CRs control CA1 and CB1. CA1 and CA2 are interrupt inputs from the peripheral. They can send an interrupt to the MPU if they are not masked. The bit 7s, IRQA1 and IRQB1 are the mask flags. The logic in bits 1 and 0 decide if the

mask is allowed or not. If the mask is set with a 1 then the interrupt is allowed. Should the mask be cleared to a zero the interrupt is not permitted to go to the MPU.

Bits 5, 4, and 3 control CA2 and CB2. The three bits are capable of assuming eight different combinations. If bit 5 is a 0 then CA2 and CB2 become interrupt inputs like CA1 and CB1. Bits 4 and 3 then control the bit 6s, IRQA2 and IRQB2. These bits are also masks. A 1 in bit 6 will allow the interrupt to go through to the MPU. A 0 will mask the interrupt.

When bit 5 is a 1, then CA2 and CB2 change direction and become outputs to the peripheral. As

221

outputs, they are used as message carriers during handshake and pulse mode data transfers as discussed earlier.

The control registers both have their own addresses in the memory map. The MPU can read their status at any time. However, the MPU is prevented from writing into the two flags, bits 6 and 7.

The logic state in bits 1 and 0 open the circuits to the flag in bit 7, while bits 5, 4, and 3 get the flag in bit 6 prepared to be thrown. However, the only way a flag can be set is by an interrupt from the peripheral. The MPU is not able to do it.

Enable Line

The enable line, E, clocks the PIA into step with the MPU. E is usually a sample of the $\phi 2$ clock. All of the action is keyed to respond to the rising edges and falling edges of the clock. During a pulse-mode data transfer for instance, CA2 or CB2 is held high but will go low on the falling edge of $\phi 2$. It will notify the peripheral with the low. Then it will go back high on the next falling edge of $\phi 2$.

During a handshake, CA2 is normally held low before the activity begins. Then on a falling edge of $\phi 2$ it will go high and conduct the handshake data transfer. At the conclusion of the transaction, CA2 or CB2 will then go low as the next falling edge of $\phi 2$ occurs. The $\phi 2$ signal is continually fed into the PIA at pin 25.

Reset Line

When pin 34, *RESET, is held low for a least eight machine cycles, the PIA goes into its own reset routine. All six registers in the chip are then reset to zero. This causes the following conditions to be arranged.

First, since all the bits in the DDRs are 0s, all the port lines in both PA7-PA0 and PB7-PB0 become inputs. Next, with bit 5 in both control registers as 0s, CA1, CB1, CA2, and CB2 all become input interrupt lines that can be triggered by a falling edge. With bits 6 and 7 of the CRs also at 0, the IRQ masks are all in place so that interrupts can not get through to the MPU.

Chapter 13

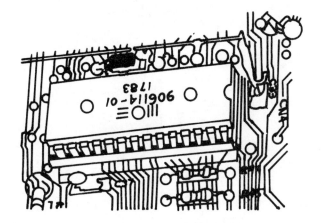

The Inbetween Chips

I N THE LAST FEW CHAPTERS, THE MICROPRO-
cessor has been pictured as a sort of central information exchange. The MPU has been shown as
the addressor and the ROM, RAM, and I/O chips
the addressees. The MPU accesses the input addressees of the I/O chips to obtain data from the outside world. The MPU then processes the data with
directions from programs and stores data in RAM
during the processing. Then the MPU accesses an
I/O output address and sends the finished data on
its way. There is one thing that all the chips involved in this process have in common. They are
all assigned addresses on the system memory map.

There is another group of chips in the machine.
They are not found listed on the memory map.
They do not have addresses. They are support
chips that perform other essential jobs in the computer. The MPU does not have any control of them.
They are just installed at strategic locations and
simply perform a job automatically as address bits
or data bits arrive at their input pins. Some of them
such as AND gates, NOT gates, buffer YES gates,

and flip-flops have already been covered in earlier
chapters. These are the type of chips I'm referring
to.

The examples that will be covered in this
chapter are electronic switch chips, timers,
decoders, multiplexers, and one 40-pin DIP known
as SAM. These are the chips that simply stand in
place and process bits that come along. You'll find
them stationed in the address bus, data bus, and
other lines that need the specialty they perform.
The simplest one of this group is an electronic
switch.

4066 SWITCH

The 4066 is a 14-pin DIP and performs its switching
with aid of both n-channel and p-channel FETS in
a CMOS configuration. From the point of view of
a user, the chip is simply four separate off-on switches. Refer Fig. 13-1. The only thing that the
switches have in common is the VDD at pin 14 and
ground at pin 7.

Each switch has two lines called I/O (or O/I) and

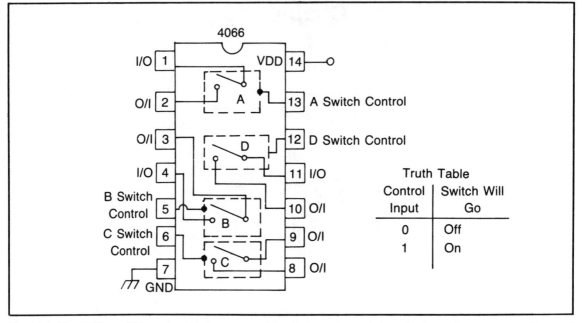

Fig. 13-1. The 4066 quad bilateral switch is a group of four independent switches. Each one has two connections and an electronic toggle switch, where a 1 turns it on and a 0 turns it off.

a control line that does the switching. The two I/O lines are connected to wires that need switching. It does not matter which I/O line is connected to what connection. They are reversible.

The control line turns the switch off and on. If a high is applied to the control line the switch turns on. If a low is applied to the control line the switch goes into the off position. The 4066 has a very simple truth table, as Fig. 13-1 shows.

A typical application is shown in Fig. 13-2. The 4066 could be in a data bus line that is carrying four bits, D3-D0. The switch can be made to act as an off-on switch for the nybble bus. The input to the switch is at pins 1, 4, 8, and 11. The output of the 4066 is at corresponding pins 2, 3, 9, and 10. That way each input sends out the correct output.

The four enable pins 12, 6, 5 and 13 are then tied together and connected to a signal line that carries the control bit to cut the data bus off and turn it back on. When the control bit is a high the data bus remains on and the 4066 acts as a piece of wire. Should the control bit change to a low, the four switches are turned off. The data bus becomes

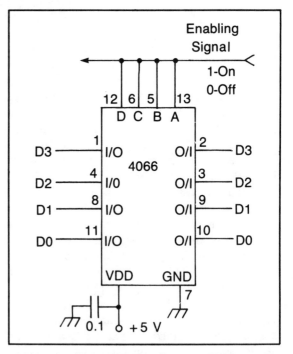

Fig. 13-2. A typical application shows the 4066 controlling the passage of signals through the data bus lines, D3-D0. The enabling signal turns them all on or off together.

open in the 4066 and any data in the line cannot proceed any further.

The 4066 is used instead of a three-state buffer YES gate chip when it is not necessary to amplify the amount of current in data bits. The 4066 acts only as wire and not as an amplifier.

555 TIMER

The 555 is a chip that is often used in computers when a time delay or an oscillator circuit is needed. The chip is able to time events as quickly as a few microseconds or as slow as many hours.

The 555 timer type circuit is based around two comparators and a flip-flop. In fact, you could fabricate a 555 type timer with comparator and flip-flop chips. Refer to Fig. 13-3. One bistable flip-flop is the center of the circuit. Two comparators input their states into the FF. The output of the FF is a state that is controlled by the states of the inputs. The inputs can make the FF hold either a high or low. The inputs can also make the FF change states at a prescribed frequency and output an oscillator clock signal. This allows the chip to perform all sorts of jobs from a one-shot timer to being a clock.

The 555 has the complete timer circuits contained in the silicon. Figure 13-4 shows the pin connections. A typical job that a timer can do is act as a bootstrap pulse to get a computer underway when it is first turned on. In Fig. 13-5, a timer is attached to the *RESET pin of an MPU. If a quick low can be sent to *RESET when the computer is first turned on, the MPU will start up. Following the low, the timer then sends a high to the reset circuit. Once started, the MPU will go into a reset routine. During the sequence, the MPU is built to load a vector address into the program counter. This vector is the start address of the program-control system. The MPU can then increment its way through the starting program and set the machine up ready for action.

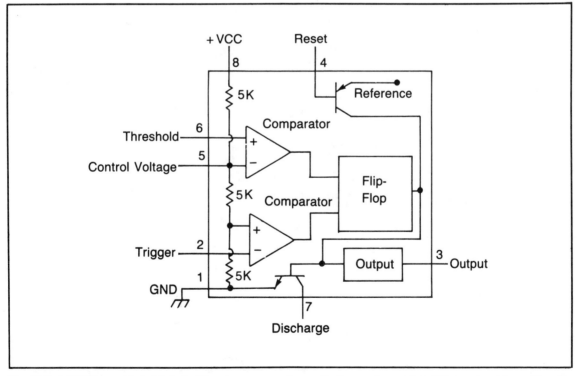

Fig. 13-3. A 555 Timer chip is fabricated from two comparators, a flip-flop, and some transistors and resistors. The chip can act as a one-shot timer, a clock or other related type duties.

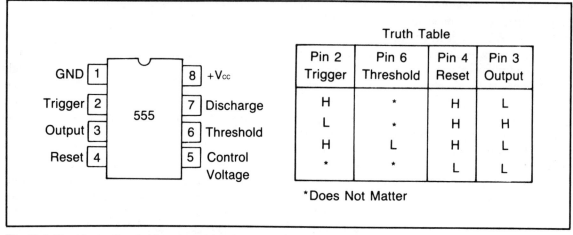

Fig. 13-4. The trigger, threshold, and reset inputs can produce various high or low outputs.

The timer chip has one of the comparators arranged with a threshold and control voltage input. For this bootstrap application, these two inputs are tied together and connected to +5 volts, a constant high. Internally the threshold connection to the second comparator connects to the first comparator's control voltage connection. This makes that connection high too.

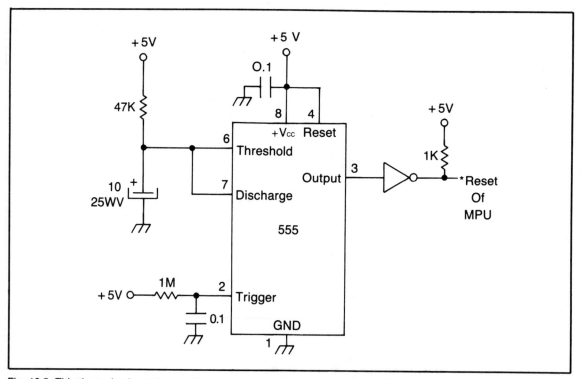

Fig. 13-5. This timer circuit can be used to get a computer underway when it is first turned on. The rise of the +5 volt source from off to +5 volts, triggers the timer and initiates the MPU with a *RESET pulse.

The other comparator connection is the trigger. The trigger is also connected to +5 volts. When the computer is first turned on, the timer powers up. As the voltage courses into the timer, it builds from zero volts to +5 volts.

The circuit is designed so the trigger has a 0.1 μF capacitor as a bypass while the other two comparator inputs use a common 10 μF. When power is first turned on the two capacitors have a charge-up race. Since the 0.1 μF is so much smaller than the 10 μF, it charges quicker. That puts a high on the trigger with the rest of the comparator pins still low.

This high results in a short pulse low onto the *RESET pin and gets the MPU started. Then the 10 μF finally charges up to a high and the FF changes states and makes the reset input a steady high. The MPU then loads the vector address and proceeds with its normal operation.

The various jobs that timers do can be controlled by connecting the correct resistors and capacitors for each job.

1-OF-8 DECODER

A very important support chip in a computer is a 1-of-8 decoder chip. It is usually used as a chip select. There are three inputs to the chip and eight outputs, as Fig. 13-6 shows. The chip is able to receive a set of three input states. Since there are eight possible combinations of bits that can be put together with three bits, the chip is able to receive one out of eight possible three bit sets.

If the three inputs are coming from three higher address lines, the three inputs are able to form eight different chip selects. The eight output pins are each connected to a different chip. By varying the input bit combinations, any chip can be selected to the mutual exclusion of the remaining chips.

The actual inputs on the pinout in Fig. 13-7 are A0, A1, and A2. The eight outputs are *O7-*O0. As the asterisk implies, the pins are held high till they are ready to select a chip. Then that one will go low and make the selection. There are three enable pins called *E1, *E2, and E3.

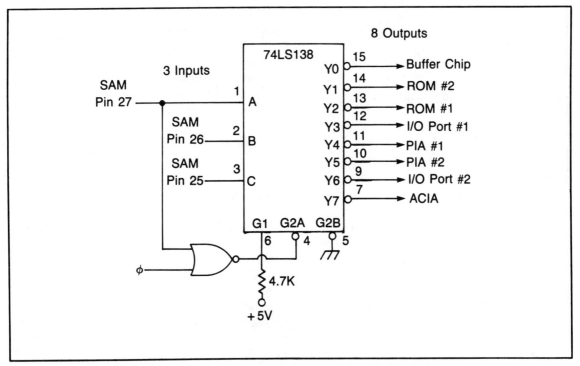

Fig. 13-6. Three inputs into the decoder chip produces the selection of 1-of-8 chips in the computer.

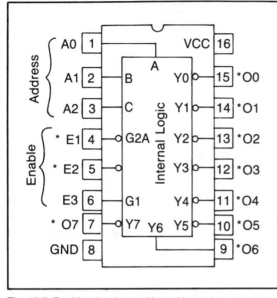

Fig. 13-7. Besides the three address bits and the eight output bits, the 74LS138 has three enable bits.

The internal wiring diagram in Fig. 13-8 shows the gate structure. The eight outputs emerge from eight NAND gates. The gates all have four inputs. Using the topmost NAND gate as an example, its bottom input is tied to one input on every other gate. They all are wired to the AND gate that has the three enable controls. This gives the three enable controls the ability to affect all eight gates at the same time.

Often the enables are wired so that they are on but do not enter into the chip activity. To turn on all the enables, so the AND gate will continually output a high, the pins have to be tied to either +5 volts or ground, whatever is needed to turn on the gate.

The three input select pins are each wired to some of the eight NAND gates. The wiring is arranged so that each different bit combination that is input will make one of the NAND gates output a low that will select a chip. At the same time all the rest of the NAND gates will remain in a dormant high state. Table 13-1 shows the truth table.

For example, suppose you want to choose a chip. The address bits are low, low, high, or 001. The high enters pin 1, a low into pin 2 and another

low into pin 3. The NAND gate that will turn low is #1. It outputs at pin 14. You can follow the logic in Fig. 13-8.

The high that enters pin 1 passes through a NOT gate and becomes a low. The low then goes to NAND inputs on gates 6, 4, 2, and 0 effectively turning them off. That same low though passes through another NOT gate, becomes a high, and is input to NAND gates 7, 5, 3, and 1. These NANDs are possible turn on choices.

The low that enters pin 2 also pass through a NOT gate and becomes a high. The high then goes directly to NANDs, 5, 4, 1, and 0. The high also passes another NOT gate and turns off NANDs 7, 6, 3, and 2.

The low that enters pin 3 also passes a NOT gate and becomes a high. The high goes directly to 3, 2, 1, and 0. The high then passes through a second NOT gate, turns into a low, and enters 7, 6, 5, and 4.

After all is said and done, there is only one NAND gate that received all highs. The rest of them each received one or more lows. One low is enough to cause the NAND output to hold at a high. Only NAND #1 was turned on and output a high.

The three address bits 001 choose a chip out of the eight that it is able to select from. The three enable selects permits increased selection ability with this chip. This chip is a staple item in microcomputers.

THREE-STATE MULTIPLEXERS

It was mentioned in the RAM chapter that the dynamic RAM chips only have eight address pins. In an 8-bit computer, there are 16 address lines. 16 lines are needed if 64K addresses are to be located by the MPU. Yet the RAM chips only have eight address pins. The addresses must be multiplexed in order to address 64K.

For instance on each 4164 RAM chip there are 64K individual bits, each with its own address from 0 to 65,535. A set of eight chips will provide byte-sized locations, with each chip donating a bit position to make up a byte of D7-D0. One data line is connected to each chip in the set.

The multiplexing of the eight address pins

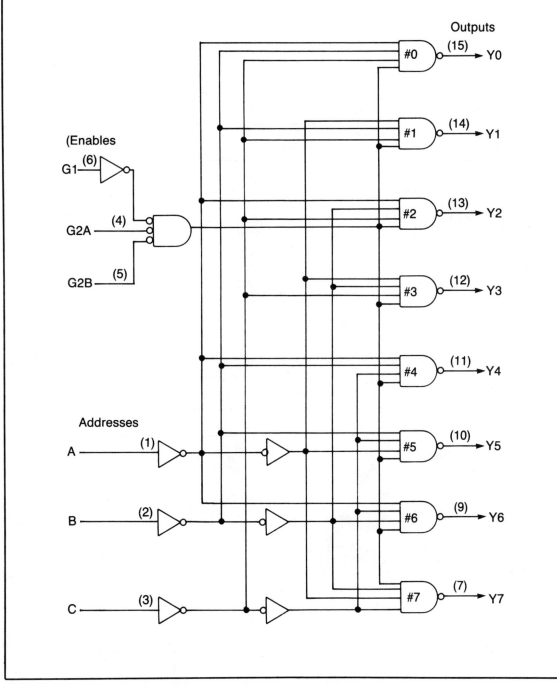

Fig. 13-8. The three enable bits are able to turn on the AND gate which in turn enables one connection on each of the NAND gates. The three address bits then selects one of the NAND gates according to the combination of highs and lows.

Table 13-1. 74LS138 Truth Table.

Inputs						Outputs *0 (held high)							
*E1	*E2	E3	A0	A1	A2	0	1	2	3	4	5	6	7
L	L	H	L	L	L	L	H	H	H	H	H	H	H
L	L	H	H	L	L	H	L	H	H	H	H	H	H
L	L	H	L	H	L	H	H	L	H	H	H	H	H
L	L	H	H	H	L	H	H	H	L	H	H	H	H
L	L	H	L	L	H	H	H	H	H	L	H	H	H
L	L	H	H	L	H	H	H	H	H	H	L	H	H
L	L	H	L	H	H	H	H	H	H	H	H	L	H
L	L	H	H	H	H	H	H	H	H	H	H	H	L

means that each pin is used twice during a single addressing operation. The 16 bits are all presented to the multiplexers at the same time but exit the circuits, eight bits at a time.

A commonly used multiplexer chip found in microcomputers is the 74LS257. The 16-pin DIP is shown in Fig. 13-9. It has eight address input lines. To accommodate 16 address lines, two 74LS257s must be used. Refer to Fig. 13-10. Some of the pins are tied together. This makes the two chips act in concert.

The common lines are the +5 volt supply and ground, the chip select, and the output control. The

lines that act independently are the eight inputs and four outputs on each chip. When they act together, they are able to receive 16 address bits and output eight address bits at a time.

A pair of 74LS257 chips working together have their output control pins 15, *OE, tied together. With this pin the two chips can be shut down. Note the output OR gates in Fig. 13-11. They are all three-state types, and they all connect to *OE. If a low enters *OE, it passes through a NOT gate and becomes a high, which causes all the ORs to three-state.

The common chip select pins 1, *CS, all

Fig. 13-9. The 74LS257 is a commonly used multiplexer chip that can receive eight bits and then output four bits at a time in sequence.

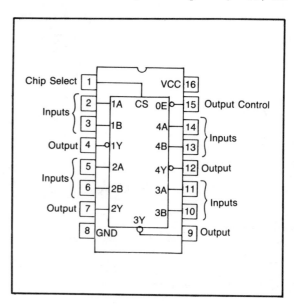

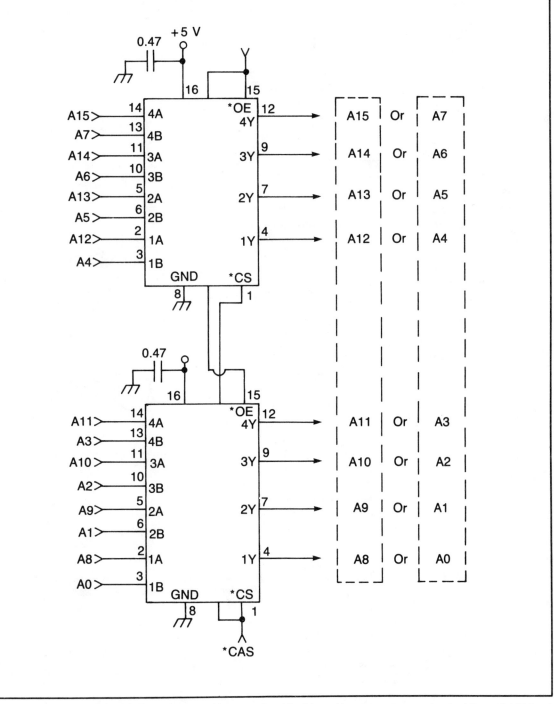

Fig. 13-10. Two multiplexers tied together are able to receive 16 address bits at one time and output them eight bits at a time. This wiring outputs A15-A8 at one time and A7-A0 next.

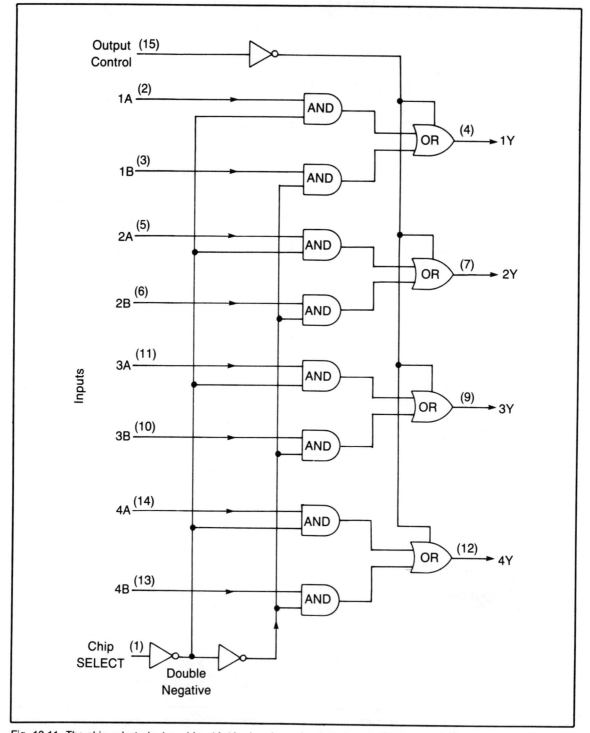

Fig. 13-11. The chip select pin 1 enables 1A-4A when it receives a low and 1B-4B as it receives a high.

232

connect to AND gate inputs. There are eight AND gates in each chip, making 16 gates in the pair. One input chip connection is made to every AND gate. The other AND attachment has four of the gates connected to one line between two NOT gates and the other four lines extend from the double NOT gate connection.

The chip select signal is *CAS the column address strobe. If you'll recall from the RAM chapter, dynamic RAM is addressed with the aid of the two strobes *RAS and *CAS. The *RAS signal strobes the row address bits into the row address decoder in the RAM, and the *CAS signal strobes the column address bit into column address decoder. Between the two, they locate an intersection in the RAM matrix where the addressed bit is found and is accessed.

The *RAS signal goes low first during the address cycle and the *CAS signal goes low afterwards. The lows are the enabling pulses. The same thing happens at pin 1 of the 74LS257 chips without *RAS. *CAS arrives to trigger the bit passage.

The actual address bits are connected directly to the eight input pins of each 74LS257. They are connected in somewhat of a staggered manner. One chip receives bits, A15-A12 and A7-A4. The second chip receives A11-A8 and A3-A0. Figure 13-10 shows the exact connections at the pins. Internally each AND gate receives one of the address bits. The address bits all arrive at the same time.

The other input of each gate is connected to the chip select, pin 1. Pin 1 is held high. While it is high, the connections after the two series NOT gates are also high since the high passes through two NOT gates. This connection is attached to four of the AND gates. The enabling high on the gate causes the output of the AND gate to be the same as the address bit input.

Meanwhile, the connection between the two NOT gates is low. The low is sent to the remaining four AND gates. This makes the output of these four gates all lows. These lows are also applied to the four OR gates.

With this arrangement, whatever state is output from the first four AND gates, which is the state of four address bits, is output from the four OR gates during *RAS. The same thing happens in both multiplex chips making a total output during *RAS of eight address bits. The bits connect to the eight input connections of each RAM chip and the row address bits are sent to the RAM's internal row decoders.

Then along comes *CAS. This low changes everything. The logic state after the two NOT gates in the chip select line goes low. This low is coupled to the AND gates that just passed address bits and cuts them off. The connection between the two NOT gates now becomes a high. This high reached the AND gates that had been off and turns them on.

The remaining address bits that are still present on these AND gates now control the AND outputs. Whatever bits are present on the AND input now shows up on the AND output. These are fed to the four OR gates which also passes them without further ado. Each chip outputs four address bits and the remaining bits enter the same connections the row address bits have just passed through. These are the bits strobed by *CAS and are passed into the column address decoder of the RAM chips.

These multiplexer chips then are nothing more than a receiver that can change 16 bits into two sets of eight. Each set of eight can then be strobed into dynamic RAM to locate the row addresses with one set of eight and the column addresses with the other set of eight.

SAM

SAM stands for synchronous address multiplexer. The 40-pin DIP in Fig. 13-12 does a lot of the jobs on one chip that are normally performed by many chips. SAM does three major jobs. First of all, it generates all of the clock signals with only the help of a quartz crystal. Secondly, it conducts all of the address multiplexing required for dynamic RAM. Refer to Fig. 13-13. This includes a refresh signal so the RAM capacitor bit-holders do not run down. Thirdly, it does the chip select work. With the help of a decoder like the 74LS138, it produces three address bits that can choose one out of eight chips. Refer to Fig. 13-14.

SAM is connected directly to the 16 address

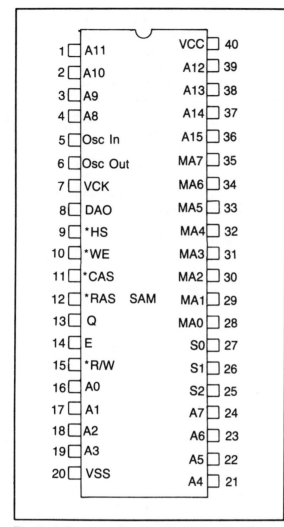

1	A11		VCC	40
2	A10		A12	39
3	A9		A13	38
4	A8		A14	37
5	Osc In		A15	36
6	Osc Out		MA7	35
7	VCK		MA6	34
8	DAO		MA5	33
9	*HS		MA4	32
10	*WE		MA3	31
11	*CAS		MA2	30
12	*RAS	SAM	MA1	29
13	Q		MA0	28
14	E		S0	27
15	*R/W		S1	26
16	A0		S2	25
17	A1		A7	24
18	A2		A6	23
19	A3		A5	22
20	VSS		A4	21

Fig. 13-12. The synchronous address multiplexer, SAM, is a 40-pin DIP that does three main jobs. It generates the master clock signals, it does all of the multiplexing for the dynamic RAM including refresh and it performs the chip selection.

bits. It has registers but they are not connected to the data bus. SAM's registers can be written to in an unusual way and be set or cleared. Without a data bus, though, the SAM registers cannot be accessed and read.

SAM has one 16-bit register. The arrangement of the bits is shown in Fig. 13-15. The register controls the entire SAM chip. Since there is no data bus to the register, other more unusual means must

be used to set or clear the bits.

Each bit in the register is given two addresses on the memory map. This gives the SAM chip 32 separate addresses that can be written to. The addresses cannot be read without a data bus. They can only be addressed, which is the extent of the writing operation.

The bits are addressed with 16 odd and 16 even number addresses. Each of the 16 bits have one odd and one even address. The addresses are all in sequence. The chip is built so that when an odd number location is addressed, the bit that it selects is set with a high. When the same bit's even number location is addressed, the bit is cleared and will contain a low.

Memory Map

The 16 bits all act in an independent manner. Refer to Fig. 13-16. Each bit is wired into internal circuitry and is able to manipulate its circuit for its own purposes. Bits 0, 1, and 2 are used to control the display mode that the video display chip can output. The bits might need other help from other chips in the computer, but it can put out a set of three bits to help in the display. The three bits can produce one of eight bit sets and thus enable one of eight video display modes. There will be more about video displays in the next chapter.

The next seven bits in the SAM register, 4-9, are used to control the starting address of the RAM that is going to contain the video display information. Bit 10 can be set or cleared to also control addresses.

Bit 11 and 12 connect into the clock circuits in SAM and control the clock frequency range. Bits 13 and 14 adjust SAM to different size dynamic RAM chips. This allows SAM to help in the addressing of 4K, 16K, or 64K dynamic RAM chips. Bit 15 gives a choice of control over two different types of memory map.

Block Diagram

Since SAM is a Synchronous Address Multiplexer, it first of all must be in sync with the MPU. At the bottom left of Fig. 13-17 are the clock circuits. The system clock is a combination of the crystal, some resistors, and capacitors as described in Chapter 8. The clock generates two signals $\phi1$ and $\phi2$. SAM is used with the 6809 MPU, which is a form of 6800. $\phi1$ is the waveshape that conducts the system addressing and $\phi2$ takes care of the data movement from MPU to memory and back. Bits 11 and 12 of the SAM register control the rate of the clock. The input from the control register block to the clock block denotes that fact.

Above the control register is SAM's address multiplexer. The 16, bits from the address bus A15-A0 all enter the multiplexer. Incidentally the 16 bits also are given entrance to the control regis-ter and the address decoder to the left of multiplexer. A15-A0 are able to set and clear a register bit, as just described, when they contain a register address. The bits are also able to generate a 3-bit set that can be sent to an external decoder like the 74LS138 as shown earlier in this chapter. The big change that the address bits go through, though, is in the address multiplexer.

The multiplexer in SAM is quite like the 74LS257 chip previously described. It works with the dynamic RAM chips. There are a number of multiplexed address lines out of SAM. They are designed to first output the row address bits for the eight RAM chips and then the column address bits

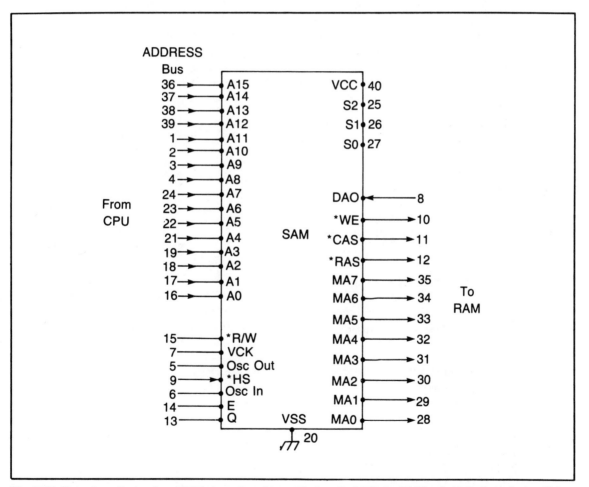

Fig. 13-13. The schematic drawing of SAM shows the address bits from the MPU, the S0-S2 select bits, the output multiplex lines to RAM and the clock and control pins. Note there are no data bus connections.

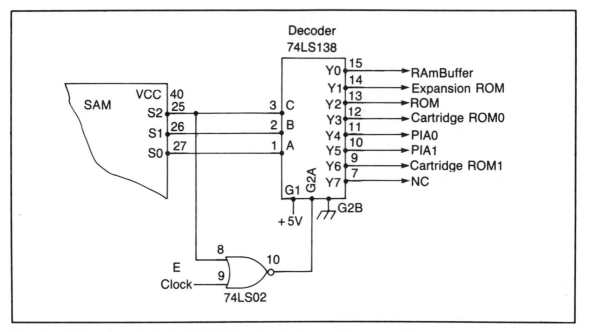

Fig. 13-14. SAM works well with the 74LS138 decoder chip to select the various chips.

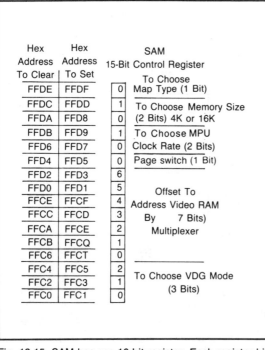

Hex Address To Clear	Hex Address To Set		SAM 15-Bit Control Register
			To Choose
FFDE	FFDF	0	Map Type (1 Bit)
FFDC	FFDD	1	To Choose Memory Size
FFDA	FFD8	0	(2 Bits) 4K or 16K
FFDB	FFD9	1	To Choose MPU
FFD6	FFD7	0	Clock Rate (2 Bits)
FFD4	FFD5	0	Page switch (1 Bit)
FFD2	FFD3	6	
FFD0	FFD1	5	Offset To
FFCE	FFCF	4	Address Video RAM
FFCC	FFCD	3	By 7 Bits)
FFCA	FFCE	2	Multiplexer
FFCB	FFCQ	1	
FFC6	FFCT	0	
FFC4	FFC5	2	To Choose VDG Mode
FFC2	FFC3	1	(3 Bits)
FFC0	FFC1	0	

Fig. 13-15. SAM has one 16 bit register. Each register bit has two addresses. One address sets the bit and the other address clears the bit.

236

of the RAM chip set. The lines connect directly onto the RAM address pins from SAM. No in-between multiplexer is needed. SAM is the multiplexer.

The multiplexer takes the A15-A0 bits and separates them to accommodate RAM. The input bits 13 and 14 from the control register tells SAM what size memory is in the computer. SAM separates the 16 address bits accordingly. If there is 16K in the RAM, then the chips are 4116 types and only need seven address bits to locate one out of 16K bits on a chip. There will be seven bits that are strobed into the row address decoder by *RAS and seven bits that are strobed into the column address decoder by *CAS.

The multiplexer block also performs the refresh needed to keep the dynamic RAM charged up. A RAM refresh signal exits the general timing circuits and is sent to a 7-bit counter circuit. The counter continually counts from 0 to 127 which are the addresses of the rows in the RAM chip set.

Each 7-bit count is sent to the address multiplexer. The multiplexer is able to send the address out over the RAM address lines during the

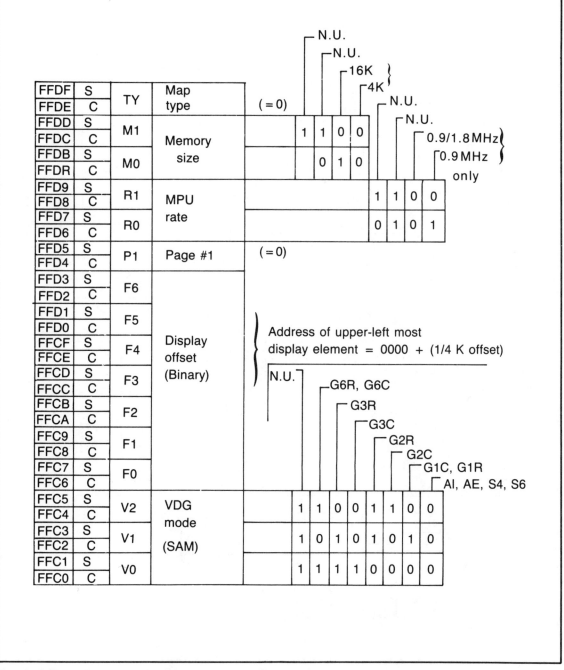

Fig. 13-16. The register has its own little memory map. The map shows what each bit or combination of bits will do when configured.

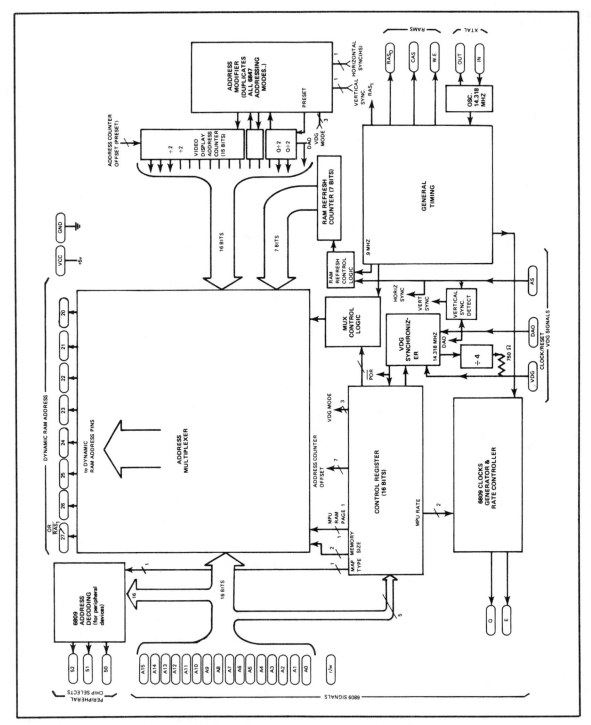

Fig. 13-17. The block diagram is centered around the address multiplexer circuits since SAM is in essence a super multiplexer chip.

238

time that $\phi1$ is low. This addressing of the rows recharges the capacitors in the rows at a time that data is being moved. This does not interfere with normal addressing.

SAM also produces signals to drive the video display circuits. They are covered in the next chapter. In order for a video display chip to run a video monitor, it needs to generate TV signals. The signals are sync, blanking, video, and color if required. SAM is able to generate both the video and color. It also receives horizontal sync and the LSB of the video display chip address lines to keep the display chip in sync with the system. The entire video RAM system is discussed in the next chapter.

SAM is in essence a super address multiplexer. It is placed in the computer in the address bus so that the complex addressing of the chips in the memory map can be handled from the single large chip.

Chapter 14

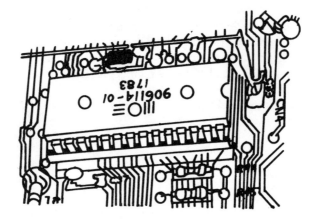

Putting Your Work on TV

THE TV PICTURE IS A NATURAL INTERFACE that the computer uses to output its results into your eyes and brain. At any instant, the TV picture, from your point of view, is a screenful of light that shows you video. The light is brightness and the video is the computer results.

The TV display at any instant, from the computer point of view, is a single electron beam that leaves a hot cathode and impinges on a piece of phosphor to create a dot of light. Why the disparity in sight of the display between the two viewpoints? It is because an instant to your eyes is about a thirtieth of a second. An instant to the computer is one clock period, which could be a millionth of a second or faster. The fastest thing you can see could be a million or more operations to the computer. To understand what is happening in the display, you must examine those lightning operations that the computer uses to get the video into the TV brightness.

TV PICTURE

The cathode ray hits one dot of phosphor at a time

(Fig. 14-1). The computer, at that instant, can cause the ray to either turn off or stay on. The dot of light, of course, will be extinguished when the beam is cutoff or light brightly when the beam is on. The cutoff and stay on happens as a low or high is applied to the cathode ray circuit. A low causes the beam to cutoff and a high keeps the beam on.

The cathode ray passes through a glass neck to get to the phosphor face. Around the neck are two coils. One is a horizontal coil and the second a vertical coil. They are able to grab ahold of the electron beam and move it anyway they please. The horizontal coil moves the beam from side to side more than 15,000 times a second. At the same time, the vertical coil pulls the beam up and down sixty times a second. The net result of this pushing and pulling is that 264 lines of light are drawn on the TV screen every 1/60th of a second. There will be more about this in Chapter 16.

COMPUTER DISPLAY BLOCK

There are many ways that computers can format the TV light or raster, as it is called, to contain the

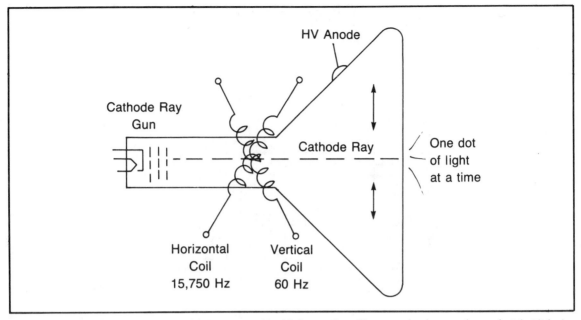

Fig. 14-1. The TV display is producing a picture one dot of light at a time. The scanning is occurring so fast that it fools your eyes into perceiving a full screen of light.

results of the computing. The idea is to layout the TV screen to handle alphanumeric characters and graphics. Some screens are able to show 80 characters across and 24 down. Others might have 40 characters × 25 down. A typical format is 32 characters across × 16 down. Refer to Fig. 14-2.

The 32 × 16 format is able to show 512 characters on the TV screen. Typically they would be placed in 192 of the 264 scan lines. The remaining 72 lines are used as a border at the top and bottom of the screen. When the cathode ray is scanning those lines, it is shut off so they appear black. There is also a black border around the display. Within these boundries is the computers display block.

The display block is arranged into 512 character locations. Each character location is the recipient of 12 scan lines. The character is able to be displayed with seven of the scan lines. The remaining five lines in the 12 are used to separate the characters. They, too, will be shut down and not light as characters are displayed.

Each character is drawn on the TV screen, five dots wide and seven scan lines high. There is also three dots that are not lit between the characters.

Therefore each line in a character location is eight dots wide. Five display the video and three are shut off to space the character. The character is fully displayed as the seven character lines are drawn. The character dot matrix therefore has 35 dots of light in a 5 × 7 layout. Refer to Fig. 14-3.

When pure graphics are displayed, the video circuits operate in a different mode and could make use of every possible dot in every character location. Graphics displays could conceivably light up the borders around the entire display block too.

VIDEO RAM

Each character location on the TV screen is assigned one byte in RAM. In a display with 512 character blocks, there would be 512 video RAM bytes. The TV blocks on the screen are constantly scanned. There is a counter circuit in the computer that scans the RAM bytes in sync with the CRT scanning. As a particular block on the screen is scanned its corresponding video RAM byte is also being read as the counter circuit increments the addresses of the bytes. Refer to Fig. 14-4. All this

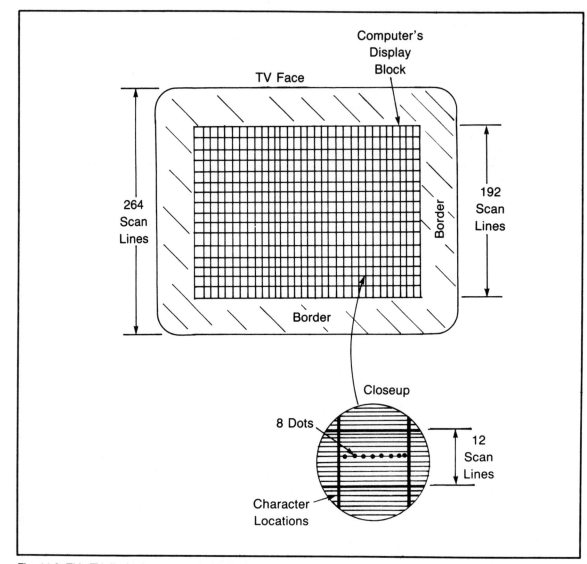

Fig. 14-2. This TV display is composed of 512 character blocks, 32 across and 16 down. There are 12 scan lines to a block and eight light dots to a scan line.

takes place at the computer rate. The only thing we observe is the TV screen constantly displaying the contents of the character blocks.

When you strike keys, the character you strike appears on the TV screen. This is because you generate an ASCII set of bits that is stored in video RAM at the location that matches up with the screen location. As the counter scans the location, it recognizes the ASCII code as an address pointer.

The computer also contains a Character ROM. In the ROM are bit matrixes for each character on the keyboard. Refer to Fig. 14-5. The matrix for a character is five bits wide and seven bits high. Each high bit is meant to light up a dot. Every low bit is designed to turn off a dot.

The ASCII code that is stored in video RAM becomes a pointer for its character matrix in ROM. As video RAM is scanned the ASCII codes address

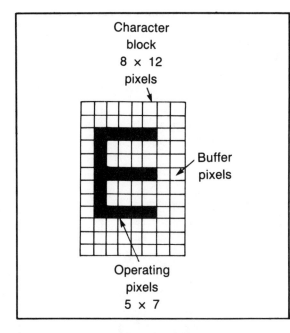

Fig. 14-3. A character is lit up in a 5 × 7 dot matrix in the character block. Each dot is called a pixel, abbreviated from picture element.

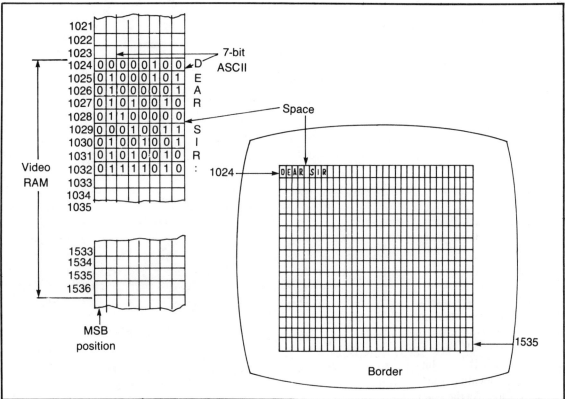

Fig. 14-4. Each character block on the screen is assigned from one byte in RAM. These RAM addresses are called video RAM.

Video RAM ASCII Bits Character Pointer	Character ROM Memory Matrix							
	7	6	5	4	3	2	1	0
53264	0	0	0	0	0	0	0	0
53265	0	0	0	0	0	0	0	0
53266	0	1	1	1	1	1	0	0
53267	0	1	0	0	0	0	0	0
53268	0	1	0	0	0	0	0	0
53269	0	1	1	1	1	0	0	0
53270	0	1	0	0	0	0	0	0
53271	0	1	0	0	0	0	0	0
53272	0	1	1	1	1	1	0	0
53273	0	0	0	0	0	0	0	0
53274	0	0	0	0	0	0	0	0

Fig. 14-5. The character ROM contains bit patterns that produce corresponding pixel patterns. The video RAM byte is a pointer to the ROM character pattern address.

the character ROM and access the matrix. The matrix contents finds its way to the electron beam. At the correct times, the beam is turned off and on to create the character on the screen.

When the ASCII code from the keystrike is placed into video RAM, the loading is conducted by the MPU. When the ASCII code is accessed (which causes the character ROM to display the selected bit matrix), the MPU is not involved. The MPU has completed its job after it loaded the video RAM location. There is another set of logical cir- cuits that continue the job. They are almost like another digital computer. They can be called the VP for video processor.

VIDEO PROCESSOR

The VP in Fig. 14-6 consists of a divider network, the character generator, a shift register, a sync generator and a video output circuit. The divider network contains the counter that must maintain the scanning frequency so the video RAM is continually accessed and keeps the characters on the TV screen intact.

The character generator is the ROM that is addressed by an ASCII byte and the scan position. The shift register is a parallel-to-serial dot data converter. It accepts the bits from the Character ROM in parallel form and converts it to serial so the CRT can use it.

The sync generator handles the horizontal and vertical sync problems that the scanning experiences. Each dot must be turned off and on in precisely the correct physical location on the TV screen. The horizontal and vertical sync pulses must be placed into the serial video output in the right places so the scanning lines are drawn, retraced, and pulled up and down at the right time.

The video output circuits mix the various TV signals together so they make sense. The signals are then amplified and the sync signals matched to the video so one is not stronger than the other. Then the final signal must be buffered so the output is 75 ohms in impedance. That is the input impedance of video monitors or rf modulators.

Divider Network

The divider network can be made up of four 4-bit counters such as 74LS93 types shown in Fig. 14-7. Each chip has four flip-flops totalling 16. The input to the divider is a clock frequency. Each chip is wired to divide the incoming frequency. The first counter divides it by 4. The resultant frequency is then applied to the second counter. The second one divides it by 14. This result is 15.84 kHz. This is a perfect frequency to use to horizontally draw the electron beam across the TV screen and simultaneously read video RAM. It is tapped off for this purpose.

The next two counters are designed to divide by 12 and 2 respectively. That produces 660 Hz. The signal is then passed to the last counter which divides the signal is then passed to the last counter which divides the signal by 11. That produces

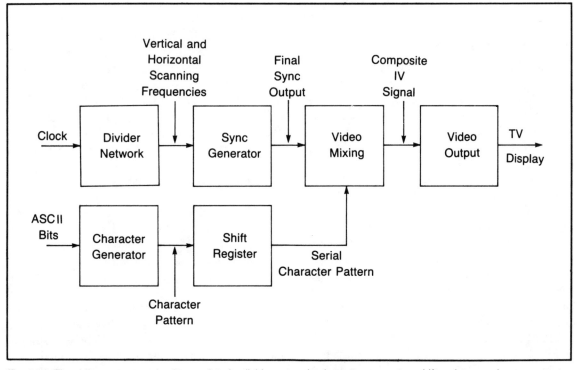

Fig. 14-6. The video processor circuits consist of a divider network, character generator, shift register, and sync generator feeding into a video system.

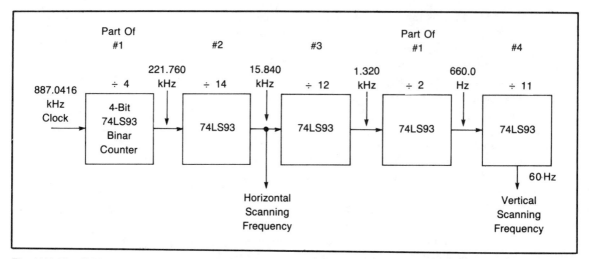

Fig. 14-7. The divider network takes the clock frequency, divides it up, and produces the horizontal and vertical scanning frequencies.

exactly 60 Hz which is perfect vertical frequency to conduct the video RAM reading and electron beam scanning. This is tapped off for the vertical sweep operation.

Character Generator

The character generator chip in Fig. 14-8 has seven inputs. Six of the inputs come from a 74LS174, a hex flip-flop latch chip. The seventh bit comes from a 74LS175 a companion latch chip. The seventh bit is needed during graphics work.

The 74LS174 latch is connected directly to six bits of the video RAM. As the video RAM is being read in time with the cathode ray scanning, bytes leave the RAM and go into the latch. The latch is able to hold them momentarily till they are to go on and get their turn in parallel-to-serial processing.

The latch is controlled at pins 1 and 9, the clock and clear pins. Pin 9 receives a clock signal that goes low every six dot scanning cycles. As the clock goes back to a high, the rising edge triggers the latch and passes the bits onto the next circuit, the character generator.

Pin 1 is a clear signal. It comes from a 74LS74 D FF. Pin 1 is held high and does not affect anything till the MPU must access video RAM. At that time, a low is sent to pin 1 and the chip is

cleared which means it has a clear output. The MPU is not to do any work with the video RAM while the Video Processor circuit is scanning and accessing the video RAM. The accessing takes place in this way.

A 74LS74 flip-flop output is connected to the clear pins of the 74LS174 latch. The signal into the 74LS74 input is a control signal that chooses whether the MPU is going to control the latch or if the VP is to control the latch. When the MPU is to control the latch, a low comes from the FF to the clear pin 1. This forces the latch to clear. The MPU can then access the video RAM without interference.

If the 74LS74 output goes back to its high state the latch is freed and can go back to processing the video bits coming from video RAM as the RAM is constantly scanned by the divider signals. The latch then feeds the video bits into the character generator. The generator in turn puts out the matrix of bits that will produce a character in a screen location.

The generator receives the seven bits of ASCII code at pins A6-A0. The generator recognizes the seven ASCII bits as an address. There are three more address bits that are multiplexed from the address bus. These bits enter pins RS1, RS2, and RS3.

Inside the character generator, which is a ROM, are the character patterns. Each character consists of seven rows of five dots each. The ten address bits, A6-A0 and RS1-RS3, become the addresses of the rows of the selected character. The addressing frees the contents of the seven rows.

The bits exit the Character ROM, one five-dot row at a time. They leave via pins D0-D4. These bits form the character in the screen location. The highs light a dot in the 5 × 7 matrix and a low cuts off the light of a dot.

In actuality the cathode ray scans the picture

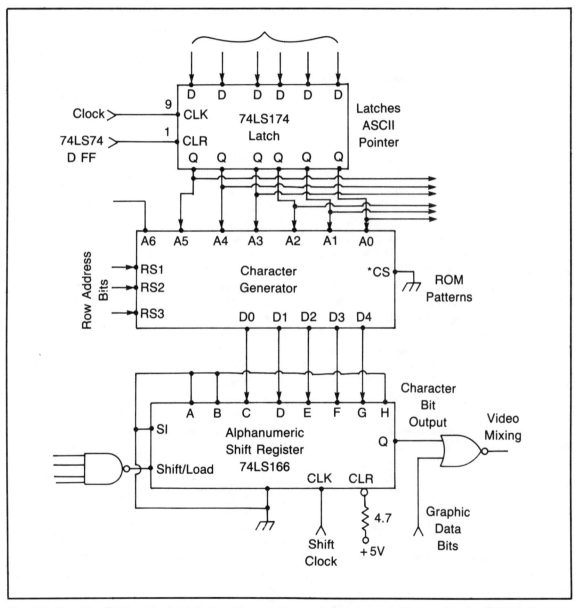

Fig. 14-8. The video RAM pointer is latched and then, at the proper time, forwarded to the character ROM. A character bit pattern is addressed and sent on to the shift register. From there, serial bits continue on to the video output circuits.

face line-by-line. In this 64 characters across format, it takes 12 scan lines to form a line of characters. There are seven rows of character dots and five rows of black dots. Starting with an ASCII 7-bit code in the latch and the cathode ray striking the phosphor at the upper left hand corner of the display, the first scan line is about to be drawn.

RS1-RS3 receives three low bits, 000. The character generator outputs the first five bits of the addressed character in the ROM matrix. The bits go on to light or darken the first five dots of the first character location on the screen. After the first line of the first character has been scanned, the electron beam arrives at the second character location.

Meanwhile the latch has received the ASCII code for the second character. The code is sent to the Character generator. The code addresses the second character. RS1-RS3 remains at 000. In fact, these bits remain at 000 for the duration of the entire first scanning line. They cause the ROM to output the first 5-bit row of the second character.

As the first scan continues the latch keeps receiving ASCII code after ASCII code for each subsequent character. The first row of every character is thus drawn on the TV screen in its location. At the end of the first scan line, the picture tube has one long line of lit and darkened dots.

Once the first scan line is finished, the electron beam is turned off and retraced back to the start point of the second scan line. The address bits at RS1-RS3 are incremented by one. They become 001.

The ASCII code for the first character is again placed into the latch. The latch again outputs to the character generator. The first character pattern is again addressed. However, this time the second row of the pattern is output. The ROM outputs the second row of bits. They find their way to the CRT and form the dots for the second row of the first character. The scan goes on and all 64 of the characters get their second rows of dots on and off.

The beat goes on. The lines get scanned, the ASCII code addresses a character, the RS1-RS3 inputs select a row of bits in a character pattern, and the display is drawn. It takes seven rows of five bits

to display each character properly. At the end of the seven rows, the electron beam is turned off to allow five dark rows to separate the characters. Our eyes are then supplied with the video to do our computing.

Alphanumeric Shift Register

The electron beam scans the picture one dot at a time in serial fashion. Every 5-bit set that leaves the character generator emerges five abreast in parallel. In order for the five bit set to fit into a scanning line, it must be converted from its parallel form to serial. A shift register like a 74LS166 is used to perform the conversion.

The 5-bit row sets are timed to appear at its appointed place on the TV screen and not during one of the five blanked out lines between characters or in any of the boundary blacked out areas around the display block. At its precisely appointed time the five bits are loaded into entry pins for the bits. These pins are shown as C, D, E, F, and G. The rest of these input pins are all disabled along with two other unneeded pins by tieing them together and connecting them to ground. A NAND gate is also connected to the shift/load enabling pin. There are four inputs to the NAND gate. They must all have the exact right timing pulses in order for the shift register to operate.

The shift register is run by a clock input. Once all the conditions have been met and the NAND outputs a low to the shift/load pin, the next clock pulse loads the dot bits into the shift register. Then one dot clock after that the shift register starts outputting the bits from Q, one bit at a time in serial form.

The NAND gate, as it goes high and low due to its inputs, turns the shift/load pin high and low. When shift/load is low, the chip receives and loads parallel bits from the character generator. As shift/load then goes back high, the chip outputs bits in serial form from Q. Incidentally the clear pin is disabled by tieing it to +5 volts. That keeps the clear control from interfering with the parallel-to-serial bit activity.

Once the serial bits are loose from Q, they go directly to a NOR gate. They pass through the NOR gate and are sent to the video mixing stages. They have to be mixed with the sync and blanking level signals.

Sync Generator

It was mentioned earlier that the divider network is set up to produce horizontal and vertical sync signals. These were the signals that are fed to the horizontal and vertical coils in the deflection yoke around the neck of the picture tube. They sync the cathode ray and conduct the precise scanning.

Two 74C04 chips, hex inverters, start the sync generating going. One is the horizontal generator and the other is the vertical generator. They each receive their respective inputs from the divider network. Refer to Fig. 14-9.

After each signal passes through two inverters, they both arrive at 100 k potentiometers. Following the pot, each side encounters two more inverters bypassed by a 330 pF and a 0.047 pF capacitor. These little networks are horizontal and vertical phase shift controls. When you adjust the horizontal pot, you change the horizontal timing slightly. The effect on the TV screen is the display will shift from side to side somewhat. This is a horizontal centering control.

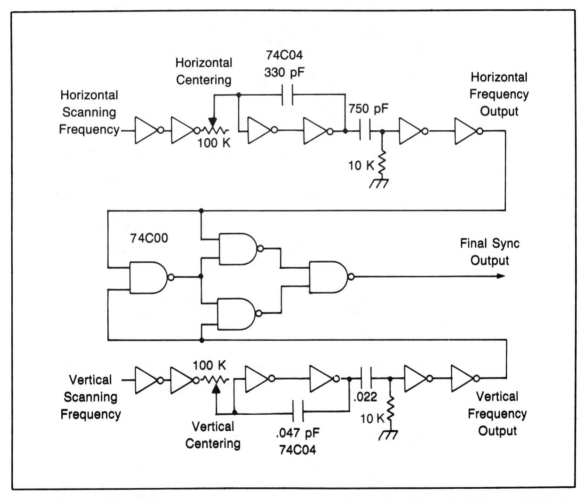

Fig. 14-9. Two hex NOT gates produce the horizontal and vertical sync frequencies. They are mixed in quad NAND chip and from there proceed to the video system.

The same thing occurs in the twin vertical network. The vertical timing is somewhat effected and the pot is a vertical centering control.

After the display block is properly centered, the shape of the pulse must be tailored to produce a linear picture on the screen. An RC network with a 750 pF capacitor and a 10 K resistor will differentiate the waveshape into the correct form. The wave is then amplified and inverted in two more inverters and then sent on to a group of NANDs in a 74C00 CMOS quad NAND chip. The processed horizontal signal passes through the group and it too is sent to the video mixer stage. The horizontal sync signal is designed to be a four microsecond pulse.

The vertical signal gets the same treatment. It is given correct phasing with the pot circuit and then sent to an RC differentiation network. The resistor is also a 10 K but the capacitor is 0.022 μF to handle the slower vertical pulse. The vertical signal joins the horizontal in the quad NAND gate.

Figure 14-10 shows what happens in the NAND gates. The horizontal input pulses are shown in the first line. The slower vertical input is shown in the next line. The two signals are then mixed and inverted. Finally the total signal is inverted once again. The final output is a designed collection of long and short pulses. These are the final sync pulses that are needed to be mixed with the video bits to produce the total display.

Video Mixer

The NOR gate mentioned before in Fig. 14-8 is the recipient of the character bit patterns into one input. The second input is used to accept graphic data bits. While the NOR gate is receiving character bit patterns the graphic input will be low. The two inputs are never on at the same time. The NOR gate outputs to an amplifier type chip that sends the bits to the video amplifier transistor in Fig. 14-11.

The total sync signal is sent directly from the output of the NAND mixer to a sync amplifier. The collector of the sync amplifier is connected to the base of the video output. The video output, and npn transistor, is going to receive and amplify the current of the composite TV signal. The npn outputs through its emitter directly to the TV display over a 75 ohm cable.

Forming the Composite TV Signal

Figure 14-11 has three resistors between two transistors acting as switches. The video is entering one transistor and the sync the second transistor. Two of the resistors, a 270 ohm and a 330

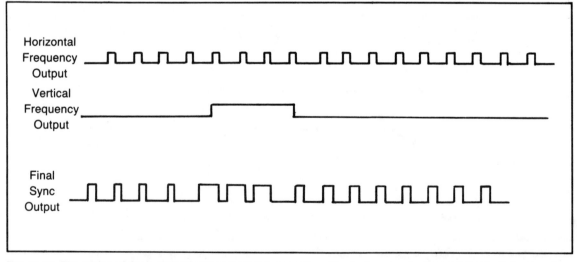

Fig. 14-10. The mixing of the horizontal and vertical pulses produce the final sync output containing both frequencies.

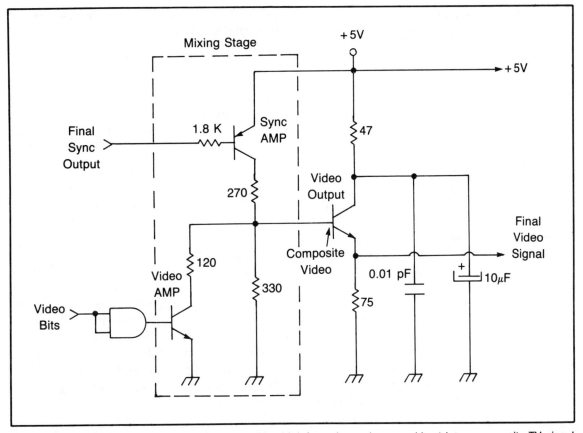

Fig. 14-11. The final sync output is mixed with the video bit information and are combined into a composite TV signal that will drive a TV monitor.

ohm, forms a voltage divider from the collector of the sync amplifier to ground. The other resistor, 120 ohms, forms a voltage divider from the video amplifier to ground. The two transistors act as a sync input switch and a video input switch to the resistors.

The sync and video outputs from these two circuits are input to the final video output current amplifier at its base. The base bias resistor, the 330 ohm is common to both inputs. This insures that the two inputs will enter the video output amplifier at the same voltage level.

The sync pulses are input to the base of the sync amplifier. The video dot information is input to the base of the video amplifier. Both the sync pulses and the dot data enter the base of the video output together. The timing of the signals have

been set precisely by the previous circuits. The sync pulses and the corresponding dot information will be arriving at this mixing point at their appointed times.

The sync pulses are varying from a zero volt low to about 1.23 volts high. The 1.23 volt level is called the *black level*, which means that the sync pulses never attain a high enough voltage to turn the cathode ray on. The sync pulses then are able to conduct their moving of the cathode ray with deflection coils, without causing any light on the TV screen. The sync pulses thus are able to operate and not produce interference. All voltage levels below 1.23 are considered in the *blacker than black* region.

The video dot data, on the other hand, are supposed to be visible on the TV screen. Therefore, the dot voltage level top is above the sync black level. When a dot is supposed to light up, the voltage input to the video output is 2.75 volts. This voltage spike mounts on top of the sync pulse and is high enough to turn on the cathode ray for the instant the dot is meant to light up. The 2.75 volts is the *white level*.

Figure 14-12 shows the various signals in the generated composite TV signal that the computer is able to produce. As the cathode ray starts at the top left of the screen, a horizontal scan line begins. As it scans, the dots that are to light get high voltage pulses. The dots that are to remain black do not have any voltage pulses.

At the end of every scanned line, a horizontal sync retrace pulse occurs that draws the cathode ray back to the left side of the picture. The ray is blanked out so the retrace cannot be seen.

All of the lines are thus scanned. At the end of the raster, a vertical retrace pulse occurs and the cathode ray is retraced invisibly back to the top of the screen once more. The scanning goes on and on, constantly displaying the characters that the ASCII code in the video RAM calls for.

In Chapter 16, the actual TV circuits are covered which will provide greater detail on the actual display mechanism.

GRAPHICS

The preceding discussions dwelled on the way alphanumeric characters were displayed on the screen. Putting graphics on the screen instead of letters and numbers from a Character ROM is quite the same except that you have to build the graphic pattern yourself instead of taking the pattern out of a ROM.

Instead of loading the video RAM with ASCII codes, the RAM is loaded with graphic dot data. The data is loaded into the same 74LS174 latch. The output of the latch however goes to a multiplexer, a 74LS153. Refer to both Fig. 14-8 and Fig. 14-13.

From the multiplexer, the graphic bits are sent to a shift register. The graphics use a different but identical shift register. Then the graphic dots are output at Q and go on to the same NOR gate that the alphanumeric video used. Either the graphics or the alphanumerics will pass through the NOR gate. Only one will be operating the computer in this circuit.

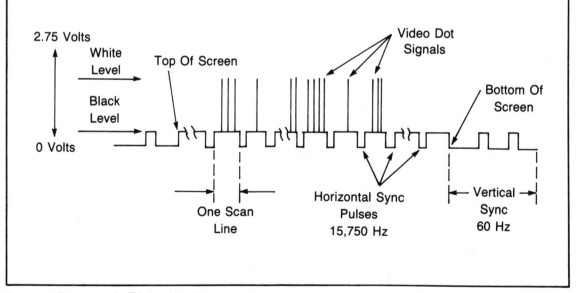

Fig. 14-12. The composite TV signal is able to turn pixels on, turn them off and blank out the screen during sync pulses.

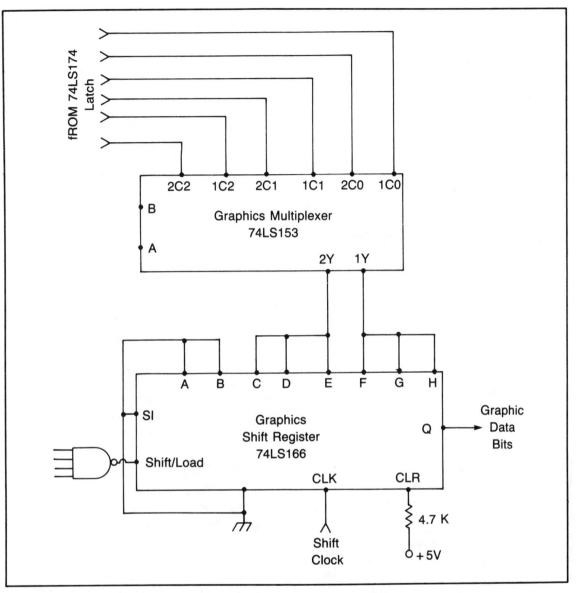

Fig. 14-13. The graphics circuits are almost identical to the alphanumeric circuits. The main difference happens due to the fact that RAM is loaded with graphic dot data rather than ASCII character codes.

From the NOR gate, the graphics video dots are then mixed with the sync signals in the same way that the alphanumerics are.

VIDEO DISPLAY GENERATOR CHIP

The video display circuits discussed in the last sec-tion are the hard way to get your work prepared for the CRT. There are many large chips, often 40-pin DIPS, that contain all the circuits just de-scribed plus more. They not only are able to pro-duce a composite TV picture, but they can install color so it may be displayed on a color monitor or TV set.

An example of this sort of chip is the MC6847. It can be found working with a chip like the SAM from Chapter 13. SAM can do its RAM addressing as described later in this section.

The 6847 is a member of the 6800 MPU family. Figure 14-14 shows the 40-pin DIP. The chip is not a resident of the memory map. It is dependent upon SAM to receive its input. The input arrives via the data bus into eight pins, DD7-DD0.

Actually, SAM is scanning the video RAM that corresponds byte-by-byte with the character locations on the TV screen. There are 512 screen locations and 512 video RAM bytes to service those locations. SAM scans the video RAM and causes the contents of the RAM to be delivered over the data bus to the VDG chip, the 6847. The data arrives in parallel bytes to a 74LS273 octal latch. Re-fer to Fig. 14-15. The latch connects the eight bits to the VDG. The latch outputs in time with a clocked *RAS signal so it is in sync with the SAM addressing of the dynamic RAM holding the ASCII character codes.

The ASCII code enters the VDG. Inside the VDG are all sorts of ROM areas. One of the ROM sections is a Character ROM, but it is all internal and not accessible through the chip pins. The ROM in response to the ASCII code that arrives is able to generate an alphanumeric character in the same way a separate Character ROM is able to. Thus dot data bit patterns are produced.

The VDG is not only able to output alphanumeric characters, it is also able to produce all sorts of graphics and combinations of alphasemigraphics. There are 14 or more possible outputs. Five control lines arrive from a PIA. The combination of bits on these control lines set up the number of different display modes. There are many ROMs in the chip that are turned off and on and accessed by these lines to develop modes.

The VDG is synced into place with a horizontal sync and one address line from SAM. The vertical sync signal is connected to the three-state control of the VDG. This blanks out the VDG output during the TV screen vertical retrace time. That way there is no interference in the display as the electron beam is brought from the bottom of the picture tube face back to the top.

The VDG is clocked with the standard color TV signal that TV men will recognize, 3.58 MHz. This frequency when entered into a color TV receiver will produce the required colors.

VDG Output

Once all the signals are input to the VDG, it goes ahead and produces the various components that make up the composite color TV signal a receiver can handle. This is all internal to the chip. The output signals exit out of their respective pins.

There is one pin that outputs the Y signal. The Y or luminance signal contains all of the dot data and the sync signals. Figure 14-16 shows the voltage levels, the black level, the blanking level, and the sync pulses. There are four levels of video

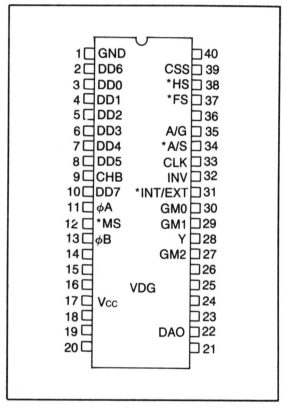

Fig. 14-14. The 40-pin video display generator chip takes the place of all the previous display circuits. It contains all the various alphanumeric, semigraphic and graphic ROMs in addition to the composite TV manufacturing circuits.

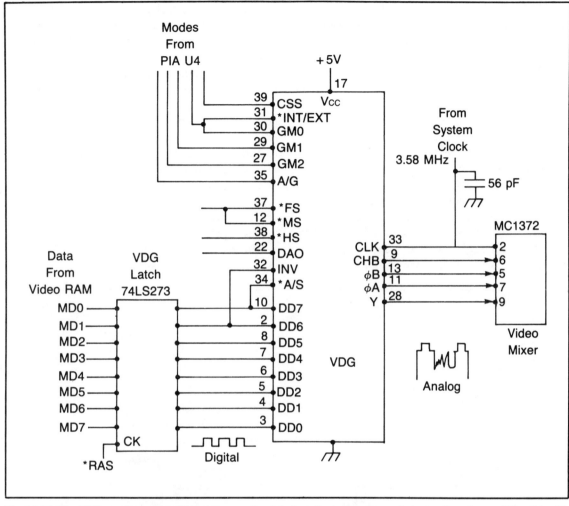

Fig. 14-15. The VDG receives video RAM data over the data bus. It receives its mode instructions from a PIA. It is able to output the ingredients to produce a composite color TV display.

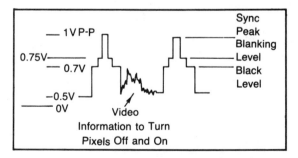

Fig. 14-16. The Y signal, also known as luminance, is nothing more than the composite black and white signal. It is easily viewable on the ordinary TV repair scope.

brightness shown from utter blackness to pure white.

Two pins output color combination signals. They are ϕA and ϕB. They are able to specify particular colors. They also specify the color burst signal developed around the 3.58 MHz color signal. The signal CHB, chroma bias is a DC level voltage. It keeps the level steady so the other signals can track together accurately. There will be more about this in the next section on the color circuits.

The four output pins are connected into a form of color TV mixing circuit. In the MC 1372 chip

255

are circuits that mix the Y, φA, φB and CHB outputs together to produce a composite color TV signal.

Color Mixing

The color mixer chip in Fig. 14-17 receives the 3.58 MHz clock signal at the oscillator input. This is the color carrier frequency. It must be very accurate at exactly 3.579545 MHz. If it is off, the TV display will be incorrect.

Inside the mixer, the circuits take the color carrier and derive a color burst of eight cycles from it. This is a precise burst of the frequency 3.579545 MHz occurring with the correct phase of the color carrier. The eight cycle sample of the carrier contains the frequency and phase information of the carrier. The rest of the carrier at this stage is

removed. The burst is going to represent the carrier till the signal arrives at the color circuits in the TV receiver that will be doing the displaying of the color picture.

In a computer's composite color TV picture, there are a number of elements. First of all there is the Y signal, which is the actual video picture containing the monochrome dot data. With the Y are the horizontal and vertical sync pulses. Refer to Fig. 14-12. The horizontal pulse occurs at a 15,750 Hz rate or once every scan line. The vertical pulse happens at a 60 Hz rate or once every raster field of 264 scan lines. This composite monochrome dot data picture is the typical output of a computer's video system.

In order to install color into the display, more information must be slipped into the composite

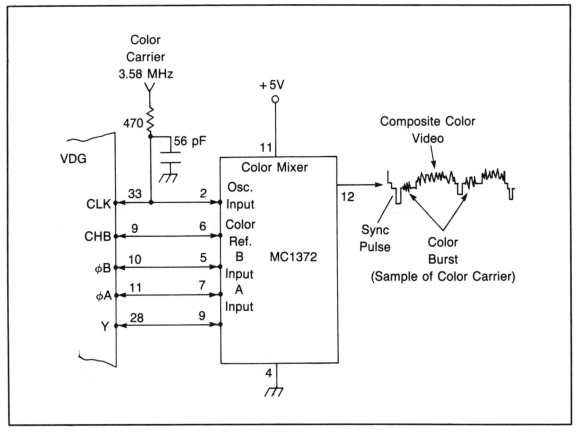

Fig. 14-17. The color mixer chip combines the Y signal with the other signals to produce the composite color signal. The incoming color carrier is processed and produces a color burst alongside the sync pulse.

structure. There is plenty of space between horizontal pulses. The Y dot data takes up very little spectrum space between the pulses. The color information is easily *interleaved* between horizontal spaces.

The first order of business is to establish a color carrier. Then the color carrier can be modulated with the color information. The color carrier of about 3.58 MHz is being produced by dividing the master clock as discussed. The color carrier is injected into the mixer chip. Refer again to Fig. 14-17. Then the color signals ϕA and ϕB are input to the mixer. The signals ϕA and ϕB are then made to modulate the carrier. The signal CHB contributes to the modulation by setting a steady level for the modulation to take place at.

It so happens that color TV sets cannot handle a signal that comes in on a color carrier. Years ago the design was set and cannot be changed. The color carrier must, after the color signals have modulated it, be suppressed. It is suppressed and a signal minus the carrier is left interleaved between sync pulses.

That is the reason for the color burst shown in Fig. 14-18. It is a sample of the carrier and contains the vital information of frequency and phase in its cycles. It will go along with the rest of the color information through to the color TV receiver. Color receivers have circuits that reproduce the color carrier so the receiver can then accurately demodulate the reconstructed carrier to retrieve the color TV signal for display. The reconstruction of the carrier is accomplished with a color oscillator in the TV. The color burst syncs the oscillator into running at the correct frequency and phase.

The color burst must be installed between horizontal sync pulses on the composite signal that the computer generates. In addition, the burst must not be installed in a place where it could possibly interfere with the rest of the composite signal.

It is installed in a spot that gets blacked out. The horizontal sync pulse is placed in a voltage level that cannot turn on the cathode ray. The sync pulse is installed on a voltage pedestal. The pedes-

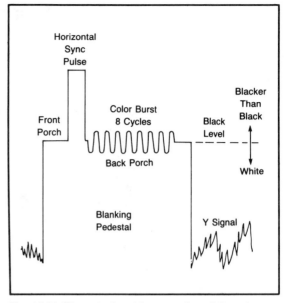

Fig. 14-18. The color burst is a sampling of the color carrier. It retains the frequency and phase information from the carrier.

tal is described as having a front porch and a back porch. The pedestal is at a voltage level that is blacked out. The color burst has been placed on the back porch of the pedestal out of the way and blacked out.

The MC 1372 mixer chip then receives the Y signal, the color carrier frequency, the color signals ϕA, ϕB, and CHB. It processes the signal by first modulating the carrier with the sidebands and then interleaving the color signal between the Y signal components. Then it removes the carrier frequency leaving only the incomplete color signals. At the same time, it produces the color burst and installs it onto the back porch of the sync pedestal.

The mixer then outputs the complete composite color TV signal containing your computing in color. This signal is finished, but it is very weak. Its current must be amplified before it can go on. In addition if the signal is going to be used in a commercial TV receiver, it must be modulated with a station carrier such as channels 3 or 4. These circuits are covered in Chapter 16.

Chapter 15

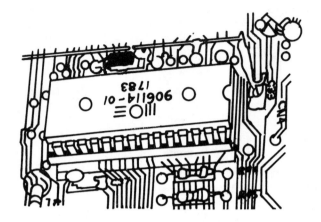

The Memory Map

EMERGING FROM THE TYPICAL 8-BIT MPU are 16 lines named A15-A0. These address lines are able to form 65,536 combinations of bits. That means the ordinary memory map that the MPU can address easily has 64K locations. At each location, bytes of data can be found.

A decoder at each location is able to receive the address bits and connect up to the location. All locations are held in an off position. Only when the decoder sends an enabling signal to that chosen location will it go on. When the addressed location turns on, all of the rest stay off. Control lines like the $\phi2$ and Valid Memory Address, VMA, help choose the locations.

Except for special situations like a SAM chip, every location on every chip in the memory map connects to the 8-bit data bus. When the location is addressed, the MPU can read the location or if possible write to the address. Bytes of data travel over the data bus to and from the location. Control lines like the read/write or interrupts help the data bus direct the flow of bytes.

The 16 bits work together to do two different types of addressing. Both types are shown in Fig. 15-1. The chips in the memory map have pins designated as CS and *CS. A CS pin is enabled by a high. A *CS pin is enabled with a low. The high order bits in the address usually do the chip selection type of addressing. The second type of addressing is the register selection. On each chip, there are a number of registers. Some chips have only a few registers while others have thousands. The lower order bits are usually assigned the task of addressing the registers on the chip.

In a chip with just a few registers, the addressing only needs a few pins for address bit input. For a chip with thousands of addresses, ten or more pins are used for the register addressing chore.

TYPICAL LAYOUT

If you were going to map a single board computer, it could have the chips or ports shown in Fig. 15-2 addressed by the MPU.

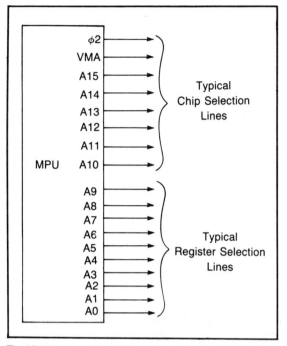

Fig. 15-1. In general, the higher address lines select the chips while the lower lines select the registers on the chips. The clock output like φ2 and valid memory address lines help the higher address lines select the chips.

8 dynamic 4116 RAM chips
2 4K ROMs
1 cartridge port with 16K
2 PIA ports

One good way to layout the addresses is with the dynamic RAM starting from zero on up to 16,383. Then the rest of the chips can be placed in the high addresses. That way if you want to expand RAM there will be address space immediately after the existing RAM.

The RAM, therefore, can be assigned addresses right off. They are placed at decimal 0-16383. This is hex 0000-3FFF. In binary, that is 0000 0000 0000 0000-0011 1111 1111 1111. The spaces between the numbers are only there for clarity. There are no spaces in the program counter register bits.

The 256 byte I/O port space is found to contain only two PIAs. The memory area assigned is

decimal 65280-65535, hex FF00-FFFF. The two PIAs have three chip selects and two register selects. The two register selects are always tied to the low bits A1 and A0. The chip select bits, one *CS and two CS will have to be tied to high significant bits in the assigned memory area.

The 16K cartridge port is assigned to decimal address space 49152-65279, hex C000-FEFF. All of the address lines are sent to the port so it can be versatile.

The two 4K ROMs are given the hex addresses 4000-4FFF, and A000-AFFF. These ROMs are going to need 12 address lines each to address their registers. These will be A11-A0, the 12 lowest address bits. In addition each ROM is going to need chip select lines.

As you can envision, the laying out of the bits to address each location individually without accidentally enabling some other location is tricky.

ASSIGNING BITS

Table 15-1 shows the memory map that has been decided on for this example computer. There are decimal numbers, hex symbols, and binary digits. The binary bits are the most referred to during the original wiring of the system. The hex is only notations of the binary, four bits to a hex symbol. The decimal is required so we humans will have an easier time of it.

The eight RAM chips are considered as one as far as the addressing goes. The addresses are all wired in parallel and are identical. There is one set of address lines on the table for all eight chips.

There are two address lines on the tables for the ROMs. They each have a separate address. There is little thought needed for the cartridge port. All of the address lines go to the port and the peripheral that plugs into the port will require addressing thought.

The PIAs though need addresses. The three chip selects will be assigned to higher bits and the two register selects go to A1 and A0 as mentioned.

The first step in the writing is to assign the register address bits for all chips. The 4116 RAMs have 16K byte locations. To address 16K locations

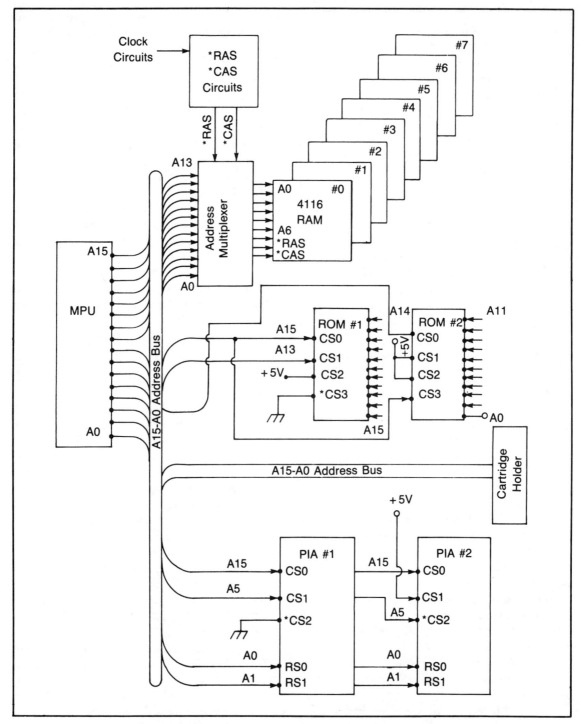

Fig. 15-2. A typical address bus leaves the MPU and goes to RAM, ROM, I/O chips and cartridge holders. To address dynamic RAM some sort of multiplexing and refreshing signals are usually required.

Table 15-1. Memory Map.

Chips	Decimal	Binary	Hex
RAM	0	0000000000000000	0000
	to		
	16383	0011111111111111	3FFF
ROM 1	16384	0100000000000000	4000
	to		
	20479	0100111111111111	4FFF
ROM 2	40960	1010000000000000	A000
	to		
	45055	1010111111111111	AFFF
Cart-ridge	49152	1100000000000000	C000
	to		
	65279	1111111011111111	FEFF
PIA 2	65280	1111111100000000	FF00
	to		
	65283	1111111100000011	FF03
PIA 1	65312	1111111100100000	FF20
	to		
	65315	1111111100100011	FF23

requires the use of 14 address lines. RAM is going to need A13-A0. A13-A0 are going to go to all eight chips simultaneously. You can x out those bits on Table 15-2.

In actuality, the 14 bits in Fig. 15-2 are going to be attached to a multiplexer circuit. A13-A7 are going to address the rows in the chips while A6-A0 will be addressing the columns. Therefore in Table 15-2, A13-A0 will be tied directly to the multiplexer to get the register addressing done.

The ROMs each have 4K. The 12 address lines A11-A0 are needed to address the 4096 registers in each ROM. You can x out those bits in Table 15-2. The PIA registers are also obvious. To address them RS1 and RS0 are connected to address lines A1 and A0.

Addressing the registers is the first part of the layout. The registers can be x'ed out because the same lower address lines connect to all the registers. When bits go out over these lines, they pass up 65,535 closed locations and only open up one. They can possibly be decoded to open up a lot more but only one chip in the computer is selected to be addressed. These bits will enable only the location on the chip selected.

CHIP SELECTS

In my example computer memory map, there are a few chip selections. The complete RAM set is one choice. Either ROM can be selected, and one of the PIAs is available by itself. The cartridge port can also be selected.

In Table 15-2, the PIA selections are calculated first. It is a good idea to figure out the highest address connections before the lower ones. You'll find this avoids accidentally addressing more than one chip at a time.

261

Table 15-2. Address Wiring Compared to Hex Address.

Chip Connections	Address Wiring A15-A0																Hex Addresses	
	15	14	13	12	11	10	9	8	7	6	5	4	3	2	1	0	FROM	TO
PIA 1	CS0										CS1				RS1	RS2	FF20	FF23
PIA 2	CS0										*CS2				RS1	RS0	FF00	FF03
ROM 1	CS0	CS1			X	X	X	X	X	X	X	X	X	X	X	X	A000	AFFF
ROM 2	*CS3	CS0			X	X	X	X	X	X	X	X	X	X	X	X	4000	4FFF
RAM Multiplexers			X	X	X	X	X	X	X	X	X	X	X	X	X	X	0000	3FFF

A good place to put the PIAs are up near the very highest address numbers. When calculating address connections, it is handy to use hex and binary rather than decimal. Table 15-2 shows the connections from A15-A0 to the chip selects and the register selects. Convenient addresses for the PIAs are FF20-FF23 and FF00-FF03. Each PIA needs four address numbers.

PIA #1 has one of its three chip selects, CS0, connected to A15. A second pin CS1 is connected to A5. The two register selects go to A1 and A0. That way, when FF20 is sent out over the address bus, the PIA register at FF20 is enabled. FF20 is 1111 1111 0010 0000 in binary. When the bits on A15 and A5 are both a 1 (CS0 and CS1 high), PIA#1 is enabled. The third chip select *CS2 could be tied to ground and be kept out of the way and enabled all the time.

The register selects with 0s on them choose the register at that address. To choose the other three registers, the bits on A1 and A0 are varied. That is the initial wiring up of PIA #1. If no other chips are wired, FF20-FF23 will dial up the four registers.

When PIA #2 is added to the system, it is connected so that FF00-FF03 will address it. CS0 can be tied to A15. CS1 is not needed. CS1 is therefore tied to +5 volts and thus kept from interfering and enabled continually. There is only one problem. With only CS0 connected to the address bus, when PIA #1 is addressed, both PIA #1 and PIA #2 will be addressed. That is where *CS2 comes in. If *CS2 is connected to A5, when A5 receives its high bit, *CS2 will not turn on. *CS2 will only turn on when a low arrives there. A low does arrive when FF00-FF03 bits are on the address bus.

These few connections are all that are required to properly address the two PIAs. The full 16 lines are not needed. The only voltages needed to enable the PIAs are three bits input to the three chip selects and two bits for the register selects. The unconnected bits can be high or low. The PIAs have no connection with them as far as addressing goes. Even though you send out 16 bits only the five connected ones perform the chip and register selection.

Wiring up the cartridge selector is not calculated. The 16 lines all go to the cartridge port. All 16 are wired to their own pins. The number of pins actually used are a function of the cartridge. Different cartridges use the address lines in many different ways.

Wiring up the ROMs is accomplished much like the PIAs. The important difference is the large number of registers in the ROMS. There are 4K bytes in each. If the ROMs have four chip selects three positive and one negative, the addressing can proceed, again with the higher numbers first.

ROM #1 is addressed from A000 to AFFF or in binary 1010 0000 0000 0000 to 1010 1111 1111 1111. Now bits A11-A0 present no problem. They are all connected to A11-A0 of the address bus. The 4K register addresses need all 12 of those bits to internally address the registers. This only leaves the four highest bits, A15-A12.

To place hex A into A15-A12, the bits 1010 are used. CS0 and CS1 are connected to A15 and A13. If CS2 and *CS3 are connected to +5 volts and ground, ROM #1 will be addressed with A000-AFFF. Next, ROM #2 must be attached. Its most significant nybble is hex 4. In binary, that is 0100. It can be addressed by connecting CS0 to A14. A high on A14 will address ROM #2.

The remaining chip selects are connected to the appropriate +5 volts or ground. The positive chip selects are tied to the voltage source and the negative selects are to tied to ground. There is an alternative measure that you could take with the negative *CS3. Instead of connecting it to ground, you could attach it to A15. This will insure the fact that a high on A15 might not accidentally enable the adjoining A14 connection on ROM #2.

Once the PIAs and the ROMs have their address lines connected, the only addresses left to attach are the 4116 dynamic RAM set. They are easy. The RAMs all have the same addresses and are wired in parallel.

There are actually two different sets of addresses in a dynamic RAM, the row addresses and the column addresses. The address numbers are the same. The difference between them is when they are addressed. First the 128 rows are addressed and then the 128 columns. It is as if the addresses are on two different chips, a row chip and a column chip.

The address numbers for both are 0-127. It takes seven address bits to locate one out of 128 locations. There are seven address pins on the 4116, A6-A0. Both the row bits and the column bits are input to these pins, in the same way but at different times.

A select pulse decides when to input the row bits and the column bits. The row select pulse is *RAS, the row address strobe. When it goes low, the row decoder in the 4116 is enabled and accepts the row bits. The column select pulse is *CAS, the column address strobe. After *RAS goes low, then *CAS goes low. This enables the column decoder in the RAM, and it accepts the column bits. The decoders then open up their addressed row and column.

At the intersection of the row and column, the bit holder is energized and either outputs a copy of its contents or receives a bit from the data bus line connected to the chip. The R/W line from the MPU decides on the action that takes place.

The two sets of seven bits leave the MPU over A13-A0. They go to a pair of multiplexers like 74LS257s. The bits are input to the multiplexers in a staggered format. The two multiplexers then output to the A6-A0 pins of the RAMs. They can then, for example, output address bits A6-A0 during the low of *RAS, and then output A13-A7 when it is the turn for *CAS.

In actual practice, all 16 of the address bits, A15-A0 are wired to the inputs of the multiplexers even though there is no need for the two highest bits, A15-and A14. This method becomes useful if and when the RAM storage capacity is increased. If you look on the memory map, the RAM ends at 16383 decimal. There is an address gap from 16384 to 32768. This is another available 16K addresses.

To obtain use of the additional 16K, all that is needed is to convert the RAM set. The 4164 chip is almost pin for pin identical to the 4116. The major difference is shown in Fig. 15-3. Pin 9 on the 4116 is Vcc. Pin 9 on the 4164 is used as the eighth address pin input, A7. It is used to receive the eighth bit A7 for the addressing and then the bit A15 for the column addressing.

In a 4164 chip, there are 256 rows and columns.

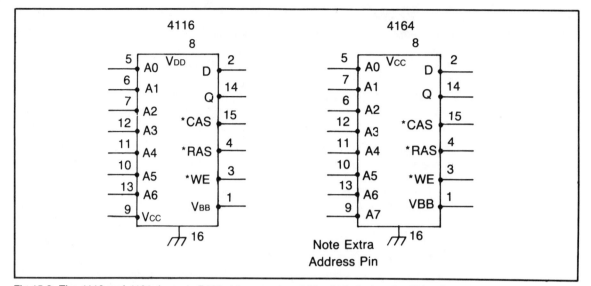

Fig.15-3. The 4116 and 4164 dynamic RAM chips are almost identical pin for pin. This allows you to convert an 8-bit MPU from 16K up to a 64K RAM.

The rows can be addressed with eight bits, A7-A0. The columns are addressed with bits A15-A8. Actual conversion instructions usually come with the new RAM set.

With the 4164 chips, the address gap between 16K and 32K is filled in with usable byte-sized registers. Yes, there are a total of 64K possible addresses on a 4164 chip. However there is only convenient room on this address map for the 32K. As a result you must disable the additional 32K so those addresses won't be enabled when a PIA or a ROM is addressed. The disabling can consist of only allowing *CAS to be active when 0-32767 is being addressed. During the addressing of any locations between 32768 and 65535 *CAS is shut down.

If you want to utilize the RAM addresses between 32768 and 65535 you could set up a banking system. This would be a logical circuit that would reenable *CAS and disable the chip selects to the PIAs and ROMs. These procedures are all custom tailoring of your computer. Simply, it is nothing more than turning chip select pulses off and on.

DATA BUS CONNECTIONS

Wiring up the data bus is fairly easy. Refer to Fig.

15-4. The data bus only goes to the chips or ports in the memory map. In my example computer, those chips are the PIAs, ROMs, the set of dynamic RAM chips, and the cartridge holder. In other computers, the data bus could go to a chip that is not in the memory map like a video generator.

In all the chips except dynamic RAM, the data bus D7-D0 is sent over eight lines to eight pins on a device. In dynamic RAM, the eight lines are separated and only one line goes to a chip.

When static RAM is used in a computer (in addition to or instead of dynamic RAM), the wiring is not like dynamic RAM. Static RAM is addressed exactly like a ROM is. All bits of a byte are on the same chip. When the RAM byte location is accessed, all of the bits give up a copy of their contents or receive a byte together. All eight bits of the data bus connect to one static RAM chip.

CONTROL LINE CONNECTIONS

Often, control lines from the MPU take part in the addressing of a chip. For example $\phi2$ of a 6800 MPU can be connected to a chip select pin. If the $\phi2$ signal is connected to a positive chip select such as CS1 then the chip will not be selected except during the times that $\phi2$ is high. When $\phi2$ is low the

264

chip will be turned off no matter what bits the rest of the address lines are indicating.

This technique is used to sync the address lines to any chip the MPU might be writing to. It is a clocked form of chip select that is often necessary.

Another way an address can be doctored is with a VMA line from the MPU. Refer to Fig. 15-5. The MPU can put out a high over this line when this line is to indicate that the address coming out from its A15-A0 pins is a valid one. The VMA will go low when the address is invalid.

The address on occasion can sometimes be

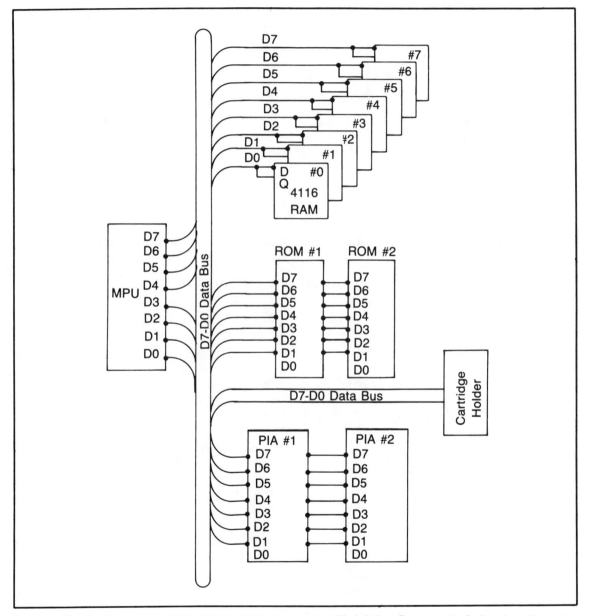

Fig. 15-4. The data bus goes to all the chips on the memory map. All eight bus lines are attached to the addressable chip. The eight dynamic RAM chips though are connected as a single chip, with one line to each chip.

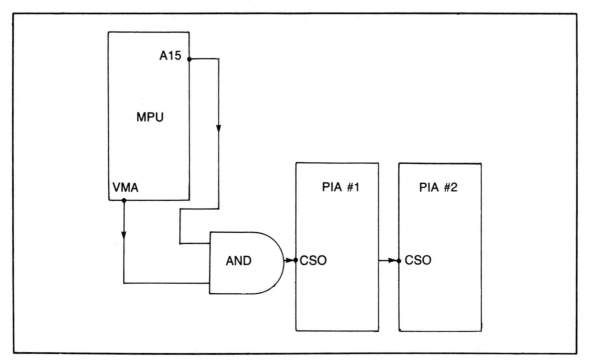

Fig. 15-5. With the aid of an AND gate and the VMA line, the PIAs can only turn on when a valid address is on the bus.

worthless as the MPU is processing data and inadvertently outputs some garbage address as the circuits are whirring. The address also has no meaning when the address is supposed to be three-stated. In these cases, the VMA pin will output a low.

These accidental addresses could possibly access a vital RAM or PIA location causing data to be destroyed. There isn't any worry with the ROMs because its data is burnt into the silicon and can't

be damaged that way.

To eliminate the possibility of trouble, the VMA line can be ANDed along with the chip selects for the RAM and PIAs. That way if the address is valid and the VMA line is high, the chip select signal will pass the AND gate fine and select its chip in normal fashion. Should the address not be valid, the VMA line will go low. This will stop any chip select and keep the memory clear of this possible trouble.

Chapter 16

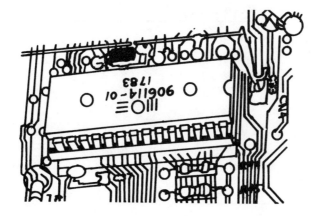

Video Monitor

IN CHAPTER 14, THE VIDEO GENERATOR CHAP-
ter, the discussion ended with the production
of a composite TV signal. The signal contained
video dot data, horizontal sync pulses at 15,750 Hz,
and vertical sync pulses at 60 Hz, all contained in
a voltage area. In order to add color to the picture,
a color carrier was derived from a 3.58 MHz clock
and the carrier was modulated with color sideband
information. Then the carrier was suppressed and
only a color sync burst was sent on with the composite signal.

This signal could be injected directly into a TV
monitor. It could also be made to modulate a channel 3 or 4 rf carrier. When it is rf modulated, the
signal can be displayed on an ordinary TV receiver.
The TV set is the subject of other books. This
chapter is going to concern itself with a video monitor that takes the composite TV signal without benefit of rf modulation.

The monitor is able to use the composite signal
directly. This saves a lot of TV circuits. The monitor does not need a tuner with a channel selector,
a strip of if amplifiers, a video detector, and all the

other circuits needed to process an rf modulated
signal. It is rather a simple affair in comparison to
a home TV receiver.

The monitor in Fig. 16-1 consists of a picture
tube, a high voltage system to apply to the side of
the CRT to attract the cathode ray, a horizontal
sweep circuit, a vertical sweep circuit, and a video
output amplifier. Then a power supply is used, but
it is not critical like the strict regulated one needed
by the computer circuits.

PICTURE TUBE

Picture tubes in monitors come in many different
sizes, shapes, and other configurations. The only
consideration that is vital is the color of the
phosphor in monochrome tubes and the spacing of
the red, green, and blue phosphor dots in a
polychrome tube.

The space between the color dots, called *dot
pitch* is measured in millimeters. The smaller the
spacing, the better the resolution of the picture. A
good monitor has a dot pitch of about 0.5 mm. The

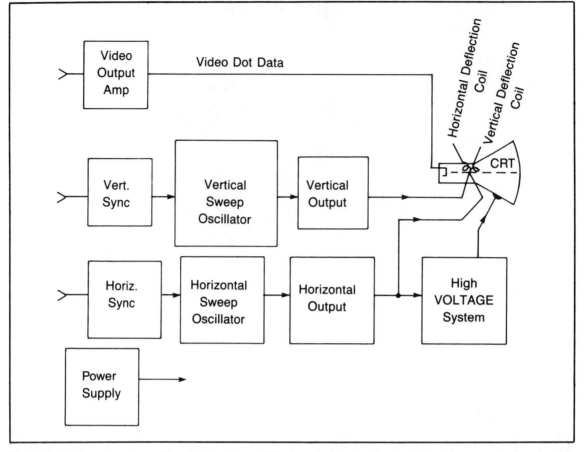

Fig. 16-1. A TV monitor places video dot data into a CRT. A vertical sweep circuit, horizontal sweep circuit and a high voltage system, causes the cathode ray containing the data, to scan the screen and light the phosphor displaying the dots.

usual home TV dot pitch is much more than that.

The spacing between the dots is the limiting resolution factor in the picture tube. The closer the dots are to each other, the greater the resolution and definition of the display.

No matter what the ability of the phosphor in a monitor's picture tube is, the resolution of the display must start with the dot matrix pattern for a character that is in the Character ROM of the computer. For instance, a dot matrix in a character block can consist of 35 dots (5 × 7) or hundreds of dots. A character with a few hundred dots will almost jump off the screen while a 35 dot character is simply viewable. An inexpensive computer will deliver a matrix with the fewer number of dots, but

expensive jobs have the ability to display more concentrated dot patterns.

Most picture tubes can easily handle a 35 or 63 dot matrix that a computer outputs to the monitor. A computer that produces a dot pattern with many more dots than these will require a special picture tube and monitor. It is important in these special cases that the monitor matches up with and can display properly the composite TV picture that the computer generates.

Black and White

The monochrome picture tube in Fig. 16-2 consists of a glass envelope, an electron gun, a high voltage repository, and a face with one color phosphor. The electron gun is an old fashioned assembly used in vacuum tubes. There are filaments that light up and heat the cathode.

Upon heating, thermionic emission causes electrons to leave the cathode. At the far end of the tube is the phosphor face. Around the perimeter of the face plate is the high voltage repository. 15,000 volts of dc is stored there. This 15 K V attracts the electrons, and they head up the neck of the envelope towards the phosphor. As they travel they must pass right through some grid structures.

The first electrode is the control grid. The control grid with the use of changing electrostatic voltage potentials between it and the cathode is able

to turn the electron beam on strong, shut it off or cause different in-between amounts of electrons to flow. If the composite TV signal is applied to the cathode-control grid electrodes, it will cause the electron beam to vary in accordance with it's highs and lows. The highs will make the beam flow strongly while the lows cut the beam off. A strong beam lights dots, and no beam keeps the dots dark.

After the beam is given the dot information, it encounters a screen grid. The screen grid is an electron accelerator. It helps the electrons on their long journey to the phosphor. Following the screen grid is a focus grid. It makes sure the beam is in a tight band and is not diffusing as it travels. The tighter the beam is, the more concentrated it will be as it

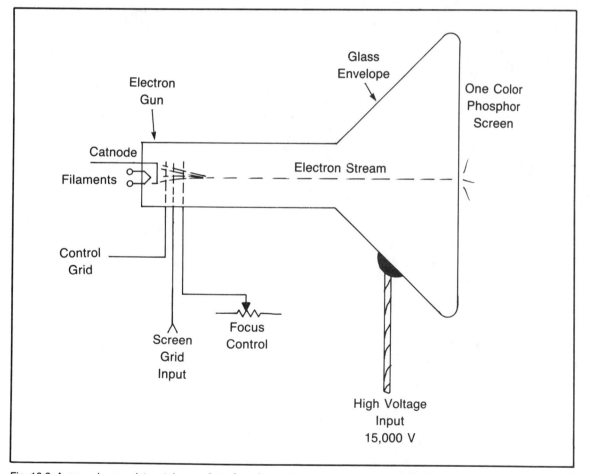

Fig. 16-2. A monochrome picture tube consists of an electron gun, a glass envelope and a layer of phosphor on the screen. The entire screen contains the same color phosphor. Typically the phosphor is white or green.

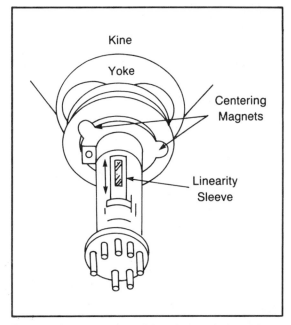

Fig. 16-3. Around the neck of the tube are electro and permanent magnets. The deflection yoke contains the horizontal and vertical electromagnets that sweep the electron stream over the TV face. The centering and linearity sleeve are permanent magnets that can adjust the picture one way or the other.

hits the phosphor. The focus and brightness will be at maximum.

Once the cathode ray clears the electron gun area, it travels down the neck from the gun to the phosphor. At the end of the neck against the bell of the envelope are the deflection coils. Refer to Fig. 16-3. The horizontal coil is putting out an electromagnetic field that grabs the beam and draws

it across the screen like writing, and then it retraces the beam path. At the same time, the vertical coil, at a slower pace, draws the beam from the top of the display to the bottom and then retraces its path. The result is the raster consisting of about 260 horizontal lines of dots on and off.

Color

The color picture tube is layed out like the monochrome tube with the addition of a few items. There are many color CRT schemes, but the following is the most common.

First of all, most color CRTs use an electron gun with three cathode rays. On the CRT face, instead of one layer of one color phosphor, a dot pattern is placed on the screen. Refer to Fig. 16-4. There are three colors of phosphor dots. All colors can be produced by adding the lights together from red, green, and blue phosphor dots. Each color dot receives the energy to light from one of the three cathode rays.

The dots can be arranged in triads. The dot pitch mentioned earlier is the distance between the dots. A metal mask is placed in front of the dot triads. Refer to Fig. 16-5. The cathode rays must encounter the mask before it can get to the phosphor. On the mask, one hole is placed in front of each dot triad. The three cathode rays are electronically aimed to converge at the mask holes, pass through, deconverge and each ray hit bull's-eye on one of the phosphor dots. The light generated can be made to be any color including black and white. Each dot in the triad can be turned on or off.

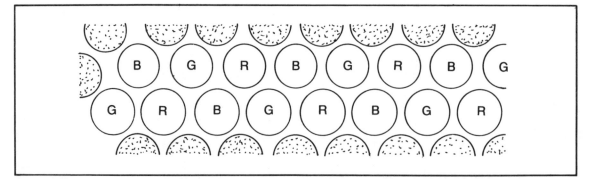

Fig. 16-4. A color CRT face, typically has a pattern consisting of red, blue, and green phosphor dots.

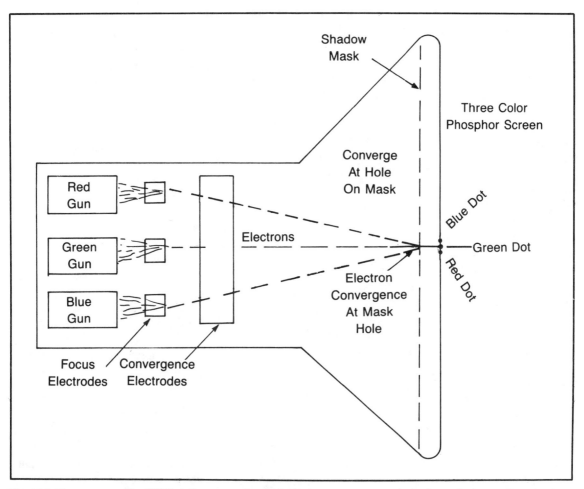

Fig. 16-5. The common color CRT has three guns, focus electrodes, convergence electrodes a shadow mask and a three color phosphor face. There is one hole in the shadow mask for every three color dot triad. The three cathode rays are adjusted to converge at each hole as they scan. That way each ray impinges on its own color phosphor dot.

Around the neck of the color CRT, in addition to the sweep deflection coils, are coils to effect the convergence of the three beams at the shadow mask. The three gun structure also has some coils and magnets to insure the intensity of each beam is correct, and the movement of the beam from the gun will result in good convergence.

The color CRT usually needs a much higher dc attraction voltage, somewhere between 20 kV and 30 kV to pull the three electron beams to the phosphor.

The strength of the electron beam and the convergence quality of the beams affect the resolution of the computer display much more than it does to an ordinary TV picture. The convergence of the rays are much more accurate at the center of the screen. As the beams are swept out to the sides or to the top and bottom, the convergence suffers. This is one of the reasons a computer display is only shown on about 190 lines instead of the full 260 lines that the sweep circuits are scanning. The borders in most displays would be difficult to show characters in.

Interlacing

Another way resolution of the TV characters

and graphics can be affected is the way the monitor interlaces its raster. Computers typically produce a 260 line raster to display its dot patterns with, then the interlacing does not matter too much. Should your computer be one that does operate with an interlaced raster, then you can obtain better resolution with a good monitor that takes pains with the interlace.

Interlacing is used in TV sets to reduce flickering. It was discovered, during early motion picture days, that the problem of flicker could easily be cured by showing the same motion picture frame twice at a speed of 24 frames a second. To the human eye, the flicker disappeared and movement seemed natural.

When TV first started, the designers copied the flicker cure. They designed a picture that was shown twice at a rate of 30 frames a second. It was called *interlaced scanning*. A TV picture was made out of 525 scanning lines. The odd numbered lines, 1, 3, 5, 7, etc. were shown 60 times a second. The even numbered lines, 2, 4, 6, 8, etc. were shown also 60 times a second immediately after the odd lines. The result, 262 1/2 odd lines were shown and then 262 1/2 even lines are scanned on the TV face. The final result is one complete flickerless picture 30 times a second. The 262 1/2 lines are called a *field* and the total 525 line picture a *frame*. These concepts are discussed later in the chapter.

In a computer that has a ROM that delivers a 35 dot character, the interlacing is ignored. Only 191 of the possible 262 1/2 scan lines are used to display the characters. The field sync pulse of 60 Hz runs at the field rate. The video RAM is scanned at a 60 Hz rate to display the dot patterns.

It takes seven scanning lines to show a character. There could be two scan lines above and three below the character, totaling 12 scan lines in a character position on the TV face. In the 190 scan lines, only 16 character rows can be placed on the screen. The resolution is more or less fixed on how well interlaced the scan lines are drawn on the TV screen. Each dot shows up first on an odd numbered line and then the same dot appears on an even numbered line. If the interlacing is messed up, the characters are going to appear with a smeary look.

Adjustments

Figure 16-3 showed the neck of a 12″ CRT where some of the adjustments are located. The deflection yoke itself determines the level of the picture. Should the picture tilt, the deflection yoke is rotated till it is straight.

Centering is made with two tabs on a permanent magnet assembly. Moving them shifts the picture vertically and horizontally without tilt.

There is a linearity sleeve on the neck of the tube. If it is loosened and moved, the character spacing on the two sides of the screen can be made linear.

There are potentiometers for the vertical size, vertical hold, and focus control. The focus is adjusted for overall scanning line thinness. The vertical size control is adjusted for a vertical scanning of about six inches.

The horizontal hold control is the horizontal oscillator coil, not a pot. The width control is also a coil. Linearity is adjusted first, and then the width coil is set so that the horizontal scan is about 8 inches.

MONOCHROME MONITOR

A typical monochrome monitor has a 12″ CRT with white phosphor. It is able to run with +12 volts input and is rated to draw about one amp of current. However, the average power used is only about 12 watts. It is designed to operate in or near room temperature near sea level. It can stand some deviation from these norms, but not too much.

A monitor needs the inputs shown in Fig. 16-6. First of all there is the composite TV signal, and if it is a color computer, it needs the color burst and sidebands along too. The monitor then needs horizontal and vertical sync pulses. Lastly the monitor needs a source of dc power. When the monitor is part of the computer system, the power can be derived directly from the system power supply. Should the monitor stand alone, then it needs its very own source.

The composite TV signal is sent to a video amplifier such as a discrete npn transistor. The horizontal sync signal is delivered to a horizontal sync amplifier another discrete npn transistor. The vertical sync pulse is also sent to a vertical amplifier, an npn. The common dc power, such as + 12 volts, is distributed in a designed manner to all of the circuits.

The TTL input level of the signals is considered to be four volts, ± 1.5 volts. The horizontal scan can be driven with positive going pulses be- tween 4 and 25 microseconds. The vertical is driven with negative going pulses between 100 and 400 microseconds.

The video input will produce white when the signal is positive going. If the signal is negative going, the cathode ray cuts off and the phosphor does not light at that spot.

A TV video signal has a bandwidth of 4.5 MHz.

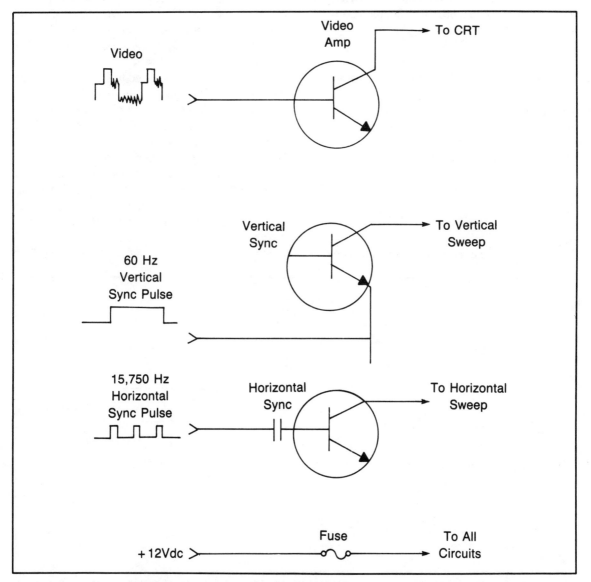

Fig. 16-6. A monitor requires the following inputs. First of all, there is the composite TV signal, either monochrome or polychrome. Then there is the horizontal and vertical sync. Lastly it must have power such as + 12 volts.

This means the TV signal can go from black to white 4.5 million times in one second. A typical monitor like this one has a bandwidth of 15 MHz of 3 dB. It will respond to a pulse rise time of no more than 30 nanoseconds.

The horizontal scanning frequency is 15,600 Hz ± 500 Hz. The horizontal retrace time is no more than 10.5 microseconds. The vertical scanning frequency is anywhere between 50 and 60 Hz. The vertical retrace is no more than 850 microseconds.

Video Input

The video input enters the monitor as shown in Fig. 16-7. It makes its way to the base of the npn video amplifier. The monitor calls for a positive going video signal. The positive signal is amplified in the npn and is inverted to negative going video dot data at the collector output.

The npn is conventionally powered. There is a forward going bias between the emitter at 0.26 volts and the base at 0.67 volts. The silicon transistor needs 0.6 volts to turn on. When there is no signal input, it is off. As the 4 volt TTL input arrives, it causes the amp to start working. The collector is given 56.5 volts. There is quite a bit of voltage and current amplification.

The collector is coupled to the picture tube cathode through a series peaking coil shunt with a resistor. A second peaking coil is in shunt with the collector output. The frequency range of the video is up around 4.5 MHz. In order for the npn to amplify the large frequency range, the peaking coil and a low value resistor must be used. Without the peaking coil and its resonant qualities and with a high resistance as a load, only a low narrow band of frequencies would be amplified. The higher frequencies would be lost.

The video is thus applied to the cathode of the picture tube. The collector voltage also arrives at the cathode. The control grid of the CRT receives a 12 volt fixed bias. This makes the cathode about 45 volts more positive than the control grid. This keeps the cathode ray more or less turned off.

As the negative going video signal arrives at the cathode, it reduces the cathode's positive voltage. The cathode ray responds by turning on. As each dot data peak arrives, the cathode ray flows heavy. The dot in front of the ray at that time will light up as the electrons smack into the phosphor.

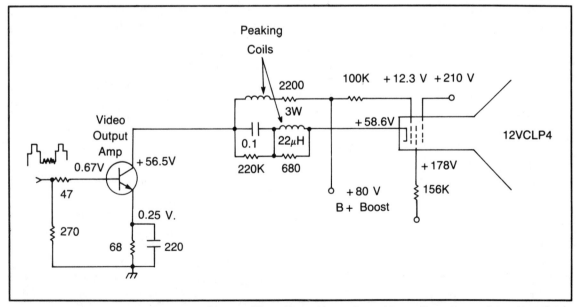

Fig. 16-7. The composite signal enters a video amplifier with peaking coils and low value output resistors to maintain the video frequency response. The video is fed into the cathode of the CRT.

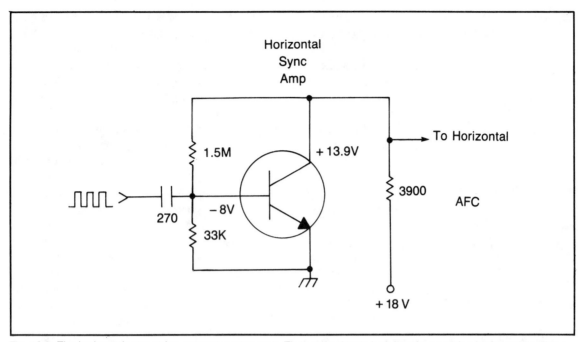

Fig. 16-8. The horizontal sync pulse enter at a sync amp. They are going to lock in a free-running horizontal oscillator.

Horizontal Sweep

In order to get the cathode ray aimed at the right dot of phosphor at the right time, the horizontal and vertical sweep must be in perfect sync with the video signal. An npn horizontal sync amplifier receives a horizontal pulse from the computer at the correct time to lock the horizontal sweep in step with the video dot data. Refer to Fig. 16-8.

Horizontal Oscillator

Meanwhile, a couple of stages ahead of the sync amp is the horizontal oscillator. Refer to Fig. 16-9. It is another npn that starts running by itself when power is applied. The transistor starts turning off and on due to the feedback components from the collector to the base and then to the emitter. In the feedback line is a horizontal oscillator coil that is tuned to the 15,750 Hz frequency.

The size of the feedback resistors and capacitors actually set the frequency to roughly the horizontal sweep value. The coil locks the frequency right on the money. The coil is adjustable and is the horizontal hold control.

Even though the horizontal oscillator is running at the right frequency, that doesn't mean it is in phase with the video. That is what the sync signal is supposed to do. After the signal is amplified, it is fed to the junction of two diodes.

Horizontal AFC

The horizontal automatic frequency control makes sure the sync pulse locks the oscillator frequency into step with the incoming video. The AFC circuit is based around the two diodes. Their cathodes are tied together and the amplified sync pulse is applied there. In addition, there is another input connected to the anode of the top diode.

This second input is coming from the flyback transformer, covered later in this chapter. It is really a sample of the frequency that the oscillator is running at. This signal might tend to be slightly out of phase with the incoming sync signal.

Since the two ac signals are input to rectifier diodes, they are changed to dc voltages. The two voltages are combined into one dc voltage. This dc is coupled into the base circuit of the oscillator. The voltage is a correction dc input to the oscillator. It is designed to change the oscillator frequency and phase slightly. It opposes any tendency of the oscillator to drift off frequency or shift its phase when compared with the sync pulse. At any rate, this comparison of the sync signal and the oscillator output waveform results is adjusting the oscillator producing the correct frequency and timing. Incidentally, the AFC-oscillator output is a square wave.

Horizontal Driver and Output

A third npn stage follows the oscillator. It is the horizontal driver. Refer to Fig. 16-10. The driver is an amplifier. It takes the 15,750 Hz square wave from the emitter of the oscillator. After the amplification, the square wave is input to the driver transformer. The transformer then couples the waveshape into the base of the horizontal output transistor, a heavy duty npn.

The collector circuit outputs to a damper diode, the flyback transformer, and the horizontal deflection coils. The finished product of the horizontal output circuit is to supply the horizontal coils with the sawtooth current shown in Fig. 16-11. A by-product of the circuit is the 15,000 volts dc that is to be applied to the high-voltage repository in the CRT and attract the electron beam.

The sawtooth current, as it courses through the horizontal coil, will create an electromagnetic field that moves the electron beam from side to side. During the rising edge of the sawtooth waveshape, 1/15,750 of a second, the beam is drawn from the left of the screen to the right. Then when the sawtooth falls quickly, in 1/140,000 of a second, the beam is retraced back to the left to begin the next scan line.

Theoretically the scan line starts in the center of the screen. Refer to Fig. 16-12. The current in the deflection yoke at that time is zero. Then the

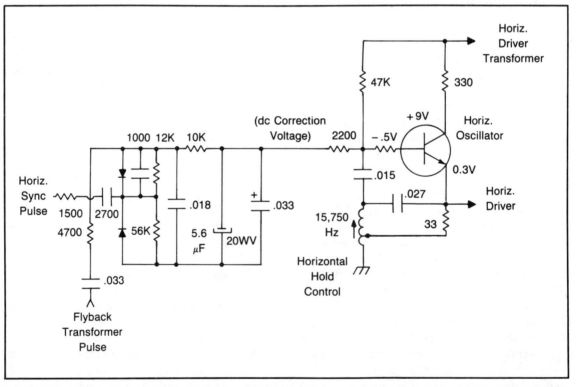

Fig. 16-9. The horizontal oscillator is locked into the correct frequency and phase with a dc correction voltage from the afc network. The afc obtains its correction voltage by comparing a sample of the flyback pulse with the computer sync input.

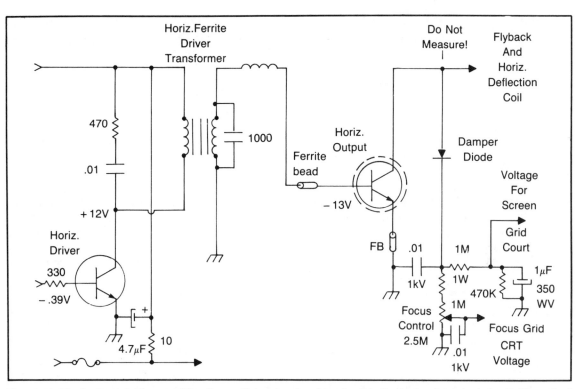

Fig. 16-10. The horizontal driver amplifies the oscillator signal and applies it to the horizontal output circuit. The output delivers a sawtooth waveshape to the flyback and yoke. It also originates the voltages for the CRT's screen grid and focus grid.

square wave, actually rectangular, turns on the output transistor. The collector current then rises in a linear fashion. The current in the yoke follows suit and moves the beam from screen center to the right hand side.

Then the waveshape ends and the transistor is driven from saturation of cuttoff. The yoke current falls to zero and overshoots even further due to the suddenness of the waveshape fall. The cathode ray is snapped back to the left side of the screen.

In series with the damper diode in Fig. 16-10 is a 1 μF filter. It is charged up from the activity. With no current exiting the collector of the output transistor, the capacitor starts to linearly discharge through the damper diode the horizontal coils, through the width coil to ground. This current in the yoke moves the electron beam from the left hand side of the screen to the center. From there, the next waveform turns on the output transistor, and the horizontal sweep continues.

The damper diode circuit also throws off as an extra +178 volts needed by the electron gun's screen grid and the +210 volts needed by the focus grid. These voltages are only potentials. Neither the screen grid or the focus grid are permitted to draw much current.

15000 Vdc

At the end of a scan line when the yoke current suddenly falls, a large overshoot pulse completely reverses the current in the horizontal yoke causing the retrace. This is called the *flyback pulse*. This pulse gets up to about 500 volts for an instant. It is coupled into the horizontal output transformer also known as the flyback.

In the flyback, the pulse is stepped up to an output pulse of about 15000 Vac. The pulse is then put into the anode of a high voltage rectifier. A pulsating dc of 15000 volts appears on the cathode.

The glass envelope repository acts as a capacitor. The glass is the dielectric. When the 15000 volt pulsating dc is placed into the high voltage entrance of the CRT, the glass acts like a 500 pF high voltage filter. This smooths out the pulsations and regulates the dc.

Boost dc

It was mentioned that the monitor operates with nothing more than a + 12 volt input. Yet there are voltages of 50 volts and more at collectors. These supplies are generated by a boost + circuit.

At the bottom of the primary of the flyback is a filter network to ground. This is a little power supply. It outputs + 80 volts. It is called the boost dc source. Some current can be drawn from it. The current rating is enough to drive a few transistors.

Vertical Sweep

The vertical sync pulse enters the monitor from the computer and arrives at the emitter of an npn transistor sync amplifier. Refer to Fig. 16-13. The pulse is amplified and sent on to the base of the vertical oscillator.

The oscillator, a pnp, is running because of feedback to its collector from the vertical deflection coil and the size of its resistors and capacitors. Refer to Fig. 16-14. The sync pulse at the exact 60

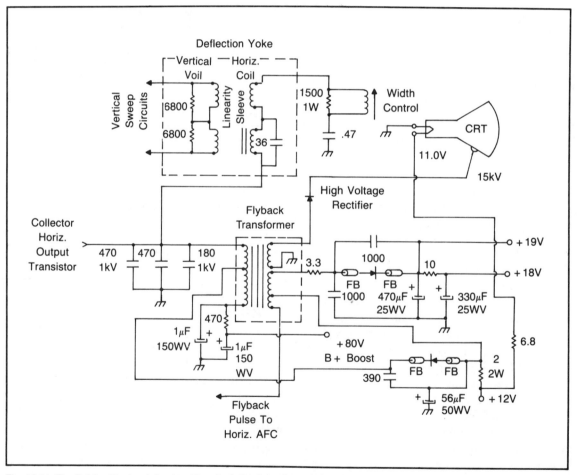

Fig. 16-11. The finished horizontal pulse drives both the flyback to produce high voltage and the yoke to cause the horizontal sweep.

278

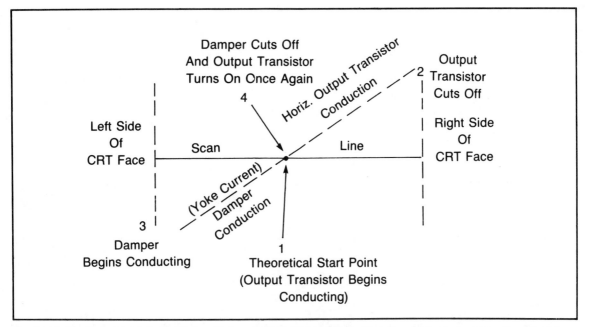

Fig. 16-12. The horizontal deflection yoke obtains current from two places. First, it receives current from the output transistor. This draws the cathode ray from center to the right side. Then retrace moves back to the left side. Next, the yoke receives current from a charged 1 mf filter through the damper diode. This draws the cathode ray from the left side back to center, where the output transistor takes over again.

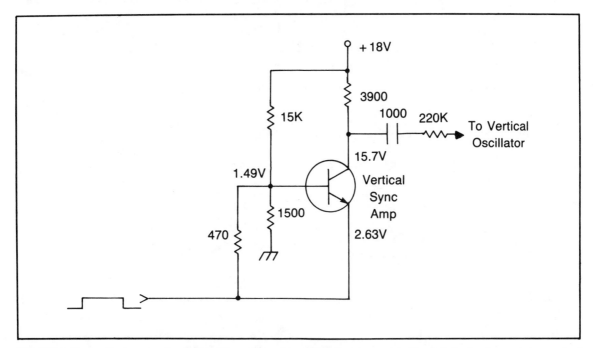

Fig. 16-13. The vertical sync pulse enters the monitor at a vertical sync amp and proceeds to the free running vertical oscillator.

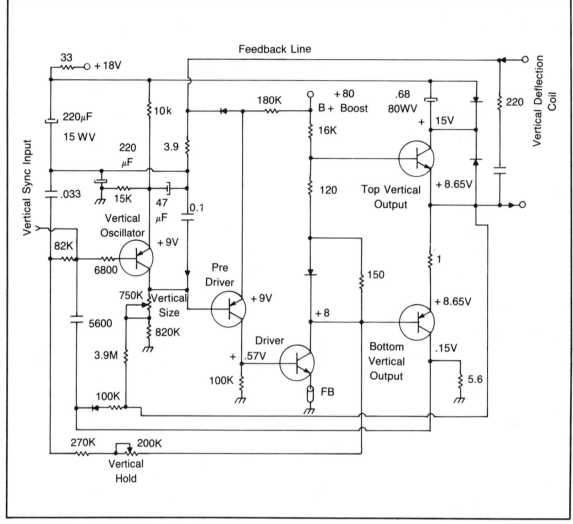

Fig. 16-14. The vertical oscillator and output is a complex little circuit that carefully creates the vertical sweep sawtooth so that a linear picture appears.

Hz system clock locks the free running oscillator into sync.

From there on, it is the job of the vertical sweep circuits to produce a sawtooth 60 Hz current that can be sent through the vertical deflection coil around the CRT neck. The vertical current can then draw the cathode ray down and then retrace up as the horizontal deflection coil is drawing the ray to the right and then retracing left.

The vertical deflection circuits are based around five transistors. Beside the oscillator, there is a predriver, a main driver, and two vertical output transistors.

Vertical Oscillator

The oscillator is a 60 Hz switch that outputs a sawtooth waveform. The vertical hold control is in the base circuit of the oscillator. As it is varied, the base bias changes slightly and the frequency that the oscillator is running at will change. The picture can be adjusted for slight variations of component values as the monitor ages.

The vertical size control in the collector can change the size of the raster by changing the peak to peak voltage of the sawtooth that is input to the next stage.

Vertical Output

The rest of the transistors are in the output stage of the vertical sweep. There are two drivers. They are needed to isolate the oscillator from the output stage. The predriver receives the sawtooth from the oscillator and amplifies it somewhat. It then passes on to the driver. The driver, in turn, amplifies it some more and passes it into the two output transistors.

There isn't any output transformer needed to couple the finished sawtooth into the deflection yoke. In old time vacuum tube circuits, it was necessary. That is because transistors have a very low impedance output. The deflection yoke like an audio speaker has an input of only a few ohms. The transistor output matches this impedance with no difficulty. As a result, the two transistors can input to the vertical coils directly.

The transistors are given the sawtooth at their bases. The two emitters are tied together and connected directly to one end of the vertical coils. The emitter connections amplify the current of the sawtooth. The 60 Hz signal then has its current course through the deflection coil and take control of the cathode ray's vertical sweep needs. The other end of the coil is fed back to the oscillator to make the oscillator run.

The two transistors are called the *top vertical output* and the *bottom vertical output*. They act as one amplifier, and with proper selection of components, the top output amplifies the top of the sweep signal as the other transistor takes care of the bottom. The peak-to-peak voltage of the output signal is about 50 volts.

There is no linearity control in the circuits. As mentioned, the vertical linearity is taken care of by a sleeve around the picture tube neck.

Blanking

As the raster is scanned line-by-line, the horizontal sawtooth draws the beam from left to right and lights the dots. Refer to Fig. 16-15 and Fig. 16-16. At the end of each line the beam must be retraced back to the left side. During the retrace the beam must be extinguished and not light up any phosphor.

At the end of each 262 1/2 lines, the beam must be retraced from the bottom of the raster to the top. Here again, the beam must be turned off and not light any dots on its way up. In lots of TV receivers, there are blanking circuits that shut off the beam. These TV sets must deal with all sorts of analog video and color signals. In this little monitor, the only video is digital dot data that only goes off and on and does not have any variations of light and color.

As a result the computer, as it builds the composite TV signal, only has to install the sync pulses that time the scanning at a voltage level that will not light the phosphor.

For example, this monochrome monitor receives a positive going composite TV signal consisting of dot data, horizontal sync pulses, and vertical sync pulses as shown earlier in Fig. 14-12. The signal varies from zero to a peak-to-peak voltage around two volts. The signal is input to the video amp. The video amp increases the peak-to-peak value and inverts it so that it is negative going. Then the signal is passed to the CRT. All of the signal arrives including the sync pulses.

The CRT has +58.6 volts on the cathode and +12.3 volts on the control grid. This constitutes 58.6-12.3 range, which equals a bias of -46.3 volts on the control grid. This negative bias is enough to stop the electron beam from getting through the control grid. The screen is thus dark or, as it is called, blanked out.

As the serial video signal enters the cathode structure, its voltage levels add to the cathode voltage. The video is now negative going. The voltage is also fairly large after the amplification. The dot data then adds its negative P-P voltage to the cathode. This reduces the -46.3 volt bias. The electron beam is then allowed to pass the control grid and head for the phosphor to light a dot.

As the horizontal sync pulse occurs at the end

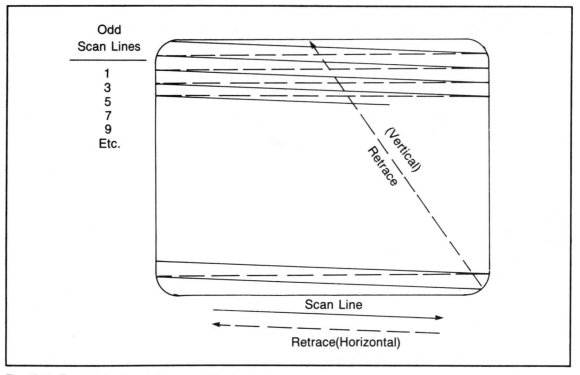

Odd
Scan Lines

1
3
5
7
9
Etc.

(Vertical)
Retrace

Scan Line

Retrace(Horizontal)

Fig. 16-15. For each horizontal line scanned in the first field, there is also a retrace line. The retrace must be blanked out so as not to interfere with the display. At the end of each field a vertical retrace line must also be blanked out.

of a scan line, the dot data ends and the P-P voltage of the sync pulse enters the cathode. Its P-P voltage is added to the cathode voltage. The sync P-P is much smaller than the video P-P. The control grid bias becomes more negative. The sync bias voltage is designed to be negative enough to cutoff the electron beam. Then as the sync pulse causes the retrace, the light on the screen is off.

The same event takes place as the vertical sync pulse arrives at the cathode. It is also set to cutoff the cathode ray as the vertical pulse retraces the beam from bottom to top.

The amount of bias voltage that separates the beam turn on and turn off point is called the blanking level. The dot data has a P-P voltage in the white level. The sync pulses have a P-P voltage in the blacker than black area below the black level.

COLOR MONITOR

There are all sorts of schemes that have computers producing a polychrome composite TV signal

rather than a monochrome type. Color in the TV display can be very useful for graphics. It is even helpful in more mundane computing such as word processing, spreadsheets, files, and the like.

The typical color monitor follows the color TV system that we have been watching at home for years. A color TV picture is actually four separate pictures, one on top of each other. First of all there is the Y signal or the black and white picture. It has a frequency response of about 4.5 MHz, which means it can go from black to white in 1/4.5 millionth of a second.

Next there are the red, green, and blue pictures. They only have a maximum of 1.5 MHz. They only fill the colors into the black and white picture. You could think of the three-gun color picture tube as producing a color picture in the following way. The three cathodes are wired together and all three receive the Y signal. Then the three control grids each receive one of the three colors. As the cathode ray containing the Y signal passes

282

through the control grids, the signals mix. The result is three beams, one with red video, one with green, and the third with blue. They all head for the same hole in the shadow mask where they converge. Then each beam impacts its assigned color phosphor dot. Horizontal and vertical scanning then produces the color display.

By varying the intensity of the three beams, the phosphor dot triads add their colors and can be made into any desired color. The colors can also adopt any brightness level. The brightness control changes the cathode control-grid bias voltage to change the intensity of the three beams simultaneously.

If you vary the tint control the phase of the color oscillator is controlled. When the color control is adjusted, the color amplifiers are varied, increasing or decreasing the intensity of the colors. These circuits are discussed in the next section.

It was mentioned earlier that the computer, when it outputs a composite color TV signal, can suppress the color carrier. The color signal is pro-

duced by modulating a 3.58 MHz color carrier with color information. The color carrier is then suppressed and a sample of the carrier called the burst is installed on the back porch of the horizontal sync pulse.

The color monitor receives the composite signal. Each color has three characteristics. One is the *brightness* or *luminance*, which is also called the Y signal. Figure 16-17 shows the conventional voltage level each color adopts for brightness. Second, there is *hue* or *tint* from green to pink. Figure 16-18 shows how the phase of the signal around the 3.58 MHz burst decides the tint. Third is the *color intensity* or *saturation*. Figure 16-18 also shows how the color is a result of the voltage level or amplitude of the tint phase angle.

The Y signal is separated from the chroma signal and sent to the Y amplifier. This circuit operates quite like the previous monochrome monitor's video circuit. The Y signal is then routed to the cathodes of the three guns. On its way, the Y signal is delayed in a delay line for about 1 micro-

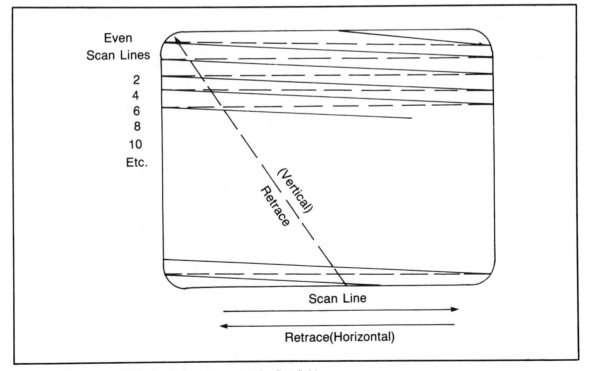

Fig. 16-16. The second field is interlaced between the first field.

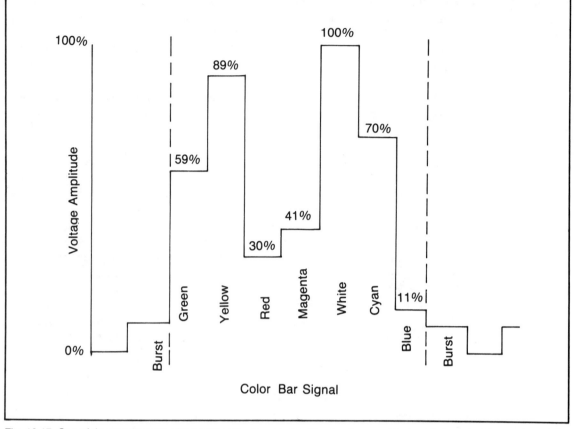

Fig. 16-17. One of the components of the total color signal is the Y or luminance. It is the black and white portion of the signal. Each color requires a different voltage level for its percentage of Y.

second. It takes the color signals about that much longer to be processed. The delay ensures that the Y and chroma signals will meet at the right time in the color matrix.

Color Amplifiers

A sample of the color signal is sent to the color bandpass amplifiers shown in Fig. 16-19. There could be two stages using two npn transistors. In the sample are the color sidebands around 3.58 MHz. The signal enters the base of the first stage. In the output of the stage is a transformer tuned to 3.58 MHz. This is called the *burst transformer*. It develops all its output energy right around the 3.58 MHz frequency, rejecting all other frequencies. As a result, the Y signal is not passed on. Only

the color burst and the color sidebands in the composite makes it to the second stage.

The only problem is the horizontal sync pulse that has the burst ringing on its back porch. This could cause interference. One way to eliminate it is to take a pulse from the flyback at the horizontal sync frequency and connect it to the emitter or some other convenient point. That way, the amplifier is switched off during the horizontal sync pulse and cannot pass on the burst. The sidebands are thus amplified and passed intact.

Burst Amplifier

Even though the burst had to be removed from the sidebands, it is still needed. There is usually a burst amplifier like Fig. 16-20 that can receive the burst signal and process it for use. The burst amplifier receives a sample of the video too. It must remove the burst from the back porch and amplify it.

The burst rings contain the frequency and phase of the color carrier. These rings are going to control an oscillator down the line. The burst amplifier is reverse biased. Another tap from the flyback is attached to the emitter. This time, though, the flyback pulse is wired to turn on the burst amplifier during the retrace. The burst amp is turned on as the sync pedestal enters the transistor. Then it goes off during the video interval.

The output transformer is a specially wound, tuned and tightly coupled burst transformer. The burst is developed across the transformer and coupled to the next stage.

Color Phase Detector

The phase detector can be a dual-diode circuit with the diodes in series. Refer to Fig. 16-20. The secondary of the burst transformer is connected directly to the cathode of one diode and the anode of the other. The centertap of the transformer is grounded.

A pair of resistors in series are connected across the diode-transformer network. Equal and opposite voltages are developed across the resistors as the burst is output through the diodes. In parallel with the resistors are two capacitors. There is a connection from the next stage, the color oscillator, to the junction of the two capacitors. It contains the free-running frequency of the oscillator, which is a crystal controlled 3.58 MHz sine wave. However, it is not in sync with the 3.58

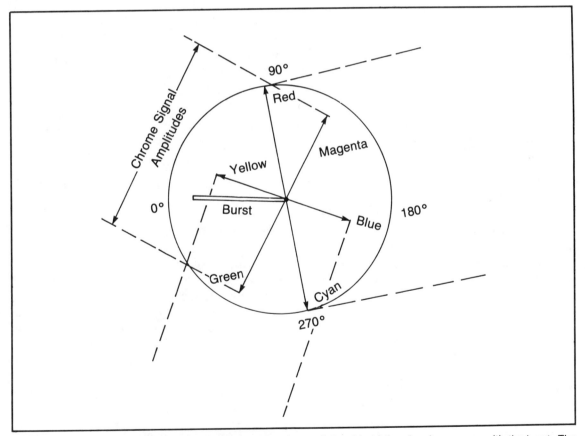

Fig. 16-18. The tint of the picture is decided by how the phase relationship of the signal compares with the burst. The intensity of the color is decided by the voltage amplitude of the chroma portion.

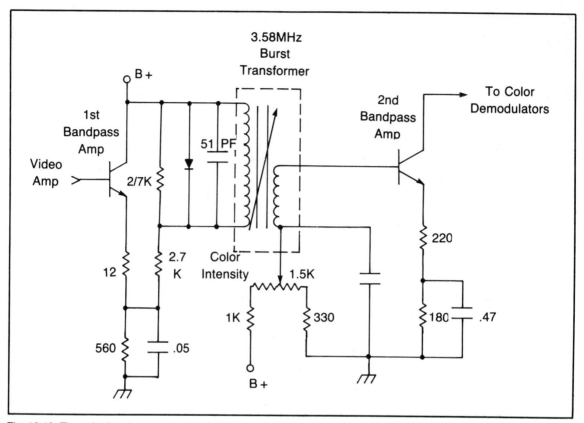

Fig. 16-19. The color bandpass amps amplify the incoming composite color TV signal and remove the Y portion and the 3.58 MHz burst with the aid of the burst transformer.

MHz that had been developed in the computer and which the burst is ringing at.

In this phase detector network, the burst from the transformer and this oscillator input are compared. If they are identical in frequency and phase, they simply add together and equal and opposite voltages will still exist at the top and bottom of the two resistors.

Should the frequency and/or phase not match the voltages developed at the resistor ends will shift. Between the two resistors, there is a tap. The voltage from this tap is a result of the top and bottom voltages. When they are identical the center-tapped voltage is zero. If the voltages are not the same a plus or minus dc voltage will be developed.

This is a correction voltage. The correction voltage is designed to be connected to the 3.58 MHz oscillator and be able to vary the oscillator slightly.

The correction voltage locks the oscillator into sync with the burst signal.

Color Oscillator

This is the oscillator that will reproduce the color carrier that was suppressed in the computer. The oscillator runs courtesy of a 3.58 MHz tank circuit in the base-emitter area. Refer to Fig. 16-21. A 3.58 MHz quartz crystal locked into step by the correction voltage keeps the oscillator at the correct frequency and phase at all times.

This signal is going to be modulated with the color sidebands to reproduce the original composite color. The oscillator circuit outputs its product to the color demodulators.

Color Demodulators

A color demodulator has to perform two jobs.

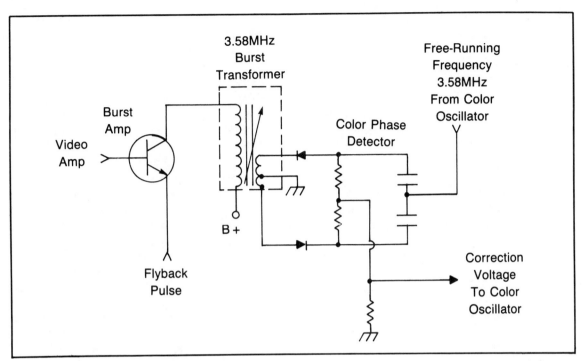

Fig. 16-20. The burst amplifier extracts the burst from the TV signal, amplifies it and passes it to a color phase detector. The phase detector compares a sample of the color oscillator with the burst to produce a dc correction voltage.

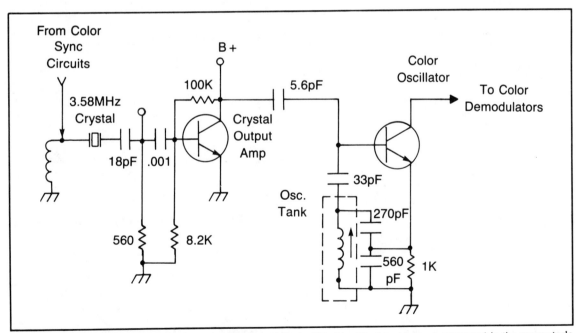

Fig. 16-21. A color oscillator is there to reconstruct the original color signal that had been suppressed in the computer's color mixer stages. It could be a crystal controlled type like this one.

The first job is to mix the 3.58 MHz color carrier with the color sidebands and restore the original color carrier structure that had been suppressed in the computer mixer chip. This process is actually modulation. Therefore, the first job the demodulaters do is modulation.

Once the modulation is performed, the circuit must then get rid of the 3.58 MHz color carrier. This is demodulation. As soon as the carrier is eliminated, the color sidebands are restored to their original characters. When the carrier was suppressed in the computer, these sidebands remained but in a distorted condition. After treatment in these demod circuits, the sidebands are reconstructed to a proper form.

A demodulator circuit can be based around an npn transistor, as Fig. 16-22. The 3.58 MHz oscillator signal and the color amp outputs are in-

put into the base and/or the emitter. The two signals mix as they modulate the electrons that move from the emitter to the collector. The collector output is the reconstructed color carrier replete with sidebands.

Getting rid of the oscillator signal is easy. A 33 pF capacitor from the collector to ground bypasses the 3.58 MHz signal to ground without disturbing the sidebands, which only have a maximum deviation of 1.5 MHz. The pure color signals can continue on to the three electron-gun control grids.

There are three color outputs. They are called color difference signals. They are R – Y, G – Y, and B – Y. When they are mixed with the Y signal, they add up to pure colors. If the configuration adds the color difference signals through the control grids as the Y signal is entering the CRT through the cathode, the following electron addition takes

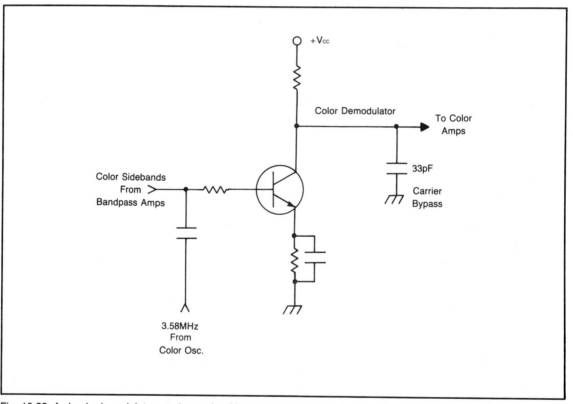

Fig. 16-22. A simple demodulator can be made with an npn transistor. It first constructs the composite color signal with inputs from the bandpass amps and the color oscillator. Then it removes the 3.58 MHz carrier with the 33 pF bypass capacitor. The color signal then continues on to the color amps and the CRT.

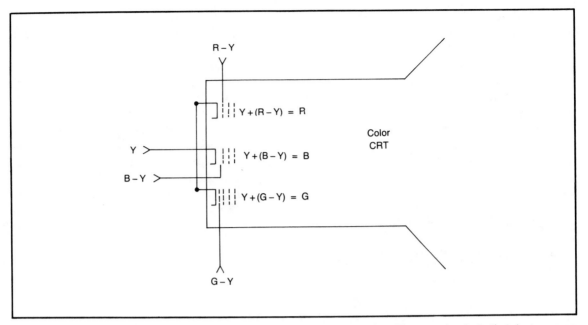

Fig. 16-23. This color matrixing scheme has the Y signal mixed with the color difference signals in the electron guns of the CRT.

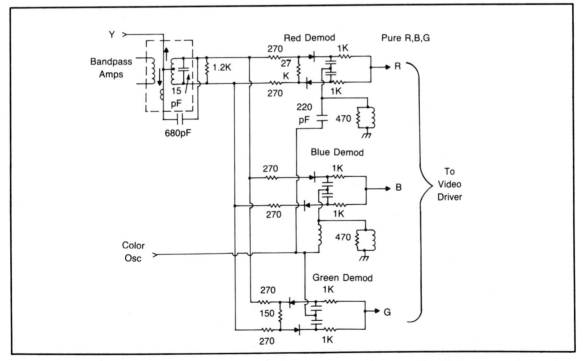

Fig. 16-24. In the so called RGB color system, the color matrixing is accomplished in the color chips on the monitor print board. Pure R, G and B are fed to the CRT, not a combination of Y and color difference signals.

place: $Y + (R - Y) = R$; $Y + (G - Y) = G$; $Y + (B - Y) = B$. Refer to Fig. 16-23.

To get the three color difference signals out of the demods, two circuits can be used. The two circuits both receive the same input from the color amplifiers. The red demod also receives the 3.58 MHz signal directly from the color oscillator. The final output of the stage is $R - Y$.

The blue demod, though, does not receive the oscillator signal directly. It gets its 3.58 MHz after the signal has been passed through a resistor-capacitor-coil phase changing network. One scheme changes the oscillator phase by 57.5 degrees. The phase change converts the final output of the stage to $B - Y$.

It so happens that $G - Y$ has a special relationship to $R - Y$ and $B - Y$. If you add them together they total $G - Y$. Therefore, if you mix $R - Y$ and $B - Y$ across a resistor, the final output is $G - Y$.

There are all sorts of designs to produce pure R, B, and G signals. The one just discussed mixed the signals in the electron stream of the color CRT. The Y signal could have been added to the color difference signals in the demodulator stages. Then pure R, B, and G can be applied to the cathode or control grid of the CRT without signal mixing taking place in the tube.

Figure 16-24 uses three demodulators instead of two. Green has its very own stage. Green has its own phase changing network to make the oscillator signal enter in the correct manner.

Chapter 17

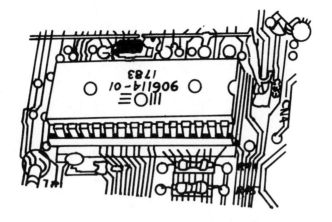

Power Supply

THROUGHOUT THE BOOK MENTION OF VARious voltages such as ± 5 Vdc and ± 12 Vdc have been made. These are the most popular voltages needed to power the chips and other components. These are all dc voltages. They must be *regulated* voltages. That is, they maintain their voltage level no matter what goes on in the circuit.

Most microcomputers plug into normal 120 volt, 60 Hz, ac wall plugs. The job of the power supply is to change the 120 Vac to the ± dc regulated voltages. If any voltage spikes or other forms of interference found in ac inputs from the electric company should manage to get through to the chips, they could cause data to become incorrect and even crash a program run. A block diagram of a typical computer power supply is shown in Fig. 17-1.

VOLTAGE REGULATION

Regulation is often described in terms of the *giant battery*. Refer to Fig. 17-2. Batteries put out dc voltages. The dc is just about perfectly regulated.

For instance, a fresh 5 volt battery, when placed into a closed circuit puts out a stream of electrons at a 5 volt level, as steady as can be. Of course over time the battery will age and its output will fail. Also, if you try to power some device that draws much more current from the battery than it is rated to deliver, the voltage level will fall and could fail completely.

The giant battery is one that is rated thousands of times greater than the amounts of current a device needs. It too could be a 5 volt type. The device that the battery is supplying draws varying amounts of current. All types of odd and data dangerous signals are generated in the power supply circuits. Through it all, in the giant battery, the voltage level holds steady. Not one voltage spike appears at the chip pins. The battery swallows them up. This is perfect regulation.

This theoretical battery, as it regulates, does so because the massive structure presents no resistance to the interfering ac that might occur. Typical ac problems crop up when the ac line voltage might fluctuate, when the computer draws

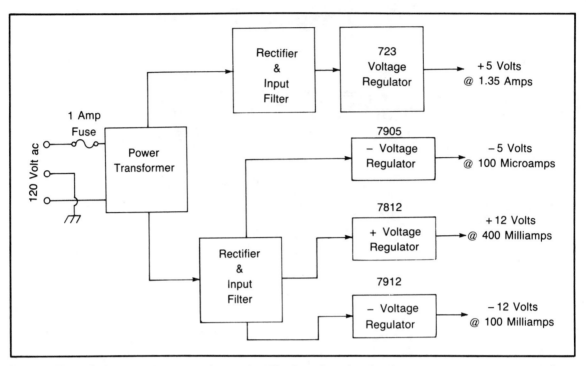

Fig. 17-1. The typical computer power supply can take 120 volts ac from the electric company and convert it to regulated voltages such as +5 volts, −5 volts, +12 volts, and −12 volts.

more or less current as chips turn on and off, and when there could be ac that manages to get through the unregulated components of the power supply. A voltage regulator like the giant battery bypasses all these unwanted ac influences to ground.

Since we cannot have the giant battery installed in the microcomputer, the ac elimination must be done through other means. Instead of a battery, electronic regulator components are used. Four regulators that will be discussed in this chapter are the 723 Adjustable Voltage Regulator, the 7905 5 volt regulato⁻, the 7812 and 7912 12 volt regulators. They are often found in microcomputer power supplies.

SINGLE-BOARD SUPPLY

A single-board supply could need four dc voltages. They are +5 volts, −5 volts, +12 volts, and −12 volts. The +5 volts goes to all of the digital chips. It is the most critical voltage since it powers the computing section where the data bits are being

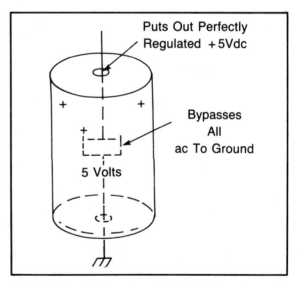

Fig. 17-2. Regulation can be visualized as the output of a giant battery. This one will maintain a perfect +5 volt output no matter how much current is drawn or how much noise or other ac interference is in the line. The battery has practically no ac resistance to ground. All ac is bypassed to ground.

processed. It is necessary not to introduce any spurious pulses that might hurt data. The +5 volt source also has the most current drain. It receives the most regulation.

The other three voltages supply a potential to fewer circuits and the current requirements are not too heavy. As an example, the +5 volts might be required to pass 1500 milliamps while the +12 volt source only has to put out 400 milliamps. The −12 volt supply could then have a 100 milliamp duty and the −5 volt only a miniscule 100 microamps.

Figure 17-3 shows the power transformer connections. The supply has a line cord that connects to the primary of a power transformer. The high side of the line has a one amp fuse that opens if a short circuit should occur and draw more than one amp through the fuse. The third wire in the line cord connects the computer chassis ground to earth ground. This includes the transformer case.

Three .01μF high voltage capacitors connect the three line cord wires together as far as ac noise is concerned. Any ac noise at the input will be bypassed to ground. The 120 Vac is generated in the primary and stepped down into the secondary windings. The two secondary windings are center tapped and connected to ground.

One secondary winding can put out 2 full amps. It is the source for the heavy +5 volt needs. The other secondary steps down the 120 volts to 18 volts. Its current requirements are minimal. It is rated to deliver 350 milliamps.

The 18 Vac output is sent to a bridge rectifier in the next area of the supply. The 16.5 Vac is rectified as it exits the winding. There is a diode in each end of the winding. The two diodes each rectify one side of the ac waveshape. The two outputs, then constitute full-wave rectification. The ac becomes pulsating dc as the two cathodes of the diodes are tied together.

A 10,000 μF filter capacitor connects from the common-cathode connection to ground. All that capacitance smooths out the pulsating dc and a somewhat, but not enough, regulated dc connects to the emitter of a pnp transistor that is going to help in the strict regulation of the +5 volt demands.

The transformer section of the power supply is the heavy part. It develops heat as well as the unregulated dc. It is often isolated from the rest of the computer. It could even be in a separate case that has to be plugged into the computer. That way, the heat and the ac that it generates is out of harms way.

+5 Volt Line

The heavy duty +5 volt line begins life as an input to the emitter of a pnp from the 10,000

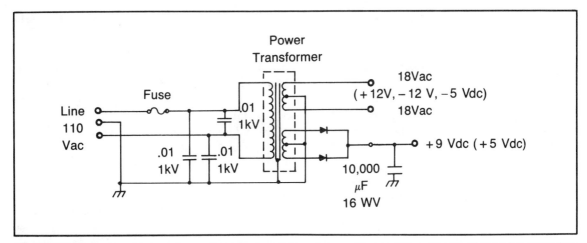

Fig. 17-3. The typical input is based around a power transformer, fuse and hv capacitors. The transformer has secondary windings that are coupled to the primary but not physically connected.

293

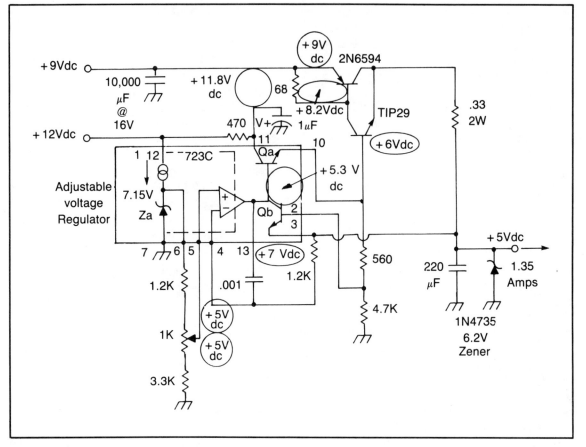

Fig. 17-4. The regulation of the +5 volt line is conducted by control circuits that operate the pass transistor. All of the output current must come through the pass transistor.

microfarad filter capacitor. This is called a *pass transistor*. Refer to Fig. 17-4. A 68 ohm resistor between the base and emitter of the pnp controls the bias and the subsequent conduction in the transistor.

The filtered but unregulated + voltage enters the emitter of the pass transistor. The transistor is to keep its voltage output constant no matter what fluctuation occurs in the unregulated input. This is done with the base input signal, which is the control electrode. The base receives its control voltage from a nearby npn transistor and a 723 regulator chip. The fully regulated +5 volts with enough current is going to be output from the pass transistor. The complications are in the control circuits.

These circuits are a feedback network. Working backwards, the pass transistor is controlled by an input from the collector of the npn buffer transistor. The npn in turn is controlled by an output from the 723 regulator.

The regulator is powered by the +12 volts developed in the other sections of the power supply. The +12 volts connects at pin 12 and is attached through a series coil. The +12 volts finds itself atop a zener diode. The diode is rated at 7.15 volts and this voltage is output to pin 6, the regulator reference pin.

Connected to pin 6 outside the chip is a voltage divider with three resistors. The center resistor is a 1K pot. The pot connects to pin 5. Pin 5 is coming from a comparator. The comparator is being used as an error amplifier.

The other comparator input is coming from the +5 volt output of the pass transistor. The two voltages are compared in the comparator. If any error occurs between the two inputs, the comparator will turn off or on according to the error.

The output from the comparator controls the two transistors in the 723. Their output then leaves pin 10 which goes to the control npn which in turn controls the pass transistor. Any change detected readjusts the pnp to a constant +5 volts with good current output.

The pass pnp output line has a small resistor to limit the amount of current the pnp will pass. Then another zener diode at 6.2 volts offers overvoltage protection. Lastly another large capacitance filter (220 μF) will absorb any noise that could have possibly sneaked into the line around this area.

Other Voltage Lines

A bridge rectifier changes the 18 volt ac inputs to one positive and one negative pulsating voltage. Refer to Fig. 17-5. The + side is going to be the +12 volts. The − side is to become the −12 volts and the −5 volts. The + side goes directly into a 7812 regulator over top of a 1500 μF filter. The filter changes the pulsating dc to a filtered but not regulated voltage.

The 7812 regulates the dc and then outputs it over another 220 μF filter where it is output as regulated +12 volts. The 7812 only has three connections to it: input, output, and ground. It is not quite so simple however. It contains all of the circuits and more discussed in the 723. It operates internally much the same way. Figure 17-6 shows the block diagram. Fortunately there are only three leads to worry about and the internals are academic.

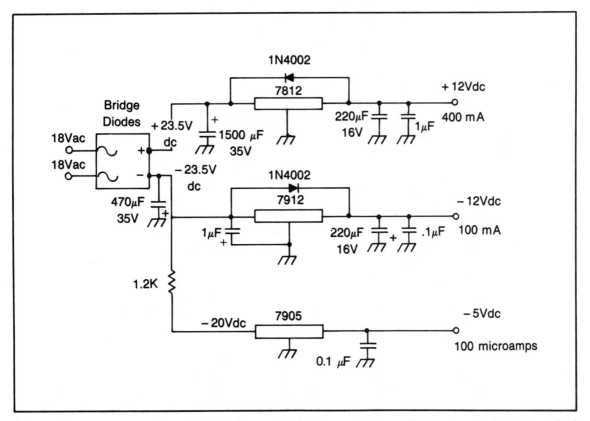

Fig. 17-5. The −5 volts, +12 volts, and −12 volts are all derived from a bridge rectifier circuit and individual three lead regulators.

295

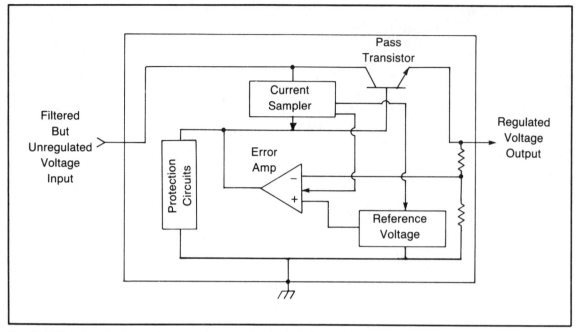

Fig. 17-6. The three lead regulators contain many circuits including a tiny pass transistor.

The input is a filtered dc voltage. The voltage is subject to variations in line voltage as the computer chips go off and on and pull different amounts of current, ac hums and pulses that could get through the bridge rectifier and filter capacitor network and other ac interferences. The input to the 12 volt regulator could change.

The output dc voltage, after passage through the series pass transistor is to be a well regulated dc without any of those input problems that could ruin the computing.

The series pass transistor, typically an npn, has the control of the output through its base. The control voltage regulates the output voltage by modulating the npn and making it act as an automatically changing variable resistor. As the input voltage tends to increase, the control voltage increases the series resistance of the npn, thus keeping the output voltage steady. When the input voltage tends to lower, the control voltage decreases the resistance of the npn again, keeping the output voltage steady.

The base circuit has between itself and the ground connection the same type of comparator

that computes the error voltage from two inputs, a voltage reference from a zener, and a sample of the output. The rest of the circuits in the regulator control current and temperature requirements. A diode is connected across the regulator in Fig. 17-5 and is wired cathode to anode in the direction of the current flow. It will pass high voltage spikes to ground through the output capacitors.

The – side of the bridge rectifiers go to the other two regulators. The – 12 volt source is a mirror image of the + 12 volt supply. Since the electrons are going the other way (from the computer to the power supply) a negative regulator is used and the protective diode is wired the other way. One input filter, a 470 μF at 35 WV is used for both – 12 volt and – 5 volt lines. Note the filter is connected with the + side to ground in contrast to the + 12 volt input filter that has the – side wired to ground.

To isolate the – 12 volts from the – 5 volt lines, a second input filter, a 1 μF, is connected from the – 12 volt input to ground also with its + end to ground. A 1.2K resistor limits the current the – 5 volt line is able to draw.

The – 12 volt line has a 220 μF filter at 16 WV

while the − 5 volt's current output is so low that it doesn't need any. The .1 μF capacitors are there to bypass ac noise.

LARGER SUPPLIES

The power supply just discussed is one that is used in single-board computers. Variations of it are found powering the MPU, memory, port, and support chips that run these type computers. As you get into machines that have their own displays, disk systems, and other peripherals connected to the computing board the supplies become much larger and more complex.

As a result you will encounter large power transformers, large filter capacitors, and other power components. They generate a lot of heat. To get rid of the heat, fans, air conditioners, and other heat elimination measures must be used. Basically though, the vital consideration of a computer supply is regulation. The supply must power the computing and storage chips with a constant dc output voltage as if it were a giant battery.

Chapter 18

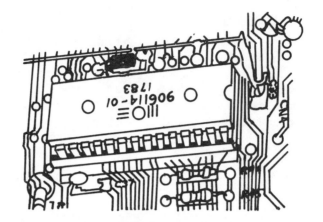

Diagnosing
Troubles and Easy Repairs

B ESIDES ENLARGING YOUR PROGRAMMING
capability, understanding how a computer
works gives you the ability to figure out what is
wrong when it fails. The same video display that
the computer uses to illustrate your work also
becomes the main diagnostic tool to clue you in on
what is wrong. The TV display is where most problems show up first. When trouble strikes in your
computer, the display, instead of portraying your
program lines or graphic pictures, suddenly goes
berserk. The strange looking information in the
display turns out to be symptoms that indicate to
the knowledgeable computer user a certain trouble. Figures 18-1 through 18-4 show general symptoms: garbage, no video with a display block,
brightness but no video or display block, no
brightness, not enough vertical sweep, no horizontal sweep and dead computer.

As a general symptom, garbage can occur in
many weird ways. Sometimes if you analyze a garbage condition there might be some secondary patterns that point to particular parts of the computer.
This type of analyzing is an art in itself and requires

a good idea of the computer's workings as well as
understanding what the program in operation is doing at that time. When you learn a lot about your
particular computer, you'll be able to sift through
a garbage symptom and often go directly to the defect without further ado.

QUICK ANALYSIS

With any symptom, the first step is to stop and
analyze. According to the what symptom is apparent a particular troubleshooting path is indicated. Figure 18-5 is a flow chart that, in general
points the way. For example, the most common
symptom is a dead computer. The first step is to
check out the power supply since it is the circuit
common to the entire print board and when it goes
out the computer stops.

When the video is missing from the display
block, the first suspect becomes the video output
transistor in the monitor circuit. The display block
is put together by the sweep circuits, and the video
circuit installs the dot data in the block.

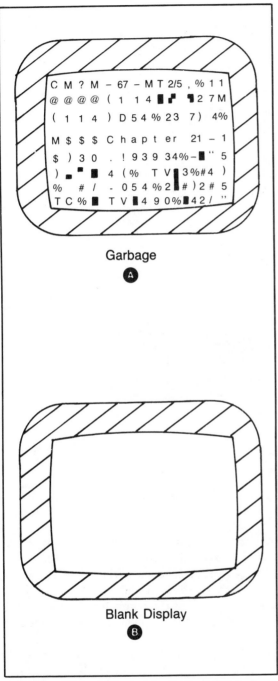

Garbage

Ⓐ

Blank Display

Ⓑ

Should there be a white line from side to side on the screen while the rest of the screen is black, the vertical sweep has collapsed and the horizontal scan line is being drawing on top of itself instead of being pulled up and down. The vertical oscillator and vertical output circuits are indicted as the trouble since they are responsible for the vertical sweeping.

The same type of reasoning takes place if there is a white line traced up and down on the screen while the rest of the screen is black. The horizontal sweep circuits are not scanning the screen while the vertical sweep is dutifully pulling the beam

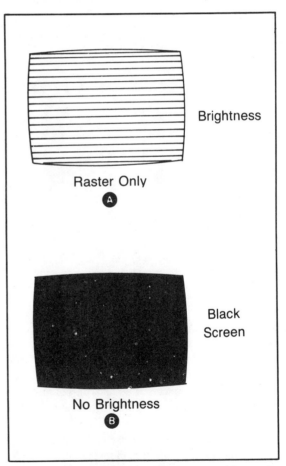

Brightness

Raster Only

Ⓐ

Black
Screen

No Brightness

Ⓑ

Fig. 18-1. A) This condition has the display full of numbers, letters, symbols, spaces and what have you. It occurs when trouble strikes in the MPU, ROM, RAM and I/O circuits. B) The blank display block trouble is a variation of garbage. It also has its roots in the same circuit areas.

Fig. 18-2. A) Brightness only, without any semblance of a display block, happens when the horizontal and vertical sync signals are gone and the display cannot be constructed. B) No brightness is usually the fault of the horizontal sweep, output or high voltage circuits in the monitor.

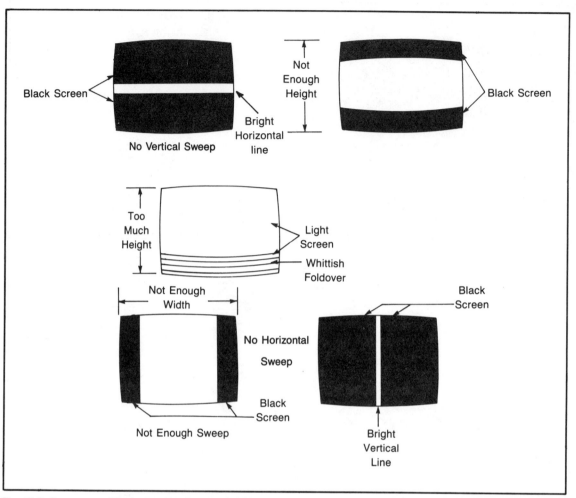

Fig. 18-3. Poor sweep. The loss or impairment of vertical sweep originates in the vertical oscillator-output circuits. Problems with the horizontal sweep occur when troubles happen in the horizontal oscillator-output circuits.

down and then back up on top of itself. The horizontal oscillator and the output circuits become suspect. Incidentally, when sweep is lost either horizontally or vertical, be sure to turn the brightness down or else the electron beam could burn a trace on the phosphor with the repeated sweep in the same spot.

The horizontal sweep circuits could also be responsible for the symptom of no brightness at all. The horizontal sweep circuits generate the high voltage for the CRT. If the high voltage quits, the lights will go out on the screen.

When garbage appears instead of logic, the en-

tire digital world is suspect. Any misfiring between the MPU and the residents of the memory map could send incorrect code bits into the video RAM bit holders. Video RAM can hold ASCII code bits. These bits address the Character ROM to send a matrix of dots to be shown in the character blocks. The video RAM is constantly being scanned by address bits and updating the TV display on every scan.

The MPU, the operating ROM, RAM, the video generating circuits, and support chips are all involved in the display. Any of them could possibly be causing the trouble. The garbage could be a

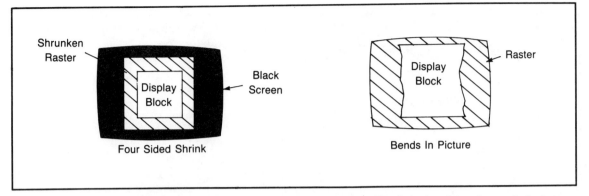

Fig. 18-4. Power supply weakening causes the four sided shrink symptom. Bends in the picture is usually bad power supply filters. The other power supply trouble, dead computer, is actually the commonest of them all.

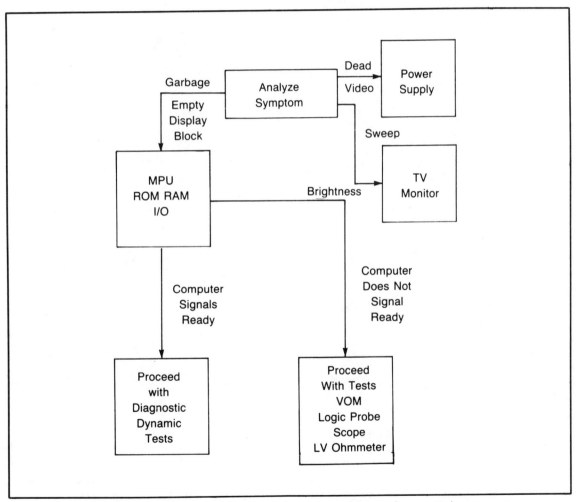

Fig. 18-5. In general, these are the common troubles, their causes, and the service approach.

meaningless jumble, have some logic but with major flaws, or could be a display block without any dot data at all. A close analysis could point out a troublemaker.

GETTING INSIDE

A single-board computer is usually easy to open up and gain access to the components. There are typically a half dozen or so Phillips head type screws holding the case together. With some do-it-yourself skills, the case will come apart easily.

Before you open the case, however, it would prove very valuable if you could obtain the service manual for your computer. Most manuals, called technical reference manuals or simply tech manuals, are available if you persist. Computer dealers are often helpful in this respect.

The computer in Fig. 18-6 comes apart, as an example, with these few instructions.

1. Cabinet Top. At the bottom front of the cabinet are three Phillips head screws. Remove them. The cabinet top will then swing back and unhinge at the rear. Unplug the keyboard cable from the main chassis. Unplug the pilot light from the main chassis. Remove the cabinet top and place aside.

2. Print Board. A copper stripping is soldered to a metal shield on the print board. Unsolder it and the cardboard shielding can be folded back. Remove seven Phillips head screws that secure the print board to the cabinet bottom. The print board and grounding plane can be removed in one section. To disconnect the grounding plane, unsolder the plane at the 10 places it is connected to the print board.

3. Keyboard. The keyboard can be disconnected from the cabinet top by removing the eight holding screws. They keyboard can then be lifted from the cabinet top.

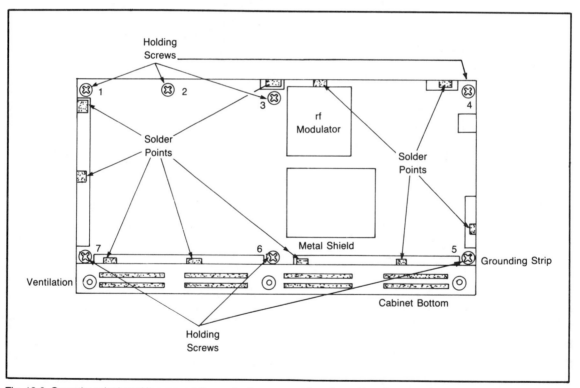

Fig. 18-6. Once the print board is exposed, it can also be removed from the cabinet by extracting more screws and possibly desoldering ground connections.

Once you have taken your computer apart, you'll find that it is just as easy to reassemble it. You just retrace your steps. Just do not rush, and when you are soldering, be careful the heat is kept away from the chips. With the computer apart, a number of quick checks can be made without undue danger.

TEST EQUIPMENT

In order to make the quick checks, you must have a voltmeter. Any little vom will do. However, only the voltmeter part of the unit is used. Do not use the ohmmeter section. The battery that operates the ohmmeter is at least 1.5 volts or more. 1.5 volts, if accidentally placed on a strategic chip pin, could provide a forward bias and turn on the circuit. This could, at the least, provide inaccurate test readings and, at the worst, blow a chip.

The voltmeter in a vom does not use any internal voltages. The circuit under test provides the voltages that are read on the meter. As far as the meter goes, the old fashioned meter type is just as good to use for testing as the newer digital meters are. Some technicians prefer the meter needle rather than the digital readout.

The ohmmeter in the vom is very useful in all the circuits in the computer except those that are based around chips. For the chip type circuits, a special low voltage ohmmeter should be used. Figure 18-7 is a schematic of the low voltage ohmmeter that can be safely used. If you are going to do a lot of digital testing, it is easy to build.

Another unit that is needed to make routine tests on digital circuits is a logic probe. A probe indicates the state of a test point, usually with three LEDs. There is one LED each for a high, low, and a pulse. When the high LED lights, the test point is being held high. If the low LED lights, the point is held low. Should the pulse LED light, either steady or blinking, the test node has a clock signal there.

A fourth handy piece of equipment that can be used to quick check the computer is the ordinary type TV service oscilloscope. The scope will let you look at the composite TV signal (monochrome or polychrome). That way the video can be traced from the output of the video generator to the input of a monitor or rf modulator.

The actual details of the way your piece of test equipment operates will be in the instruction manual of the particular make and model you use. In general, the voltmeter is attached by connecting the negative probe to the print board ground. Then, when you touch down on a test point, the positive voltage at that point attracts electrons from ground through the meter movement and deflects the meter. The needle reading is a close approximation of the voltage that the test point is held at.

The low voltage ohmmeter has an npn transistor acting as a switch for a light bulb. The comparator output turns the transistor on and off. If the comparator is outputting a low the npn is biased off. The bulb will not light. When the comparator switches to a high output, the npn turns on, the bulb gets current and the light goes on.

With the two input leads not touching or open, the biasing resistors produce a negative reference voltage at the − input. The output is a low. When the input leads touch or are shorted together by a low resistance between them, the reference voltage goes more positive than the + input, the comparator outputs a high and the bulb goes on. Therefore a state of GO occurs when the leads are shorted and a state of NO GO happens when the resistance between the leads is very high.

The handy thing about this arrangement is only 0.2 volts goes through the component being tested. This places the voltage well below the 0.6 volts a silicon pn junction requires to turn on. Transistor junctions can be safely tested with this low voltage continuity tester.

The logic probe has a slight complication upon attachment. While the vom and ordinary scope only require one ground lead to be connected for a test, the logic probe typically needs one ground lead and a +V lead attached for the test. Then the probe itself can be touched down on a test node.

The +V connection is usually attached to the +V line that powers the chips such as +5 volts. The probe becomes a part of the circuit. The voltage being checked will read out by lighting up an

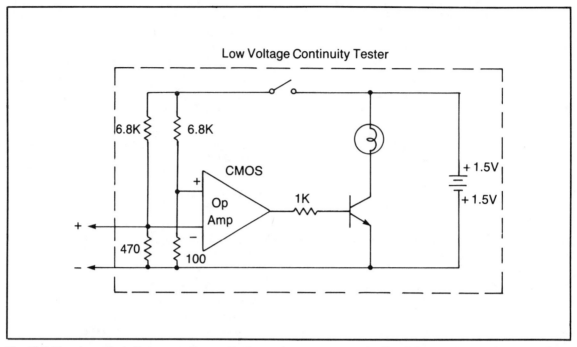

Fig. 18-7. The ohmmeter in the vom can be used in the monitor or power supply. For digital circuits though, a low voltage continuity tester such as this one is safer.

LED. Should you connect the +V lead to a line that is not the same as the line under test, then the LED lighting could be incorrect. For instance, if you connect to a +12 volt point, the probe will be looking for a voltage that is proportional to +12 volts instead of the desired +5 volts.

The scope is a form of picture of the voltage it receives at its vertical input. There are sweep circuits in the scope something like the ones in the TV monitor. However, you can adjust the frequency of the sweep oscillators in the scope. The scope draws a horizontal scan line and also can make the line be drawn in a vertical plane.

If you set the horizontal frequency around 15,750 Hz and the vertical at 60 Hz and touch down on the video generator output, a representation of the composite TV signal that is operating at those frequencies will be seen on the scope face. It will look something like Fig. 18-8 and can be examined for defect. Actually the most used test is to see that it is present. If it is, it can be traced through the video circuits and monitor if one is being used.

QUICK CHECKS

If you armed with at least a vom, there are a lot of quick checks that can be made. First of all, the most common trouble is the dead computer. The

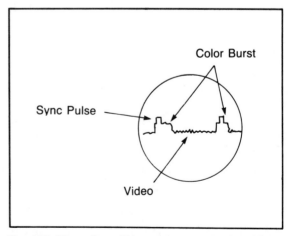

Fig. 18-8. The ordinary TV service type scope is useful to test out the TV signals the computer produces and the monitor displays.

first check, after the fuse, is the test points in the power supply.

It is important that you are able to locate the test points on the print board. The schematic diagram or a detailed print board drawing is handy. Without them, it is very difficult to read the actual print board. Lots of manufacturers are placing all sorts of information on the boards that can substitute for service notes.

If the symptom is a dead computer, the chances are good that some part in the power supply has died. In a single board computer that uses a home TV for the display, the supply is small and typically outputs voltages such as +5 and −5 volts and +12 and −12 volts. Find these voltage output points, take the vom and take readings. If the four supply voltages are all present, then the power supply itself is indicated to be ok.

The next step is to take readings at the VCC or VDD pins on the chips. Chances are you'll find one or more of the voltages missing. If a voltage is missing, then the trouble is in the special line that goes to that chip or the chip itself could be shorted. Further, isolation of where the voltage line is broken can be made. Follow the line, test point by test point, until the voltage suddenly appears. The trouble is then between the node that the voltage is still appearing and the node where it disappeared. All the components and connections between those two points become the prime suspects. Test them one by one.

If one or more of the voltages are missing at the source test point, then that line is indicated as the troubled one. All the components in that line, especially the voltage regulator could be causing the condition. The voltage regulator can be tested at its input and output. The voltages that are supposed to be there must be.

Testing the single-board power supply for the presence or absence of voltages is straightforward with few surprises. When missing or lowered voltages are uncovered, the circuit components can be tested and the bad one logically reasoned out through trial and error. It is then replaced, and operation is restored.

In the larger supplies that must provide volt-

ages for peripherals such as disk drives and TV displays, the circuits are more extensive. However, the TV display can be a help. Besides the fact that the computer goes dead, symptoms can appear on the TV screen. First of all, the main symptom is when the TV screen goes black. That verifies the power supply itself has conked out and not some digital component. Other symptoms area four-sided shrink of the raster when the voltage falls off, and bends in the raster with or without thick horizontal black stripes. This symptom directly indicates the large power filters located near the power transformer and the rectifiers.

When an empty display comes up on the screen, the power supply is also tested first, but once it is exonerated, the digital circuits are quick tested. The first such test is with the logic probe. Test the data pins D7-D0, the address pins A15-A0, and any clock input or output pins. The probe should show pulses on all those pins. If any are missing, that is a valid clue and requires further investigation of those circuits. If you know how those circuits are working, you will be able to intelligently come up with some theories of why it failed.

With one of the scenarios you develop, you then make further tests to verify or shoot down your theory. That is what troubleshooting is all about. For example, Fig. 18-9 is the pinout of a typical MPU and the voltages and pulses that should be present under normal operation. *RESET is usually held high. When the reset button is pressed, the pin should go low and then go high again after the circuits are reset. If *RESET does not perform exactly that way, then trouble in the reset circuit is indicated.

Another pin, R/*W is usually held high and does not go low unless it is responding to a write instruction the MPU is performing. In addition, R/*W is clocked to sync with the rest of the reading and writing that is going on. If you touch down on R/*W and if either it is held low or the clock pulse is missing, the circuit could be in trouble and needs further examination.

The *NMI and *IRQ interrupt pins should be held high. They go low when an interrupt is to take place. If a logic probe reading shows one or both

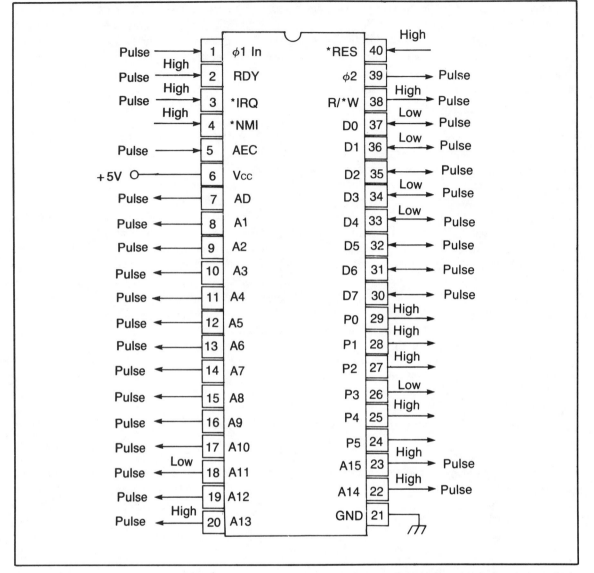

Fig. 18-9. To test the inputs and outputs of a chip like this MPU, a logic probe will read all these input and output logic states and pulses.

of them low, then the indicated pin is connected to trouble. They are inputs, so the chips they originate from and the circuit lines from those origination points become suspect. Also, the MPU itself could be shorted and pulling the pins low.

Each pin on every chip is a test node. With the service notes for your particular make model and your understanding of the circuits, troubleshooting the digital circuits should isolate the bad component or connection without too much time lost.

COMPONENT TESTS

In computers, as well as other electronic gear, there are only a few different types of components. They are resistors, capacitors, coils, diodes, bipolar transistors, FETs, chips, and the connections and copper traces on the print board. All that computing takes place on just those few general items.

For the most part, pinning down the seat of the trouble and the few components that become the suspects is performed with voltage, logic probe, and scope tests. Once the suspects are identified and lined up for individual testing, then the ohmmeter becomes the main test tool. The ohmmeter is the quickest means to test resistors, capacitors, coils, diodes, transistors, and the traces and connections on the print board.

FETs are best tested with a transistor tester. Chips for the most part can only be tested on expensive test equipment available to professionals only. Chips are quick tested only by substitution. Usually the vom and logic probe input and output tests will give some indication of whether a chip has failed or not. For example, if all of a chips inputs and source voltages are correct but one or more outputs is missing, chances are good the chip is internally defective.

These various ohmmeter and transistor tester measures are usually started with the suspect component still wired on the print board. Whether the component is in-circuit or disconnected from the circuit is a major consideration during the tests. In-circuit tests must be interpreted one way and out-of-circuit tests a different way.

Resistors and Capacitors

In-circuit, a suspect component could have all sorts of other components in series and parallel with it. When you place an ohmmeter across the suspect, some battery current from the meter flows through the suspect. Also, some current will flow through components that are not suspect but in parallel with the one being tested. This could cause the test readings to be wrong. A good capacitor could read as if it had a shorted dielectric. In those cases, the only way to be sure of the test reading is to lift one side of the capacitor to make the test. Refer to Fig. 18-10. With nothing in parallel the test will then read the real condition of the capacitor.

Resistors are read directly with an ohmmeter out-of-circuit. In-circuit resistors can be read as long

as any parallel resistance is considered. For example, if a 2K resistor is being read and there is another 2K in parallel with it, the ohmmeter is putting test current through two parallel resistors at the same time. The reading according to Ohm's Law should be 1K. Refer to Fig. 18-11. If it is, then chances are good the resistor under test is ok. However, the only sure way is to remove it from the circuit and test it while it is unencumbered by other components.

Small capacitors out-of-circuit should read infinite resistance. The dielectric is supposed to be as close to a perfect insulator as possible. If a capacitor reads any resistance, even in megohms, it is not a good one and should be replaced.

Filter capacitors with a lot of capacitance, when first connected to the ohmmeter will shown a large deflection of the needle towards zero. Refer to Fig. 18-12. Then the needle will stop and retrace a path back towards infinity. The larger the capacitance, the more the original deflection and the slower the needle will retrace.

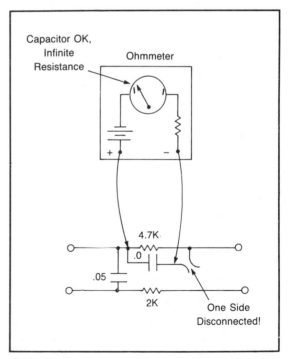

Fig. 18-10. The ohmmeter will make a valid resistance test of a capacitor only if one end is disconnected from the circuit.

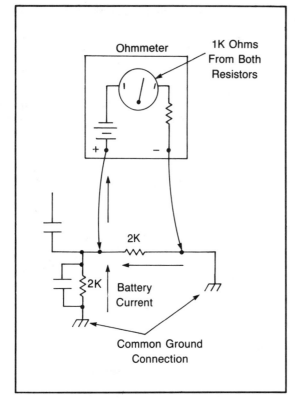

Fig. 18-11. When reading the resistance of components in a circuit, be sure to take into account the effects of adjoining components on the test current from the meter.

PN Junctions Tests

Discrete silicon diodes can be tested with the ordinary ohmmeter in the vom. The battery voltage will not hurt them. The test is simple and is best done with one lead disconnected from the print board. The fact that the pn junction in the diode will pass current when forward biased and halt current if reverse biased is the basis for the test.

Connect the two ohmmeter leads to the diode without regard for polarity. One of two events will take place. Either the battery voltage will forward bias the diode or reverse bias it. If you forward bias the junction, then the needle on your ohmmeter will read near zero ohms, a dead short. Should you reverse bias the diode the needle will read infinity, an open condition. Note which of the two readings occur. Refer to Fig. 18-13.

Next reverse the connections to the diode. The needle will point again. A good diode will cause the needle to point to the opposite reading compared to the first reading. If the needle read zero ohms for the first reading, it will read infinity for the reversal reading. If the needle indicated an open for the first reading, it will show infinity as the second reading. The battery is allowed to pass current during one reading but not allowed to for the opposite reading.

If the diode is shorted, then the needle will read zero during both readings as the battery current can pass both ways. Should the pn junction be open then the meter will read infinity both ways as the battery current cannot surmount the open junction.

Transistors, from a resistance test point of view, are nothing but two diodes attached back-to-back. An npn is two diodes with the two anodes attached, and a pnp is a pair with the cathodes attached. The ohmmeter test is very much the same

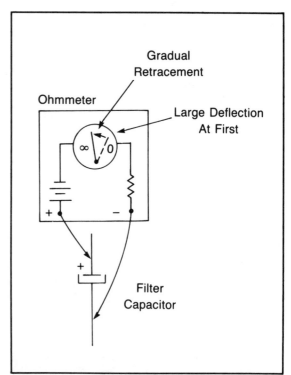

Fig. 18-12. Testing a filter capacitor with an ohmmeter has the meter show low resistance as the capacitor fills with a charge. Then the meter needle will start a gradual retracement towards a higher resistance.

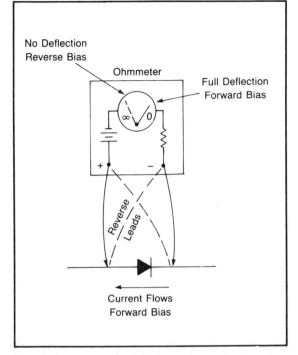

No Deflection
Reverse Bias

Ohmmeter

Full Deflection
Forward Bias

∞ 0

+   −

Reverse Leads

Current Flows
Forward Bias

Fig. 18-13. A pn junction will show a low resistance when the ohmmeter is connected to forward bias the junction. Reversing the leads then reverse biases the junction showing a very high resistance.

as the single diode test except that two pn junctions must be tested instead of one.

The ordinary ohmmeter can be safely used for discrete npn and pnp tests too. The technique is simple. Take either one of the test leads and attach it to the base of the transistor. This is the common connection for both internal diodes. Do not concern yourself about whether the transistor is an npn or pnp or which lead to connect. Just attach one of the leads to the base.

Touch the other lead to the emitter and note the needle reading. It will be zero or infinity. Next touch that lead to the collector and note the reading. If the opposite reading comes up, the transistor is bad and needs replacement. A good transistor will show the same reading, but that is not the entire story.

When the readings are the same, reverse the leads. Attach the other lead to the base. Touch down on the emitter again. A good transistor will

show the opposite of the above readings. If the reading is the same as the above, then the transistor is bad. When the base-emitter reading is ok, connect the collector with the lead that touched the emitter. It should read the way the emitter did.

Actually, the test is fast after you do a couple. Instead of the ohmmeter you can also use an ordinary continuity tester. This test is also useful to identify unmarked transistors. You first find the base. It will be the common lead by which you can get short type readings between the base-emitter and base-collector. The resistance between the emitter-collector is very high no matter which way the leads are attached.

In addition, you can determine whether the transistor is an npn or a pnp. An npn will show an open to both emitter and collector if the negative lead is connected to the base. A pnp will read short to the emitter and collector when the negative lead is attached to the base.

FETs and Chips

FETs and chips are not as easy to test. Resistors, capacitors, silicon diodes, and discrete transistors are fairly rugged and can stand a certain amount of normal handling and soldering. They can be removed and replaced without undue hardship. The FETs and chips can be a major handling and soldering problem.

The major enemy of these more sensitive components is static electricity. The insulated gates in MOSFETs are the vulnerable sections. A small shot of static electricity and the gate dielectric will fail. All sorts of elaborate precautions must be taken to insure the safety of the gate insulators.

A professional technician uses the arrangement in Fig. 18-14 when he must handle these IGFET items. First of all, he locates an earth ground. He connects his bench to the earth ground, preferably a cold water pipe type.

Next he rigs up a metal bracelet and connects it to the earth ground too. However, he installs a one megohm resistor in series with the line that goes from the bracelet to ground. This prevents an accidental contact with a power supply voltage like

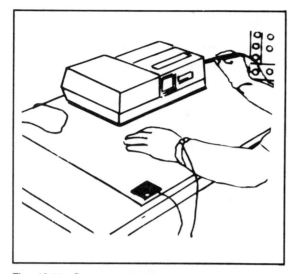

Fig. 18-14. Great care must be taken when handling MOSFET components. Here is an antistatic kit put out by RCA to keep you and your workbench static free. It consists of a static dissipative mat, a lightweight wrist strap, and coil cord, and a six-foot grounding cable that constantly drains static electric charges to ground.

120 Vac from passing current through him. The current will be absorbed by the resistor.

Then he follows these rules.

1. A device must never be inserted or removed from circuits with the power on or even plugged in.

2. During handling all leads of a device must remain shorted together.

3. The device must only be handled by the hand that is grounded with the bracelet grounding attachment.

4. All tools such as chip pullers, chip inserters, pliers, screwdrivers, etc, must be grounded.

5. The soldering iron used must have it's tip grounded. The iron should not be connected to electricity during the time the actual soldering takes place.

The idea when testing and handling FETs and chips is to take your time and handle them correctly. The MOSFETs, once they are snug in the circuit are quite rugged and reliable.

A MOSFET can be tested somewhat with a low voltage ohmmeter. Do not try to test it with an ordinary ohmmeter. You can use an electronic vom. Most electronic digital volts are low voltage. They only use a 1.5 volt supply and can be used except for the $R \times 1$ scale. The $R \times 1$ which will put out a short circuit current of 100 milliamps. This can damage the sensitive components. A short circuit current of less than 1 milliamp must be used. The $R \times 10K$ to $R \times 100$ put out a short circuit current of less than 1 milliamp. They are safe to test with.

With a MOSFET that is under suspicion, the forward and reverse resistances can be tested with the highest R scale. There should be infinite resistance both ways on all combinations of leads. If there is any resistance at all that shows there is leakage between the source, drain, or gate.

This test only shows up short circuits. If any of the electrodes have broken, open resistance tests will not show it. However you could try bridging the suspected open MOSFET with a replacement. If the unit is open and is causing trouble, the trouble will disappear when the new MOSFET is bridged in as a test.

Most quick checks of the solid state components are performed with an ohmmeter, preferably an electronic one. For more sophisticated testing, there are many transistor testers on the market that will check out all the discrete solid state devices both in-circuit and out-of-circuit.

Testing of chips in the factory can be accomplished with a chip tester in the same way a tube tester can check out a vacuum tube. However, the factory tester is especially built to test that one type of chip and is very expensive. There is no such counterpart outside the factory or special supply houses.

You are, under most circumstances, only able to test a chip in one of two ways. Number one is by direct replacement with a known good replacement. Number two is by understanding the operation of the chip and taking input and output readings with a logic probe, vom, or scope.

In computers, it is the practice to install a number of chip sockets on the print board. Usually, only the large chips will be socketed. The smaller chips do not have sockets. Some computers use a lot of sockets and others only a few. When a suspect chip is socketed and you have a replacement, then you can test the chip by sticking a new one in its place. During the replacement test great care must be taken during the removal of the suspect and the installation of the replacement. Use a grounded chip extractor and chip installer. These should be used as often as practical to avoid actually touching the chip. They are available at any electronics supply store, including Radio Shack.

Your body contains 100 to 200 volts of static electric potentials at all times. On a dry day, the potential could build up into a thousand or more volts. If this is discharged through a chip during handling, odds are the chip will be destroyed. Chips like dynamic RAM are especially susceptible.

When a suspect chip is soldered into the board, then the chip must be unsoldered and removed. This can be a tricky job that is best performed by a technician who is an artisan. Since most of us are not lucky enough to be artisans, when you decide to remove a chip, it might be a good idea to take the attitude that removal is going to be the death of the chip whether it is actually bad or not. For-

tunately, the chips that are soldered in place are the small, inexpensive ones. Often they are under a dollar.

When you purchase the replacement, buy the socket for it too. Then desolder the chip, pin by pin and remove it. It is still a good idea to take care, but in case you do harm the chip there is no problem. Use a well tinned, pencil type iron of no more than 30 watts. the solder must be 60/40 (60% tin, 40% lead). Take care not to burn the print board or anything else.

If you want to save the chip, use a heat sink. Just grasp the end of the chip leg being heated at the chip body with a long nose pliers. The heat will be bypassed into the pliers instead of into the body of the chip.

Once the chip is removed, secure it and reach for the socket you bought. Install it in the same pins the chip came out of. The socket is installed fairly easily, just don't relax your soldering hand too much. Once the socket is soldered into place, the replacement test can take place. The socket is to remain on the print board. It will make the board a bit easier to work on from then on in. The suspect can be installed or replaced with ease.

Chapter 19

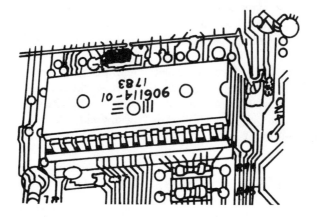

Safety First

MICROCOMPUTERS ARE RELATIVELY SAFE machines to work with. Their peripherals are also fairly safe. However, they operate on electricity and there is always a certain amount of potential danger. Electricity must be handled properly, or else it can hurt or even kill.

Every electronic tech knows the basic safety measure to take when he must put his hand into a circuit area that could possibly contain a surprise damage voltage potential. Electricity must have a closed circuit in order to have current move through the circuit. When you get an electric shock, its because you close some circuit. You become a resistor in parallel or series with the circuit.

There are a number of possible paths through your body. The common ones are from hand to hand across your chest, left hand to a leg, right hand to a leg and from leg to leg. The paths that lead through your heart are the potentially lethal ones. Other paths might shock or burn you, but they probably won't finish you off.

Therefore, techs try to work in a way that if a shock does happen, the current does not go through the heart. When he is working with high voltages and possible high currents, he keeps his **left** hand in his pocket. That keeps the possible current paths away from the heart. If you ever have to stick your hand into a circuit where an accident could happen, remember that tip.

DANGER WHILE CHANGING CHIPS

In the single-board computer, about the only problem area is the power supply. The machine is receiving 120 Vac, and if you get across it, a shock will result. For instance, in the last chapter it was mentioned that the handling of MOSFET chips was best performed while the tech was wearing a bracelet connected to earth ground. The bracelet is used to drain off any static electricity that develops as the tech moves around. Normal activity usually keeps a couple hundred volts of static charges in the human body. These static charges can possibly kill a chip. The bracelet keeps the static charge at near zero volts as it drains off the charge to earth ground. The chips are thus safe from the static charges during handling.

However, the tech is connected to earth ground. If he should accidentally get across the 120 Vac line, the voltage will push a lot of current through the bracelet to ground. This could be very dangerous and even deadly.

Therefore, a 1 megohm resistor is installed in series between the bracelet and ground. If an accidental shock should occur, the current will be absorbed in the high resistance and not the low resistance of the human body. The important thing the tech does however is to avoid the possible shock. The piece of equipment that is receiving the replacement is **never** plugged into electricity while parts are being replaced.

In addition, the bracelet is only worn while handling chips that are not installed in the computer. Once the chip is plugged into a socket or soldered into place, the static charge crisis is over and the bracelet is removed before the machine is energized. It is vital that the procedure is performed in this way to avoid trouble.

OTHER POTENTIAL DANGERS

Electric shock, fire, CRT implosions, and X-radiation are the dangers that are possible in computers, peripherals, and TV displays. The main shock sources are the house current inputs and the high voltage circuits in the TV displays. Fires can start in any electrical appliance. CRT implosions can occur with any display at any time. X-radiation is a problem if you work too close with TV displays and the high voltage gets too high. Accidents can happen at any time. There are ways though that you can minimize the possibility of harm and damage.

Electrical Shock

When you plug the computer system into electricity, for the most part, you are plugging in the primary of a transformer. The transformer primary is physically isolated from the secondary with heavy insulation. The ac is transferred from primary to secondary but the secondary isolates its ac from the electric company's. This protects the computer and anyone who is working on the computer from lethal electric shock.

In general, there is the dangerous side, with the isolation transformer's primary and the safer side with the transformer's secondary. Refer to Fig. 19-2. On the danger side are items such as the power cord, the power plug, and possibly a fuse and some isolation high voltage capacitors. Be on the lookout for frayed insulation on the cord, cracked plugs, and cords that are stretched taut. Refer to Fig. 19-3. They are all dangerous.

Lot's of units use interlocks. When you open up the machine, the power line opens up at the interlock. Refer to Fig. 19-4. If an interlock is not used, the device will probably employ a strain relief. The strain relief can take the form of an insulating bushing, clamp, strap, knotted power line, etc. It is used to keep tension off of the internal connections. Do not defeat any of these measures. They are all there for your safety. Without the interlock or the strain relief, power supply trouble could eventually happen and shock or fire becomes a distinct possibility.

Most power plugs in computers are polarized. Refer to Fig. 19-5. The polarized plugs are often three wire. There is the ac high wire which contains 120 volts, the ac low wire which is at 0 volts, and the ground wire that goes to earth ground. It

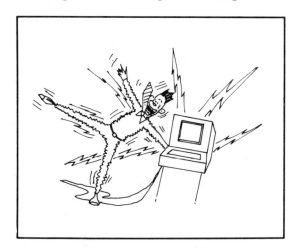

Fig. 19-1. Experienced techs would not have had their LEFT hand in a place where heavy line current could possibly have gotten them like this poor guy. Their left hand would have been in their pocket.

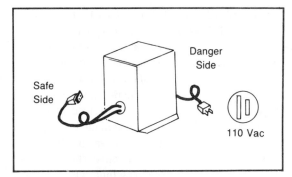

Fig. 19-2. The dangerous side of an isolation transformer plugs into the wall. The safe side goes into the computer.

is easy to defeat the plug with adapters or other measures. **Don't do it!**

The least that could happen is a fuse will blow. The most is the computer could have all its chips blow out. Be especially careful of strip type outlets. The two wire polarized plug will fit into it. If you plug it in the wrong way, blooey!

Some monitors have their own power supply and do not use an isolation transformer. This is especially true when the monitor is a home TV. Without a transformer, the unit is entirely dependent on the polarized plug. The plug connects the print board and chassis ground to the external earth ground. The point is, never defeat the polarized plug for your sake and your equipment.

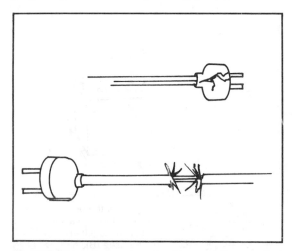

Fig. 19-3. The ac line can be quite dangerous if you contact the copper wire inside. Be on the lookout for frayed insulation, taut lines, and cracked plugs.

High Voltages

There isn't any need for high voltage in the computer itself. The high voltage is only needed to be applied to the well in the side of a picture tube to attract the electron beam to the phosphor. This high voltage could be as low as 12,000 volts in a monochrome monitor or as high as 30,000 volts in a color TV used as a monitor.

Fortunately, this high voltage is usually not lethal. There is practically no current being drawn as it is applied to the CRT. About all that is drawn is the current in the cathode rays which is, from a danger point of view, negligible.

The danger is the high voltage will cause you to move violently and jump away. You could knock everything over and cut yourself on sharp chassis

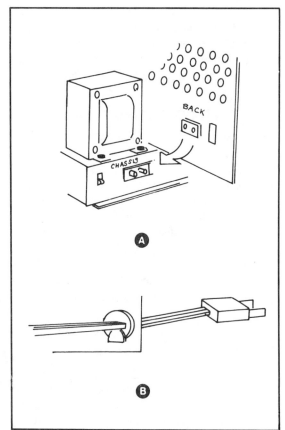

Fig. 19-4. Lots of equipment use interlocks (A) or strain relief systems (B). Do not defeat any of these measures. They are carefully designed safety controls.

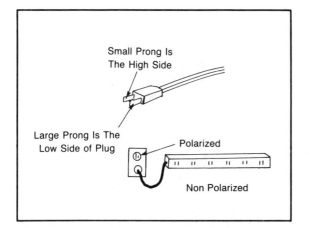

Fig. 19-5. Most computer equipment has polarized plugs, either three wire or two wire. Be careful not to defeat the polarization. If you do, you could blow out the chips and transistors and also get hurt.

edges or bruise yourself in falls. If you have a heart condition, it could be serious.

It is a good idea not to get into the high voltage system unless you receive some training. During training, you'll become familiar with the system including the flyback transformer that produces the high voltage. The flyback is subject to heat, melting wax, cracks, and HV arcing from point to point. These are all fairly visible to the trained eye. Sometimes the problem can be repaired and other times a new flyback must be installed. Often a special type of flyback is used and must be changed only with the exact replacement. This is in the realm of TV service and should be treated as such. Just be careful in the HV circuits.

Besides those kilovoltages, there are some other voltages, not as high, but fraught with danger that are called B+. These are voltages between about 50 and 500 volts. They are dc voltages produced by both the power transformer and the flyback. They are distributed throughout computer circuits and will shock you if you contact them. Needless to say, learn where they are so you won't accidentally touch them.

Fire

When your computer and peripherals leave the factory every reasonable precaution is taken to

avoid fire hazards. As time goes by the machine receives a certain amount of wear, tear, and repair. The factory safety measures could be degraded.

First of all, certain special parts are used to avoid trouble. When one of these parts breaks down, it is replaced. The replacement could be fine electronically and restore operation to the device. However, the replacement might be made by a different manufacturer whose own machines do not need certain safety measures. For instance, the part might overheat slightly in your machine while it is fine in another machine. The overheating over a period of time could result in a fire. Be sure to use only direct replacements and not one that defeats some safety measure.

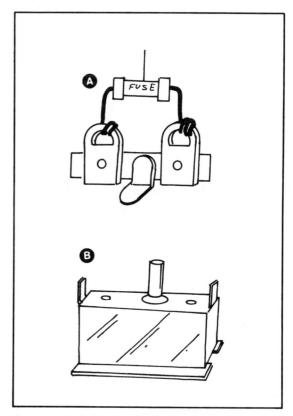

Fig. 19-6. A common type of fuse is the pigtail (A). Good replacement technique dictates soldering in a new one and not jerryrigging the two connections together. Instead of a fuse, a circuit breaker could be used (B). Always replace the breaker with one that is rated the same. Don't take chances with one that has more or less current carrying ability.

Another thing to be careful of is the way the wires in your device are dressed out over the chassis. There are some components in most electronic gear that get hot. The manufacturer will dress out the leads in the machine in such a way that they do not get near the hot components. During repairs and maintenance, leads can get moved. If a lead falls on a hot component, the insulation will melt and who knows what will happen then. A fire is a good possibility.

The fuses in your equipment are carefully designed. Fuses must be replaced only with the same size and ratings. Fuses come in many different sizes, shapes, and ratings. A fuse can be a snap-in, a pig tail, a resistor or even a fusible link which is just a piece of wire. Instead of a fuse a circuit breaker is often used. Refer to Fig. 19-6. Whatever the configuration, the only right fuse is the one the factory specifies. The fuse information is usually printed right near the fuse itself.

If you install a fuse that is too small, it will keep on blowing. Should you install one too large or use a piece of wire to short it out, chances are good you'll be rewarded with a fire.

X-Radiation

There is a lot of confusion about X-radiation from computers and their TV displays. The truth of the matter is, dangerous X-radiation is possible from large picture tubes and some of the components in the HV circuits. In a color TV, the high voltage rectifier tube and the high voltage shunt regulator tubes were the villains. There are still a few of them around in old color TVs but not in the latest TV sets. If you use an older color TV as a monitor, then stay away from those tubes while the TV is on.

X-radiation is completely dependent on the level of high voltage. If the high voltage is at or near 30 kV X-radiation from the CRT and those high voltage tubes is a distinct possibility. If you must be near those items try to limit the amount of time actually exposed. Should you encounter a TV that has an HV above 30 kV, stay clear till the HV is brought down to its prescribed level.

For the most part, it has not been shown that there is any problem with today's computers and monitors as far as X-radiation goes. It would be sensible though to avoid placing yourself against a lighted TV display. If you are separated from it, even by as little as 18 inches, there does not appear to be any particular hazard.

Cathode Ray Tubes

While the CRT is in its cabinet, the danger is minimal. CRTs can implode. They are under a great deal of atmospheric pressure. Inside the glass envelope is almost a perfect vacuum for the electron beam to travel in. If it implodes in the cabinet though, odds are, not one shred of glass will get out. The danger appears when a CRT must be removed from the cabinet. If it implodes outside its enclosure glass can fly and create a hazard. Replacing a CRT is best left to the professional.

Index

Index

OTHER POPULAR TAB BOOKS OF INTEREST

TAB   TAB BOOKS Inc.

Blue Ridge Summit, Pa. 17214

Send for FREE TAB Catalog describing over 750 current titles in print.